IMAGES AND ELOQUENCE
Photographs for Composition

IMAGES AND ELOQUENCE
Photographs for Composition

Photographed, written, and designed by
AHMED ESSA
University of Nevada

HOLT, RINEHART AND WINSTON, INC.
New York   Chicago   San Francisco   Atlanta   Dallas
Montreal   Toronto   London   Sydney

Copyright © 1972 by Ahmed Essa
All Rights Reserved
Library of Congress Catalog Card Number: 70–165030
ISBN: 0–03–085289–7
Printed in the United States of America

2 3 4 5   032   9 8 7 6 5 4 3 2 1

ACKNOWLEDGMENTS...

I do not believe I would have become proficient in photography were it not for the valuable lessons and advice of the Ohio University Department of Photography (particularly Miss Elizabeth Truxell) and the Athena Yearbook photographers for the 1955 and 1956 issues. Miss Truxell permitted me to work at my own pace and, as a result, I was able to accomplish more in the courses I took under her. My relationship to the Athena photographers was that of an apprentice and I know of no better way to learn photography than under the guidance of people more experienced than oneself.

I am grateful to Dr. Robert Gorrell of the Department of English, University of Nevada (Reno), for his help, advice, and (most important) encouragement.

I am indebted to Dr. Edward Hodnett, former chairman of the English Department at Ohio University, who has been a mentor to me since my undergraduate days. His wisdom, compounded with common sense, has been responsible for many of my achievements. Other advisers I am indebted to are Dr. Eleazer Lecky and Dr. Allan Casson, both of the University of Southern California, and Dr. Ronald Freeman, formerly of U.S.C. and now at U.C.L.A.

My appreciation also goes to Jamie Arjona, University of Nevada photographer, for his advice and help, especially regarding color photography, and to Frank S. Kinsey, of Silver State Cameras, for his assistance in solving darkroom problems and in obtaining many photographic supplies.

It is becoming axiomatic that a husband who works on a book owes much to his wife: she is encouraging when the goal appears too distant, patient when things become too exasperating, and always ready with counsel when it is needed. To my wife Eva goes my gratitude.

Editors are patient, too. Jane Ross of Holt, Rinehart and Winston patiently answered many questions and offered practical suggestions. Moreover, she proved very encouraging through her enthusiasm for this book—an enthusiasm that proved contagious. I also appreciate the advice and technical assistance of Wyatt James, Howard Leiderman, and John Finnerty, all of Holt, Rinehart and Winston, who worked with me in the final stages of this book.

...AND A DEDICATION

This book is dedicated to my two favorite, but not necessarily most cooperative, subjects:

FIONA
and
EUGENE

Reno, Nevada
July 1971

A. E.

Contents

Introduction 8
Observation 10
Assumptions 44
Contexts 62
Contrasts 104
The World of the Child 130
Environment 164
People 192
Imagination 218
Miscellaneous 242

INTRODUCTION

The title means two things: the word *Images* refers to the photographs in this book; but since they are subjects for composition, the implication is that the student provides the *Eloquence*.

Images and Eloquence offers a solution to a perennial problem in writing courses. The English teacher constantly complains that the student is always sent to the library, from which he returns with a rehash of what he has read. Practically every composition turns out to be an assignment in rewriting someone else's work. Photographs enable the student to rely on his individual verbal ability.

Photographs serve two other purposes in the English composition course. Since the student is limited to the picture in front of him, he is subjected to paying more attention to the words he is going to use, a discipline so very necessary to the act of writing. In addition, the photograph becomes a topic that is identical for all the students. This puts the instructor at an advantage. He is fully familiar with the "topic" and, since all the students have written on the same thing, he can grade all the papers on an equal level. At the same time, however, photographs differ from other "identical" topics. Photographs do not evoke common responses. Like many other art forms, they lend themselves to different interpretations. The students therefore have a certain amount of intellectual freedom, one that depends on their intelligence.

This book relies on the student's intelligence. It avoids the chief weakness underlying the use of photographs in the English composition course: invariably the instructor places a photograph before the students and asks them to describe it. I do not believe photographs have such a limited role in the classroom. This book goes beyond merely asking the student to describe what he sees. The assignments are based on the fact that there are four sources of all writing: research, observation, experience, and imagination. Most of the photographs, especially those taken in other countries, can lead to research, since the student would want to know more about the backgrounds of the pictures. The entire book depends on the ability to observe details, although only the first section concentrates on this particular aspect of writing. The second and third sections ask the students to draw on their experiences. In addition, most of the photographs provide some vicarious experiences to add to those the students already have. Toward the end of this book, there is an entire section devoted to the stimulation of the imagination through the medium of photographs.

In fact, I hope that all the photographs in this book will act as catalysts to the student's

imagination. We are losing our ability to visualize. Television, despite McLuhan's boosting of the medium, is stifling to the imagination. The audience does not even have to know when to laugh: the canned laughter does that "thinking" for them. Television is also responsible for the fleeting attitude most people have toward a picture. They give it a cursory glance, without paying attention to the signficant details. If they cannot see what is before them, how much more impoverished must be their imaginations? People are too preoccupied with abstractions. The particular, the concrete, is necessary if their imaginations are to recover. The photographs in this book should prove valuable, I am sure, in fulfilling this need.

The sections in this book are ordered toward this end. The first section draws attention to details in the photographs. The second will help the observer guard against making too many assumptions. The third reminds him of the significance of context, and the fourth takes the context, the background, and demonstrates how a change in the viewpoint can change the tone or mood of a place. In each subsequent section, the student draws upon what he has learned in the preceding ones. The lessons of the first four sections are then applied to different areas in the next three sections—the world of the child, the environment, and people. The last of the ordered sections is the one on imagination; here the section resorts to "visual thinking" to interpret the pictures. All the preceding sections will have, by then, aided the student's imagination, so that he will be better prepared to use it.

In the first eight sections, the photographs appear first; words that are pertinent to these pictures come at the end of each grouping. The student should carefully look at the photographs and then return to them after he has read the instructions and the questions. One section in particular, the one on contexts, relies heavily on the student's cooperation. The section is divided into two parts. The first part consists of portions of photographs taken out of their contexts. These pictures are restored to their backgrounds in the second part. The student should refrain from looking at the second part until he has carefully worked out the exercises that ask him to determine the context on his own. Only then should he refer to the background of each picture to see whether his conclusions are accurate.

There is one more section, titled *Miscellaneous*, at the end of the book. Since these are times when students are called upon to do their "thing," the last group of photographs provides them with the opportunity to do so; there are no instructions or questions assigned to any of these pictures.

OBSERVATION

11

37

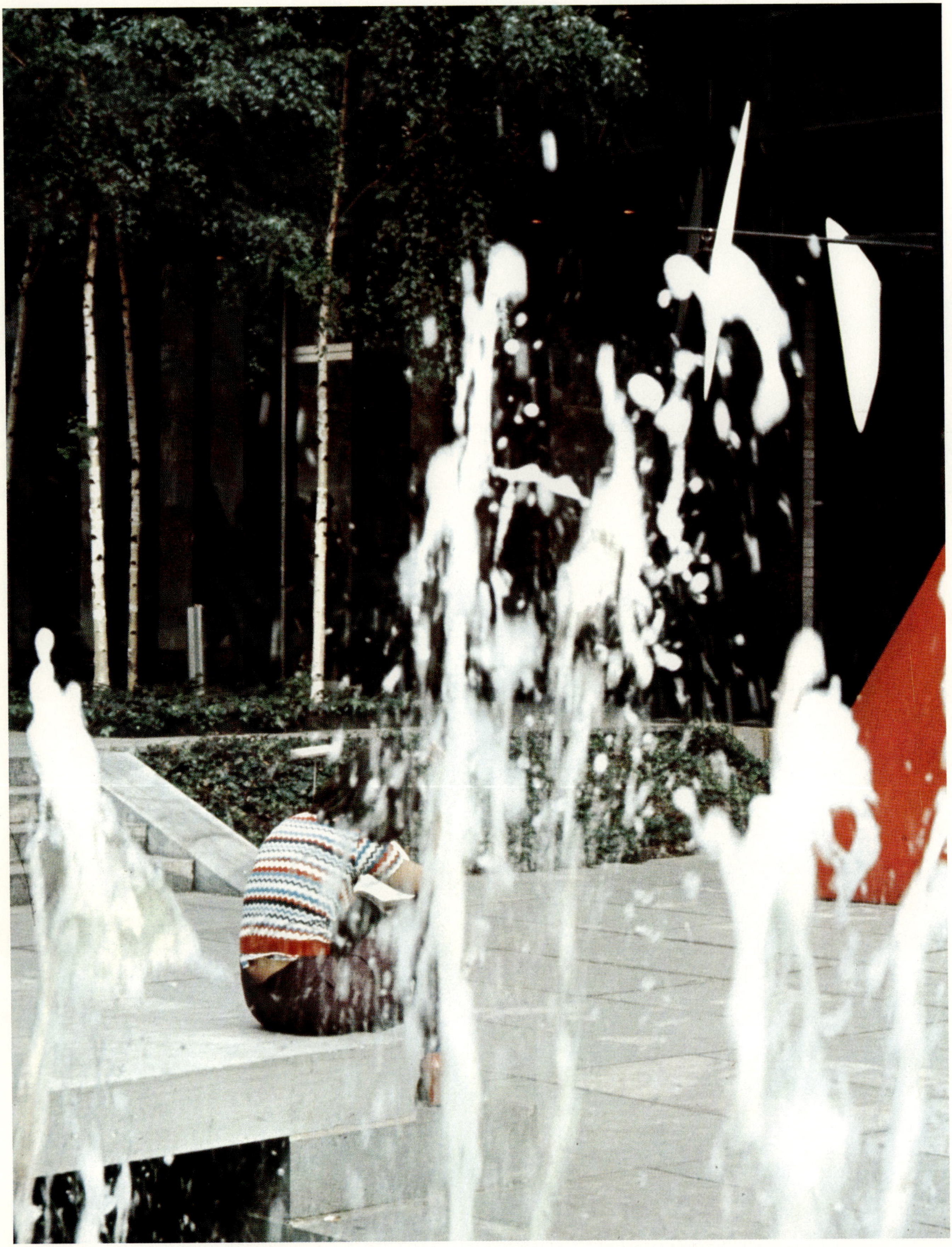

39

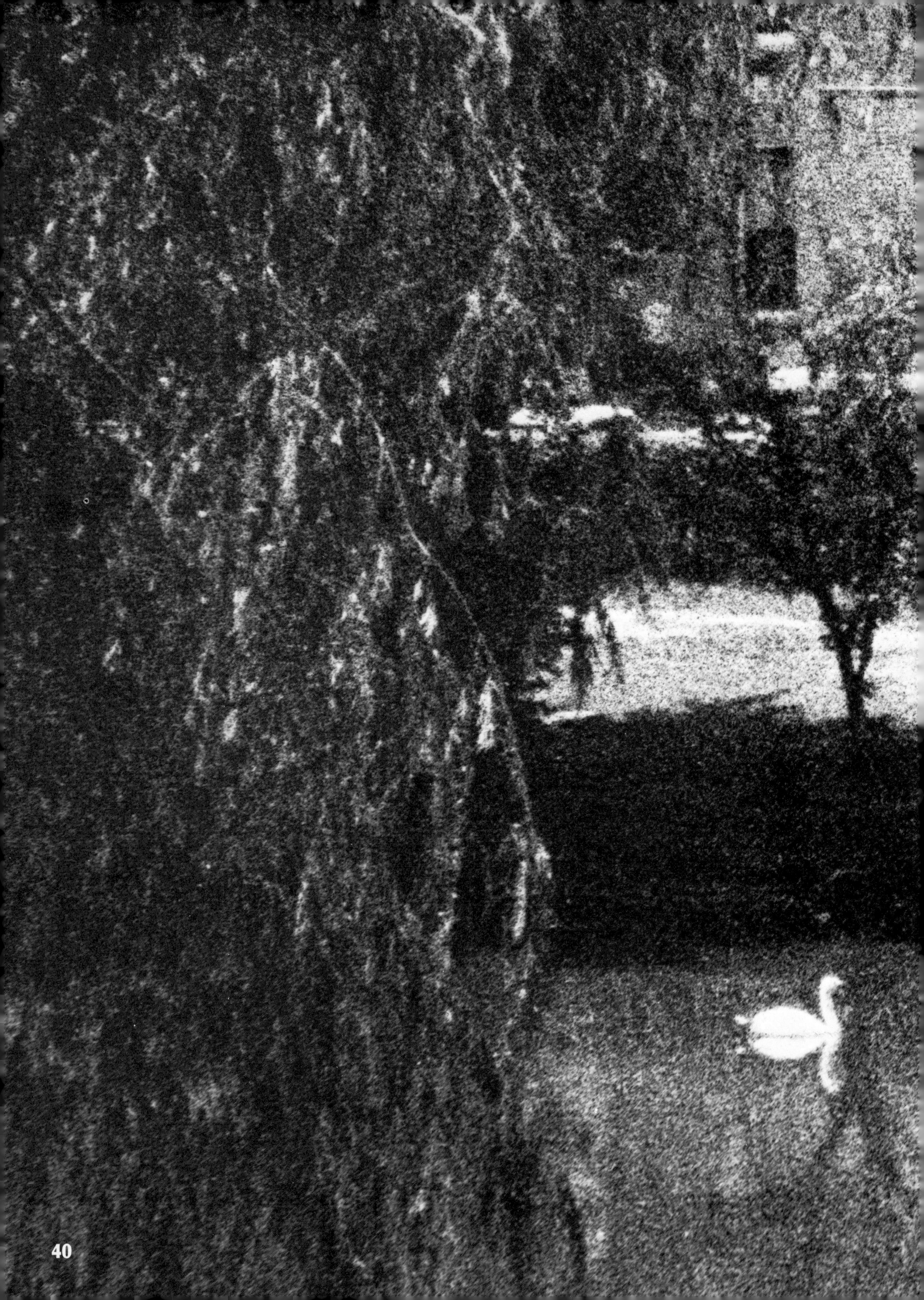

41

Most people look at a photograph and attempt to perceive it as a whole. This, of course, is how to begin observing a picture. The photographer aims at a central impact and the observer's eyes should immediately center on that point of interest. But most people do not go beyond the initial stage. For them, the first and invariably cursory glance is enough. As Aldous Huxley pointed out, people must learn to observe if they are to *see*. He clarified what observation is in a chapter heading in his book *The Art of Seeing*. Seeing, according to Huxley, is sensing plus selecting plus perceiving.

This section concentrates on the selecting aspect of Huxley's formula. Except for the first one, the photographs here are arranged in such a manner as to train the observer's eye. What Huxley called "analytical looking" means paying attention to details in the picture. Each photograph here emphasizes some significant aspect of observation. The student should therefore consider the pictures in sequence, so that by the end of the section he will have learned to *see*.

The first photograph was chosen for its complexity. The student should write on this picture alone, without paying any attention to the rest of the section. The results should be "diagnosed" by the instructor to determine the level of the class and its strengths and weaknesses. The instructor should then know what to emphasize in the photographs that follow.

In the beginning, the questions should be answered in the form of paragraphs. If the instructor prefers, he can ask for sentences that express the essence of the photograph. These sentences, in turn, can be used as topic sentences for the paragraphs. A few of the pictures in this section call for a longer treatment than a paragraph. The length of the composition, however, is at the discretion of the instructor.

1. Lahore Morning, pages 12–13: What does this picture tell you about a city in Pakistan? Draw on your experience in your own town or city of early morning when people are going to work. What are the similarities? What are the differences? Would it help you understand the picture better if you did some research about cities in Pakistan?

2. Black Man, page 14: There is one detail in the background which tells you where this man is standing. What is that detail? What does it tell you? Is it significant?

3. Boy and Bicycles, page 15: Does the background in this picture make a difference? What if it were left out?

4. Girl and Typewriter, page 16: What are the similarities in the two important parts of this picture? Do the two parts work together to make a comment on the situation? How much does the mural on the wall tell you?

5. Women and Statue, page 17: There is an implied similarity between the statue and the women. What is implied? Does the implication apply to women only? Is the statue that of a man or a woman?

6. Steps on the Banks of the Seine, pages 18–19: Here, several details have to be considered to determine the locale of the picture. What are those details? They form a pattern. Does this pattern convey any information? Across the top of the picture is something important that a hasty observer would ignore. Look at the top part of the picture: what does it say? How is that information related to the two rings in the lower right-hand side of the photograph?

7. Man with a Blowtorch, page 20: You have to focus on one particular point if you want to know what this man is doing. The background, in this instance, is of no help. Does the detail tell you anything about the occupation of the man?

8. Tables and Chairs, page 21: Sometimes a pattern, pleasing to the eye, is the sole reason for a photograph. In some cases, however, the pattern may hide a detail that adds a touch of significance to the picture. There is such a detail in this picture. What is that detail?

9. Registration Scene, pages 22–23: How often students go through registration, absorbed with their individual problems! Here is a photograph that shows part of what you may have missed. Does the picture convey a different idea of registration?

10. Old Chair, page 24: The old chair says a lot about how its owners lived. Taking into account the various details, discuss that life.

11. Group of Zulus, page 25: Each person in the photograph is wearing a different type of clothing. Here is one place where a single glance is not enough. Consider each person and his or her clothing individually and you can tell something about the life of the Zulus. Would research help you understand better?

12. Tree Trunk, pages 26–27: How long has this tree trunk been lying on its side? Do you need to know botany to answer this question? Do the details in the photograph convey sufficient information?

13. Goats on Building, page 28, and Pakistani and Bicycle, page 29: In both these pictures, something appears out of place. The first picture was taken in India and the second one in Pakistan. Incongruous detail at times makes a very significant statement, as it does in these two photographs. What kind of statements are made here?

14. Street Scene, pages 30–31: Driving absorbs a person's attention, especially on a route he drives every day and especially when he is heading home tired and late. Is this picture restricted to the driver's viewpoint, or does it convey more information?

15. Zulu Barbers, page 32, and Zulu Tailors, page 33: These pictures are like the one in page 25: they give the observer a glimpse of life in Zululand. But in this case, you are asked *not* to do any research. From these photographs, tell what you can about the life of the Zulus and the land in which they live.

16. Zulu Dancers, pages 34–35: The foreground and background complement each other here, although the focus is on the person in front. People often glance at this picture and make a mistake in determining the sex of this person. Can you tell? What else can you say about this person? Does the picture reveal the relationship between this person and the other dancers?

17. Waiting for the Train, page 36, and Waiting for the Ferry, page 37: These two photographs, taken in India and in Seattle, face each other so that you can compare them and note the differences. What are these differences and what is their significance?

18. Color Photograph, page 38: An overwhelming detail can sometimes distract you from the subject of the picture, as it does here. But this particular overwhelming detail tells us of the importance of the photograph as a tool for observation: what can you see in the picture that would evade you when you look at the real thing?

19. Library Tables, page 39: The absence of details can be important too. What do you expect to find in a setting such as this? What does their absence tell you?

20. Lake Scene, pages 40–41: There are very few details here but careful observation is still necessary if you are to penetrate the texture and see more. How much more do you see when you pay careful attention to different parts of the picture?

ASSUMPTIONS

ASSUMPTIONS

ASSUMPTIONS

ASSUMPTIONS

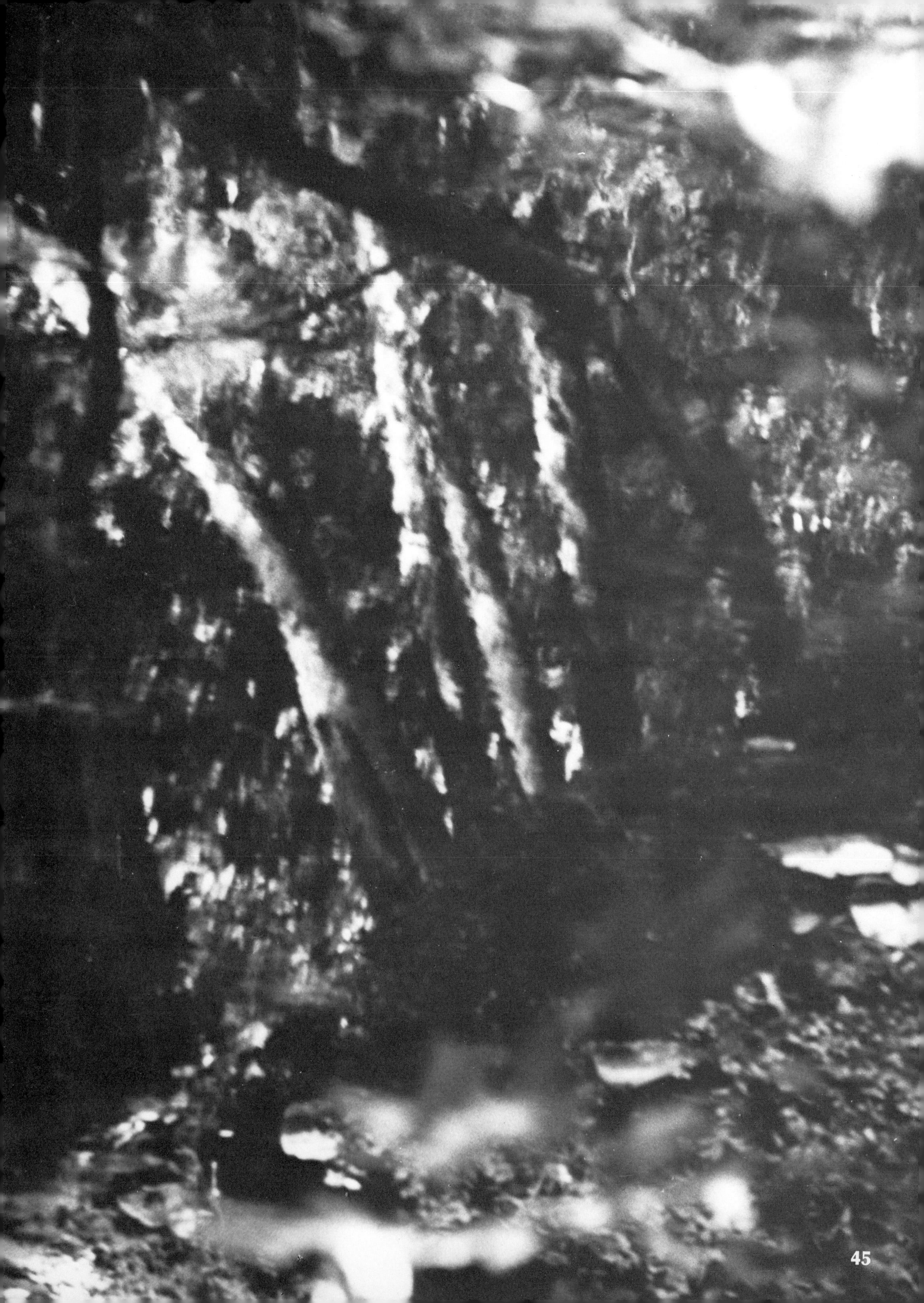

46

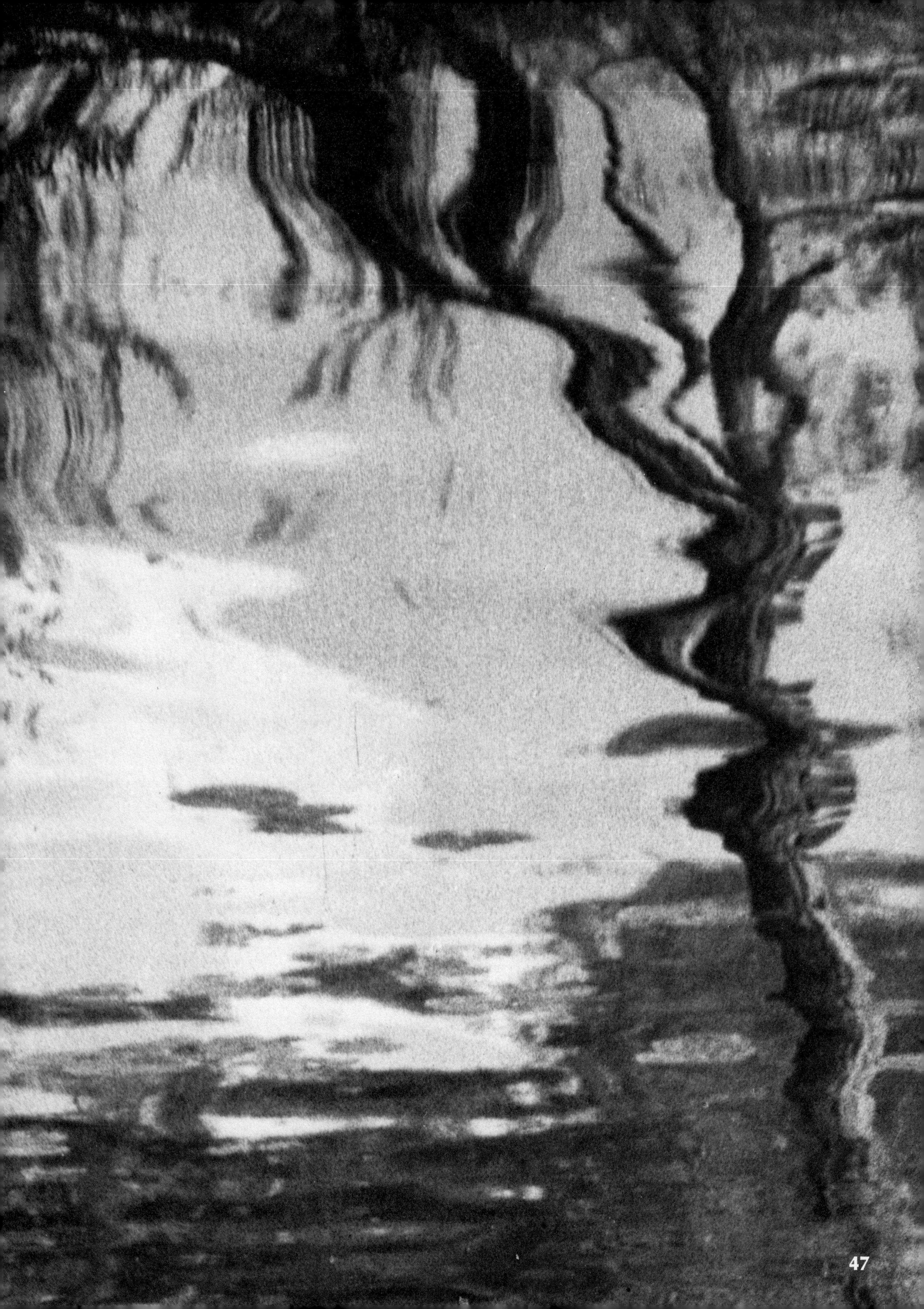

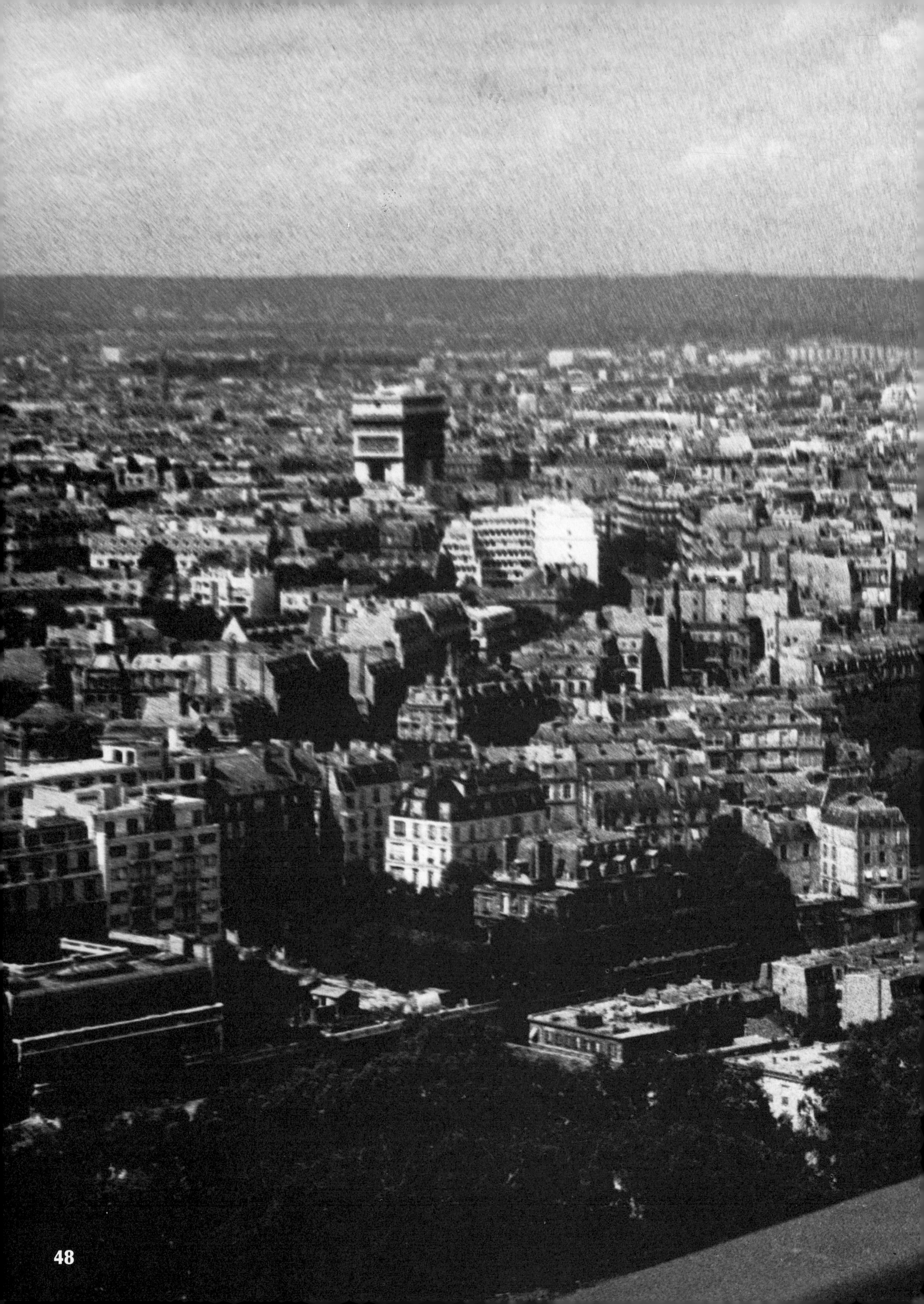

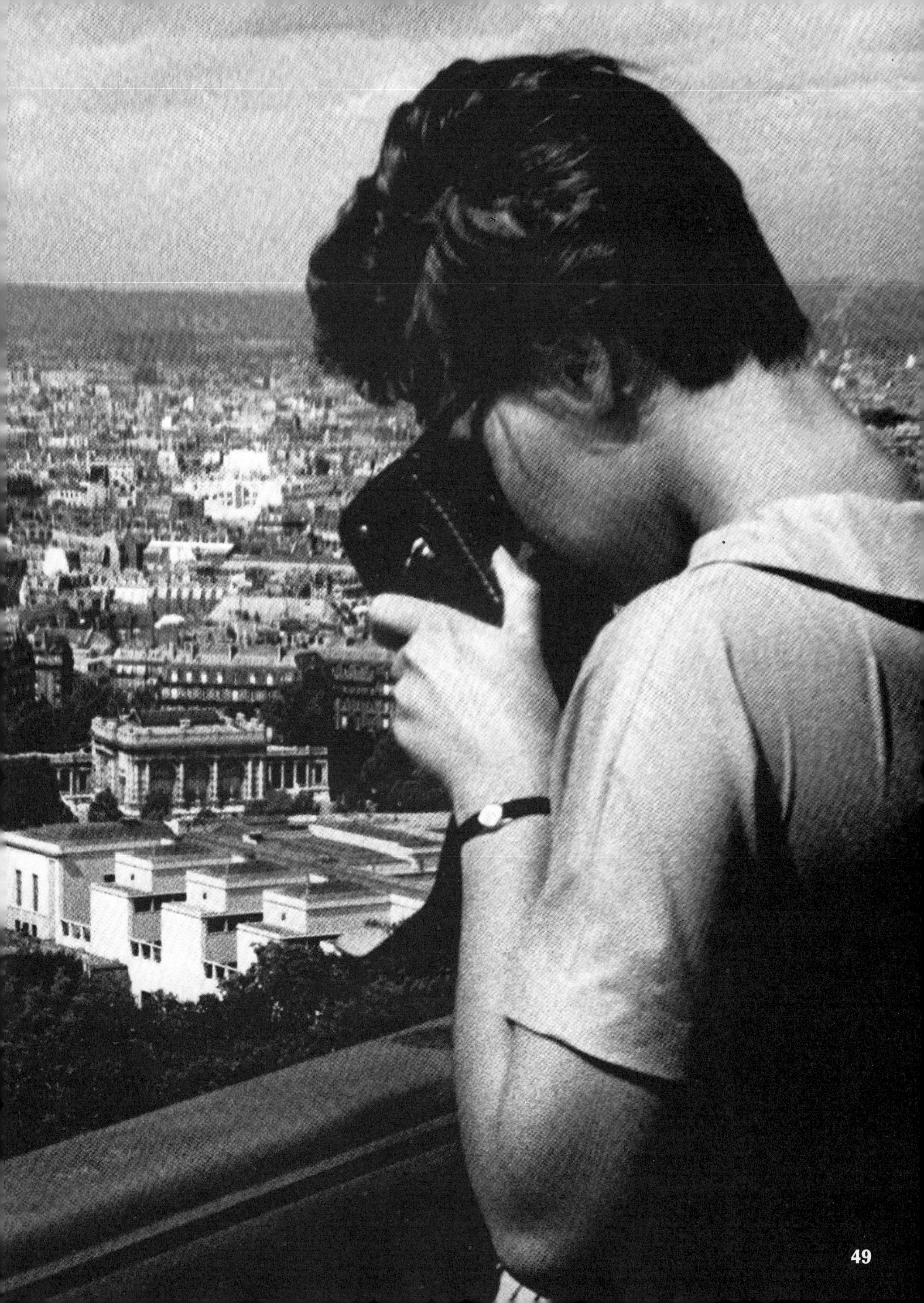

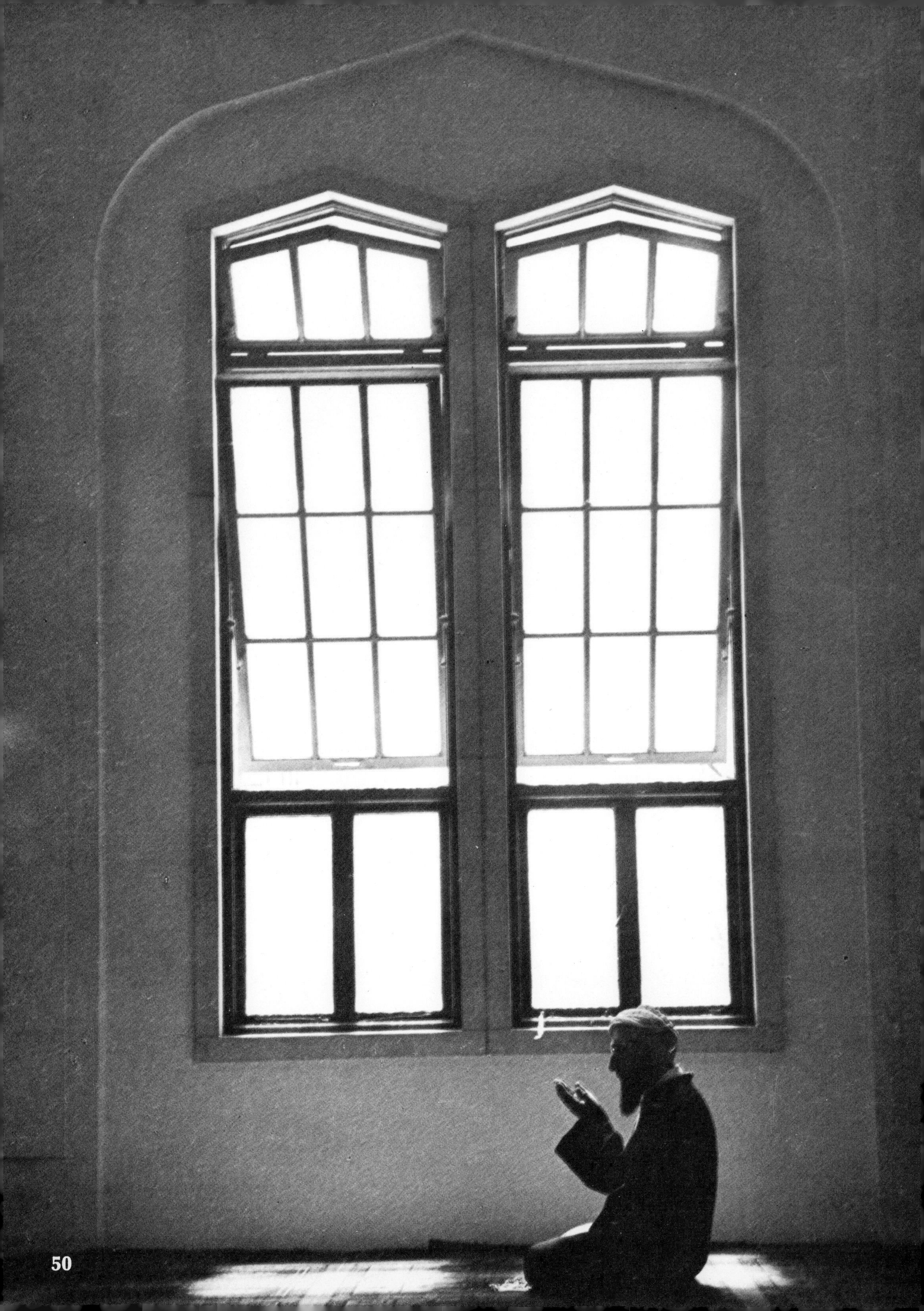

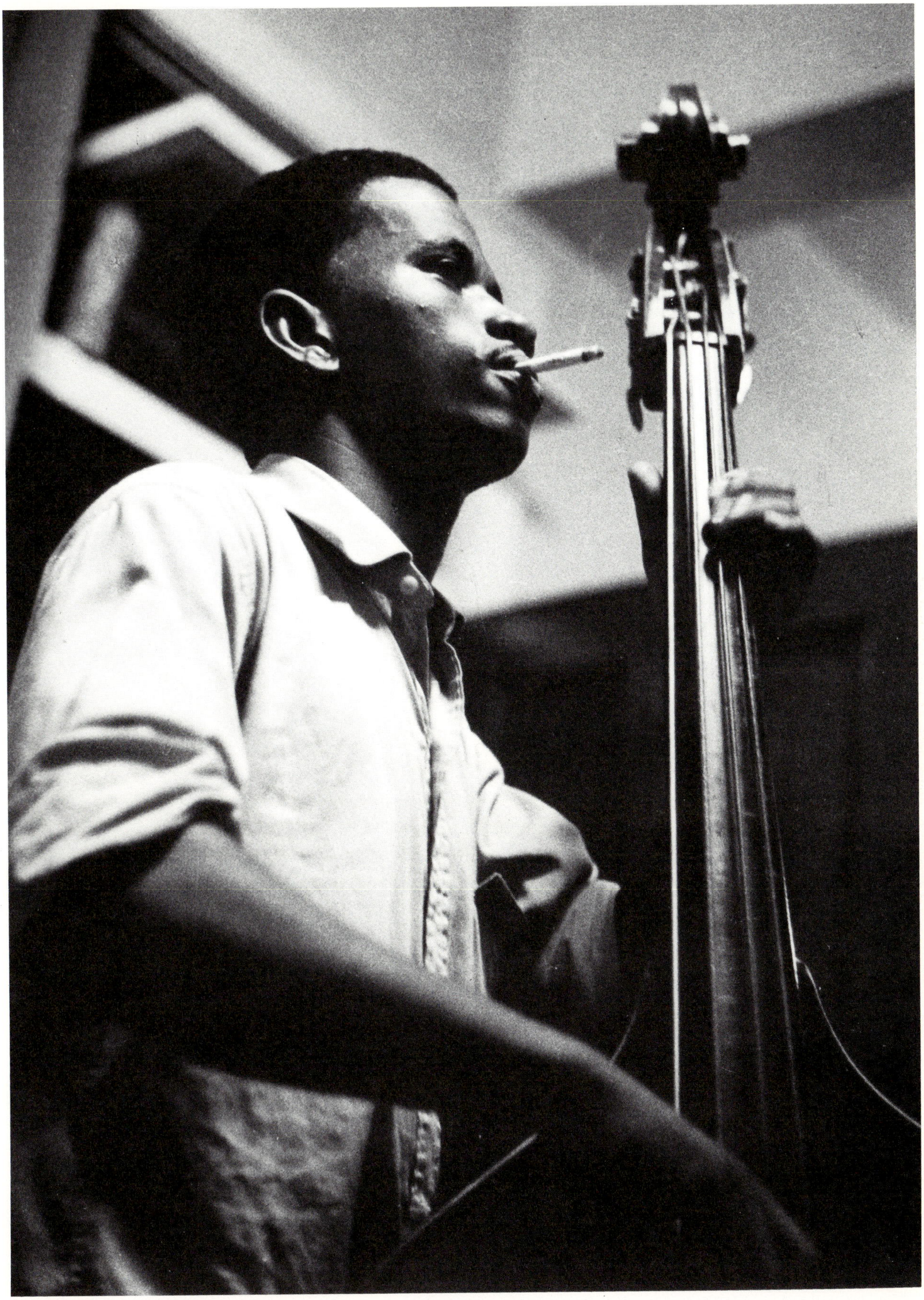

52

53

54

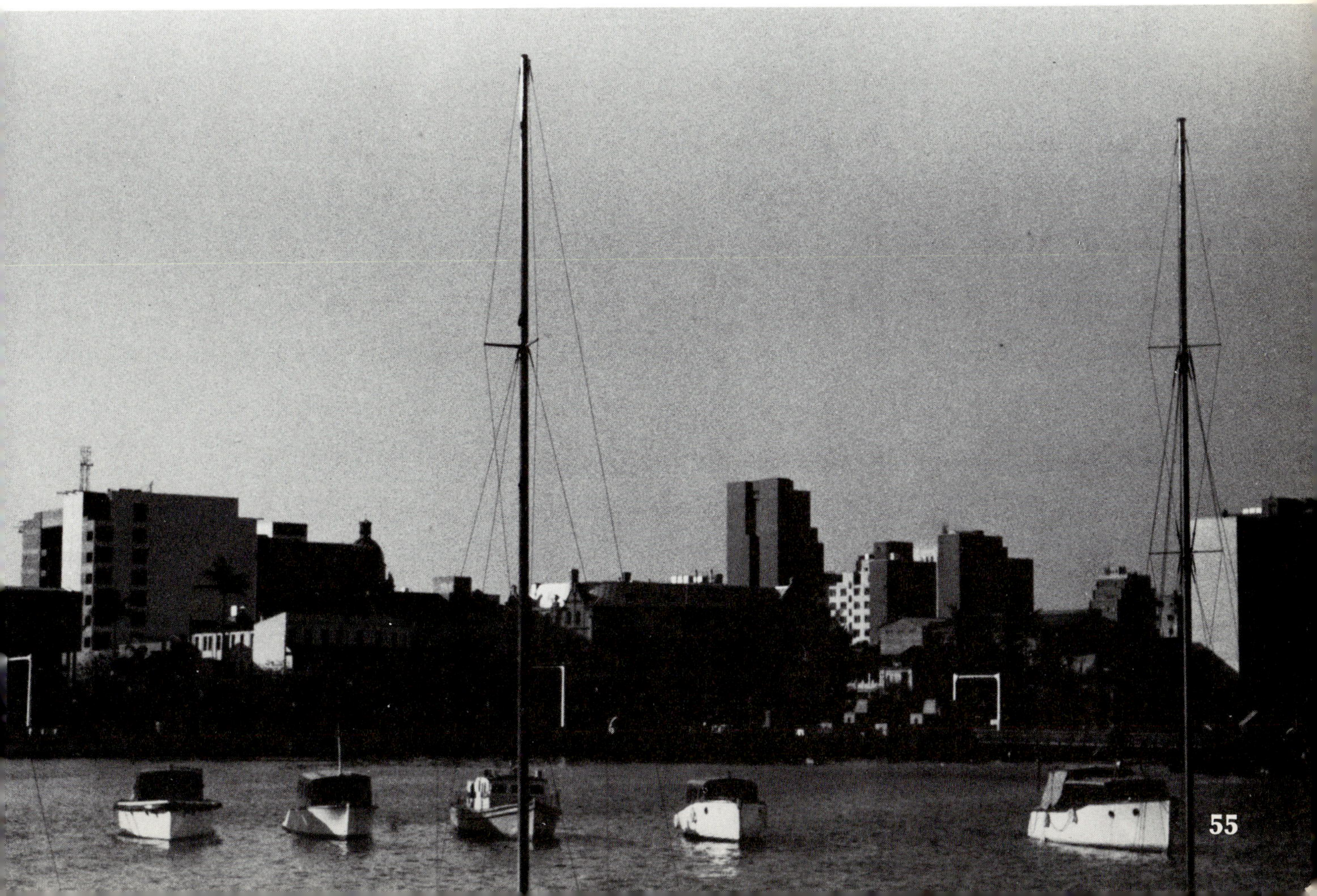

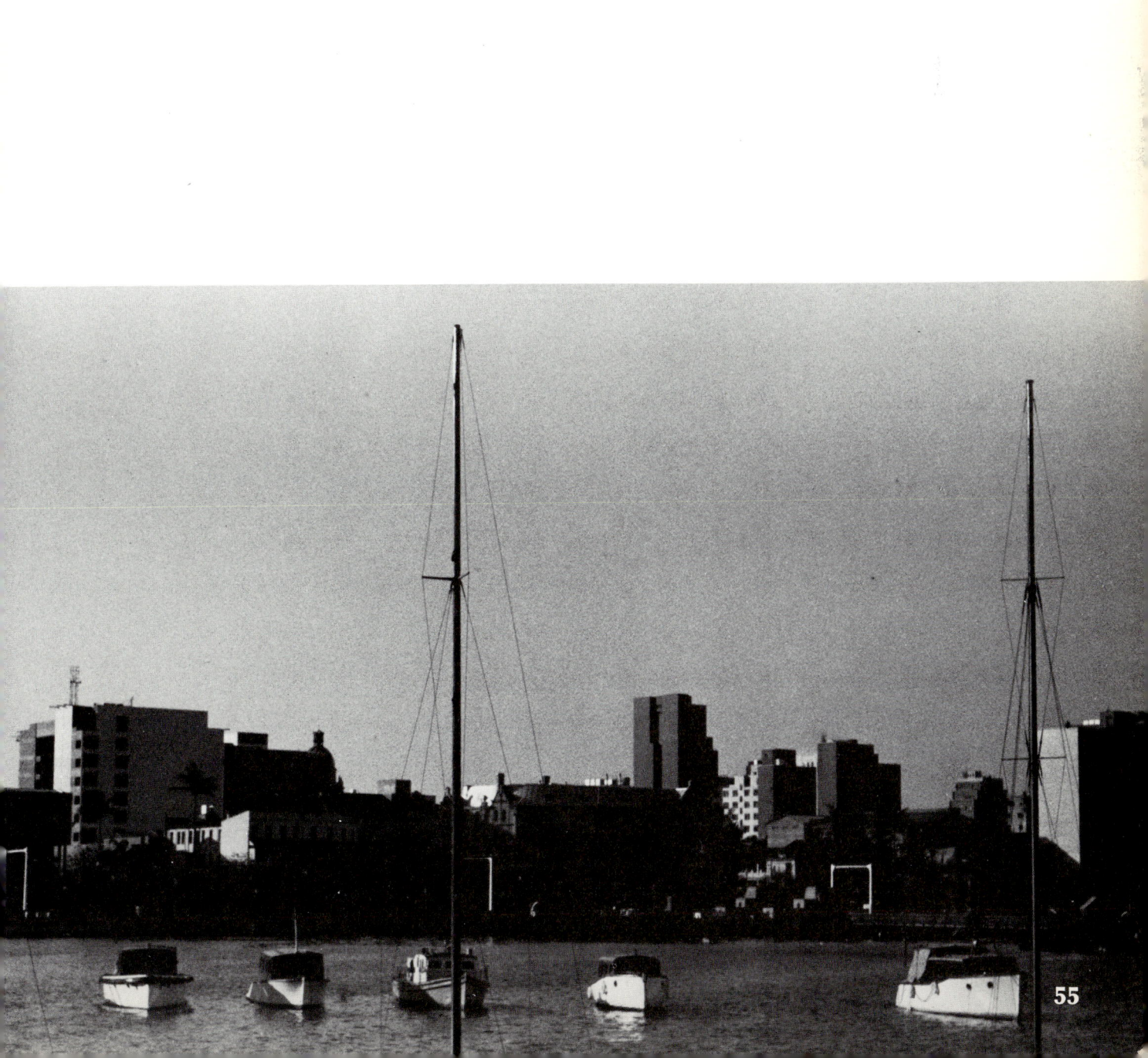

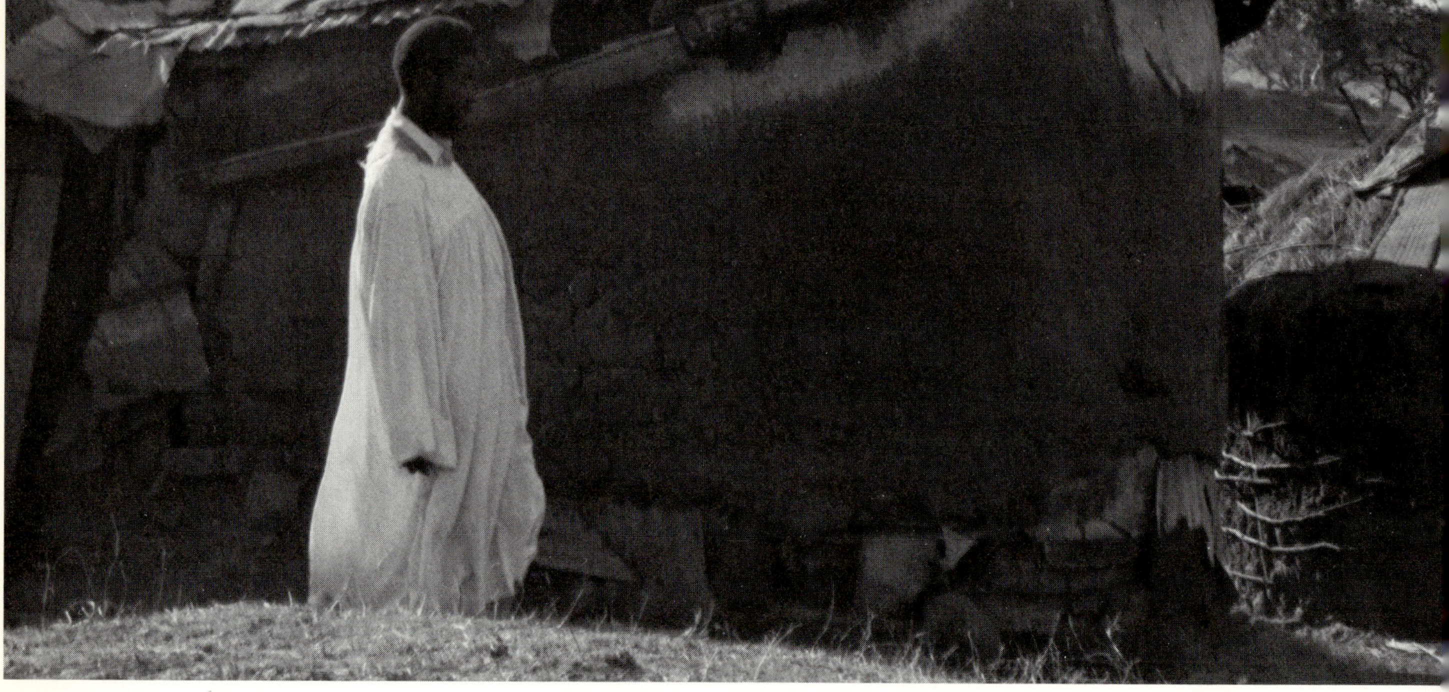

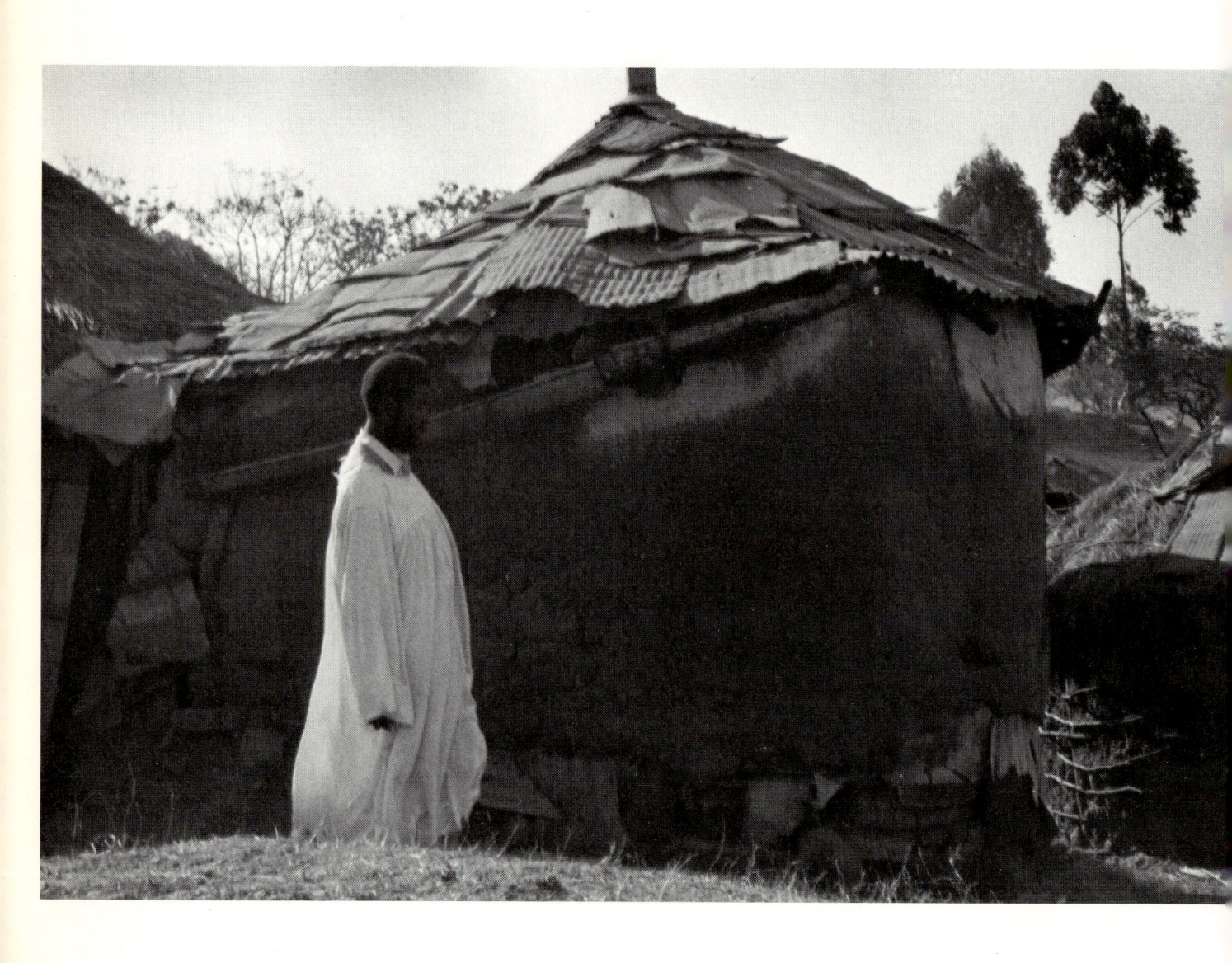

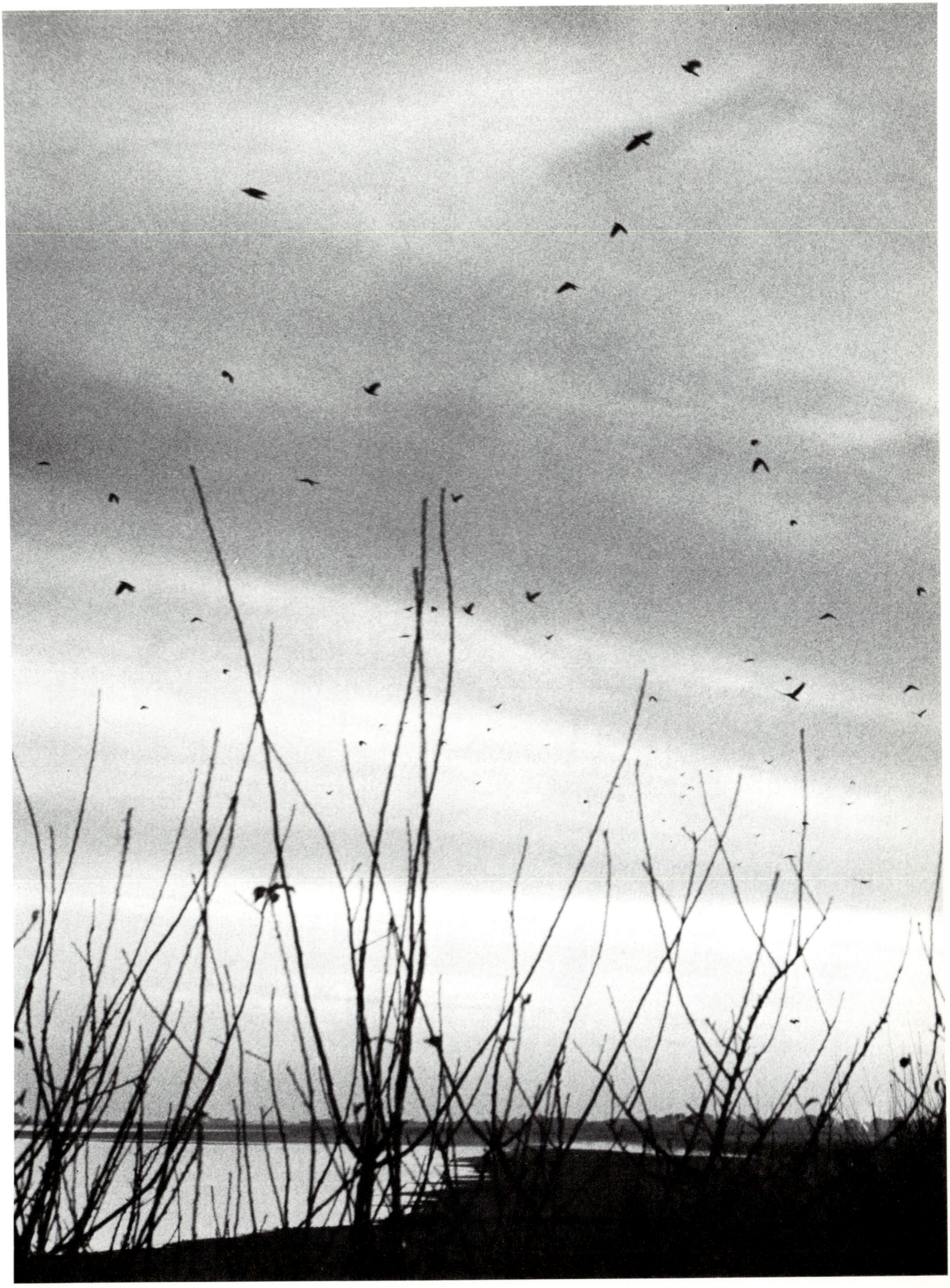

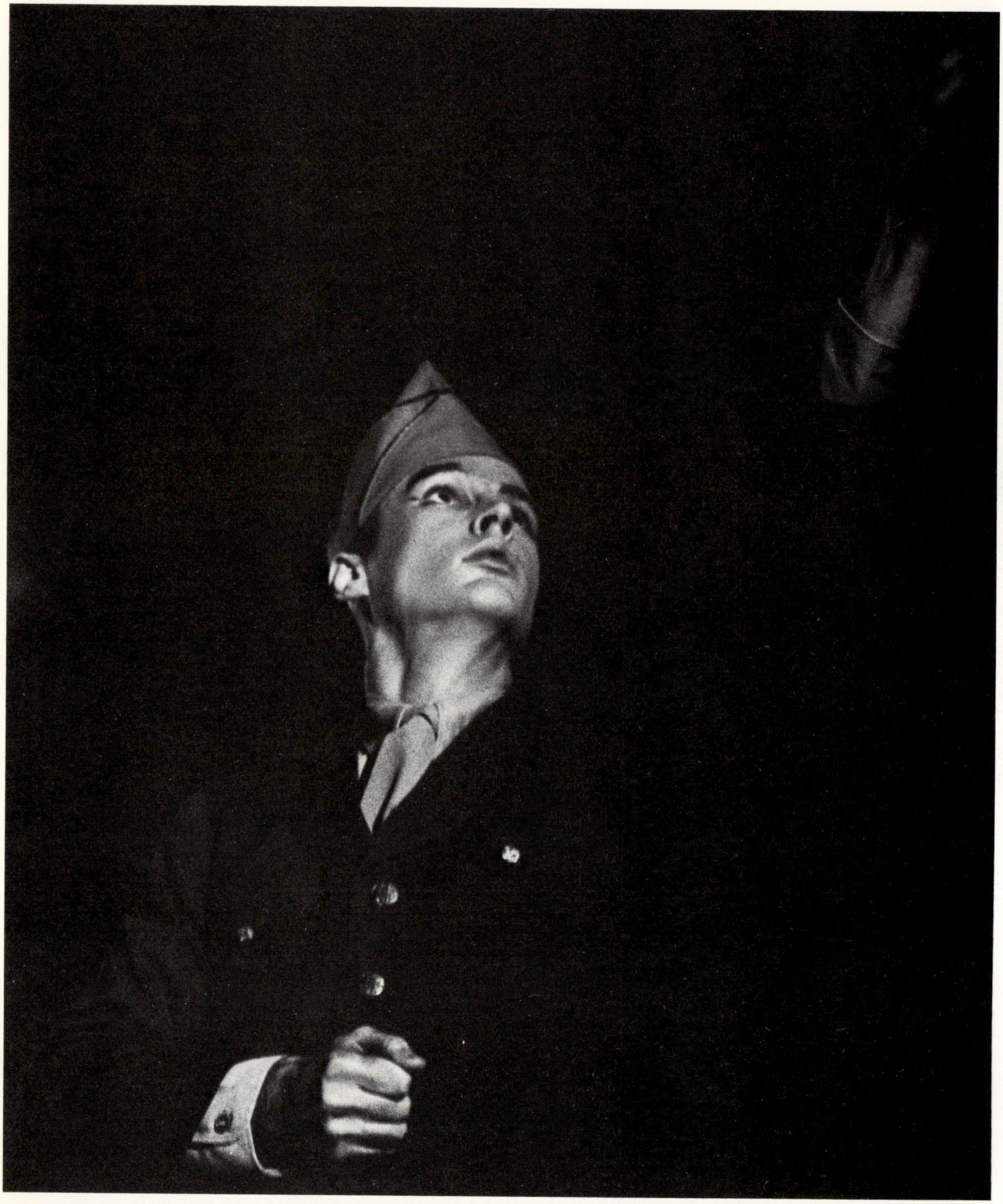

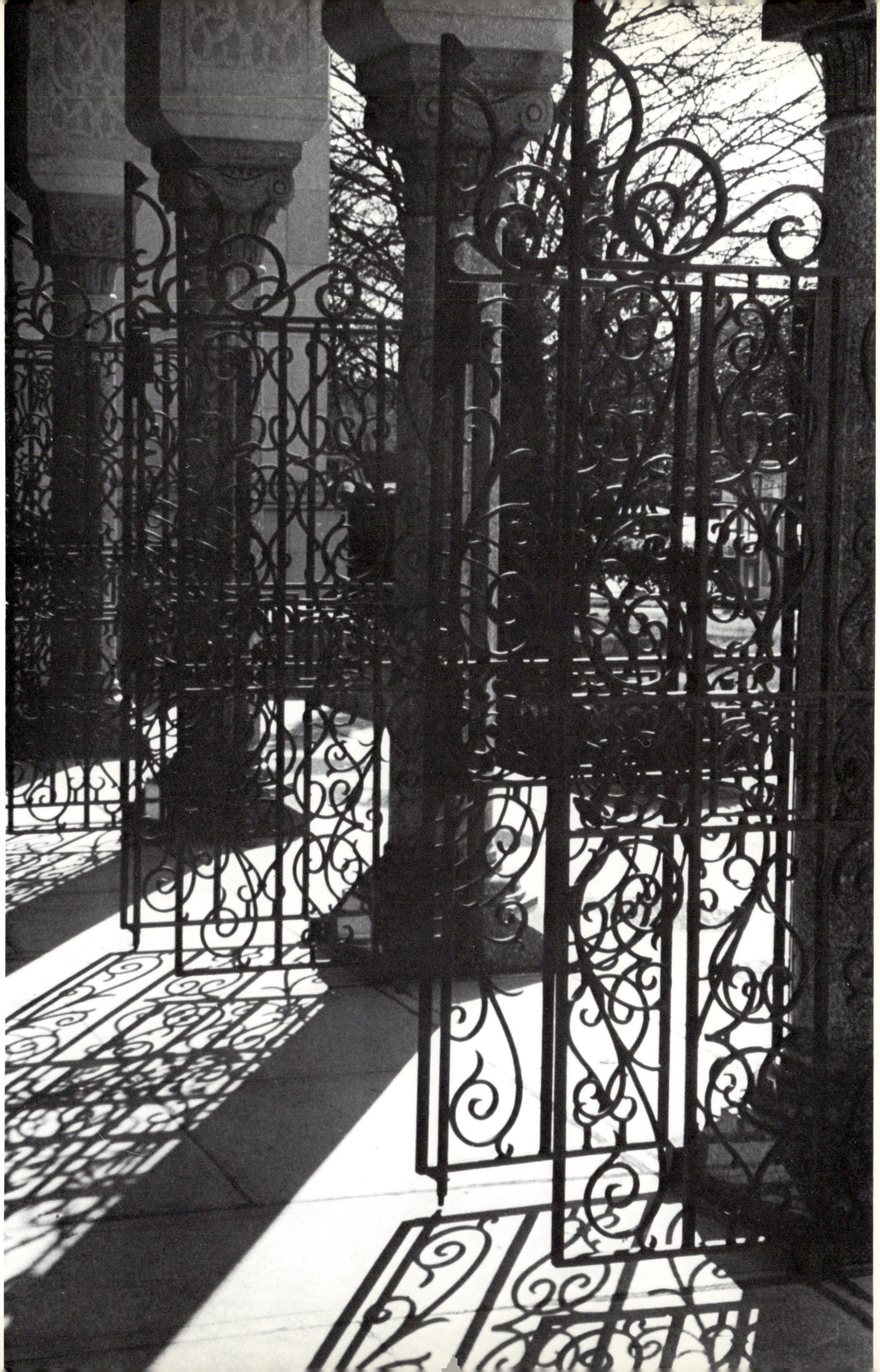

It is easy to make assumptions when confronted by only a photograph and no explanatory text. The observer all too readily projects into the picture his preconceived notion of what he thinks it depicts. But when a person has learned to observe and to pay attention to individual details, he is less likely to make sweeping statements about the photograph. The ones in this section have been chosen to test the student's observation and, consequently, to guard against his making assumptions without supporting evidence in the form of significant features.

There is another kind of assumption that results from pictures—of all kinds, including movies and television. Persons exposed to the same image of a people or an area eventually think of those people or that area in terms of stereotypes. Because I lived in Africa most of my life, people ask me whether there are cities on that continent. Some of the photographs in this chapter can be used to eliminate the kind of assumptions that lead to stereotypes.

The answers to the questions can be either paragraphs or full-length compositions. The simple approach is the best: the student can begin by stating, "I believe this is a picture of...." He can then proceed to supply reasons for his belief. Where the response to the questions includes a discussion of stereotypes, the answer can be either a composition or a longer research paper.

Page 46: Here is a group about whom it is easy to make assumptions. What are those assumptions and why does one tend to make them?

Page 47: Does this picture remind you of a painting? What kind of a painting? What is the subject? Is there anything in the picture that would help you answer these questions?

Pages 48–49: Can you tell what city this is? Does the inclusion of the young lady in the picture give you any idea? Look at the buildings: are they clues in identifying the city? Is there one particular structure which provides the significant detail necessary to answer the first question? Have any of your responses been due to stereotypes? What are the stereotypes and how do you think they should be eliminated?

Page 50: What is the man in the picture doing? To answer this question, pay particular attention to the background. Where do you think this building is located? Many people have stereotyped ideas about the situation and background of this photograph; discuss the matter in some detail.

Page 51: This photograph is demanding because of the absence of any clues to answering the following question: where do you think this picture was taken? In class, extensively discuss the implications of the answers offered by yourself and the other students.

Pages 52–53: A student of art or architecture will find much to interest him here. But for most students the question to be answered is simple. Where do you think this building is located? Try to be as specific as possible and give reasons for your answer.

Page 54: What are these men making? There is a significant detail here to help you in answering this question.

Page 55: Any city on an ocean front? or lake? The clues here are subtle. This picture also lends itself to a discussion of stereotypes.

Page 56: There is an abundance of details here to tell you about the area that forms the background. Does the presence of the man help you, or does it put you off? Why?

Page 57: To determine where this picture was taken, you will have to guess. There is nothing in the picture to give you any indication. The question on this photograph, however, is: where do you think the birds are going? What makes you think so?

Page 58: What is the situation here? Three details act together to provide the information.

Page 59: Any idea what kind of building this could be an entrance to? What keeps distracting you from getting an answer?

CONTEXTS

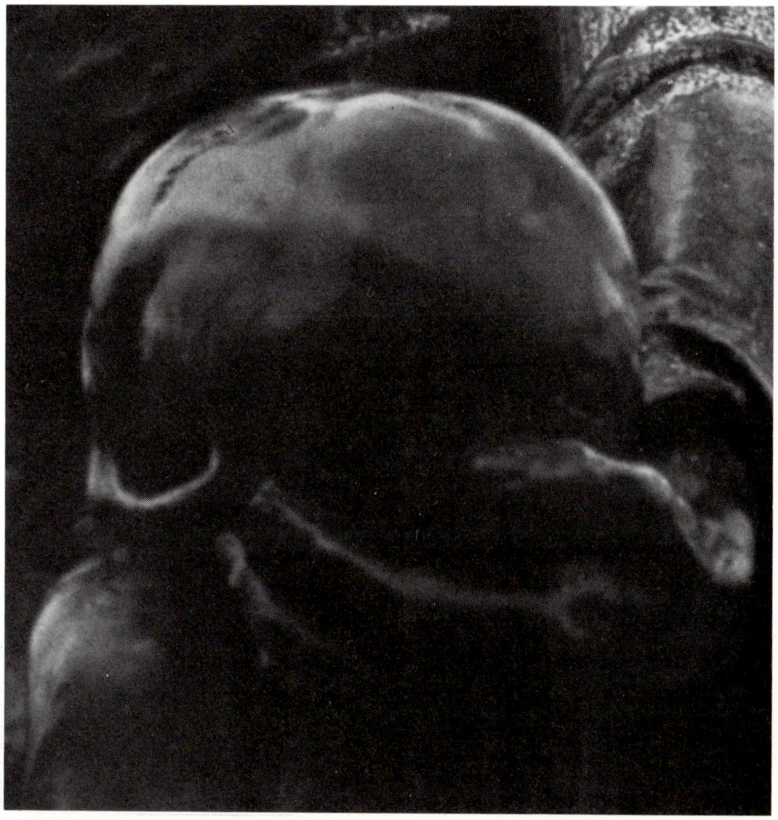

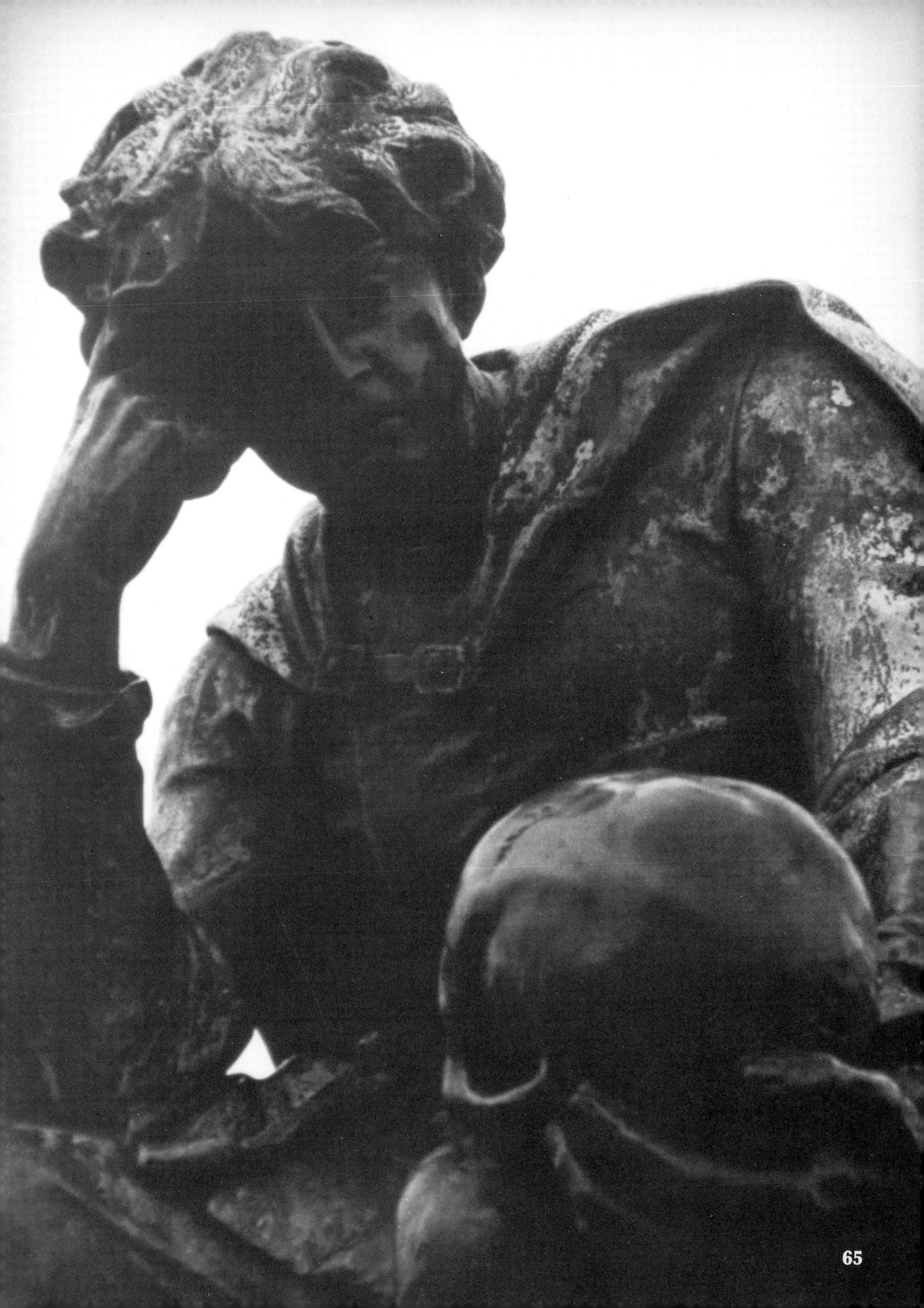

Do NOT go
beyond page 83
until you have
read the
instructions on
that page.

The purpose of
the photographs
on pages 67 to 82
is for you to
determine the
context of each
picture.
For more
details on this
procedure, see
the material
on page 83.

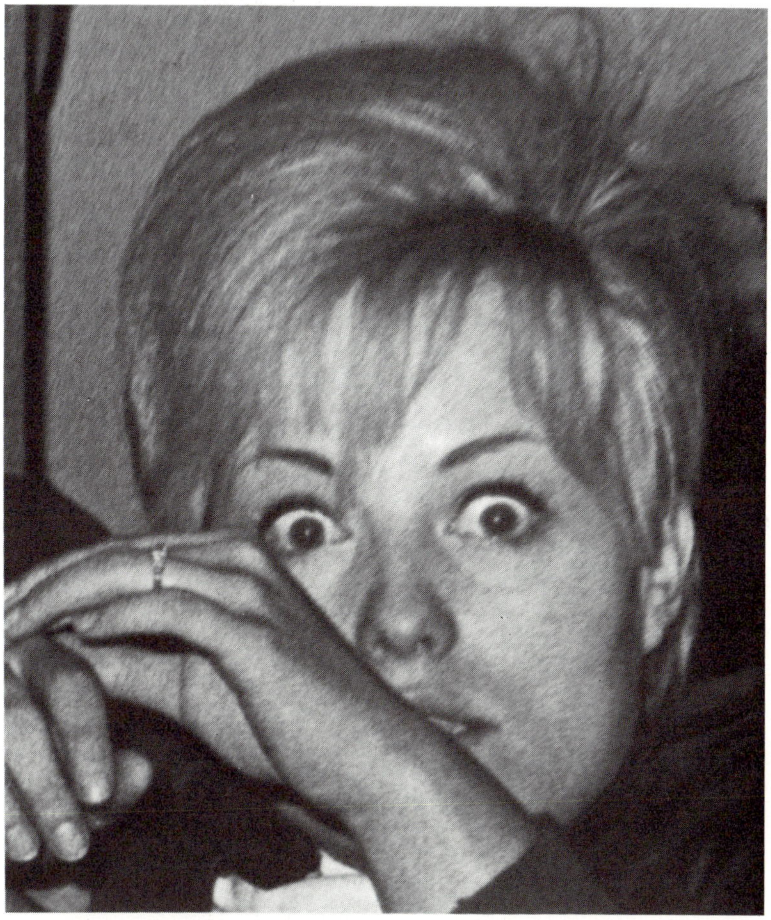

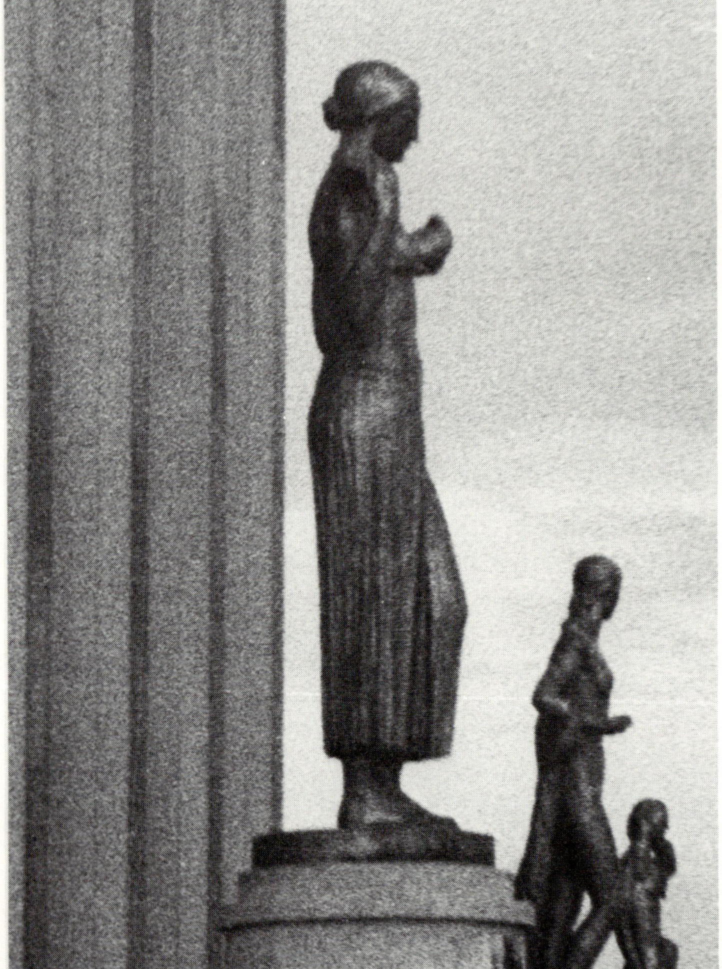

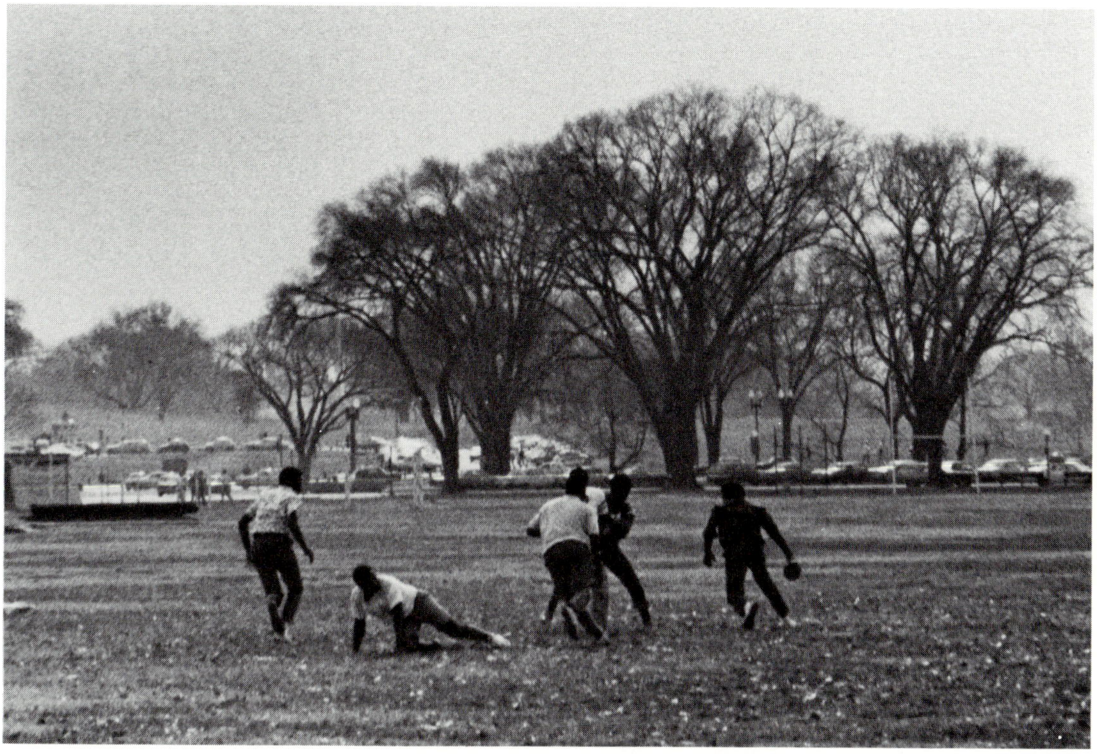

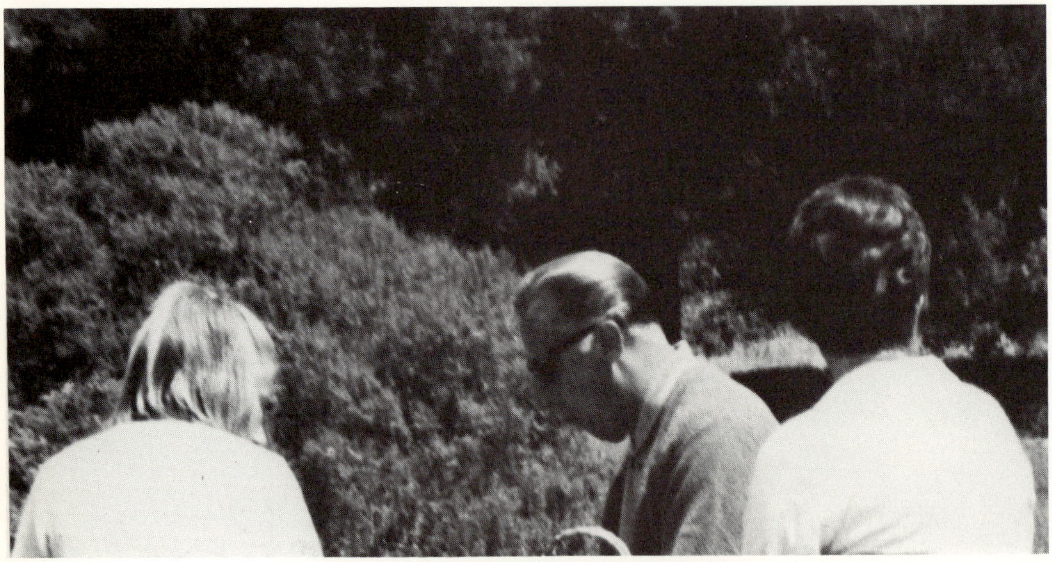

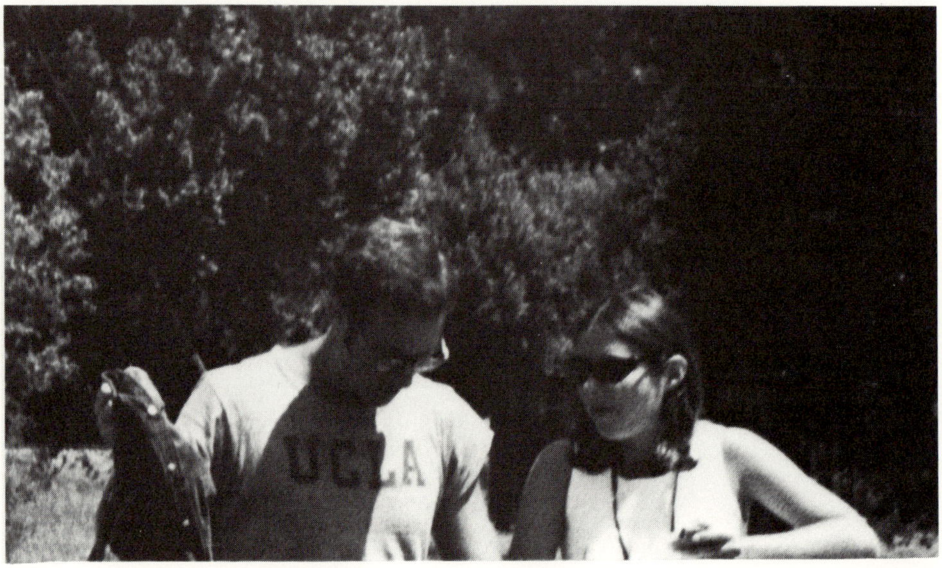
UCLA

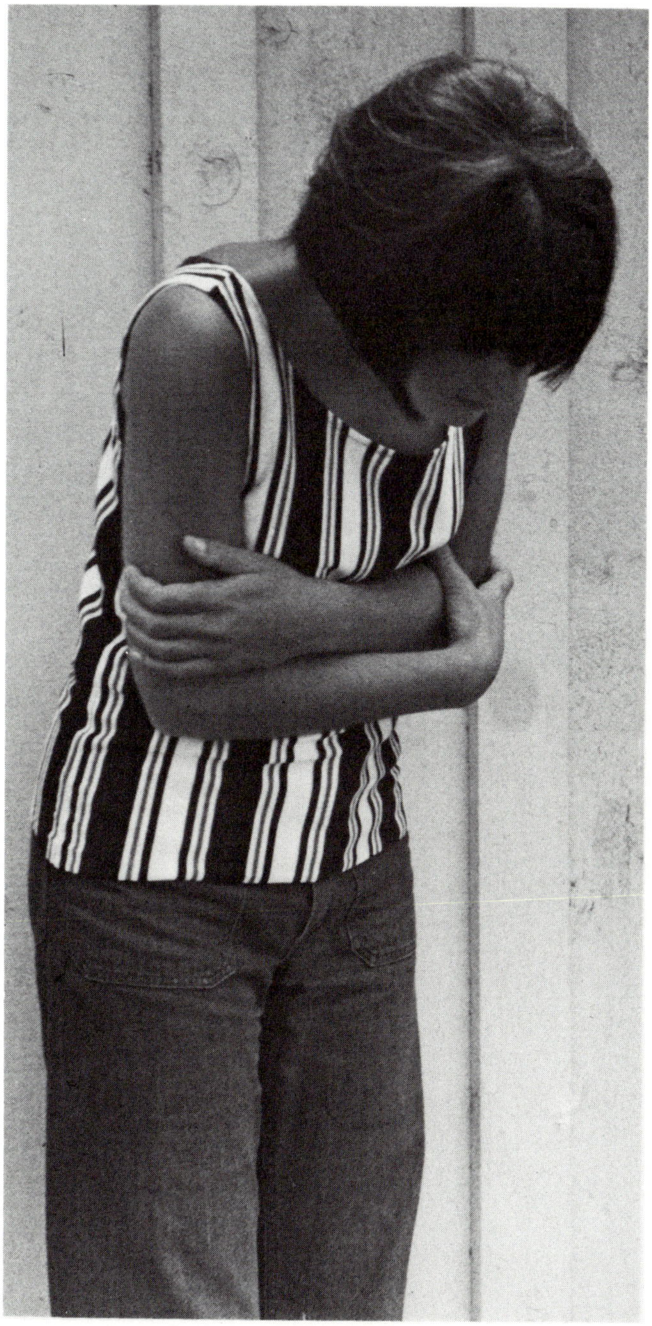

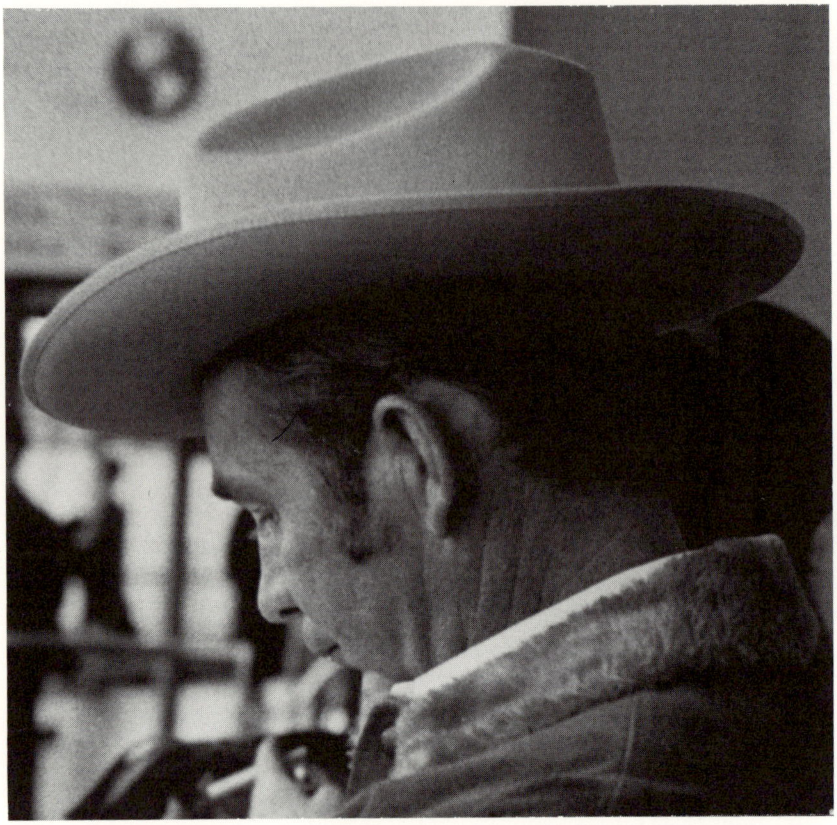

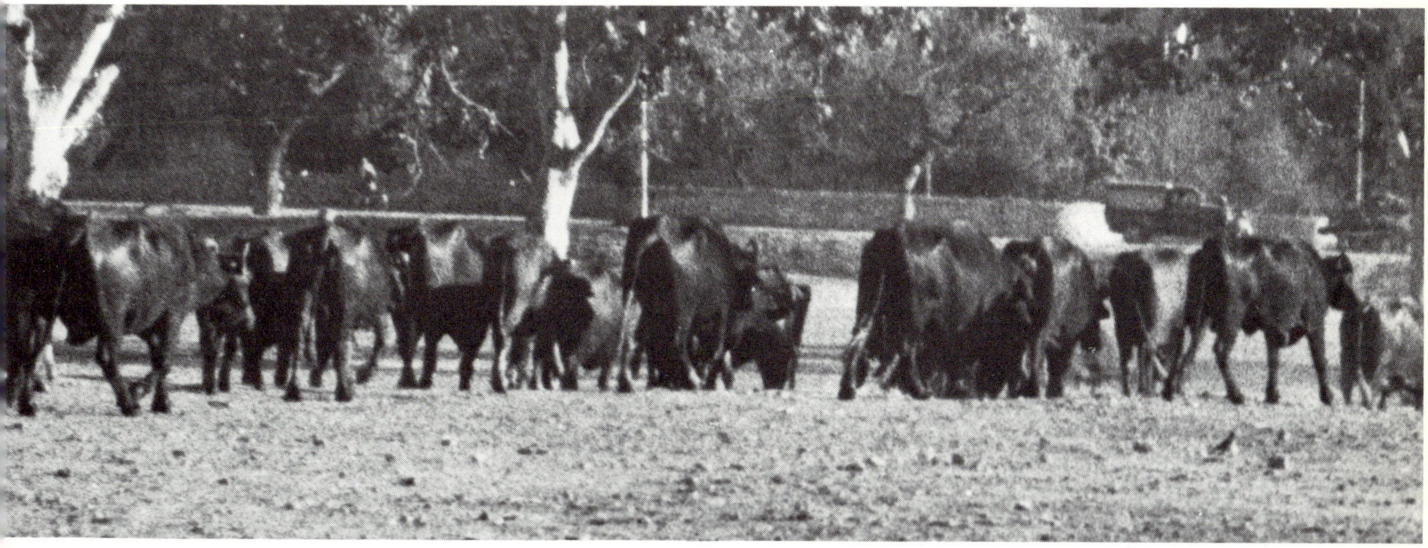

74

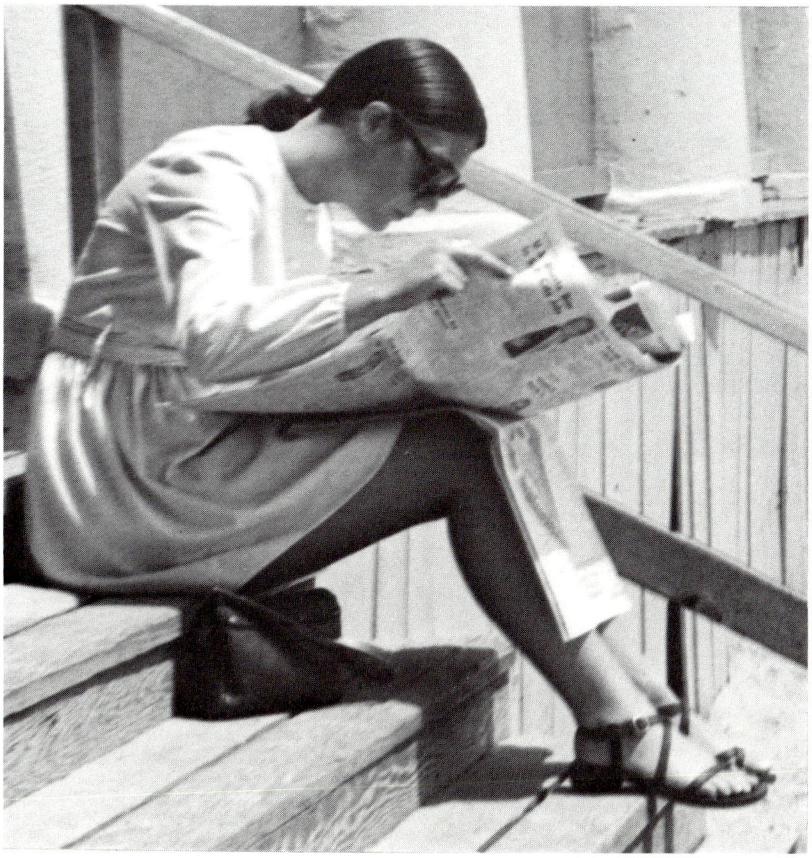

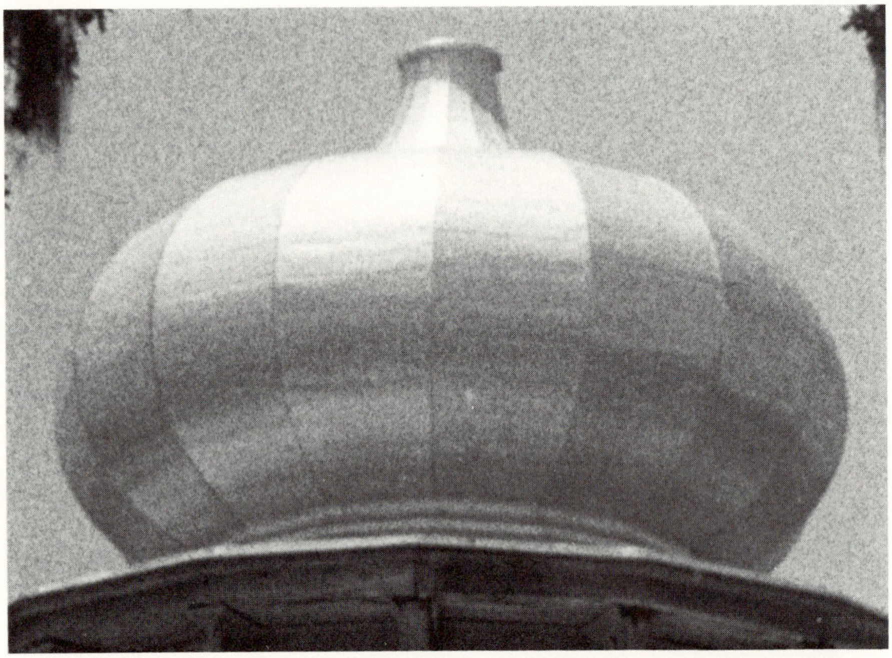

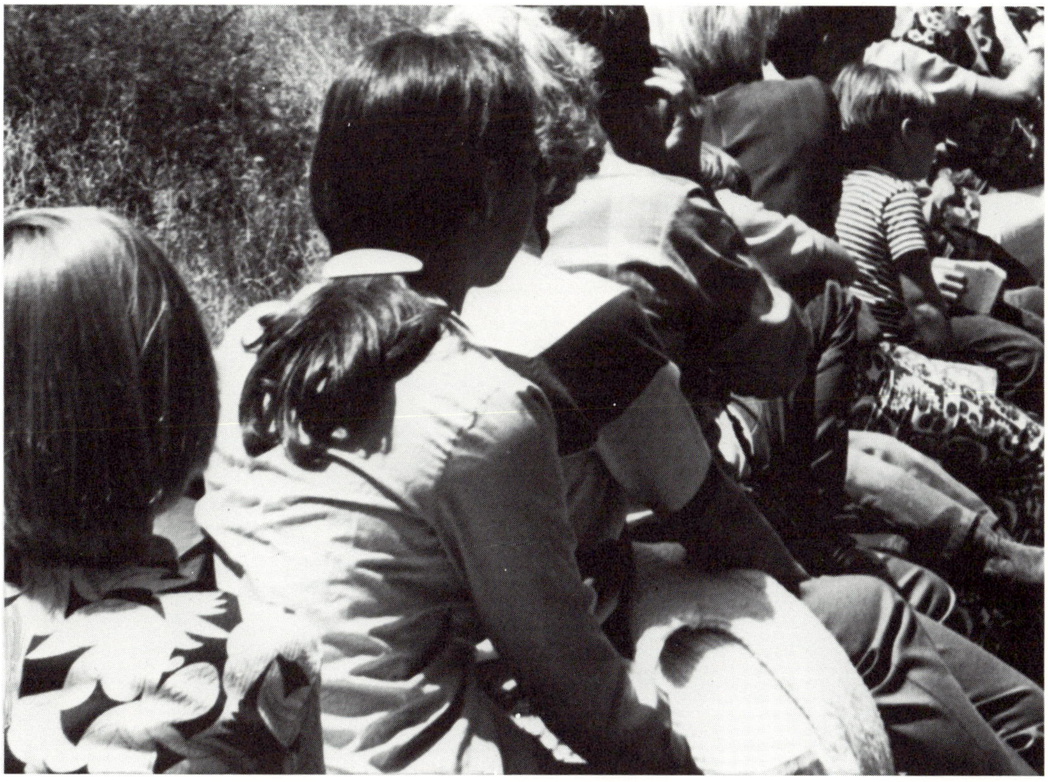

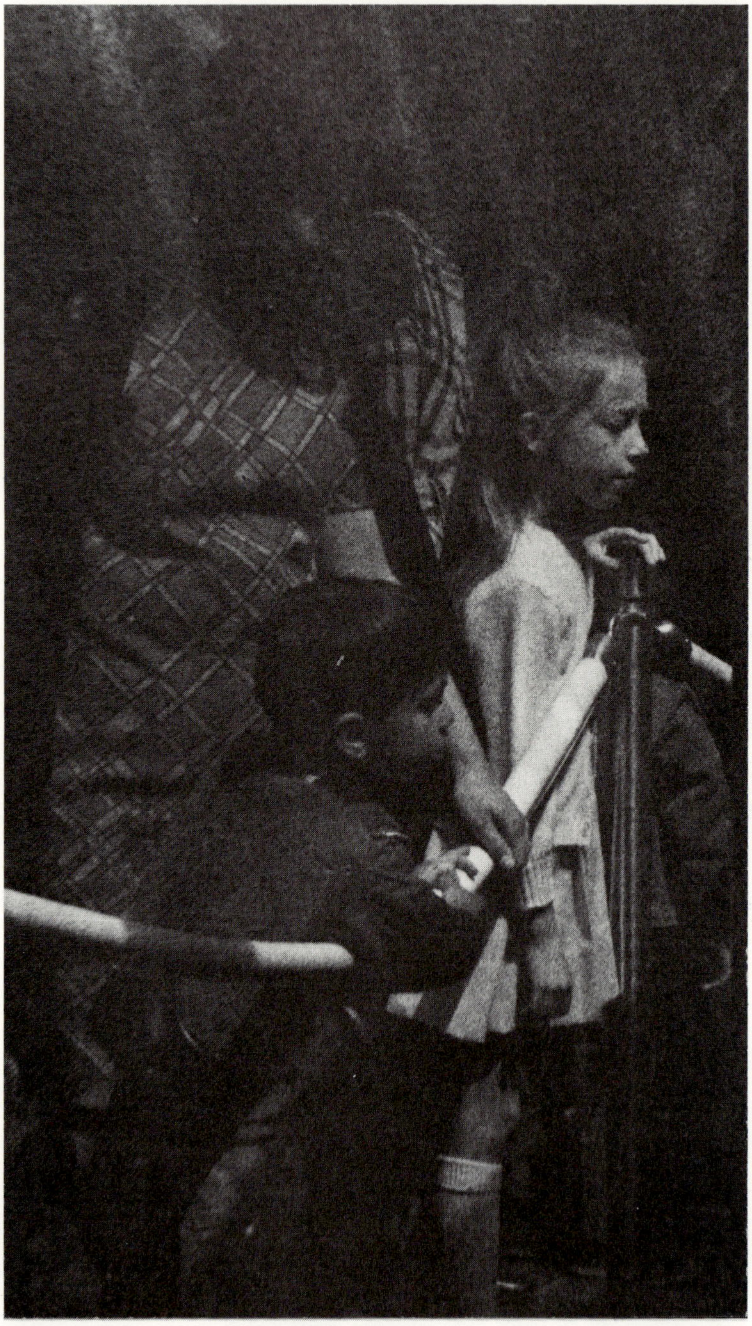

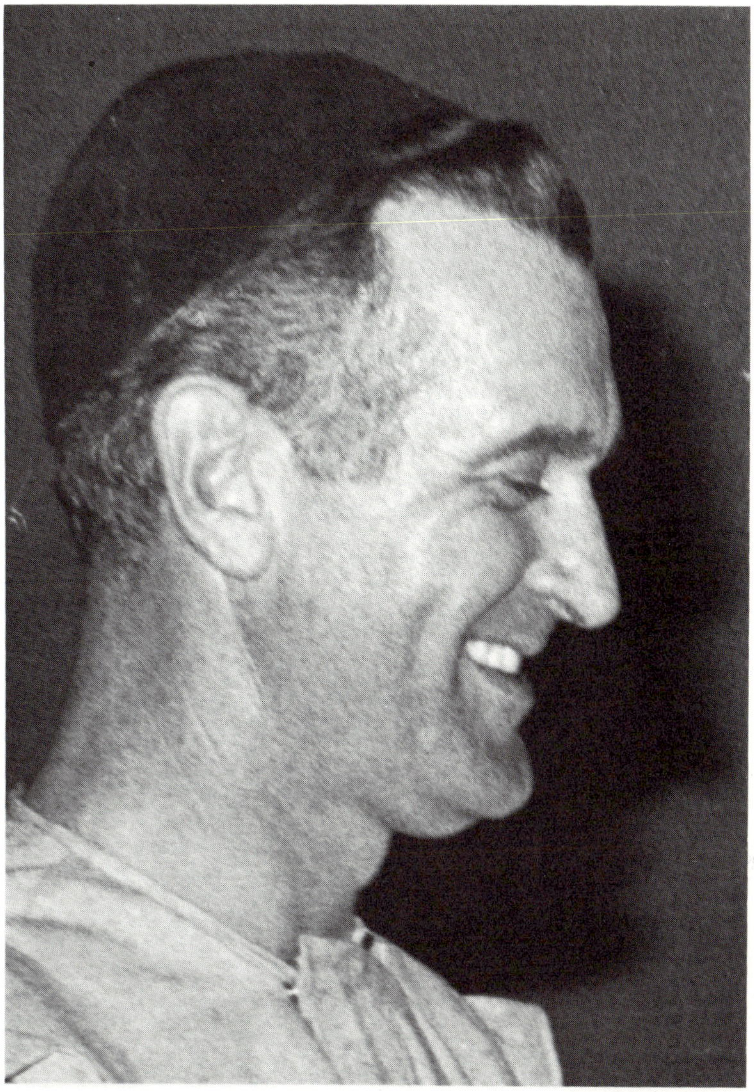

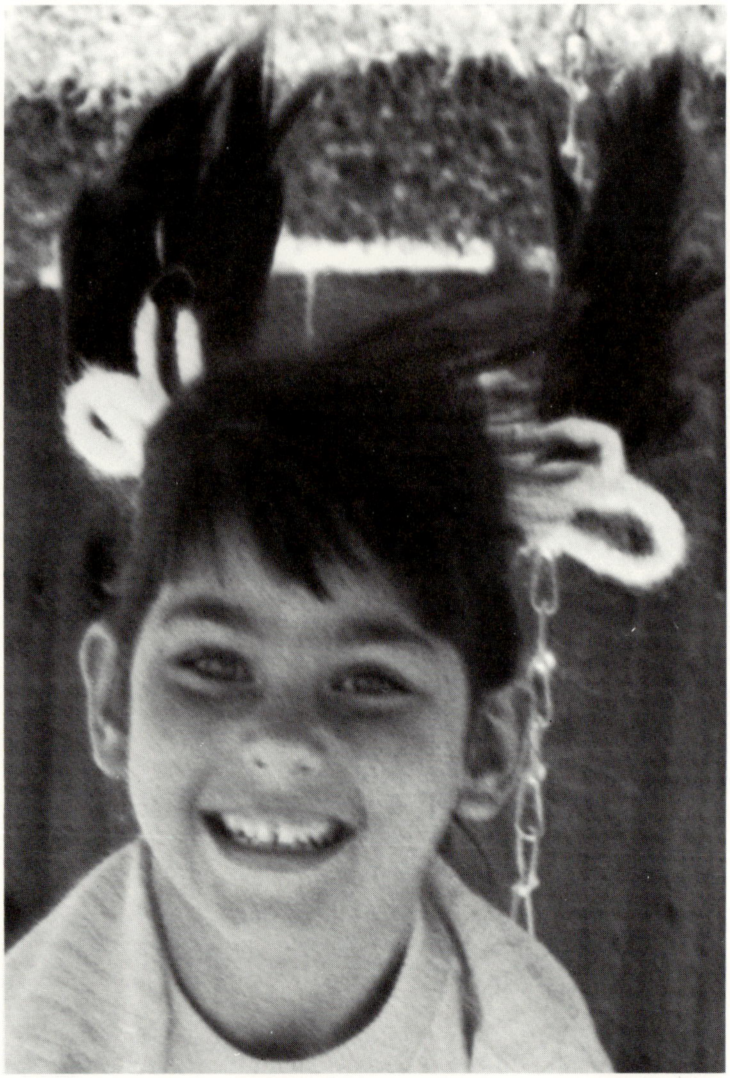

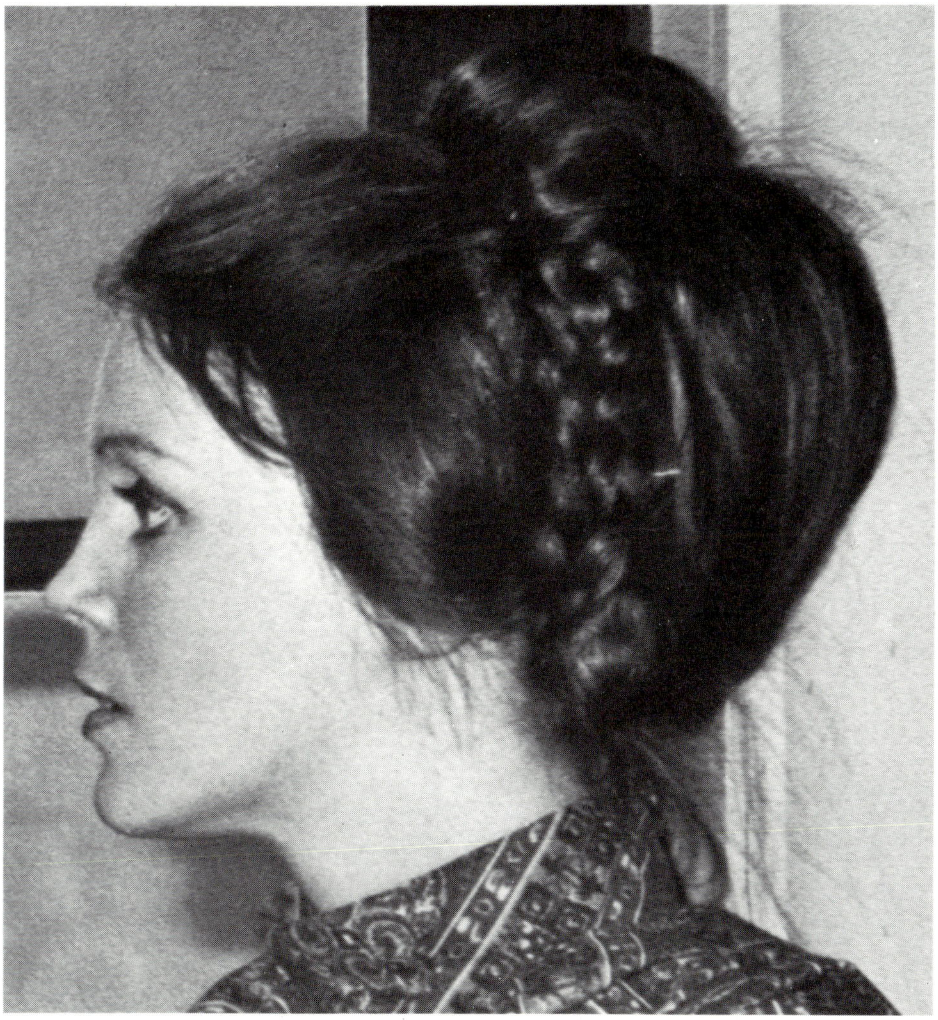

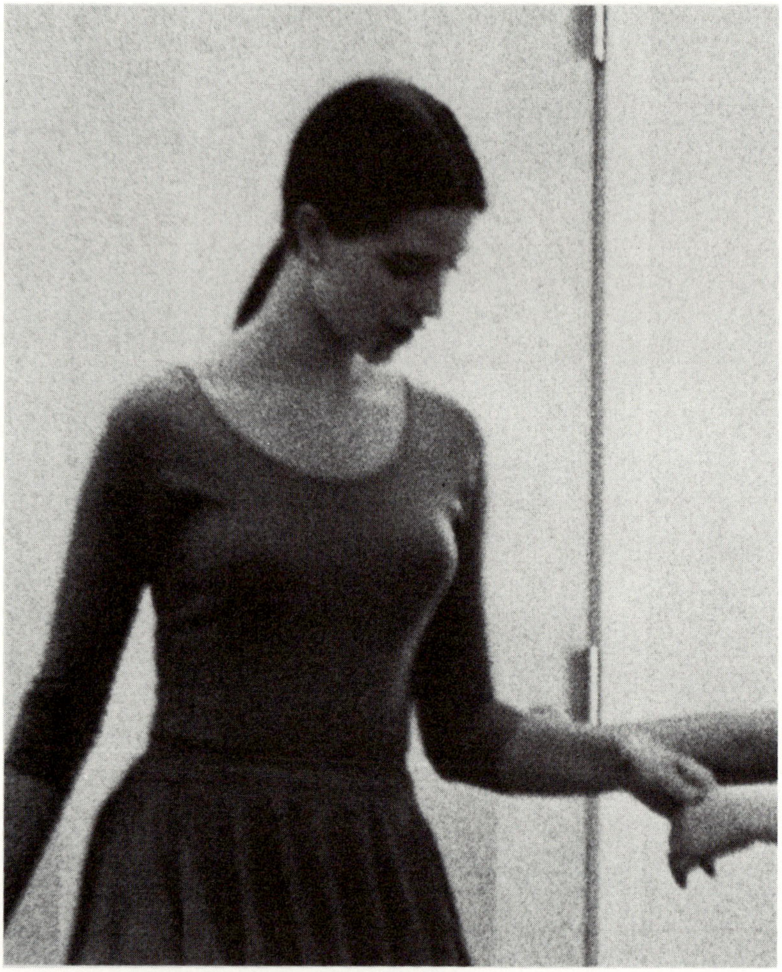

DO NOT LOOK AT THE REMAINING PHOTOGRAPHS IN THIS SECTION UNTIL YOU HAVE ANSWERED THE FOLLOWING QUESTIONS. Then you can check the contexts and see how close your answers are.

    The importance of context cannot be emphasized enough. Some statements mean very little until put into context. There are photographs that would lose their significance, or have very little, if the background were taken away. The contexts have been removed in the preceding photographs in order to tax the student's observation, as well as his knowledge and ability to visualize situations.

    This section complements the previous one. There is a greater danger, here, of making assumptions, since there are very few or no clues to help the student. If the whole thing turns out to be a guessing game, this section will not serve its purpose. The student should make an attempt to determine the context from the photograph before him, even though there is a likelihood that his conclusion may be farfetched. The main aim of this group of pictures is to emphasize the importance of context, and the extent of this emphasis will be made clear when the student looks at the pictures restored to their backgrounds.

Page 67: What does the girl's expression reveal about the situation she is in?

Page 68: What kind of a background should there be for these statues?

Page 69: Where is this game of football being played?

Page 70: Where are these people sitting?

Page 71: What is this girl looking at?

Page 72: Where is this man sitting?

Page 73: In which country do these cows belong?

Page 74: What is the owner of these feet doing?

Page 75: Where is this girl reading the newspaper?

Page 76: What kind of a building does this dome belong to?

Page 77: What are these people so intently looking at?

Page 78: What kind of an exhibit is this group watching?

Page 79: What does this person find so amusing?

Page 80: What situation is this girl in?

Page 81: What has attracted the attention of this woman? What does her expression convey?

Page 82: What is this girl doing?

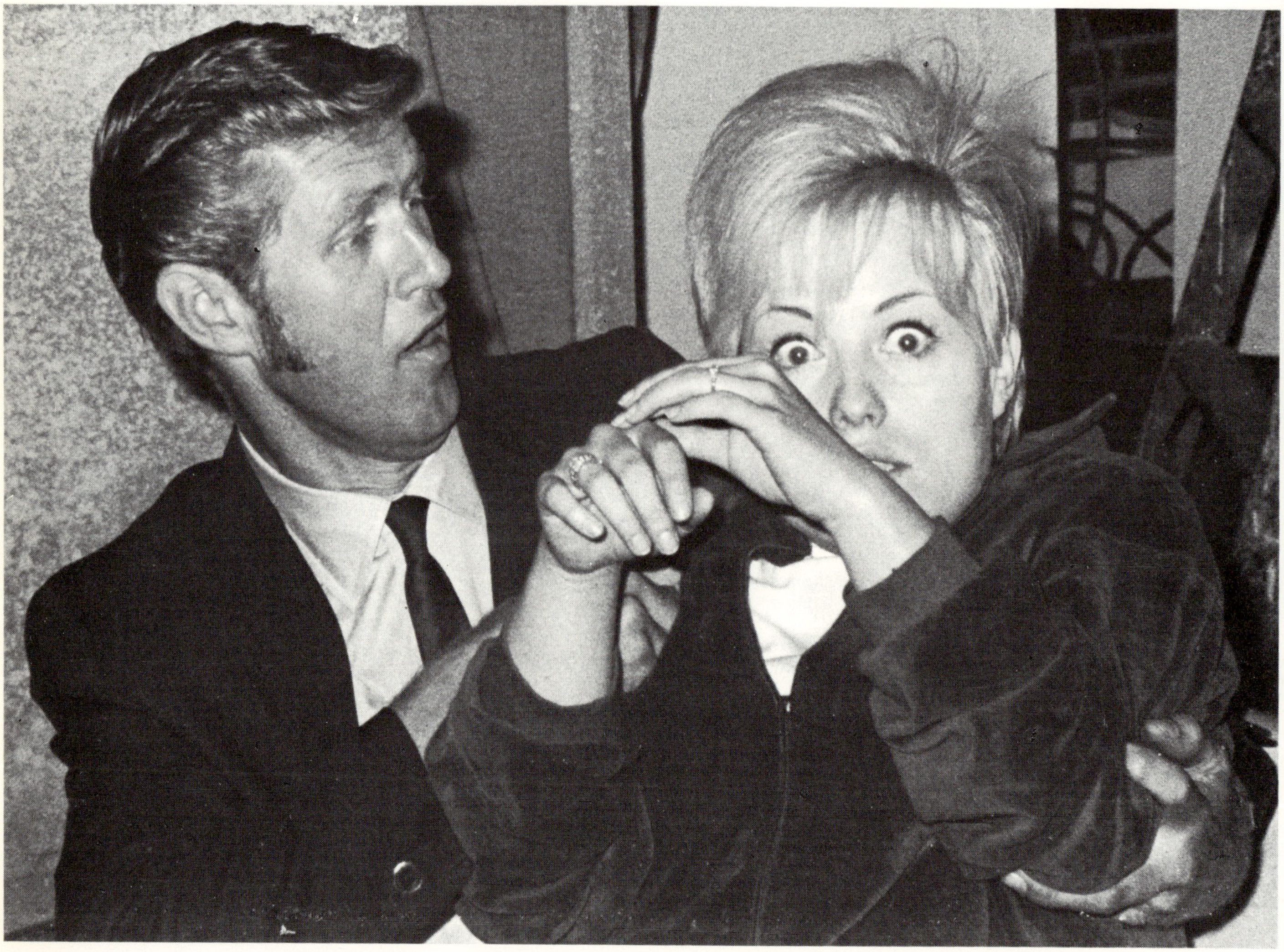

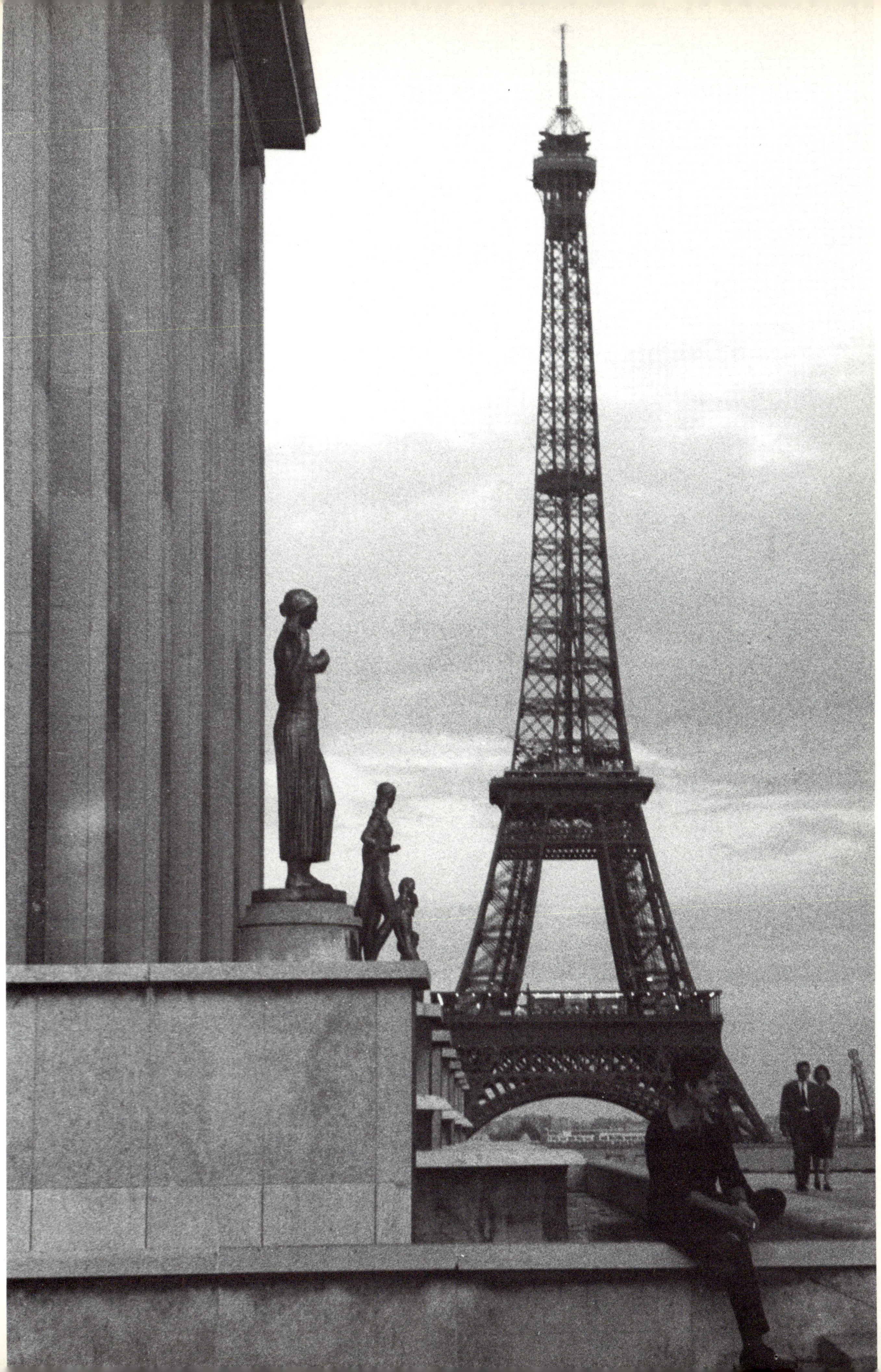

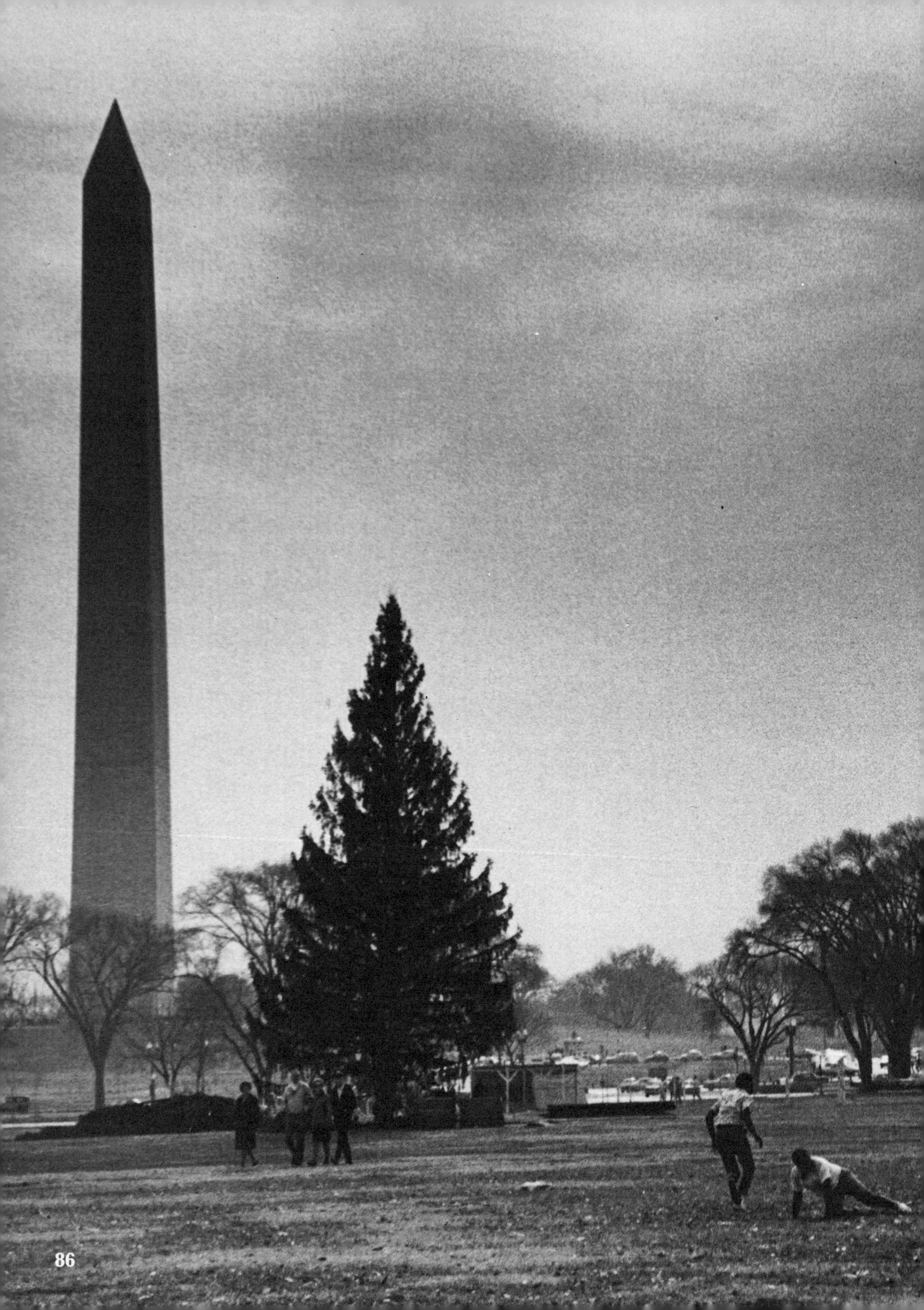

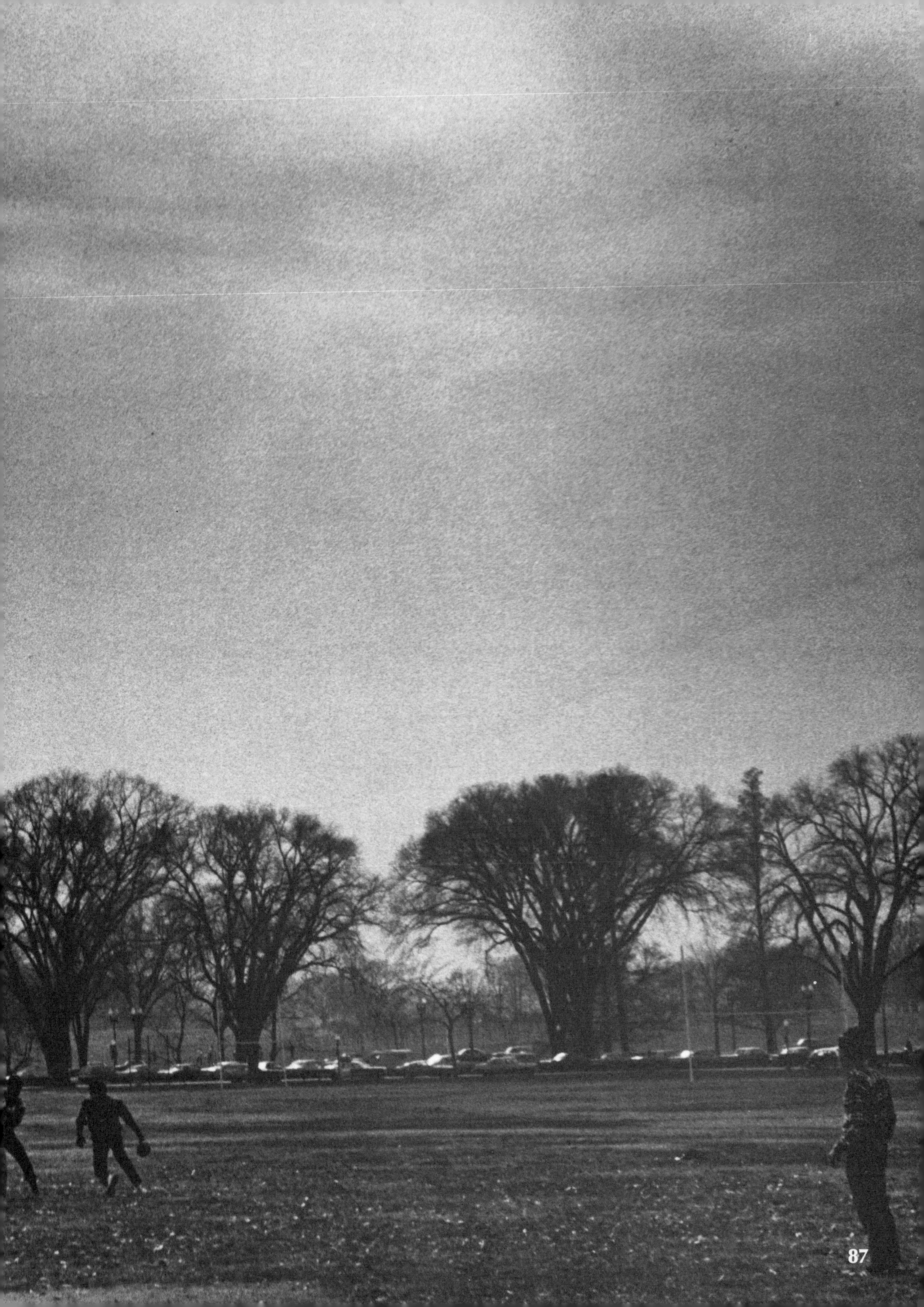

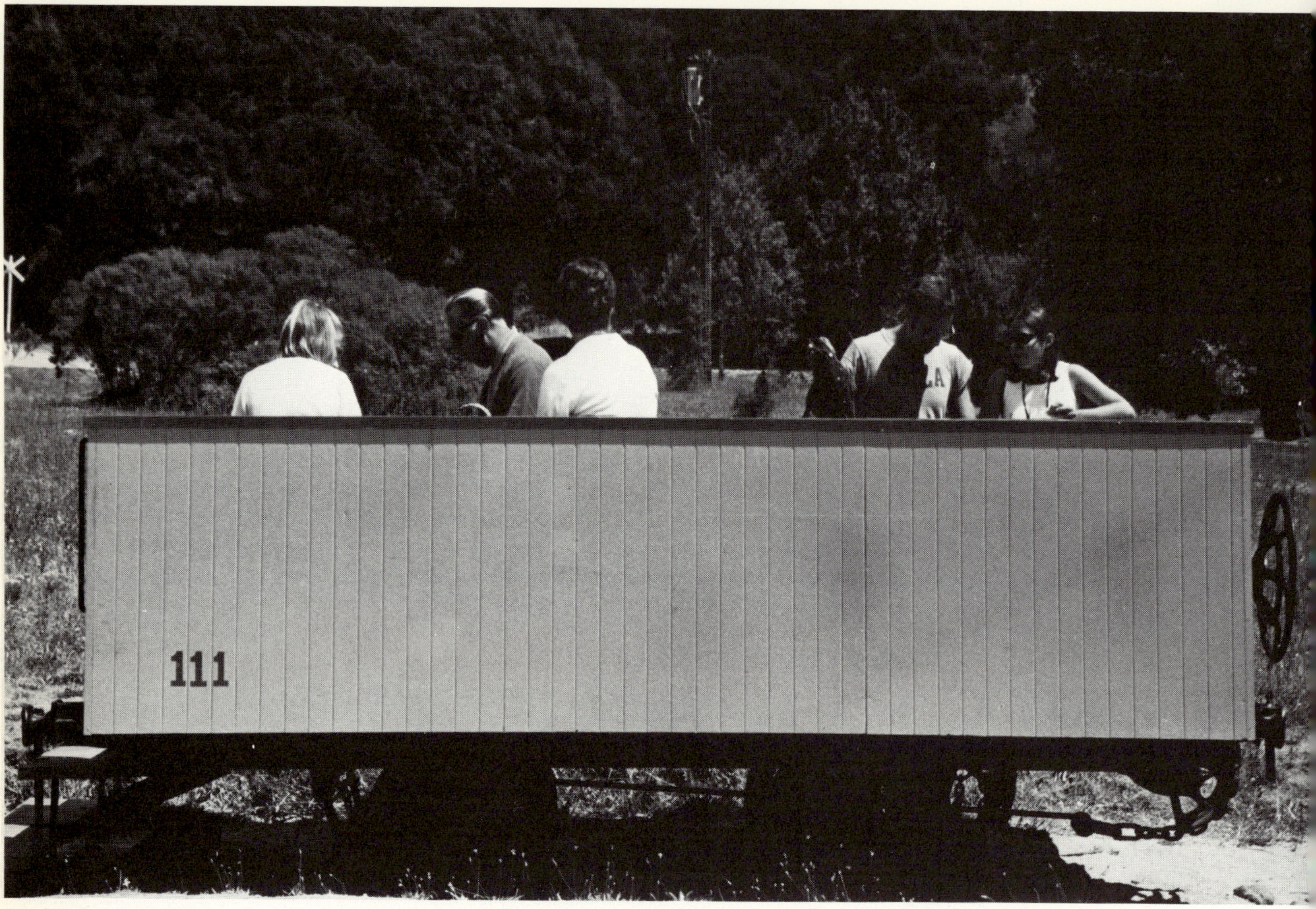
111

89

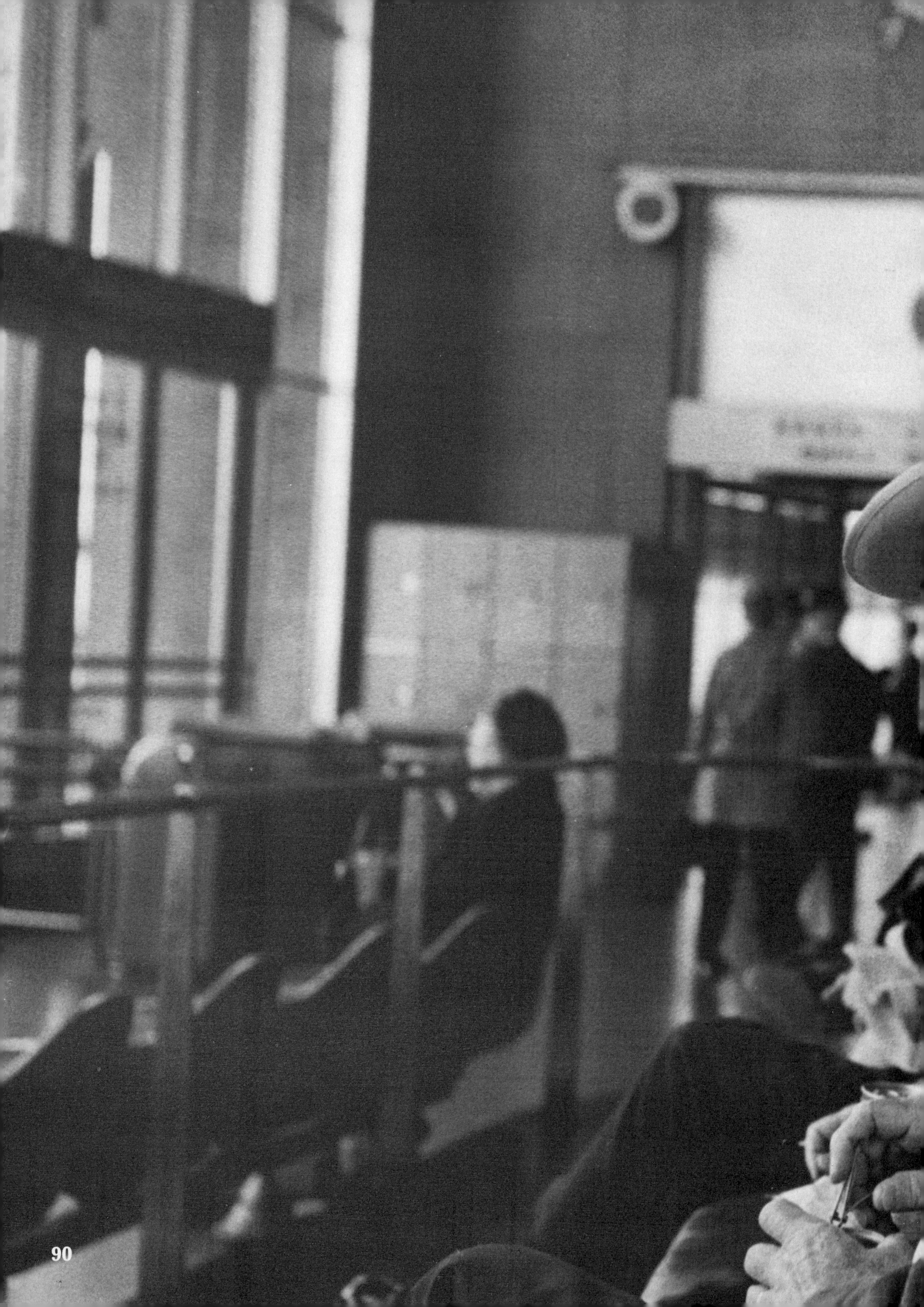

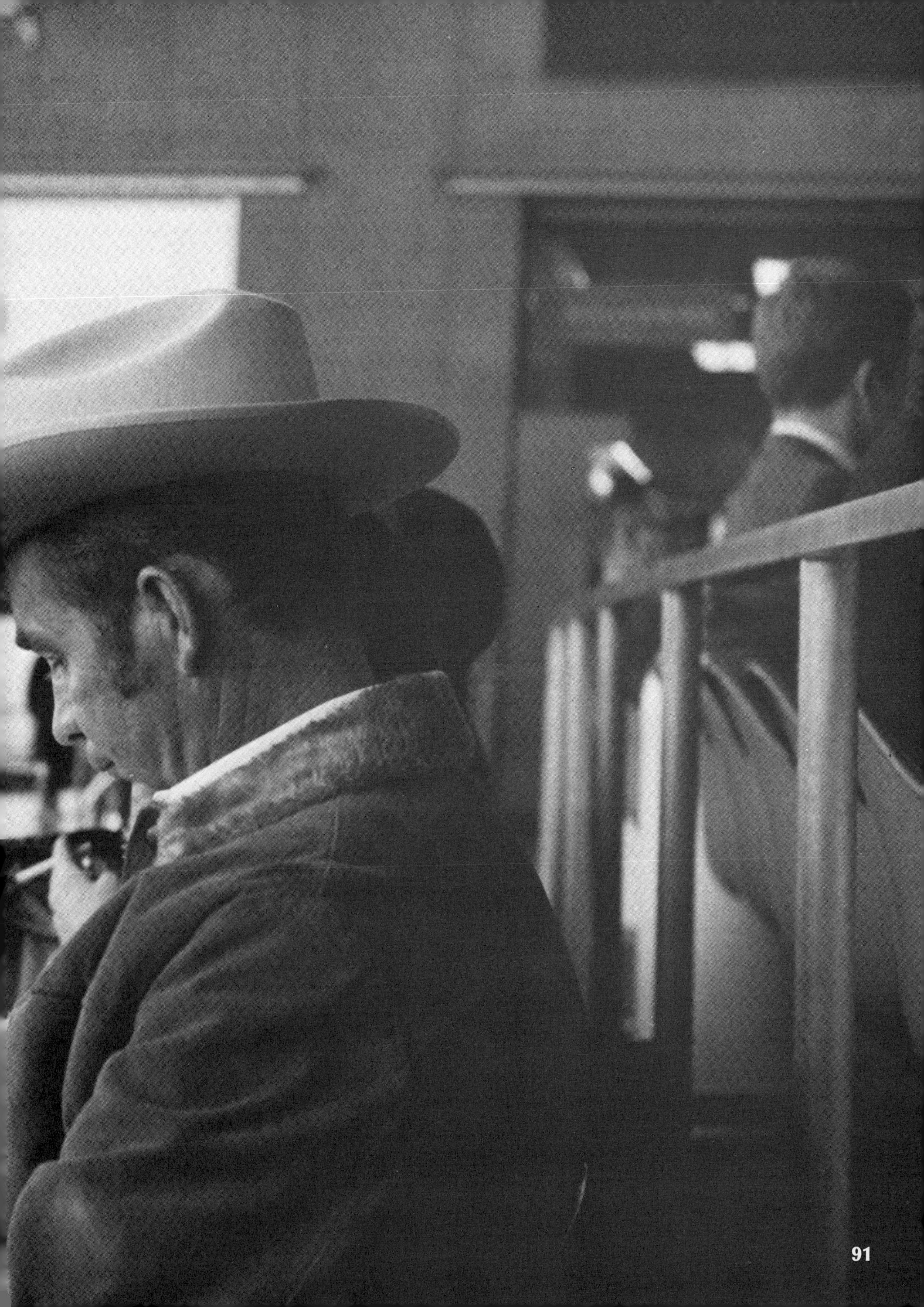

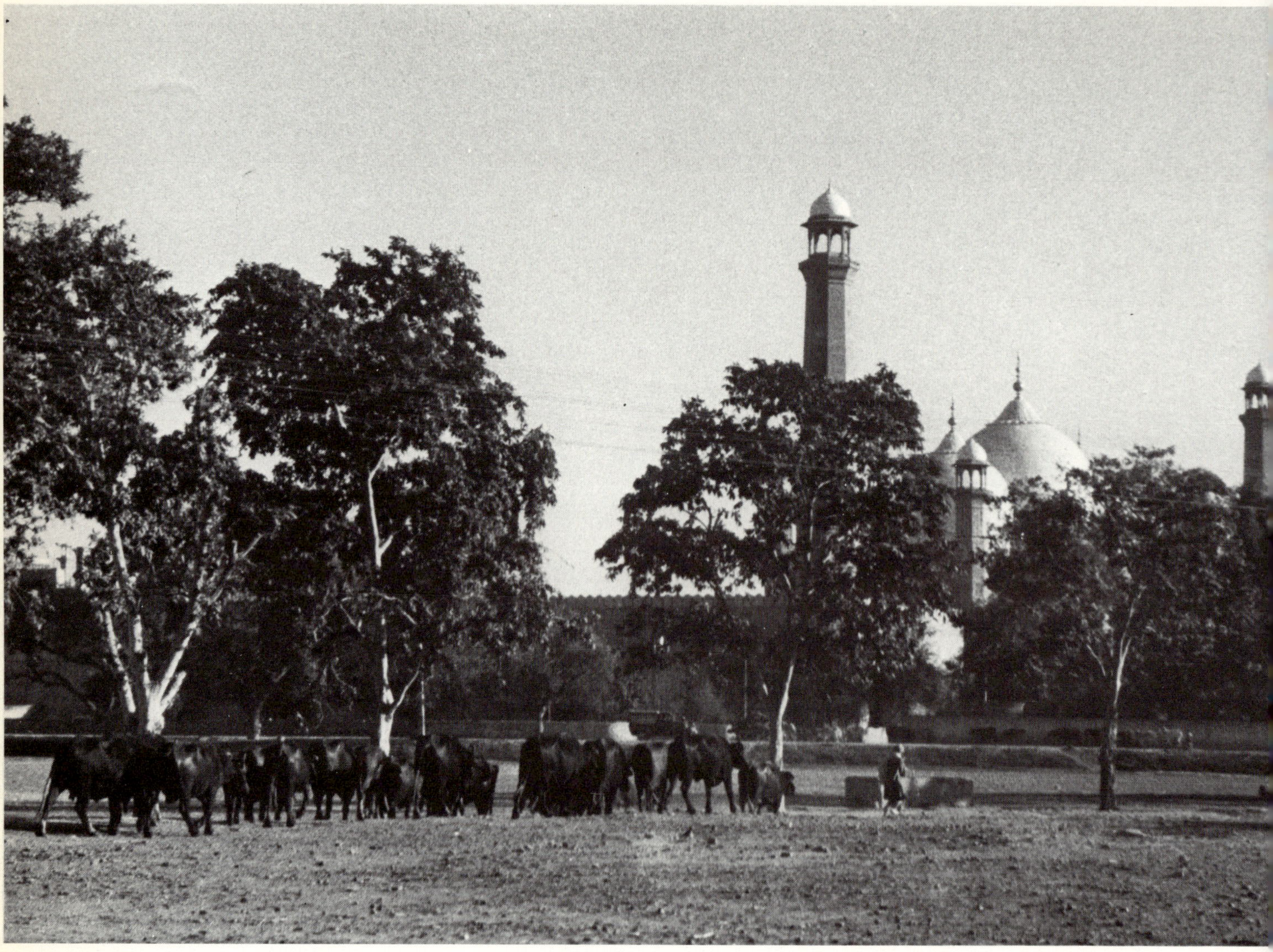

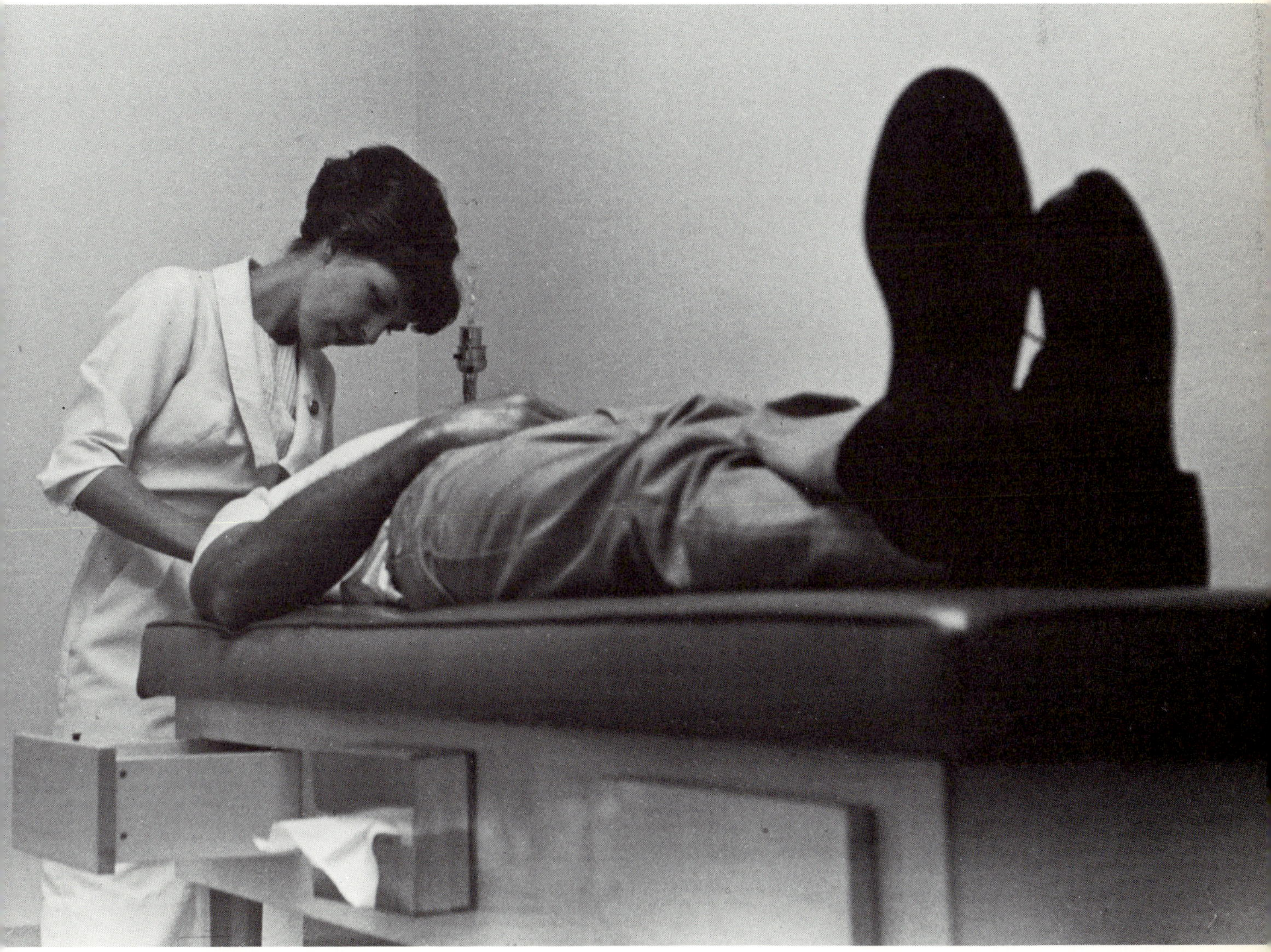

94

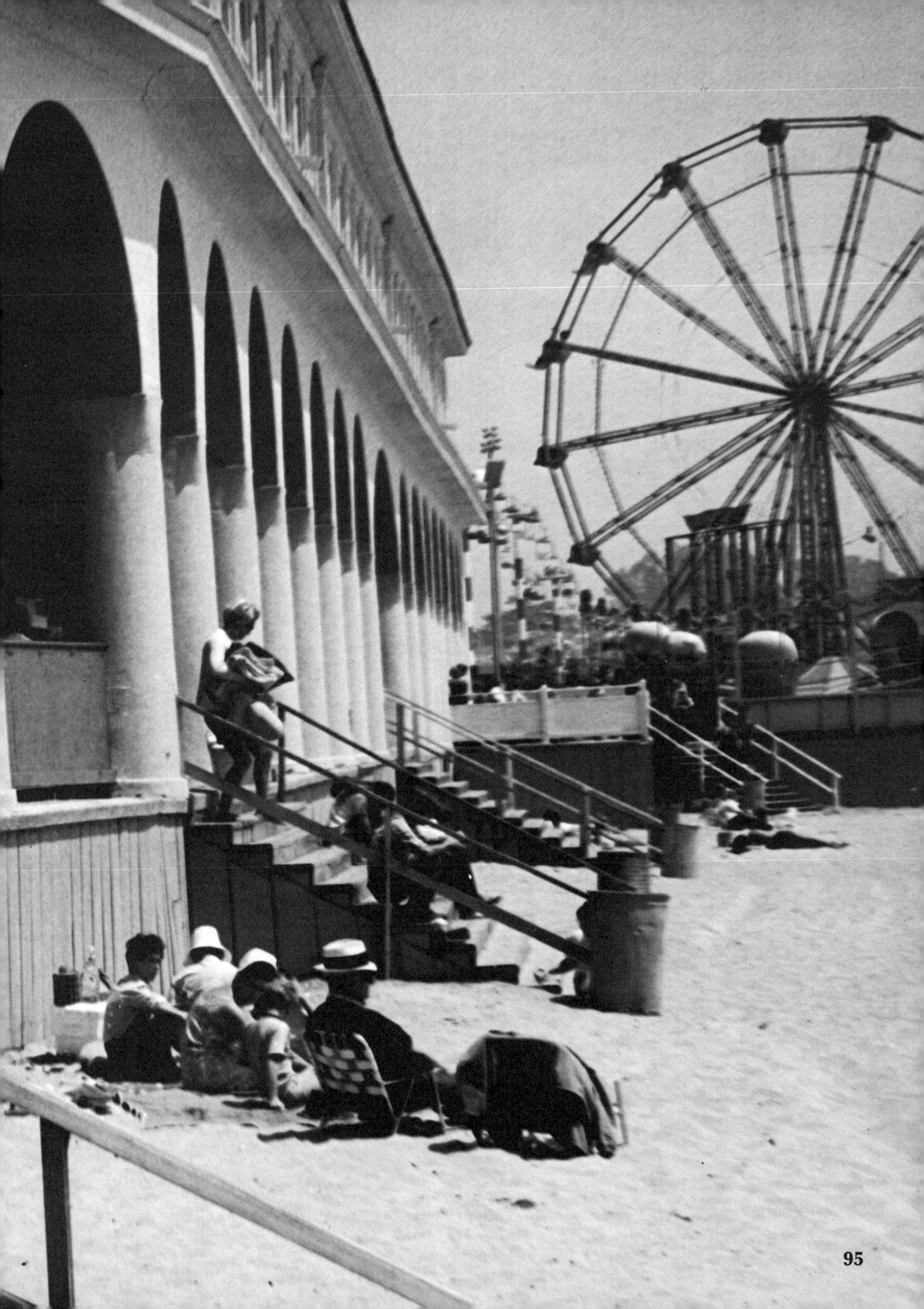

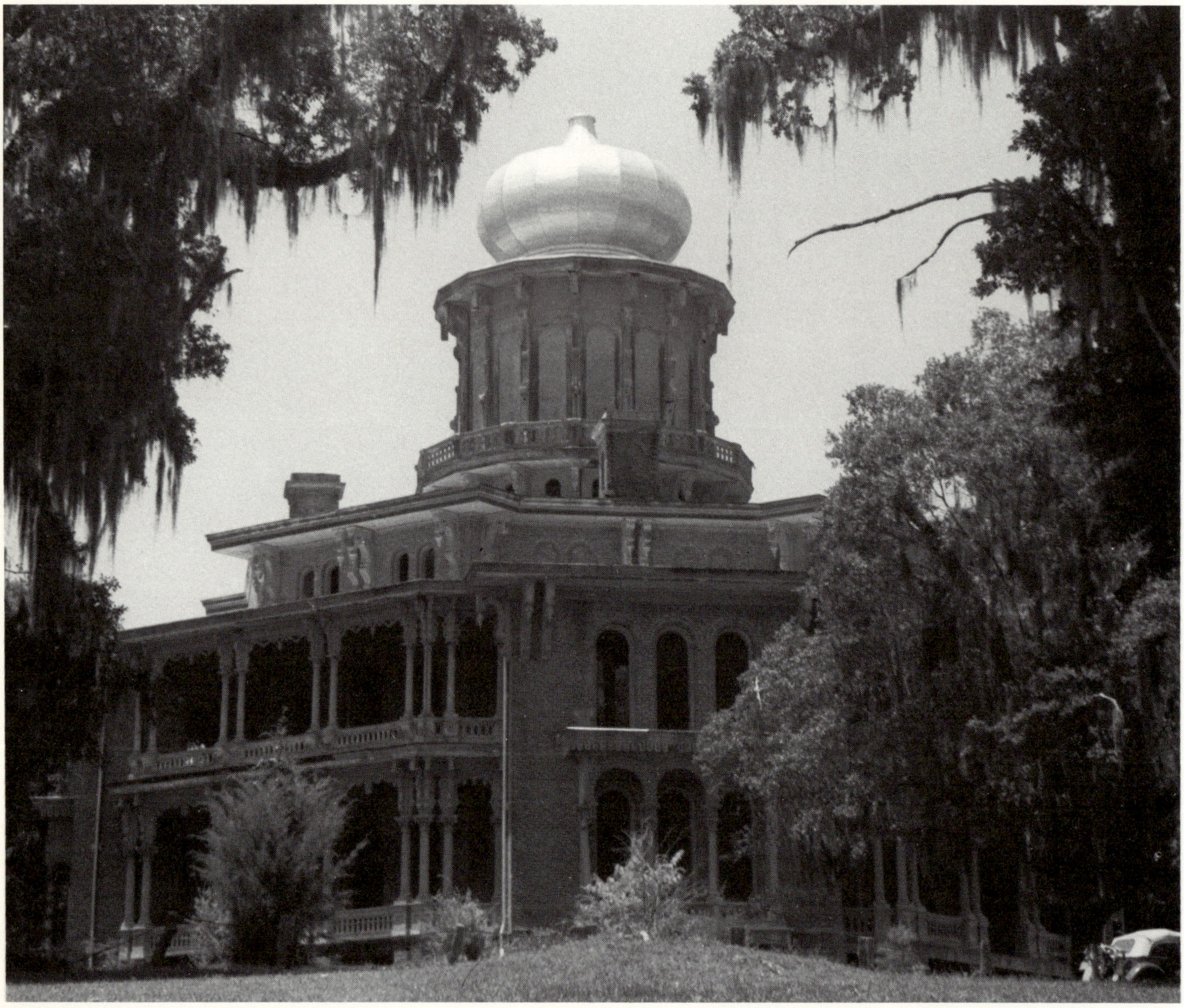

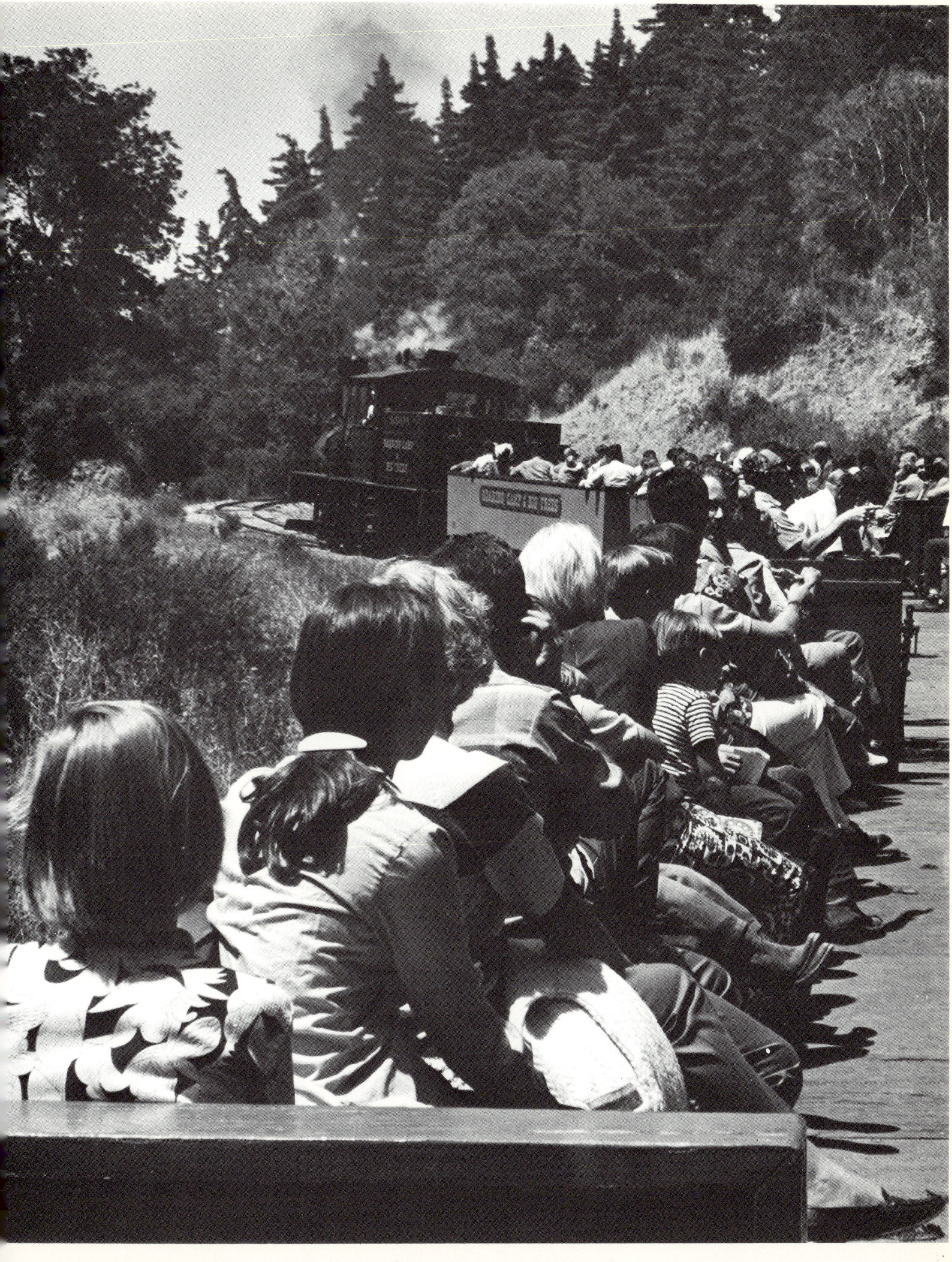

BOTTLE-NOSE DOLPHIN

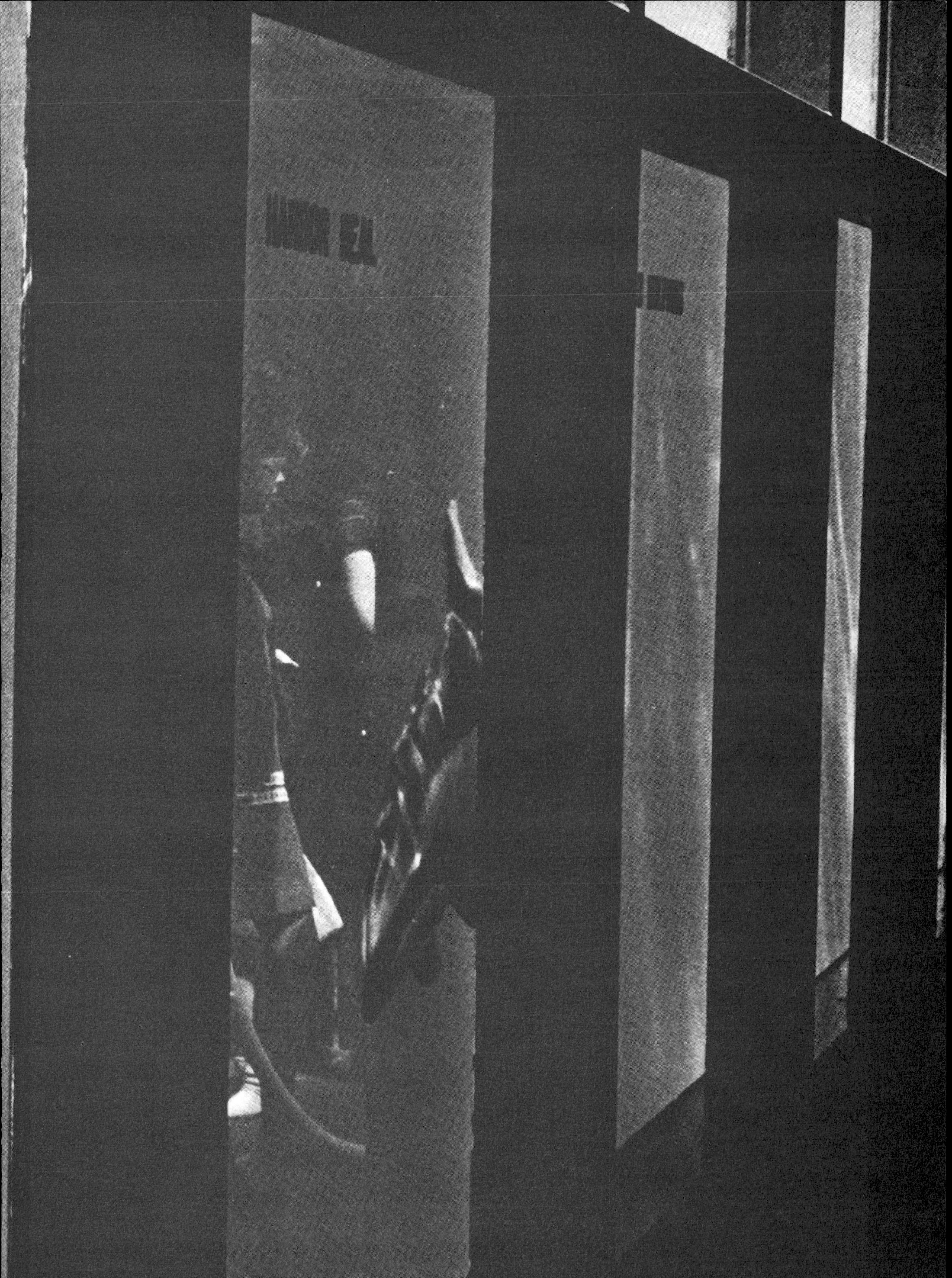

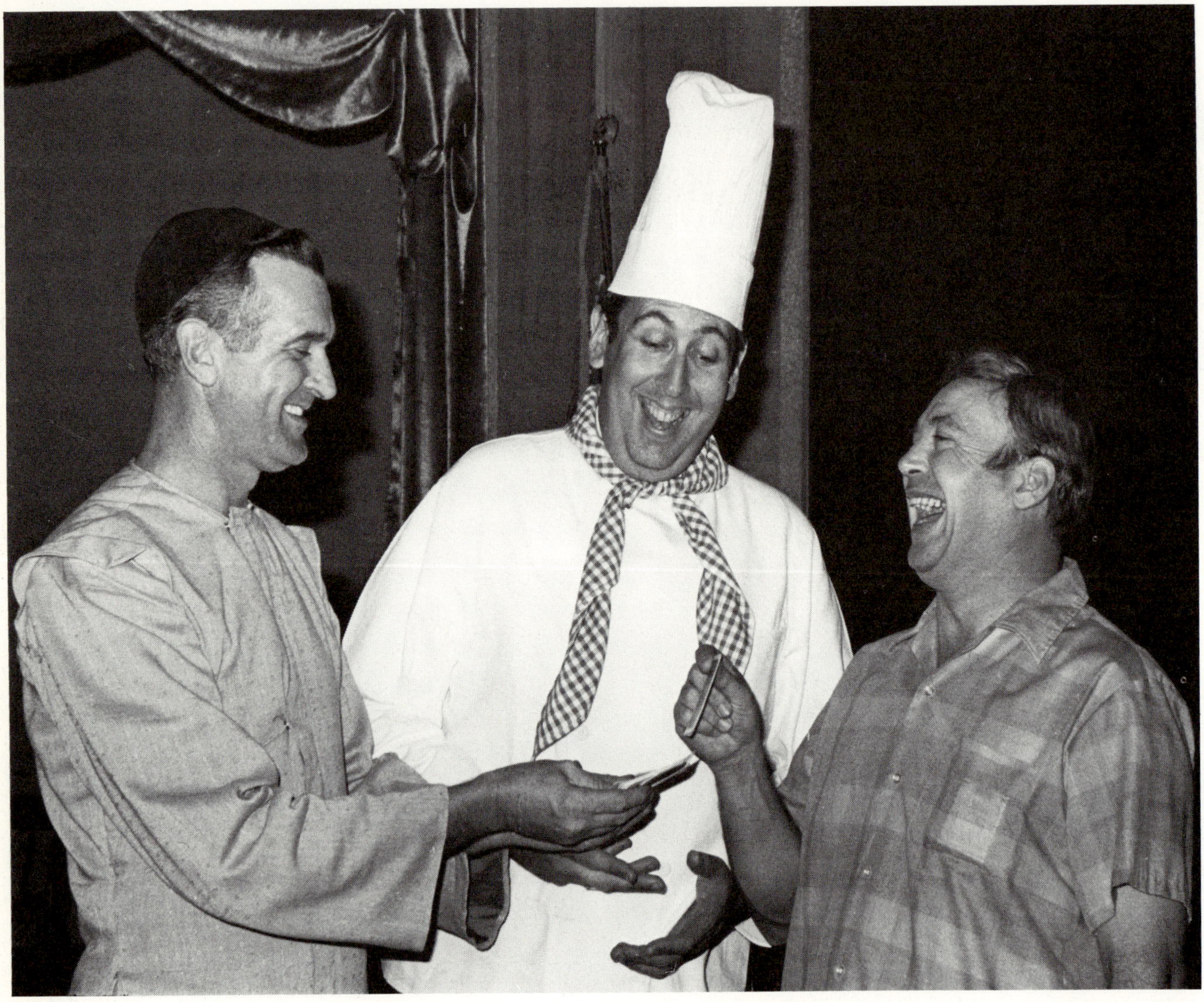

101

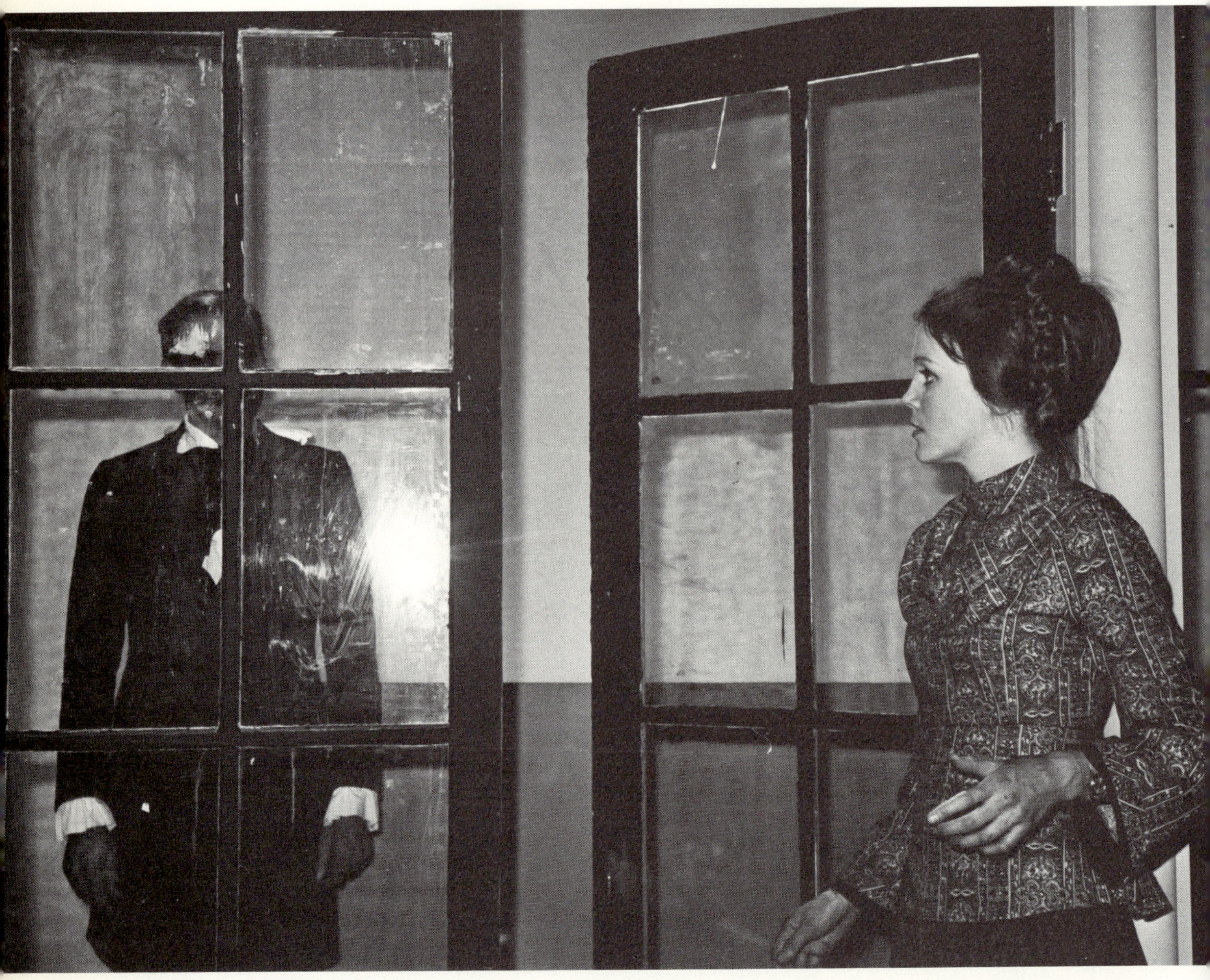

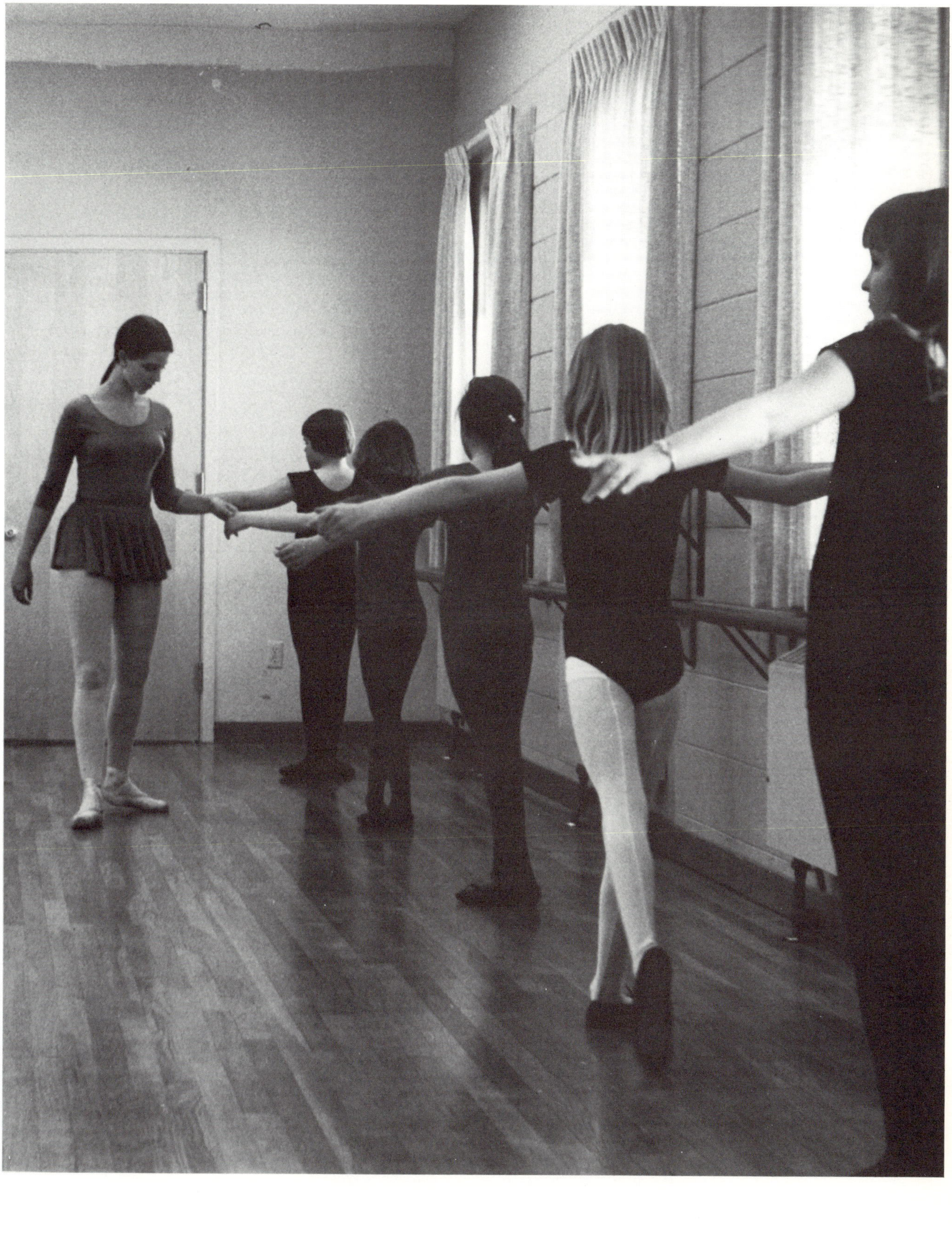

CONTRASTS

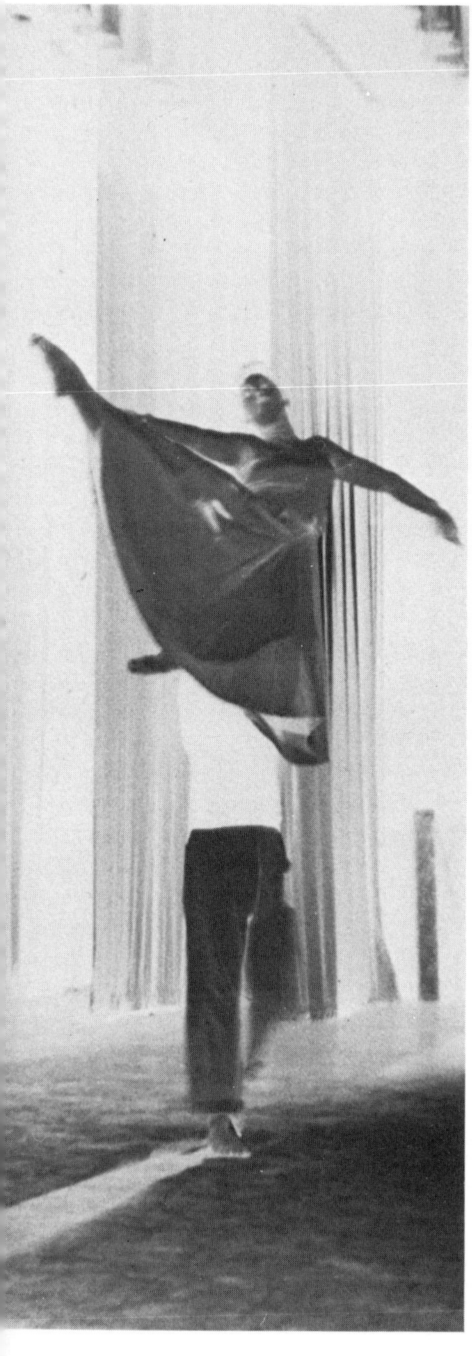

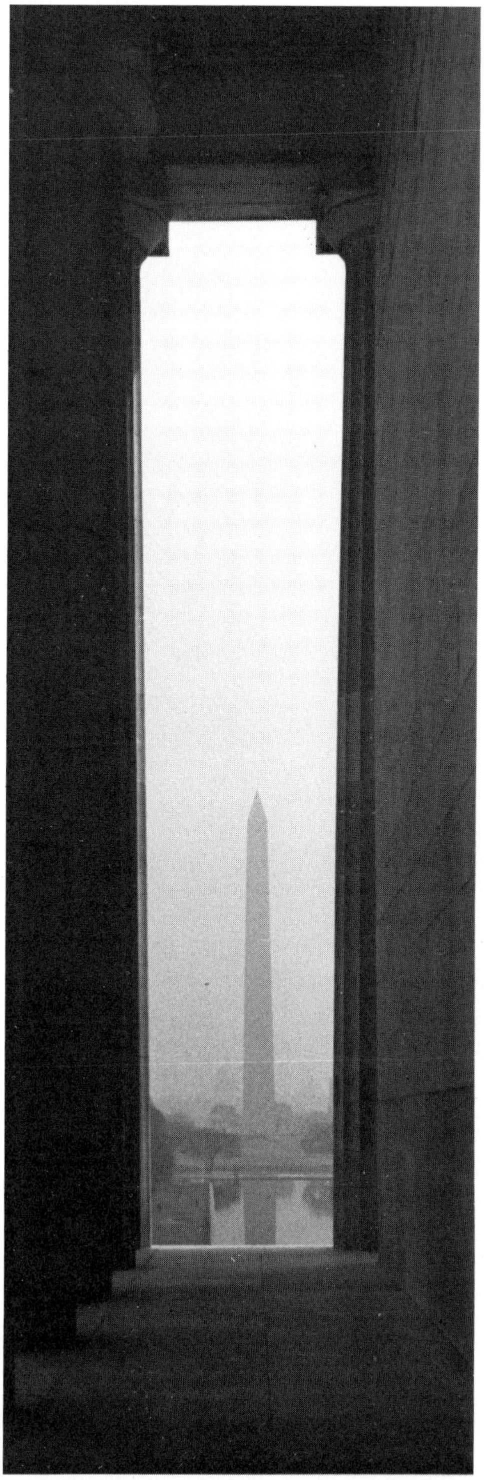

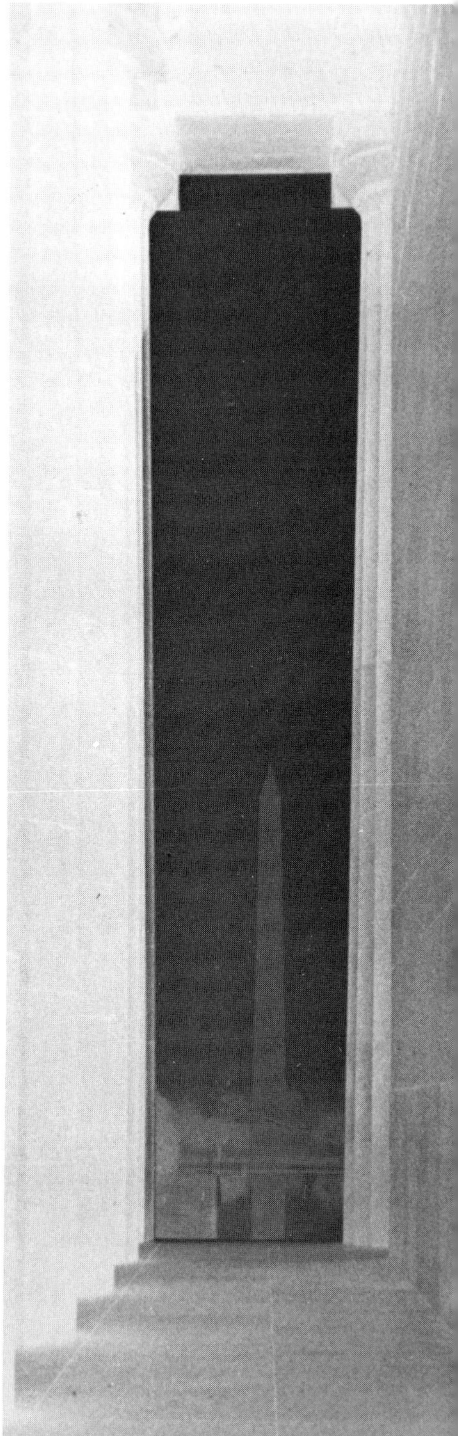

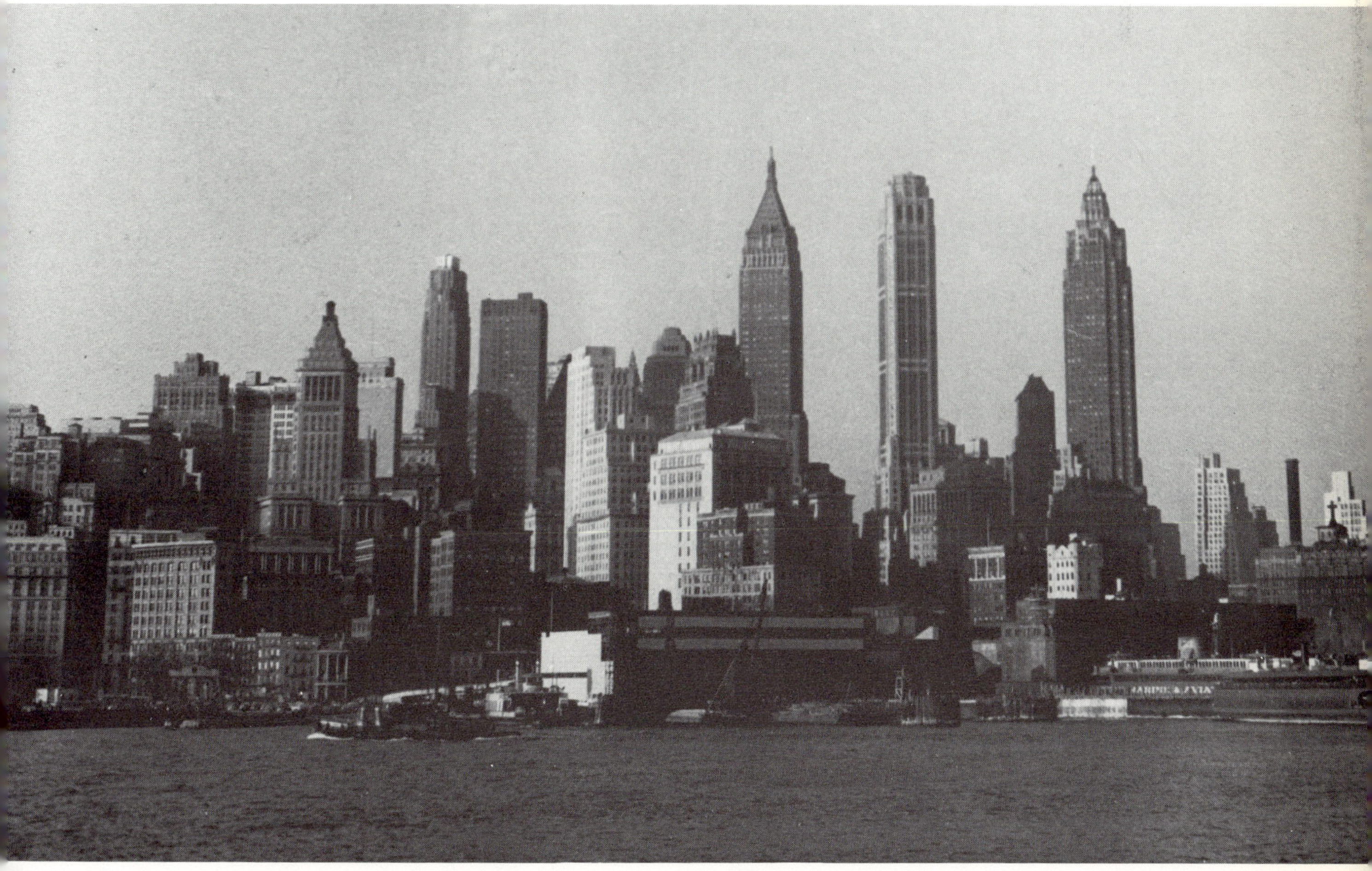

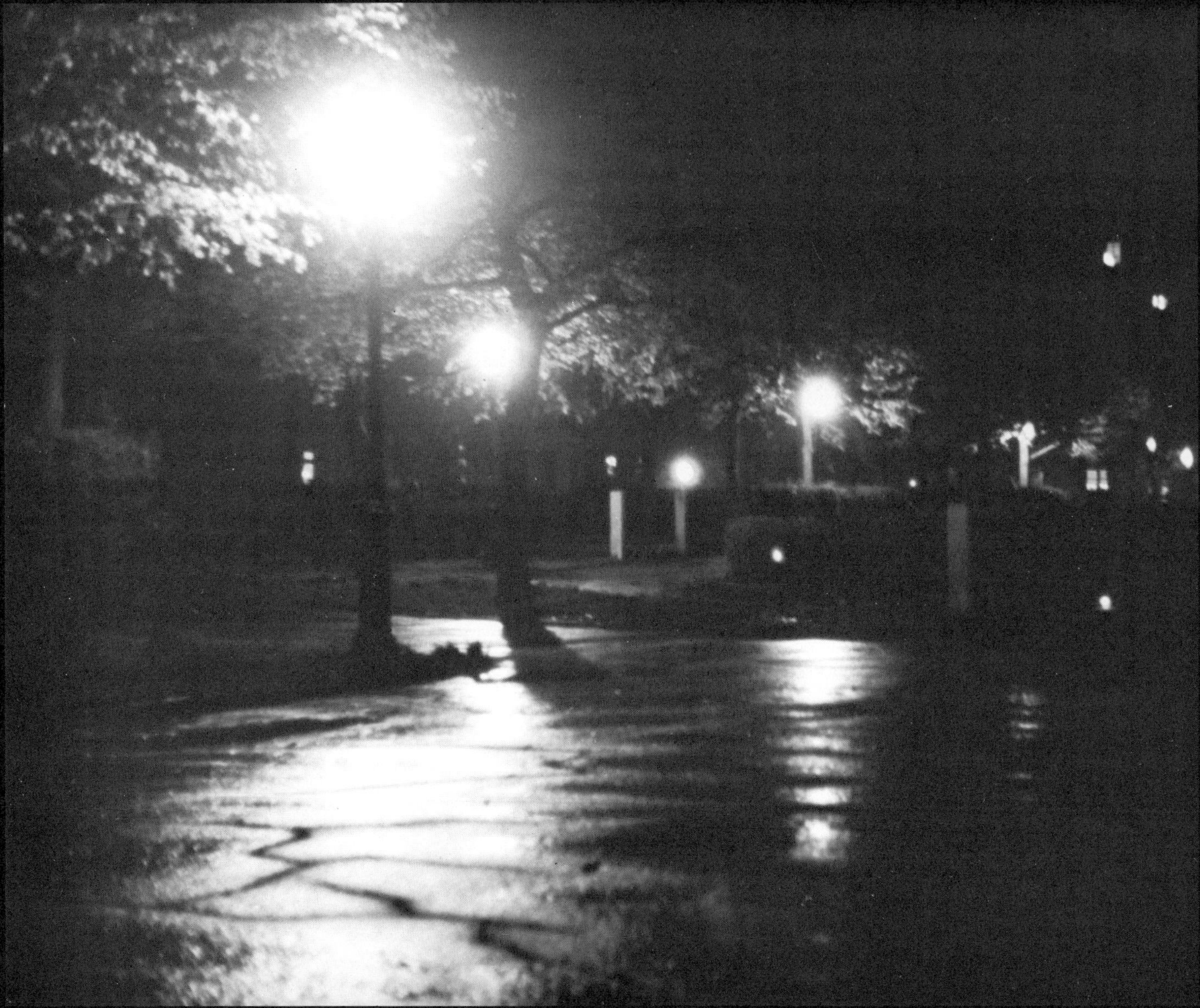

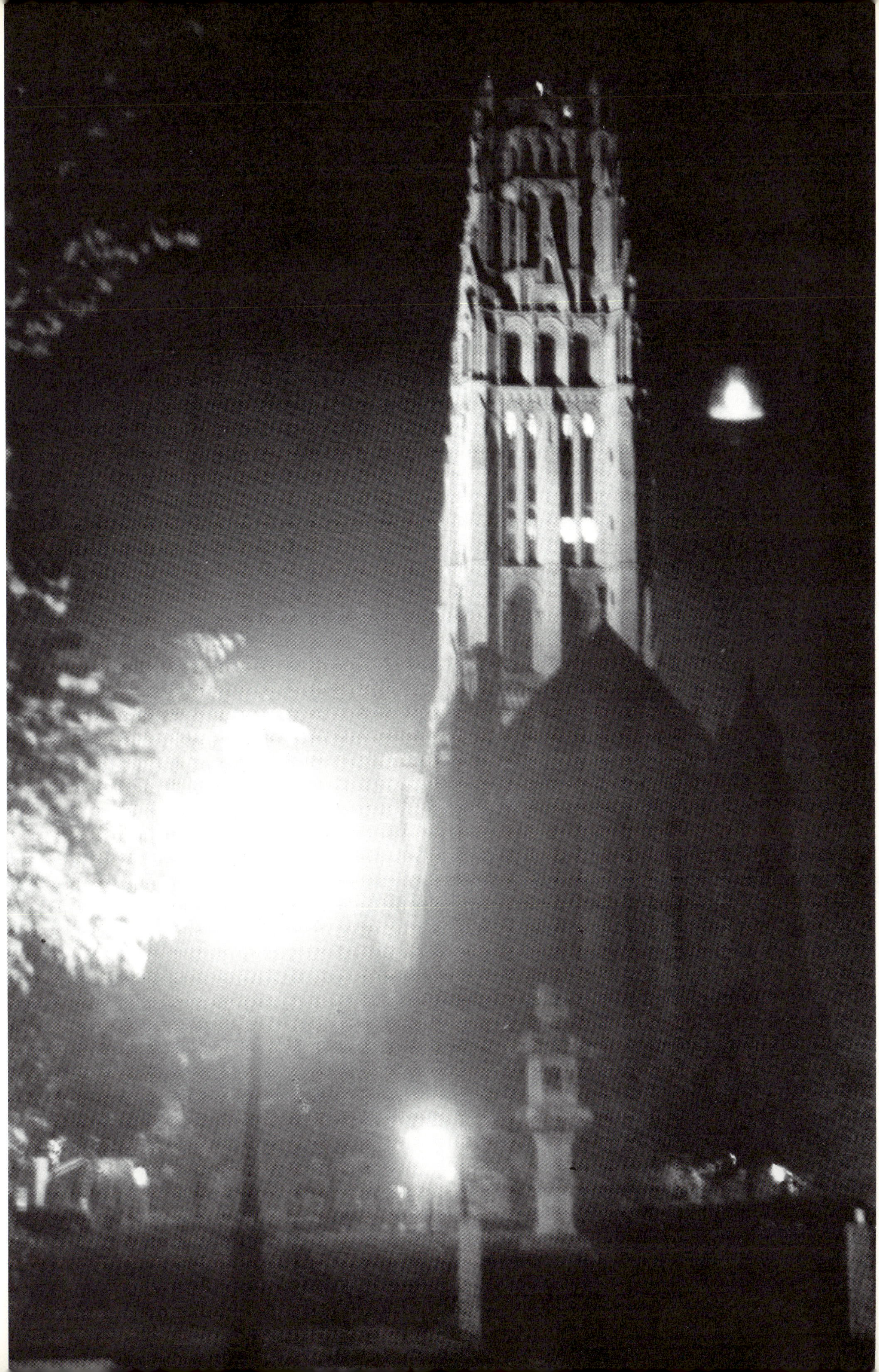

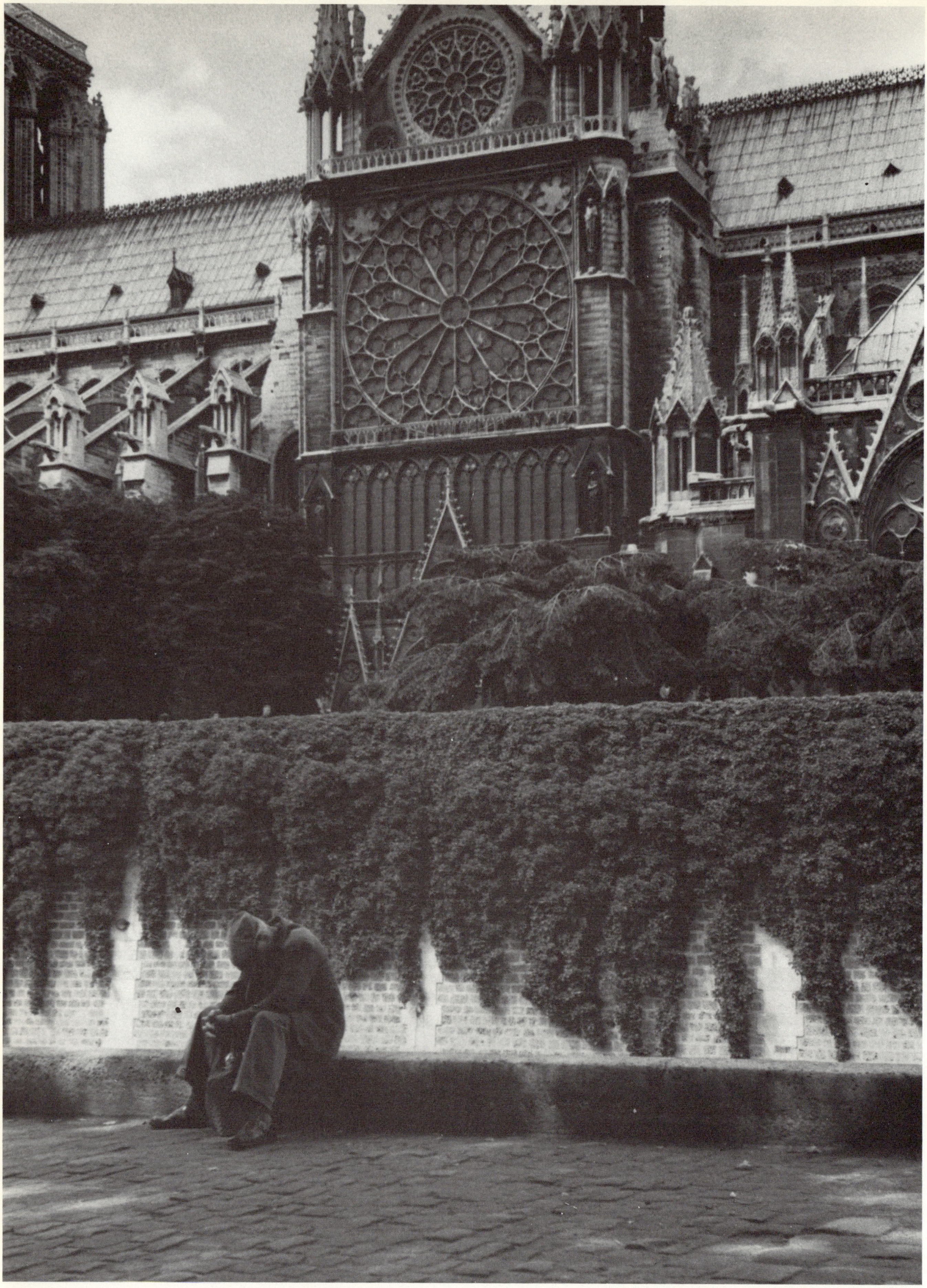

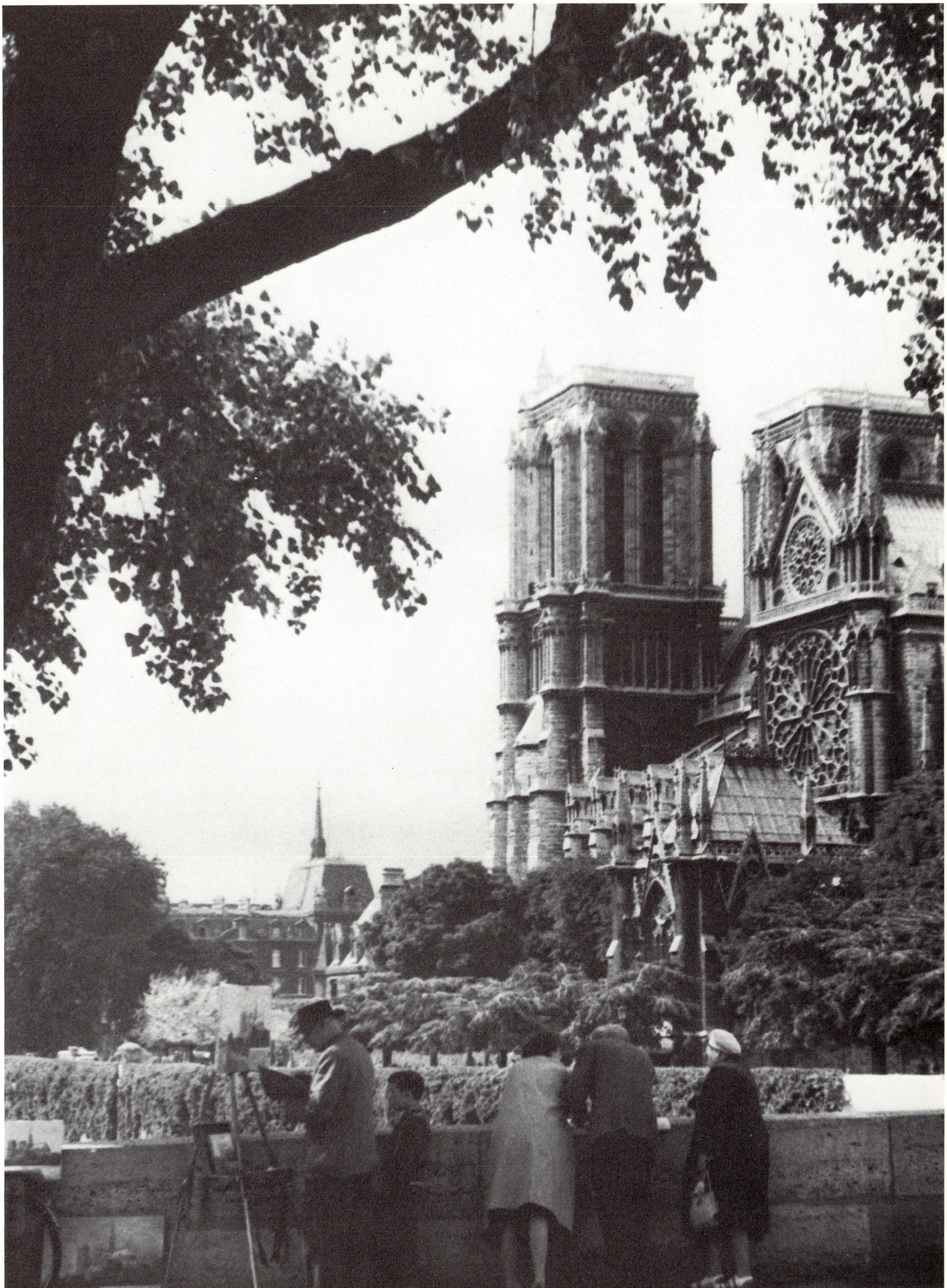

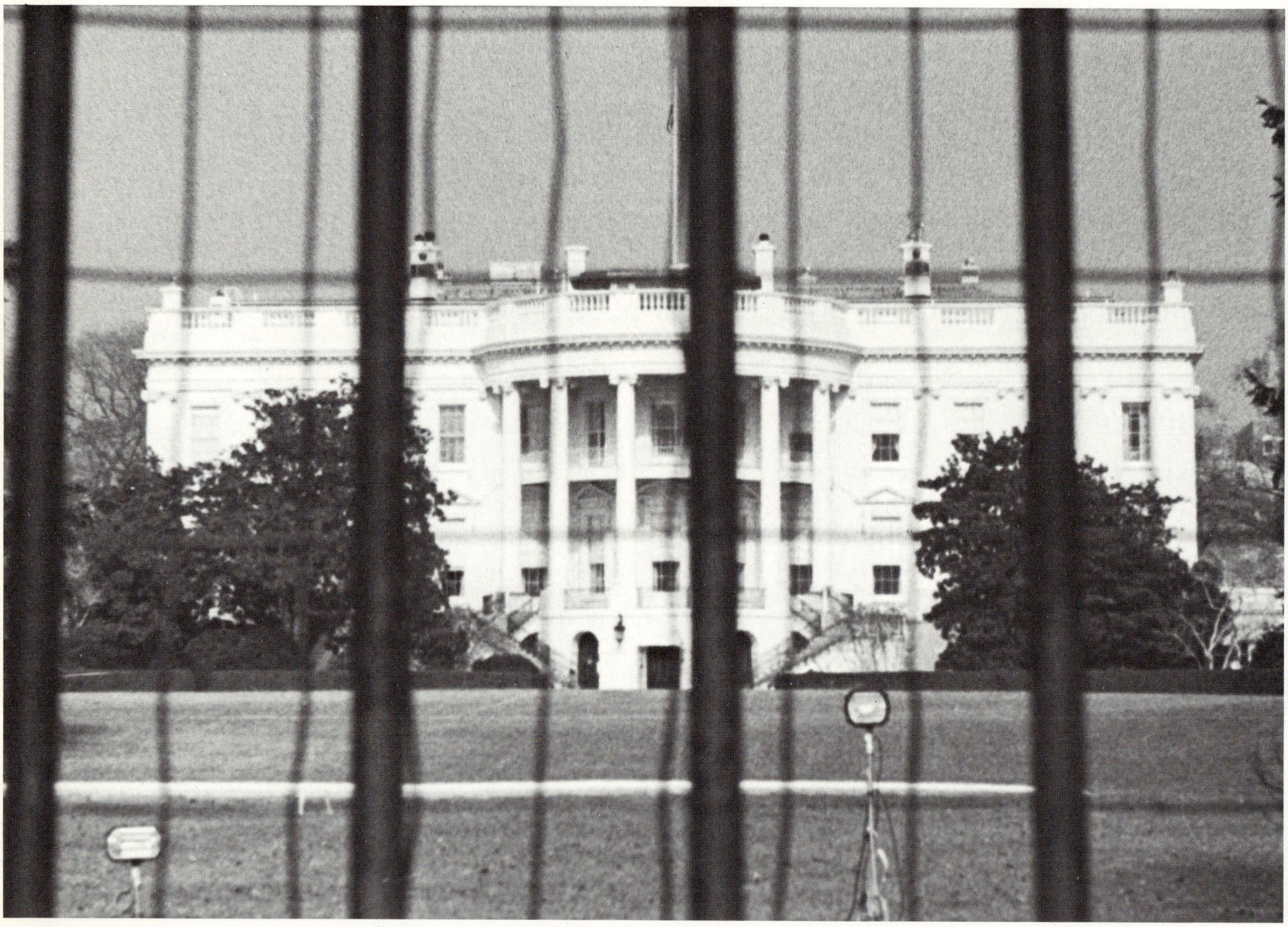

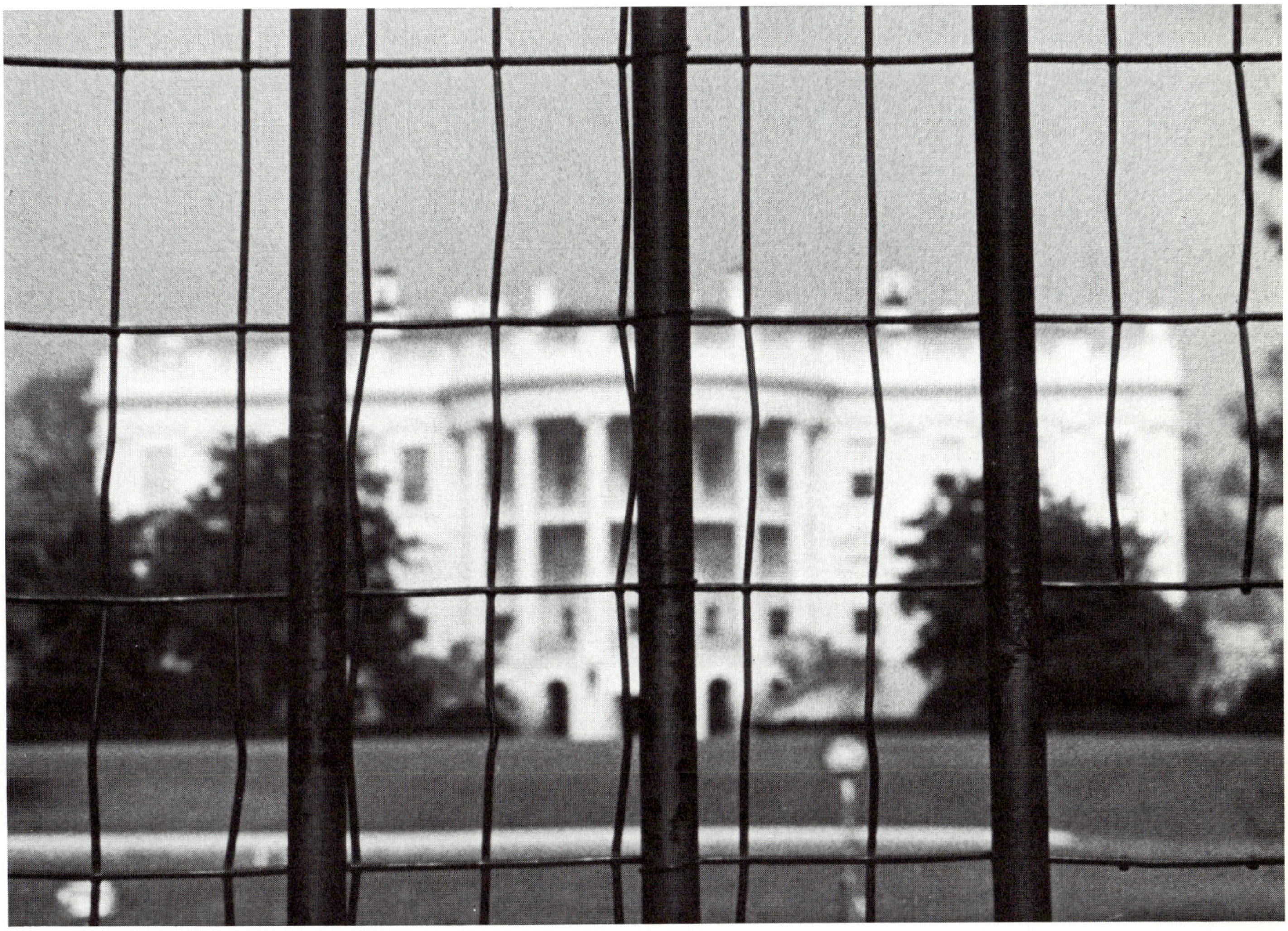

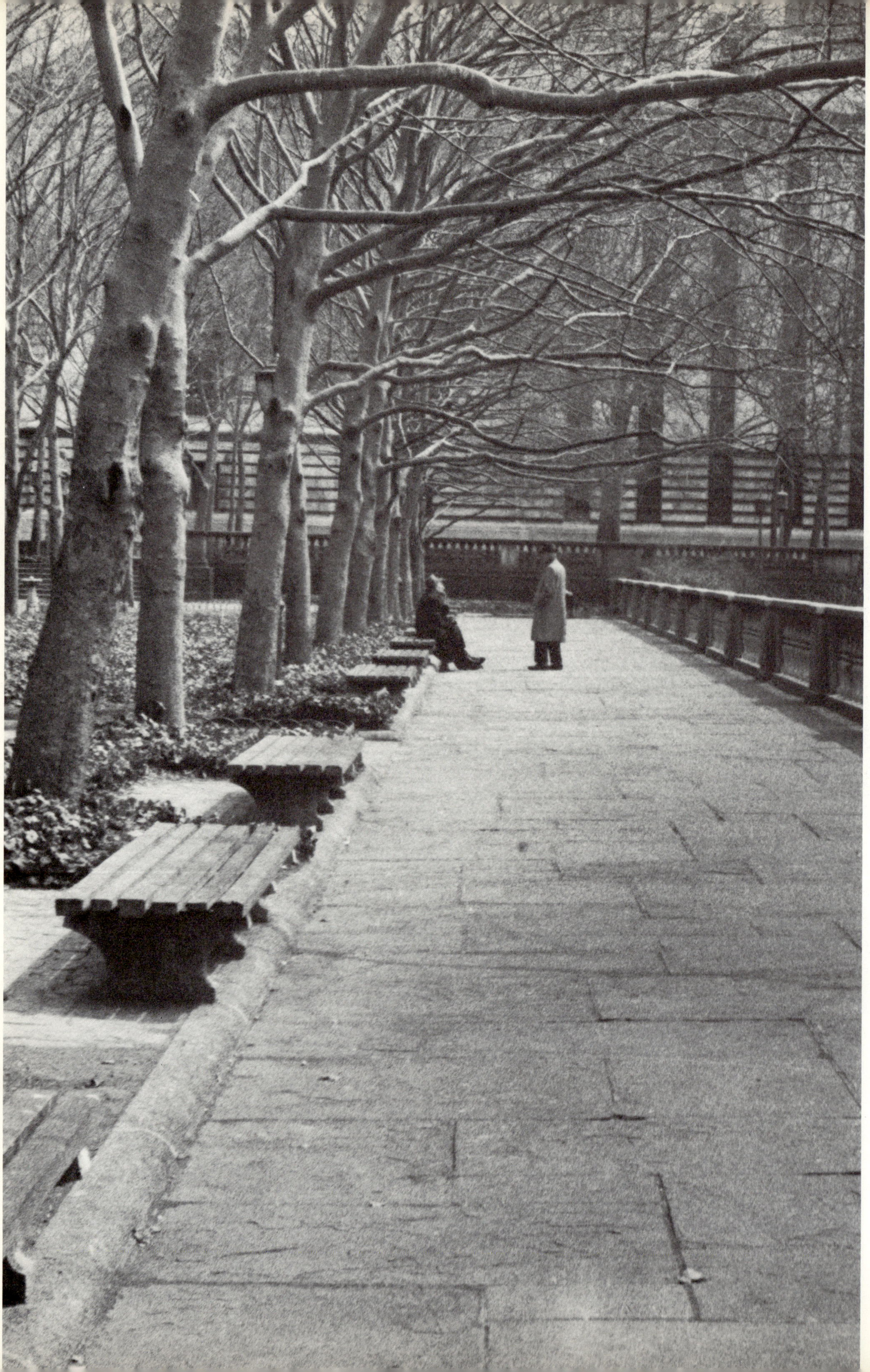

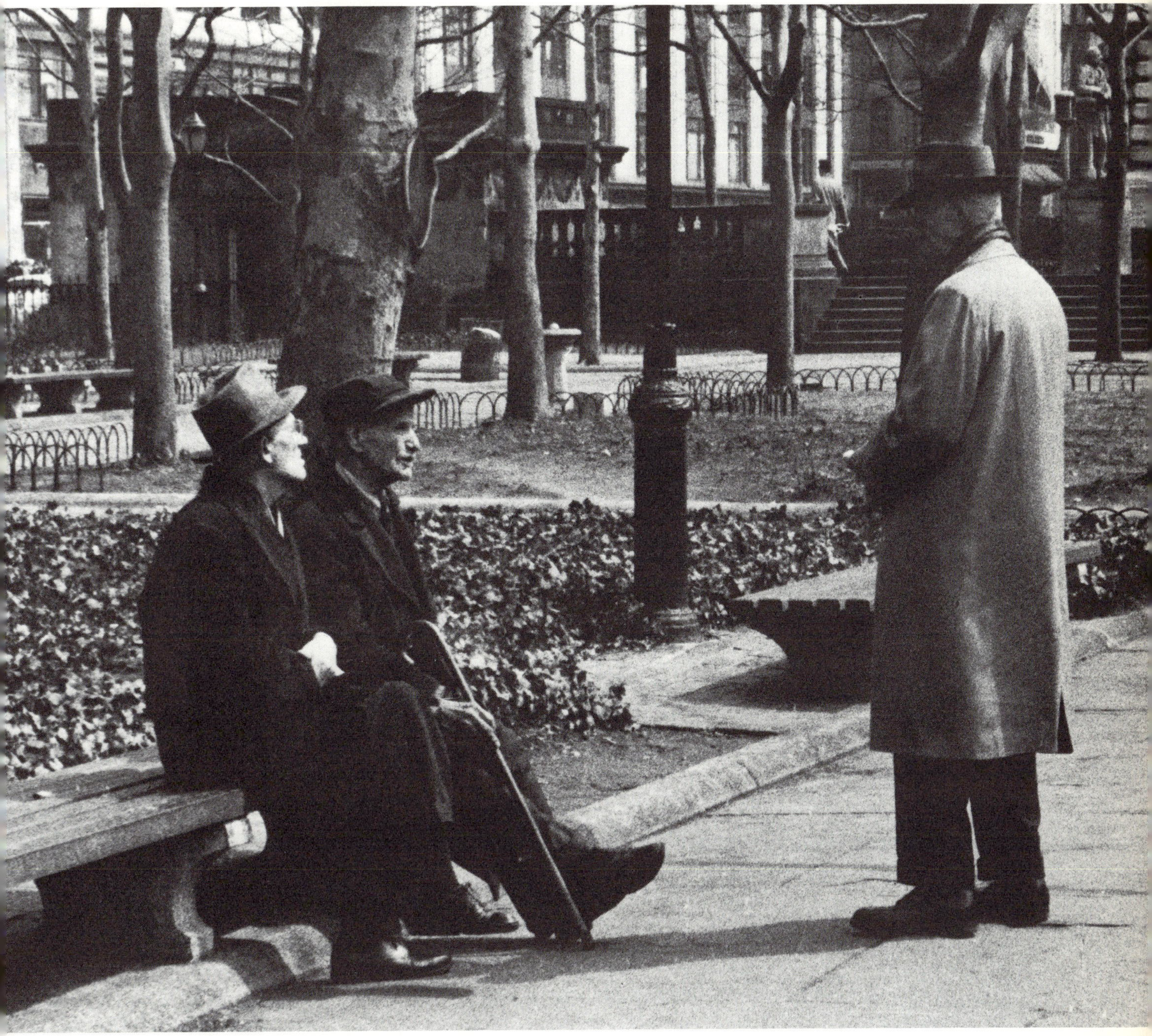

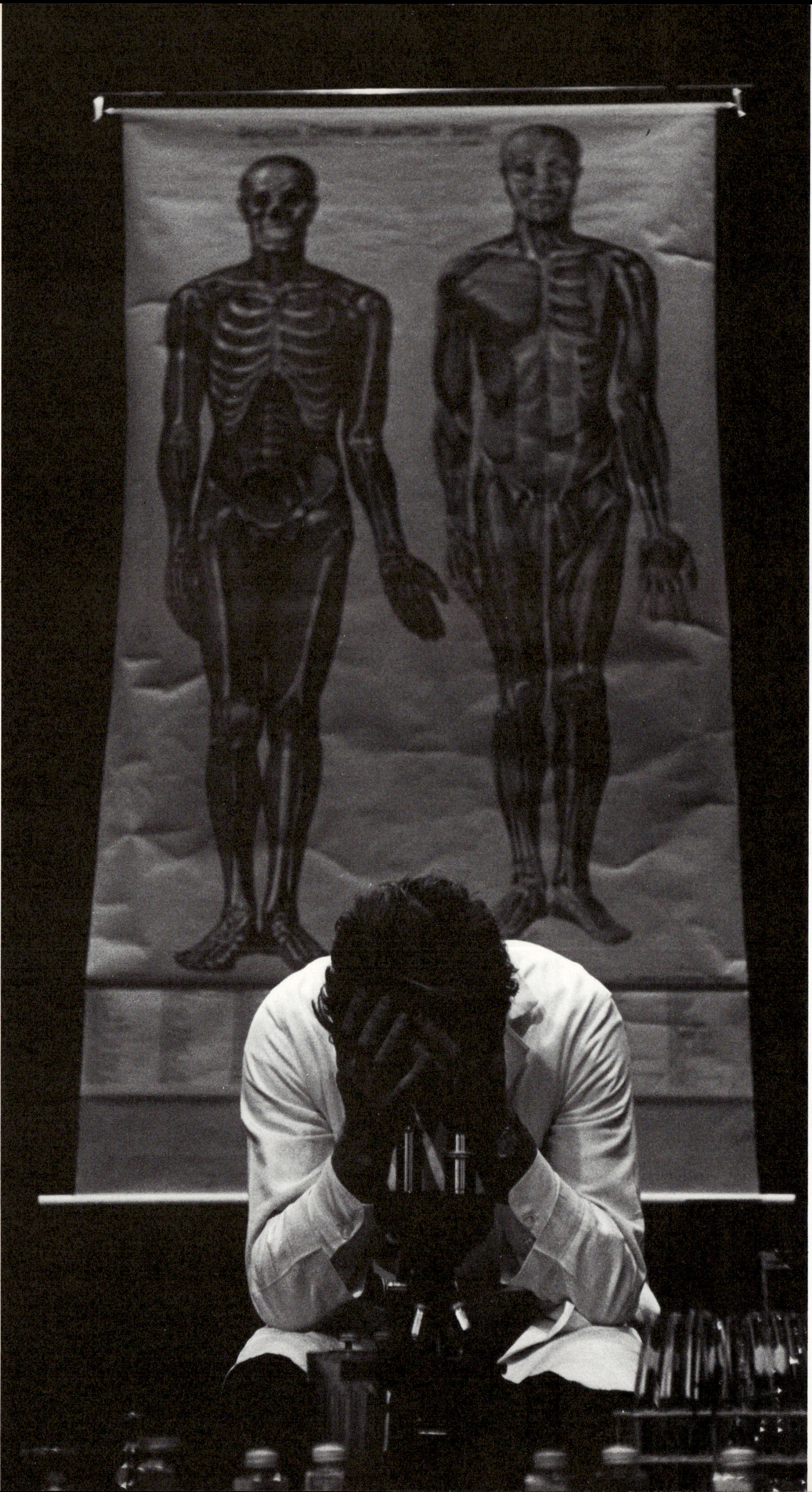

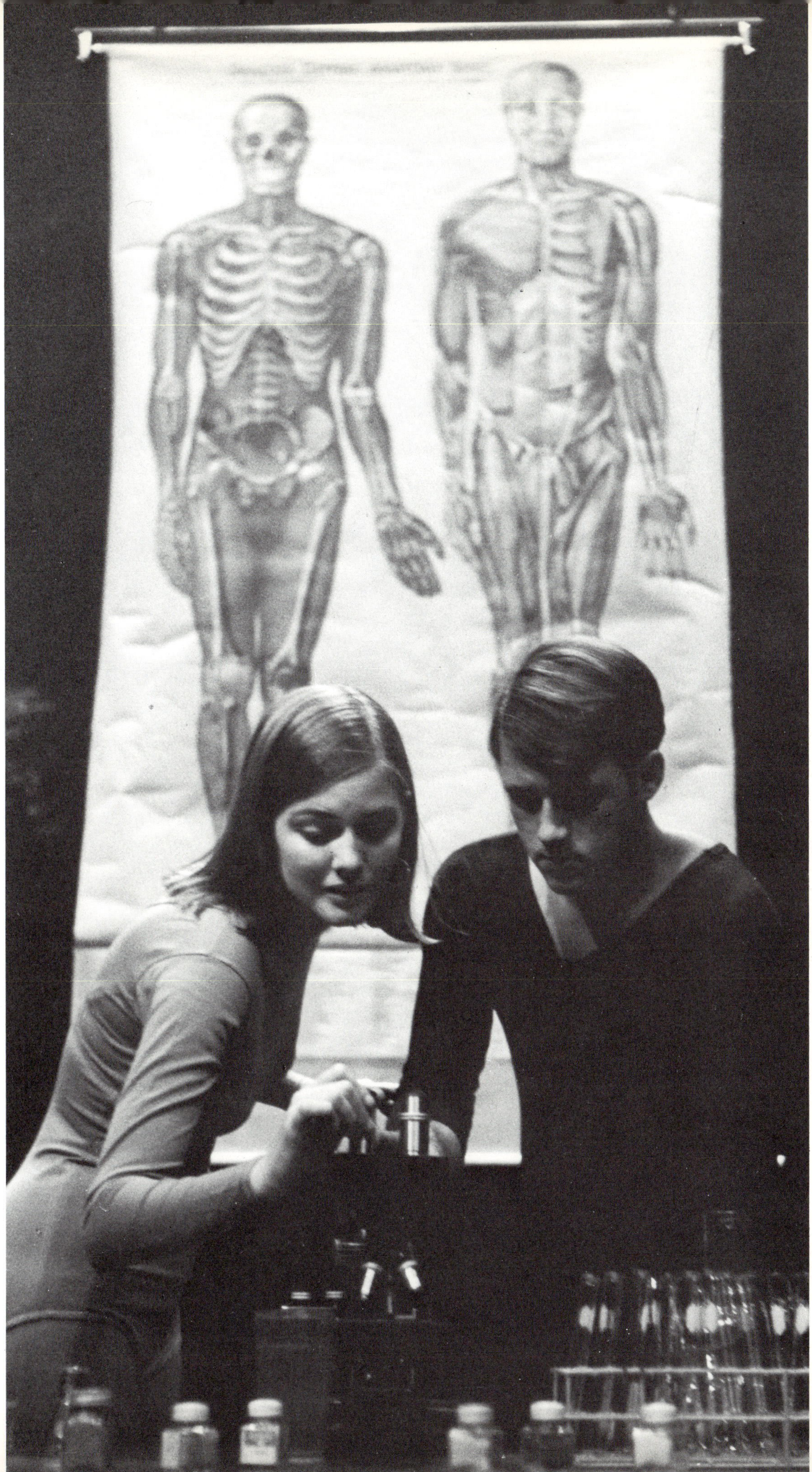

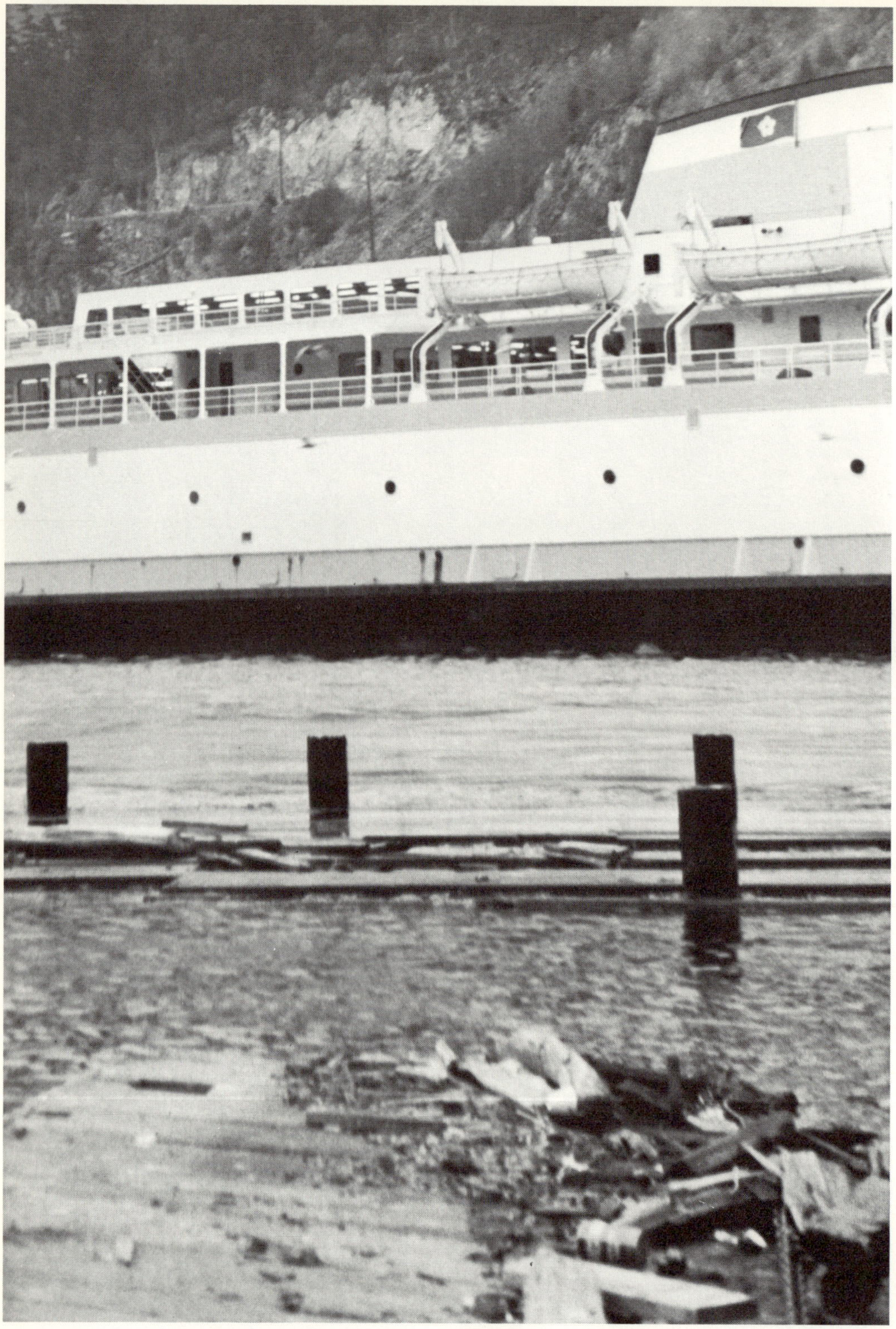

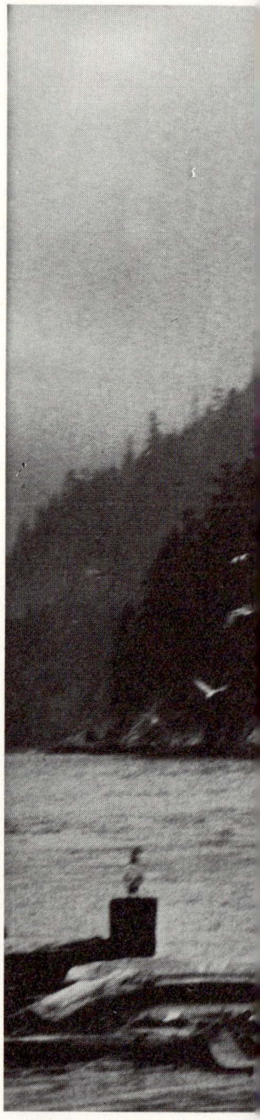

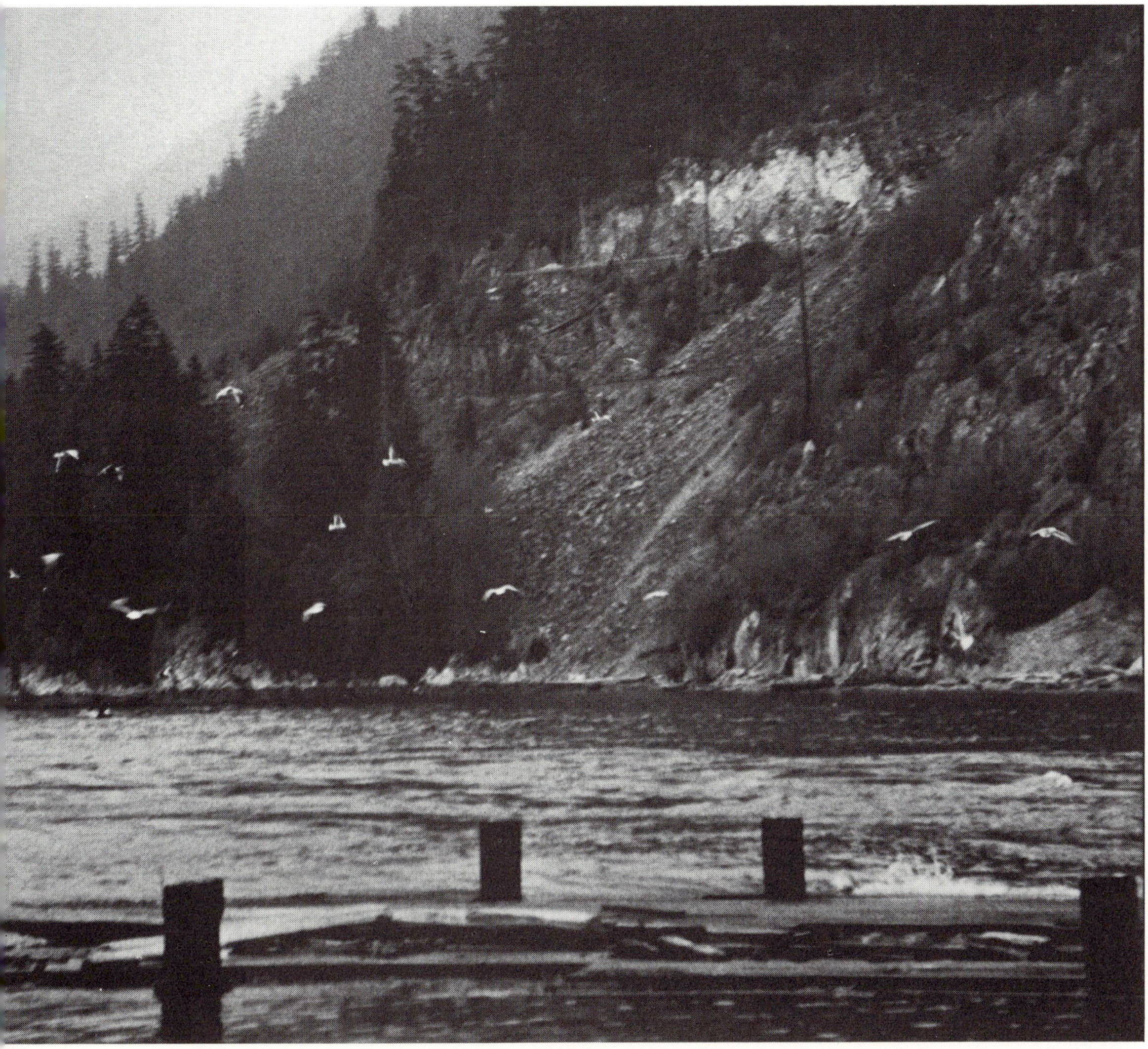

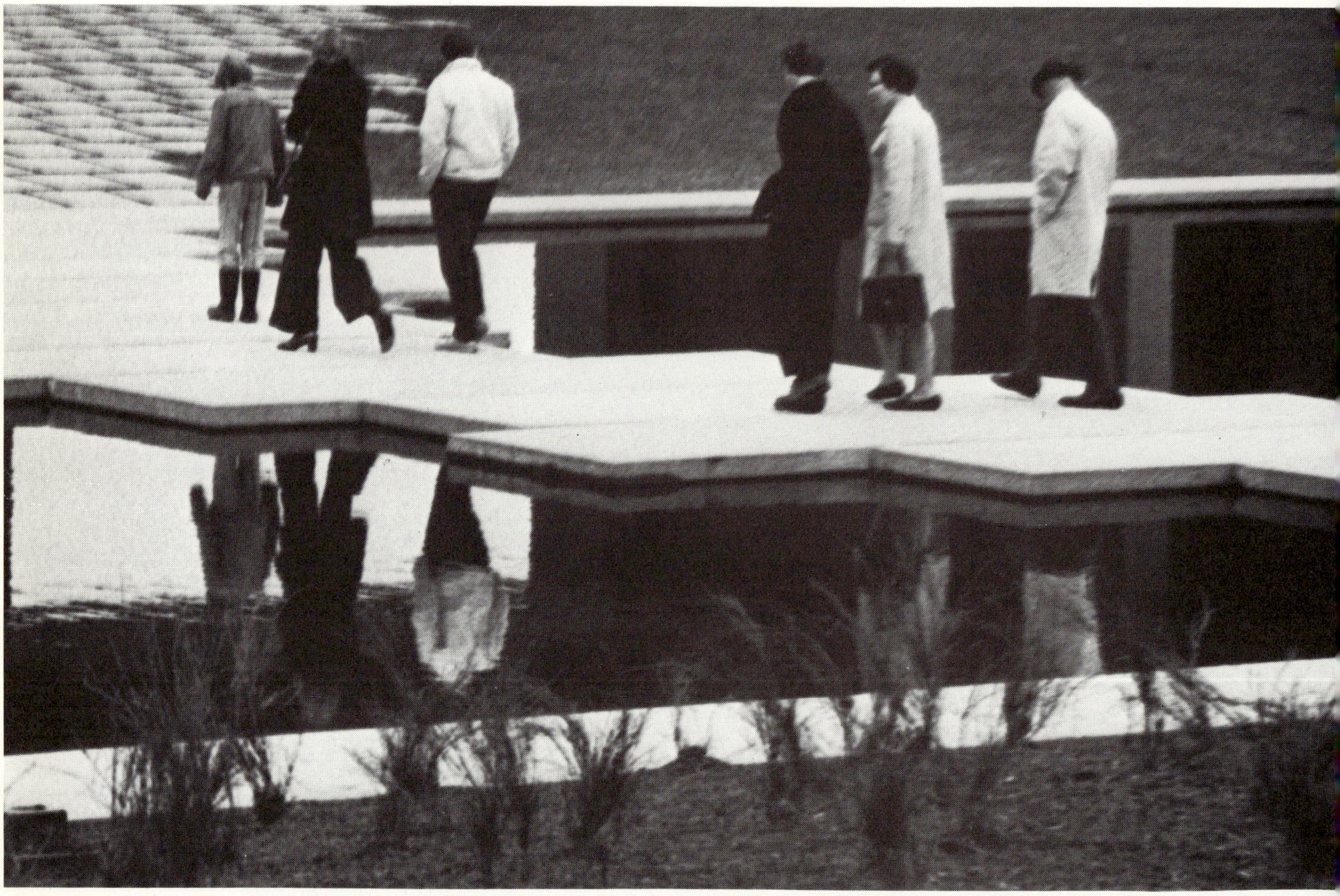

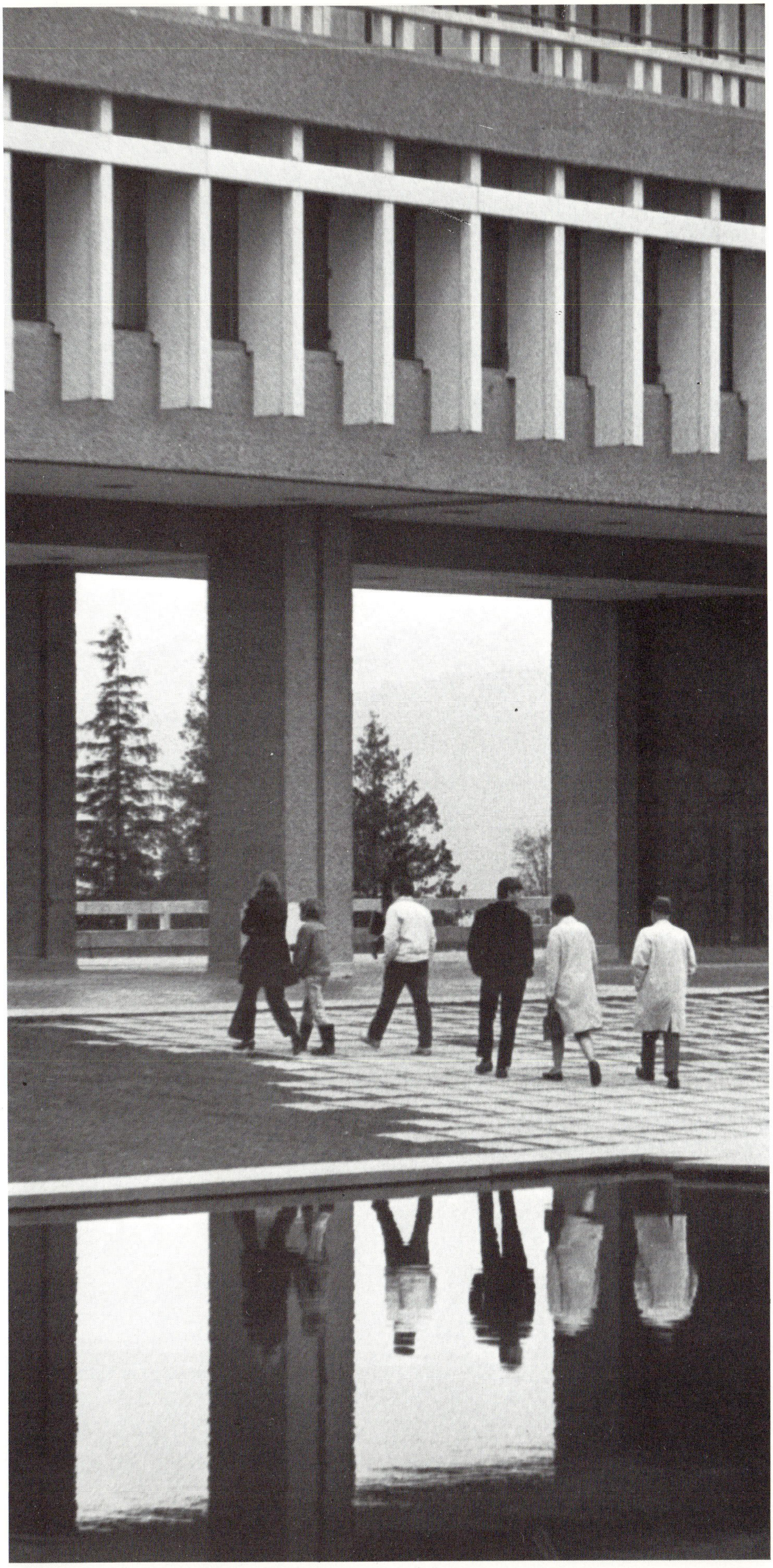

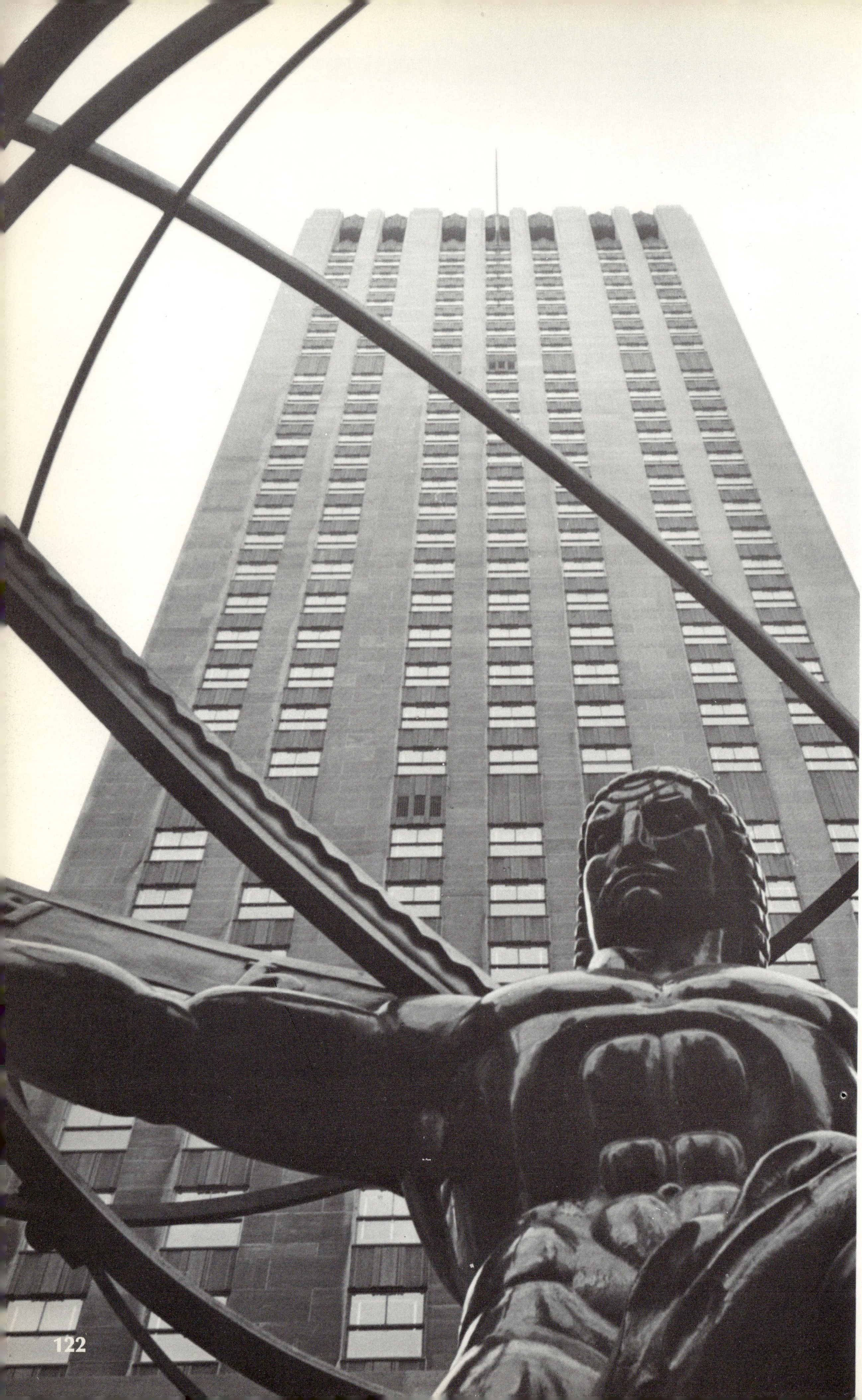

123

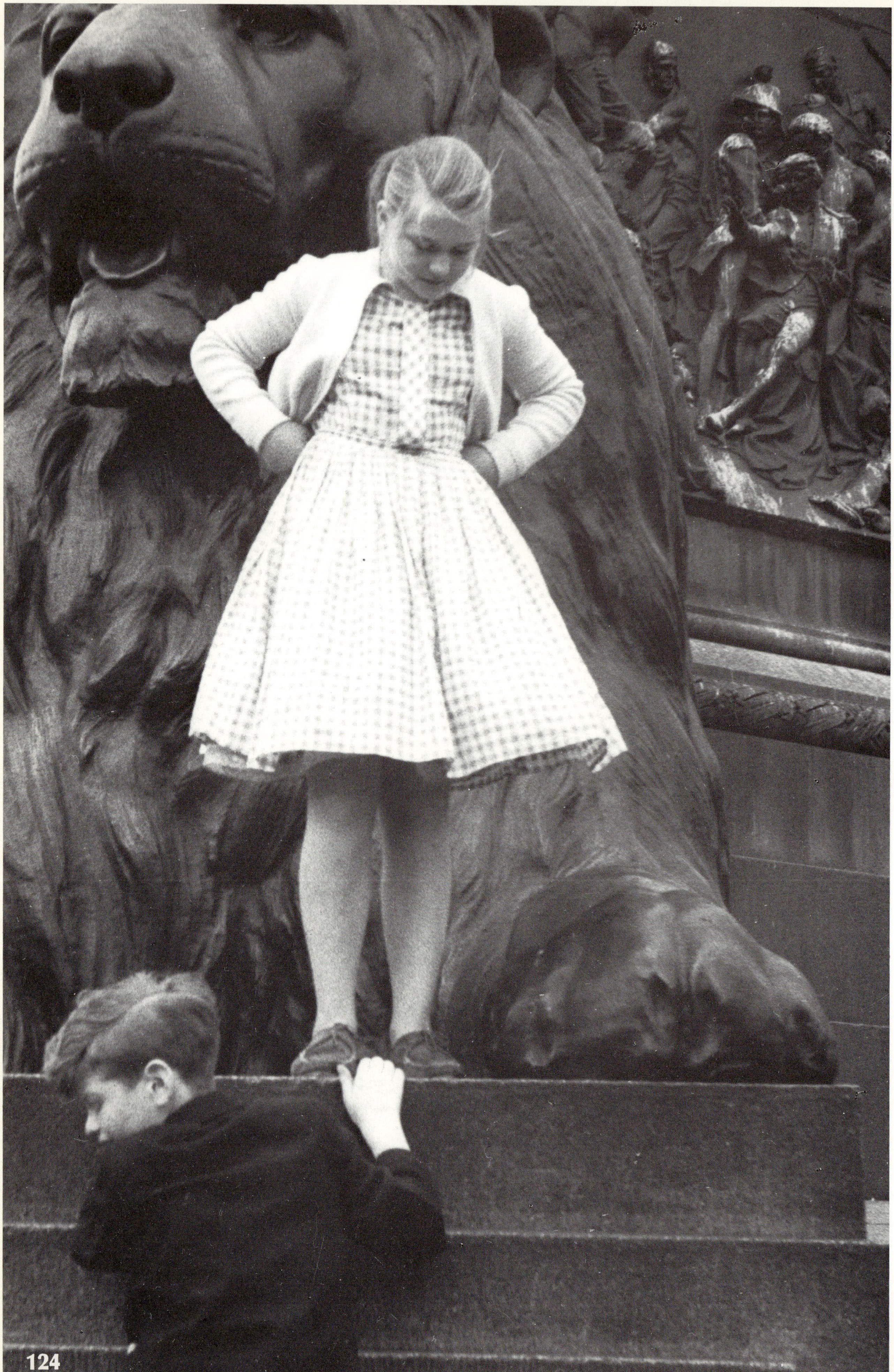

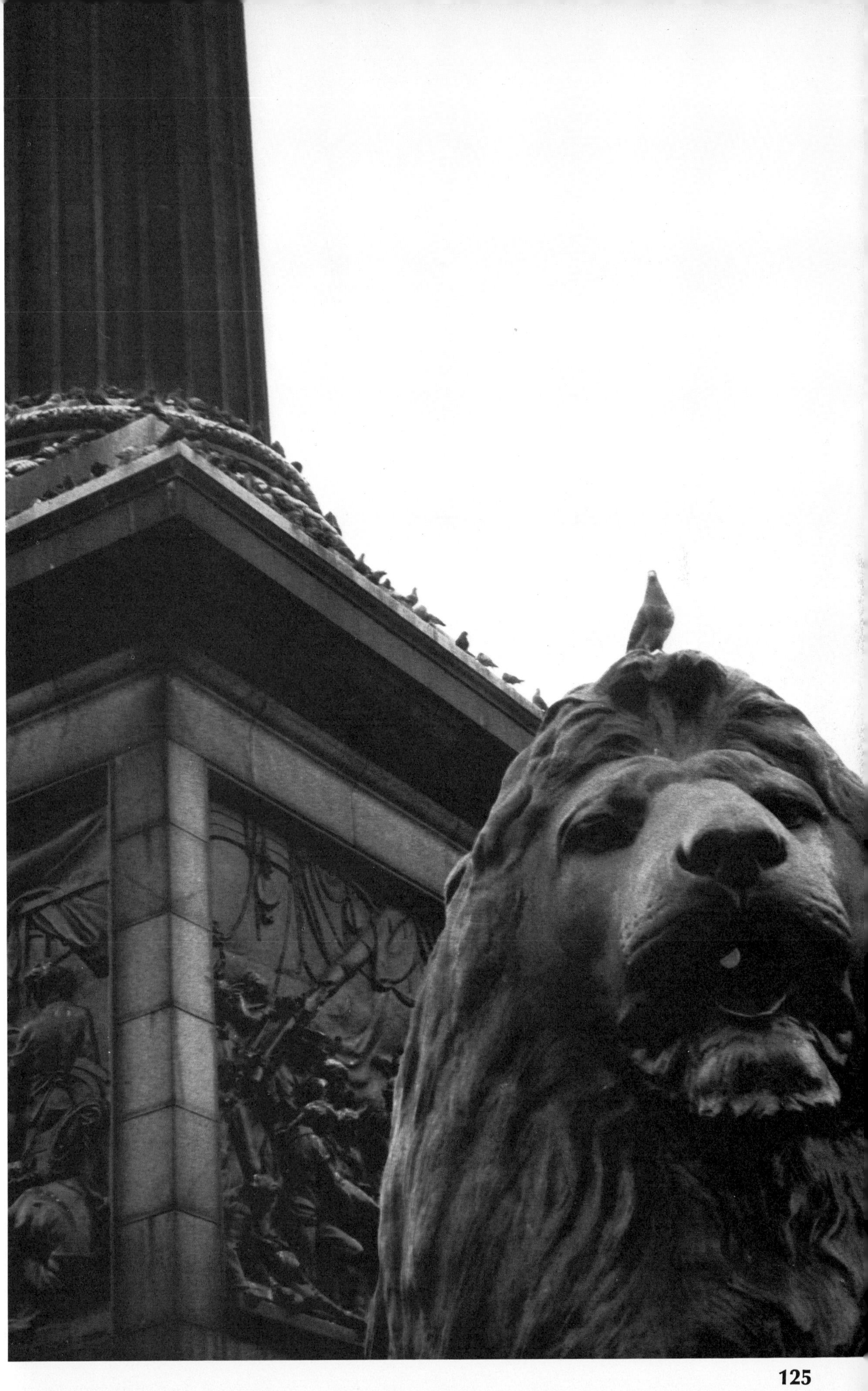

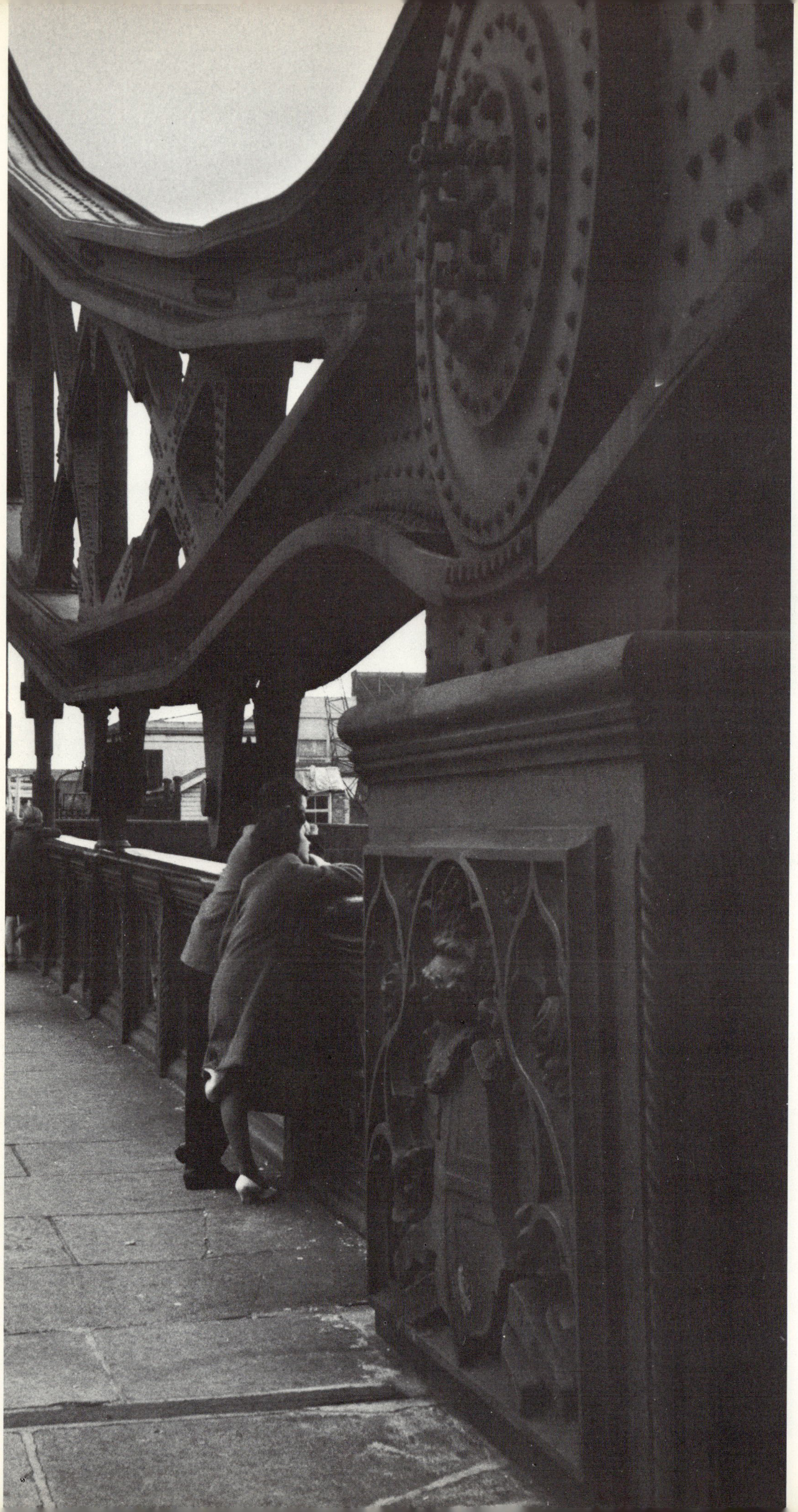

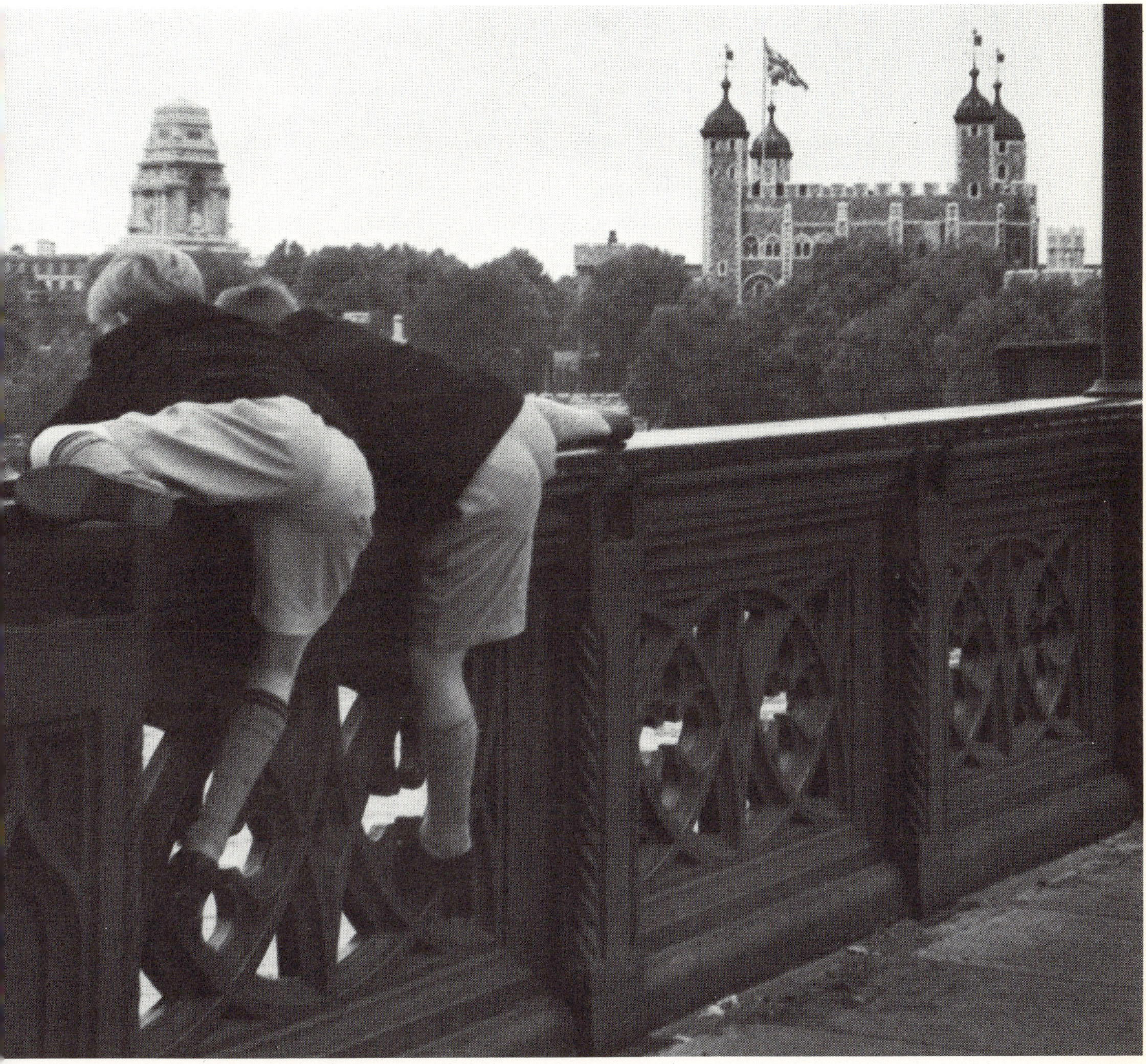

Due to its overuse in all kinds of courses, the comparison and contrast approach to any topic has lost its effect. Yet, in practically everything we evaluate, we are comparing one thing with another, or with an ideal. Even when we are not evaluating, we rely on comparisons. We realize it is cold because we know what warmth is. In the academic world, we need to compare and contrast in order to learn more about the world around us. The photographs in this section, it is hoped, will provide a refreshing way to return to the comparison and contrast approach.

The contrasts in these pictures are also meant to demonstrate viewpoint. The way a person looks at something depends on his attitude. Two people may look at the same situation differently, or at different things in the same setting. The attitude may be expressed in terms of mood or tone. The attitudes reflected in these photographs—as well as the mood or tone—should be translated by the student into words. This can be done in one of two ways. The student can write about a set of pictures in a single composition and discuss the differences. On the other hand, the student can write an entire composition on a single photograph and reflect the viewpoint depicted in it. He will, in the latter case, have to resort to words and phrases to convey the mood or tone. The second approach is the more demanding of the student's writing skill. In addition, the following questions suggest other ways of writing about the photographs:

Pages 106–107: Of these two ways of looking at lower Manhattan, which do you prefer? Why?

Pages 108–109: If you find yourself walking alone at night, which of these two settings would make you feel uneasy? The reasons for the way you feel about the two settings are significant. Analyze those reasons.

Pages 110–111: One of these situations is familiar to people who have visited Paris, or seen the city in movies or on television. The other presents an aspect of the city not ordinarily seen in travelogs. What do these two pictures say about the same city, about the romantic notion people have of Paris? In both pictures, what is the significance of Notre Dame?

Pages 112–113: Unless a person enters the grounds of the White House, this is how the building appears to him when he is passing it. What he sees depends on how he focuses. If he gazes at the building, the fence is fuzzy in the foreground. If he looks at the fence, the building is lost in a haze. Analyze these two ways of looking at the White House and also at any building.

Pages 114–115: What do these two pictures—one a distant view and the other a closer look—tell us about the way we see things that make us uneasy?

Pages 116–117: The anatomy charts in the background attempt to reveal what man is made of. The figures in the foreground of both pictures, however, expose the limitations of the physiological approach. They also provide almost opposing viewpoints on man: discuss these viewpoints against their backgrounds.

Pages 118–119: Which of these two pictures appeals to you? Why?

Pages 120–121: One way of looking at these two photographs is to consider the esthetics of the situation. Is it a matter of taste which one pleases you most? What factors are responsible for the pleasing effect? Why is one of the pictures more effective than the other?

Pages 122–123: The statue is that of Atlas carrying the world on his shoulders (in the original myth he carries the sky). Two ways of looking at the world are depicted in the two photographs. How do these ways differ from each other? Does it make a difference that you cannot see the face in the second picture?

Pages 124–125: You can look at this lion as the one in Trafalgar Square in London (where these photographs were taken), or as representative of any statue. In either case, the two pictures make some pertinent comments on the British lion in particular and statues in general. What are those comments?

Pages 126–127: The Tower Bridge in London is a huge structure. In one picture, this structure is emphasized, in the other it is minimized. Keeping in mind the importance of size, what do you believe these two pictures say about technology?

THE WORLD OF THE CHILD

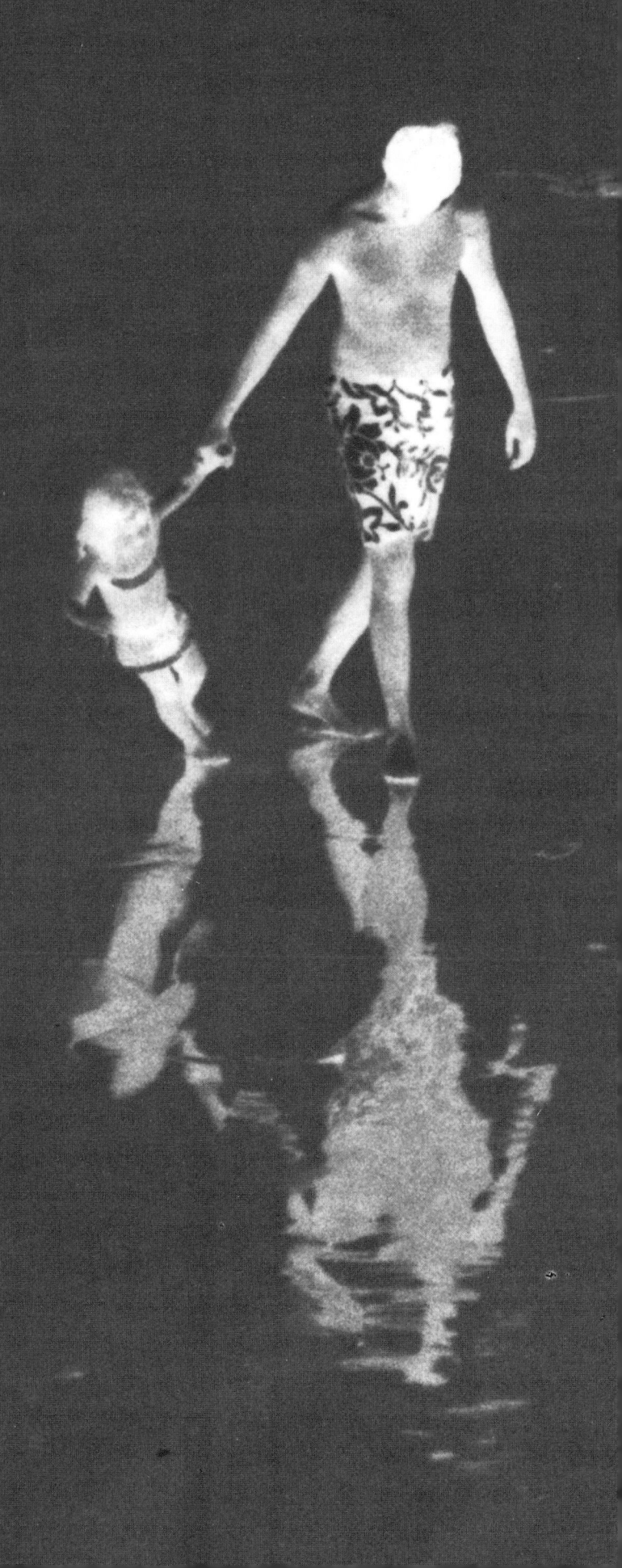

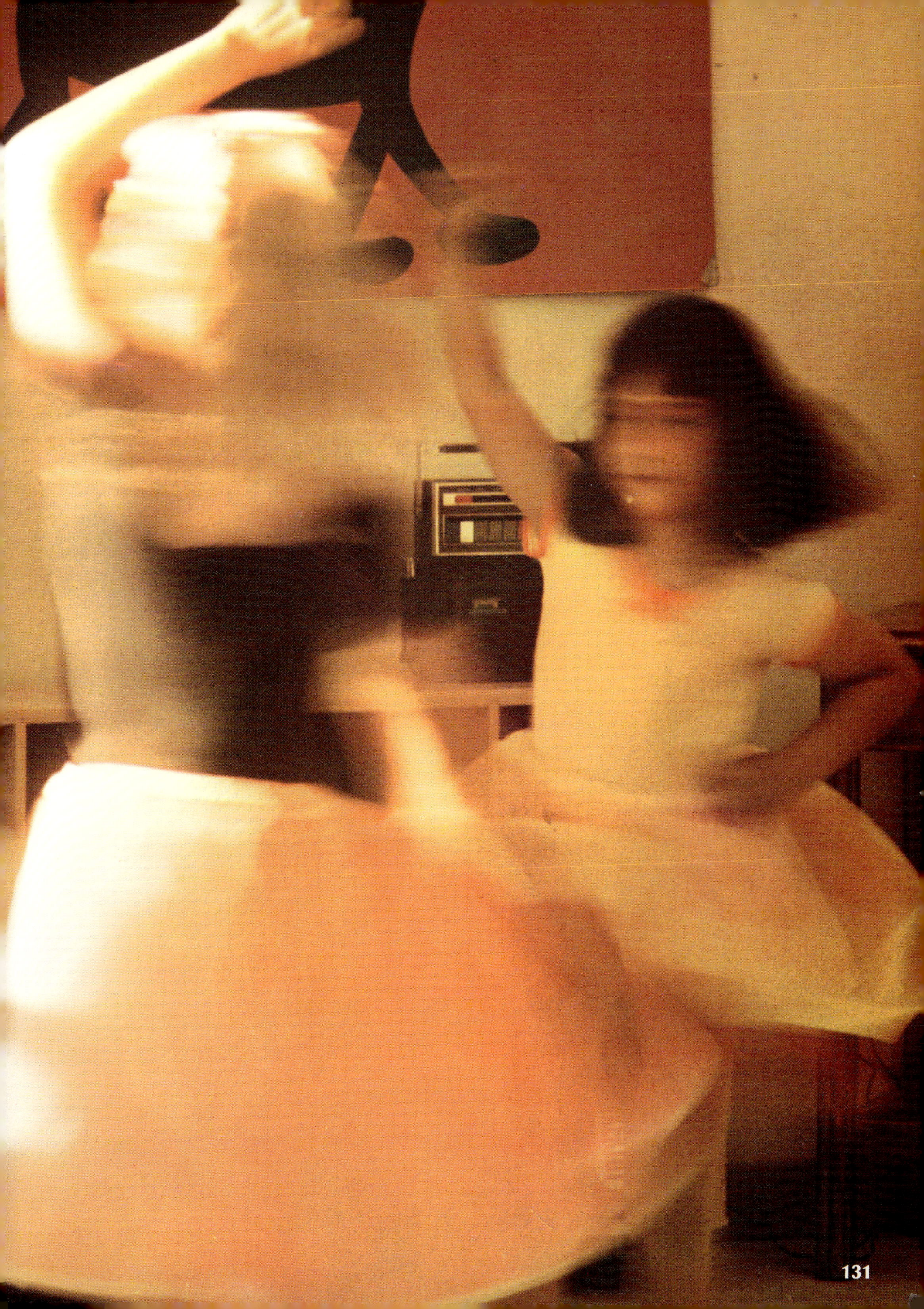

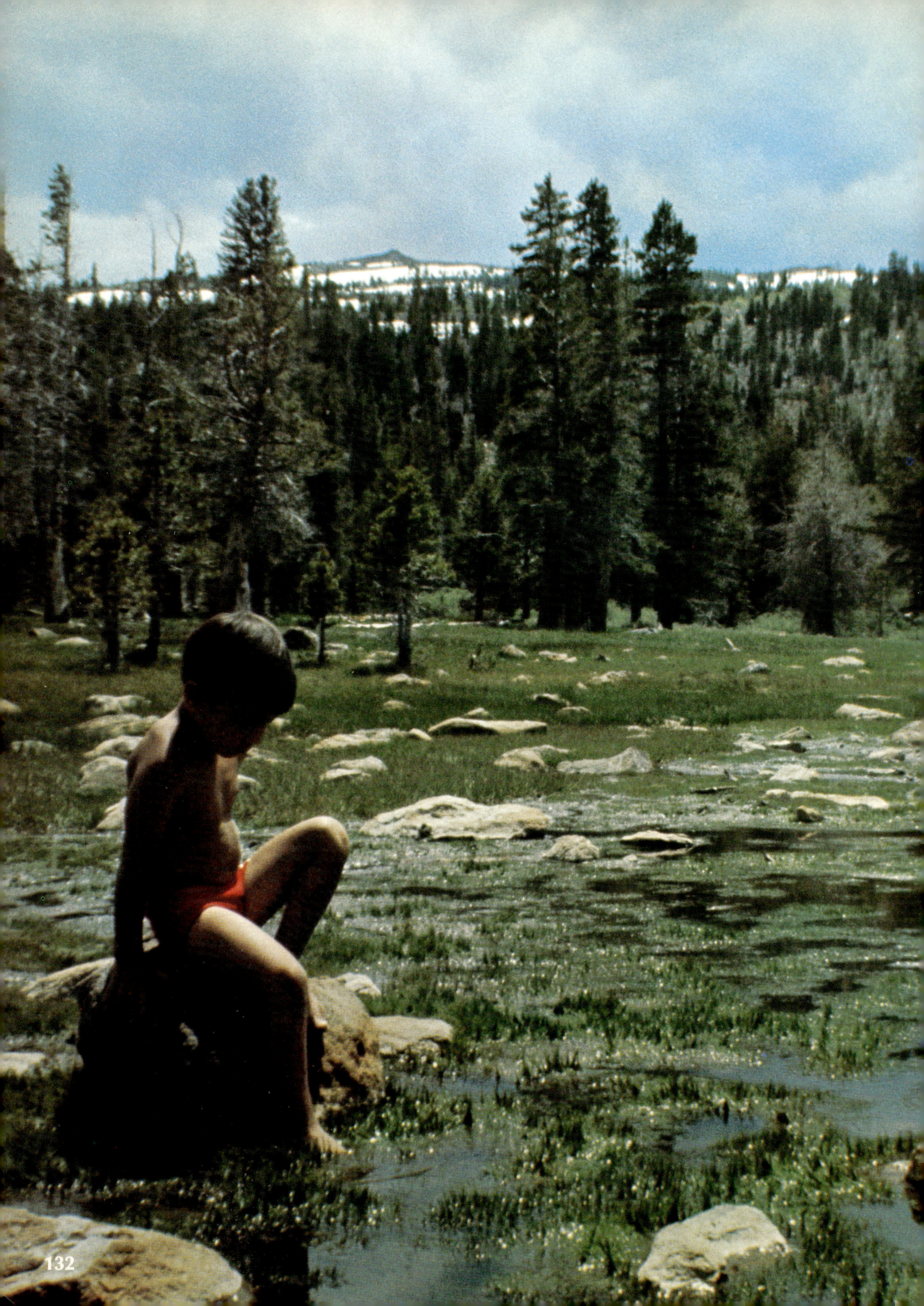

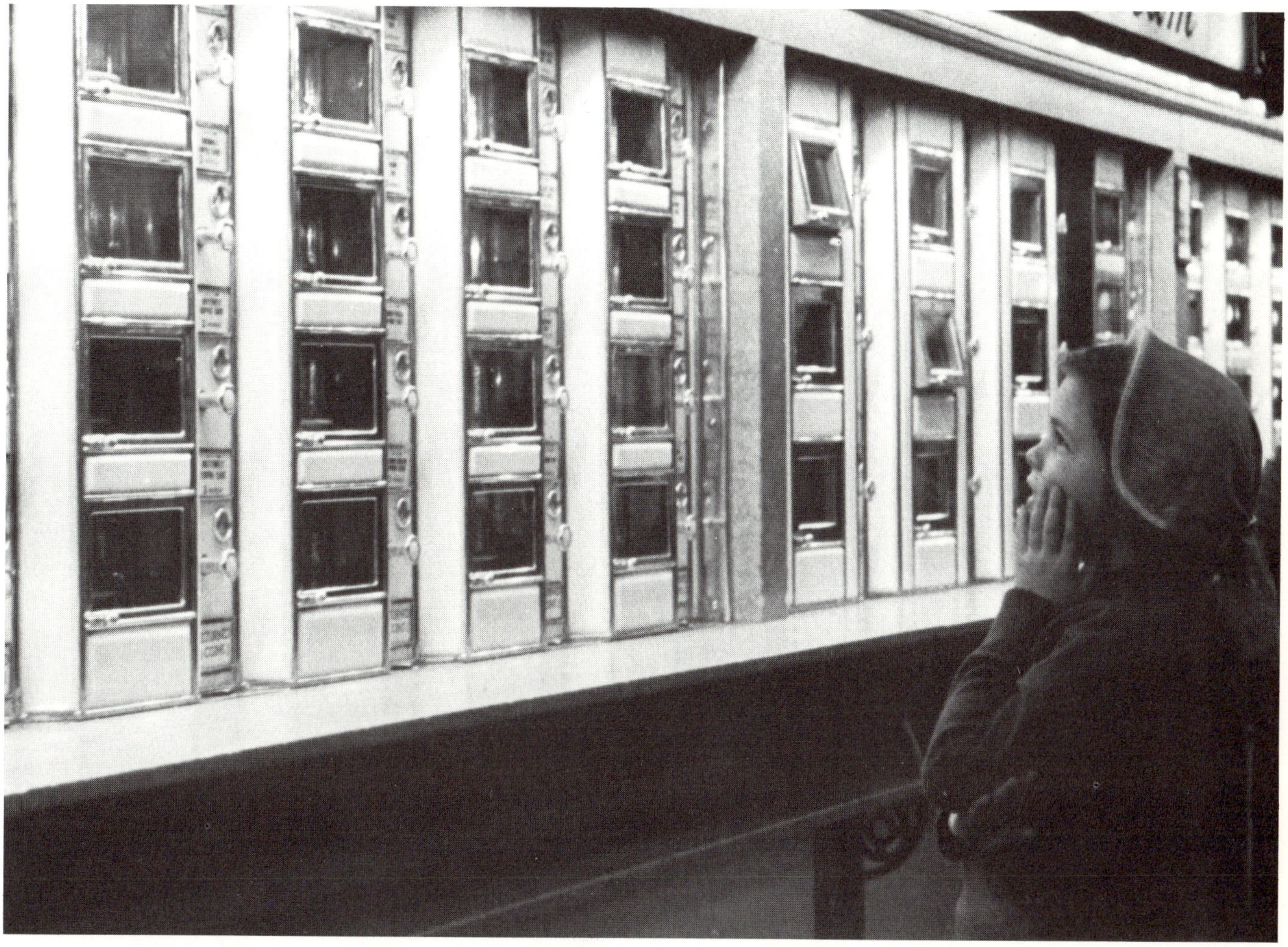

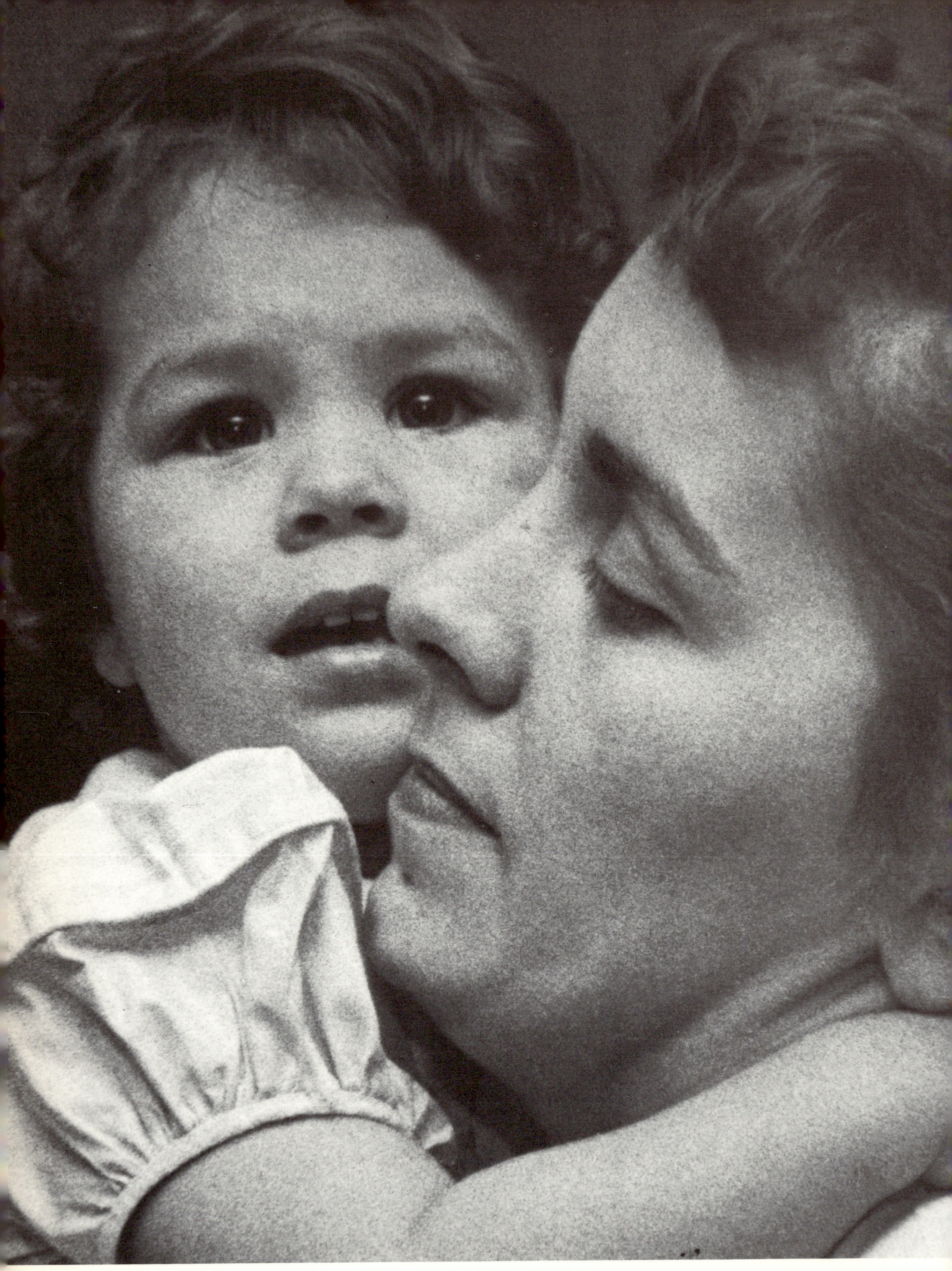

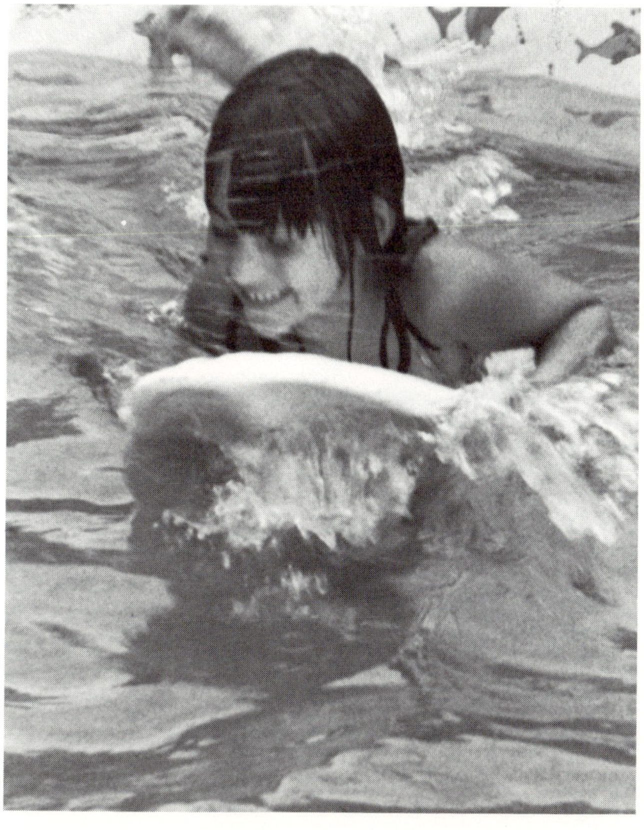

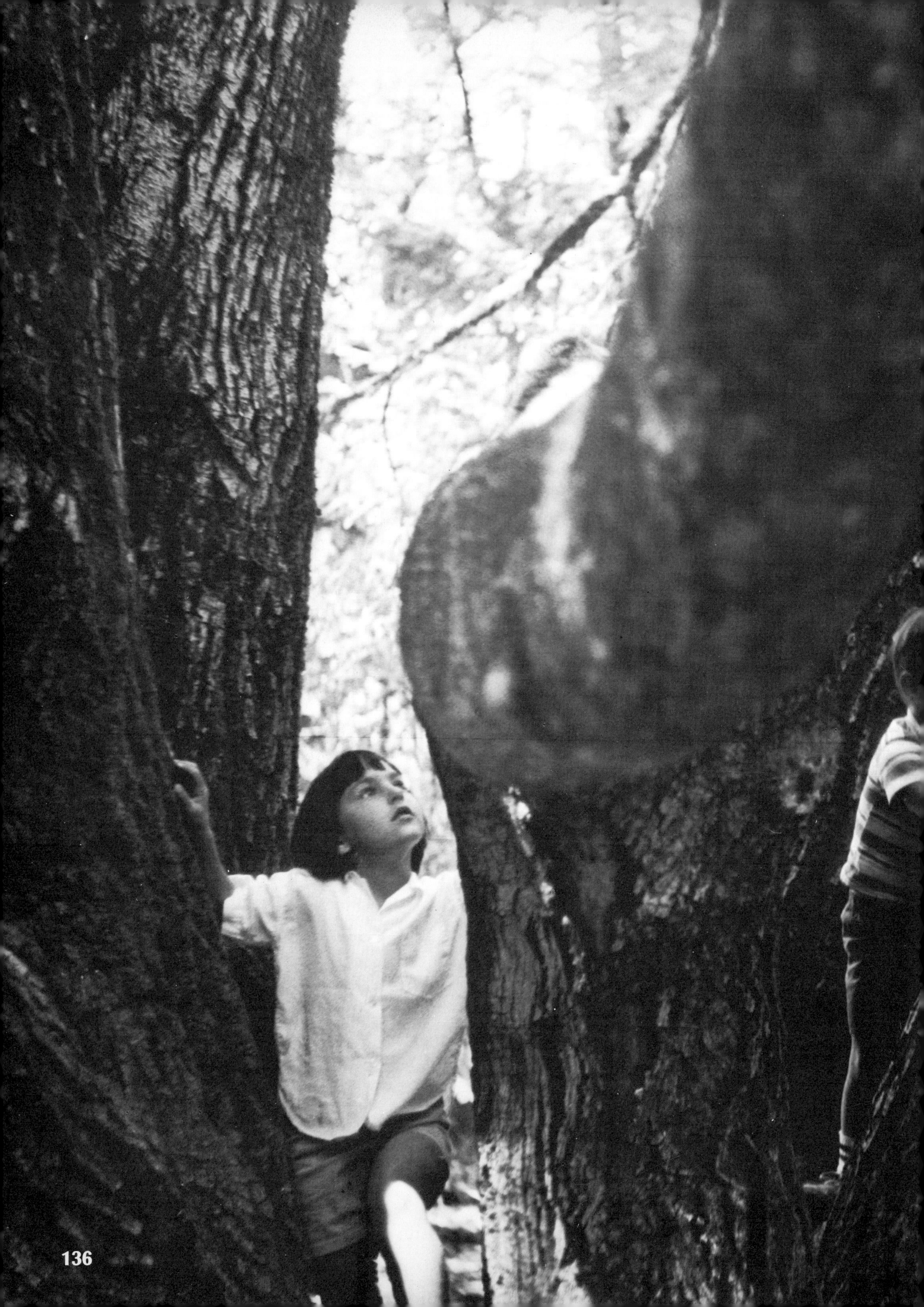

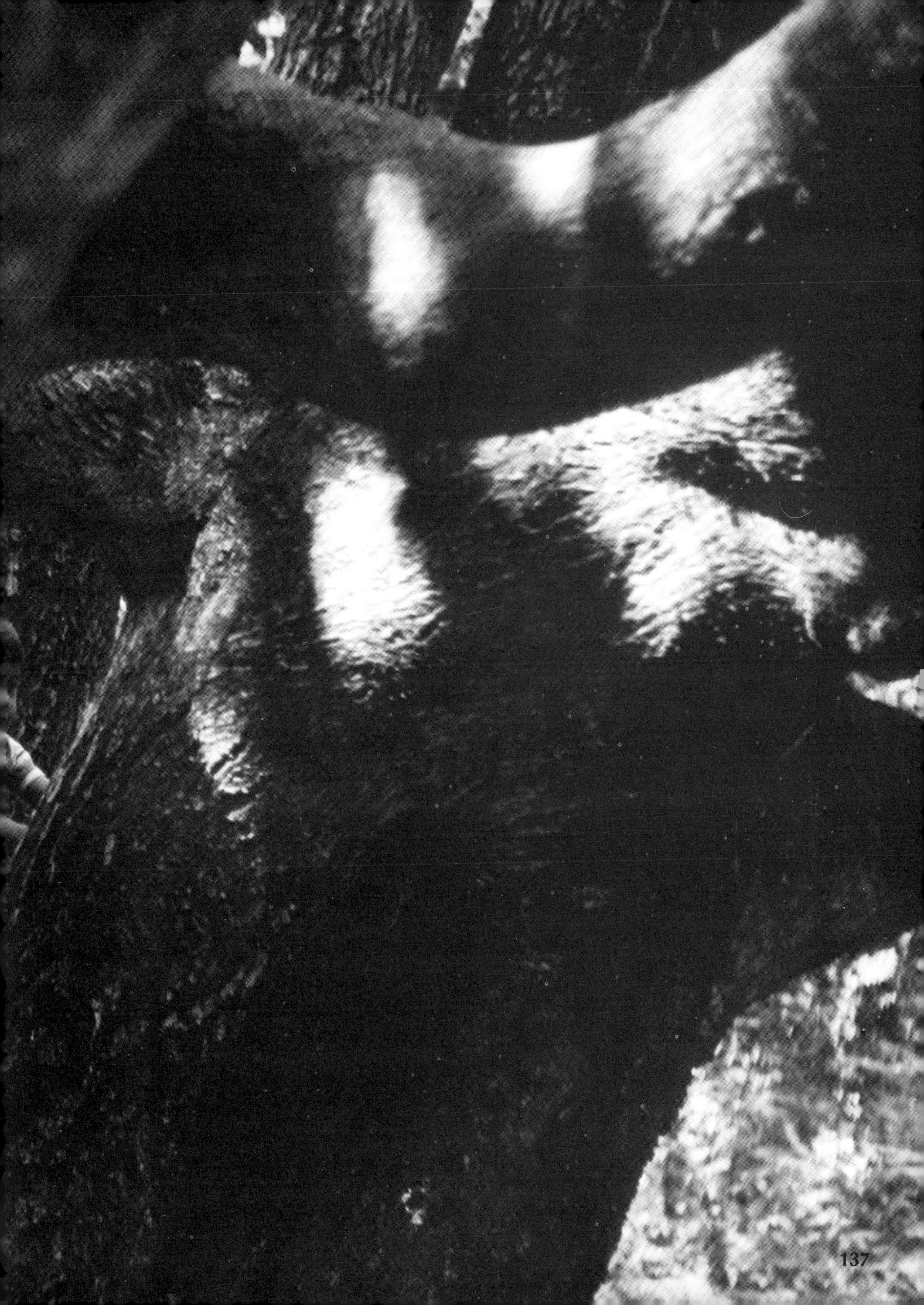

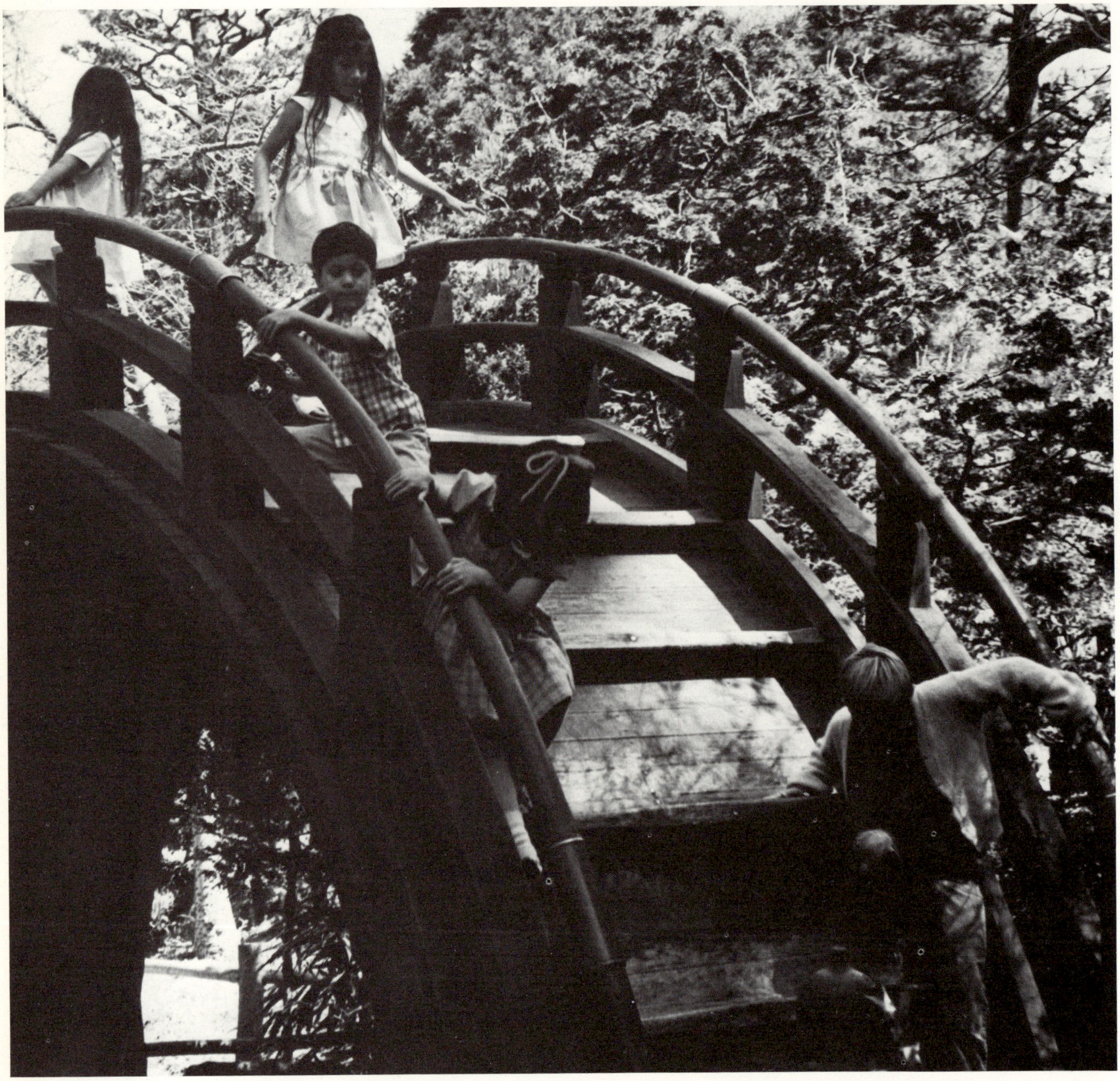

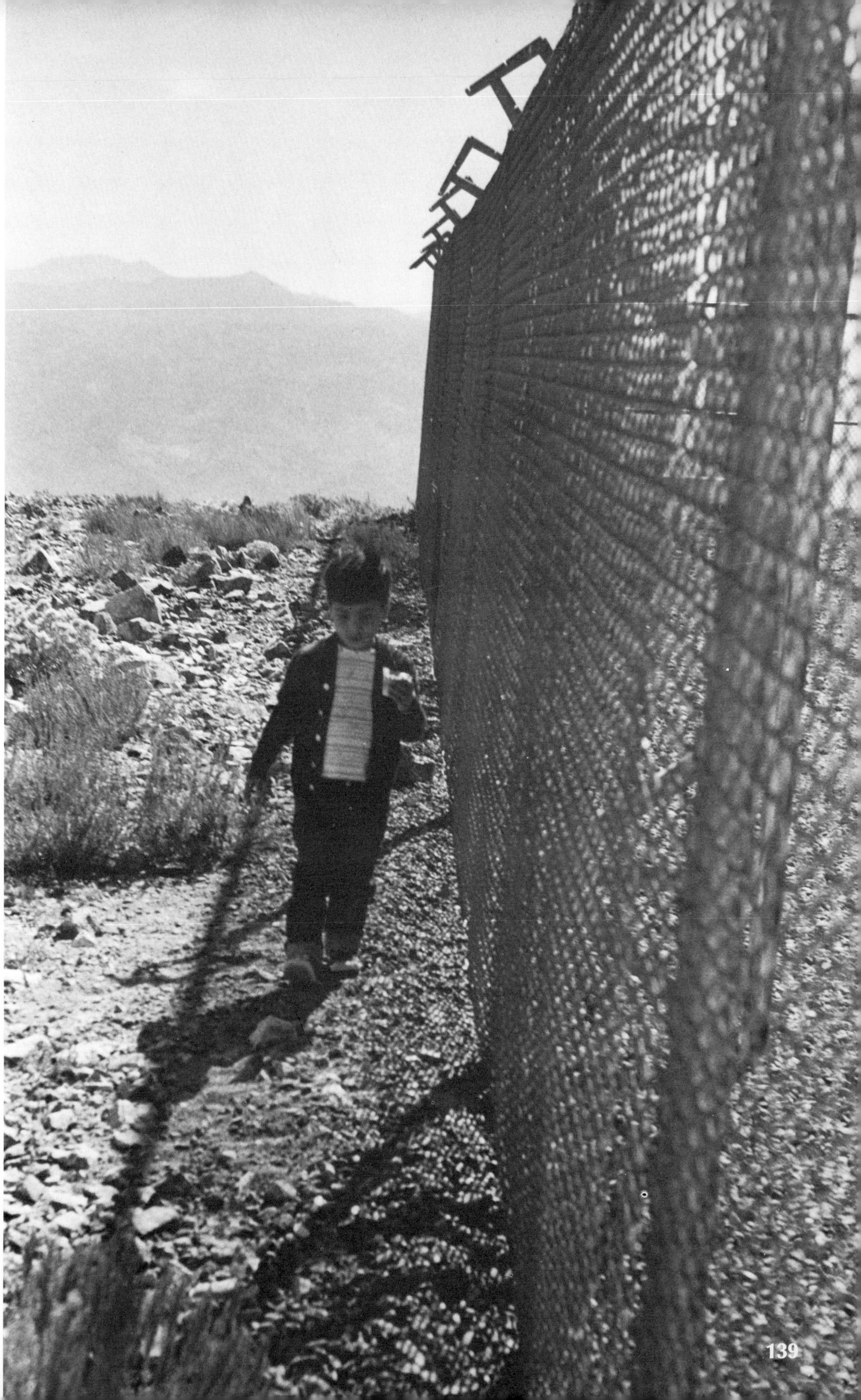

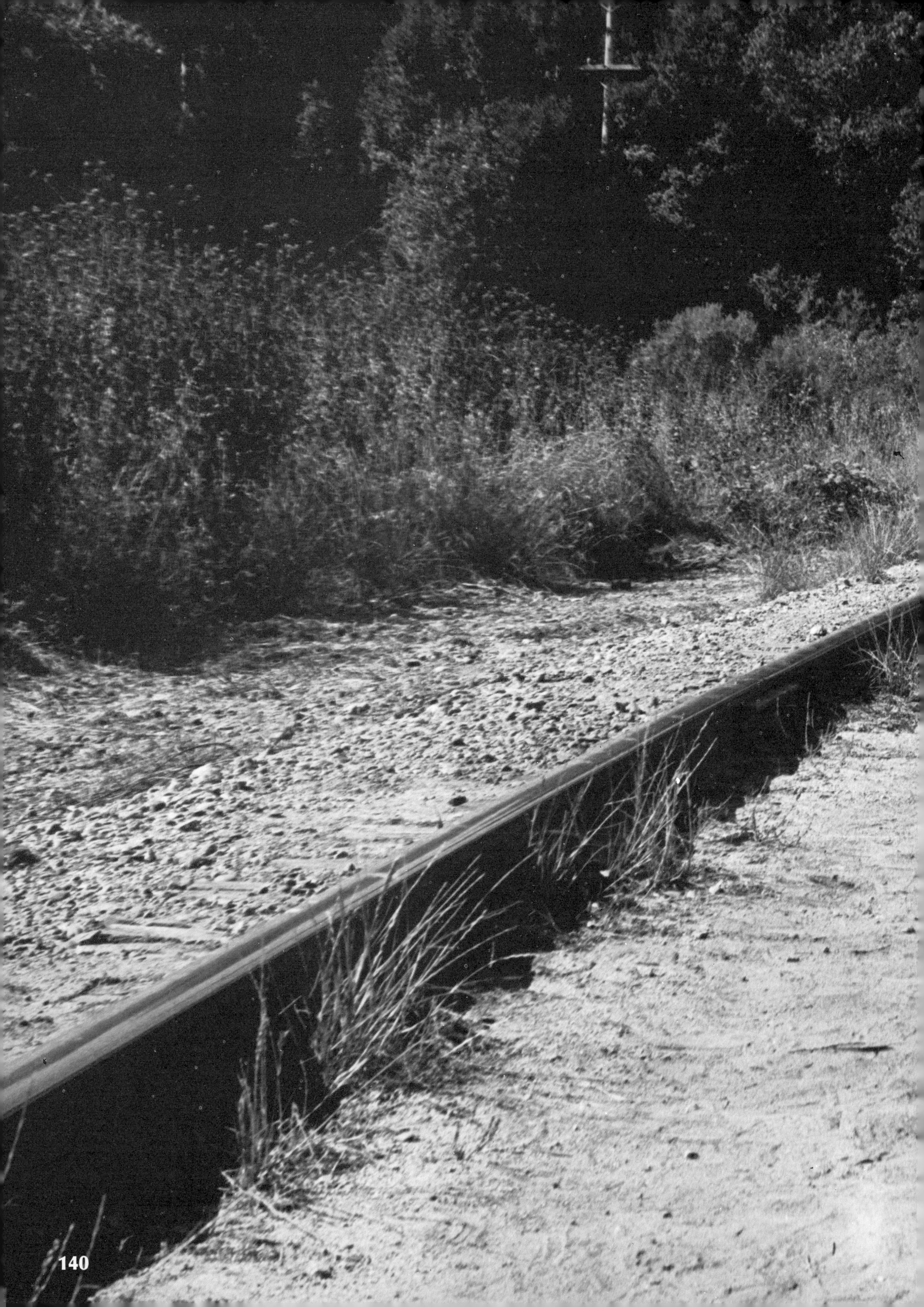

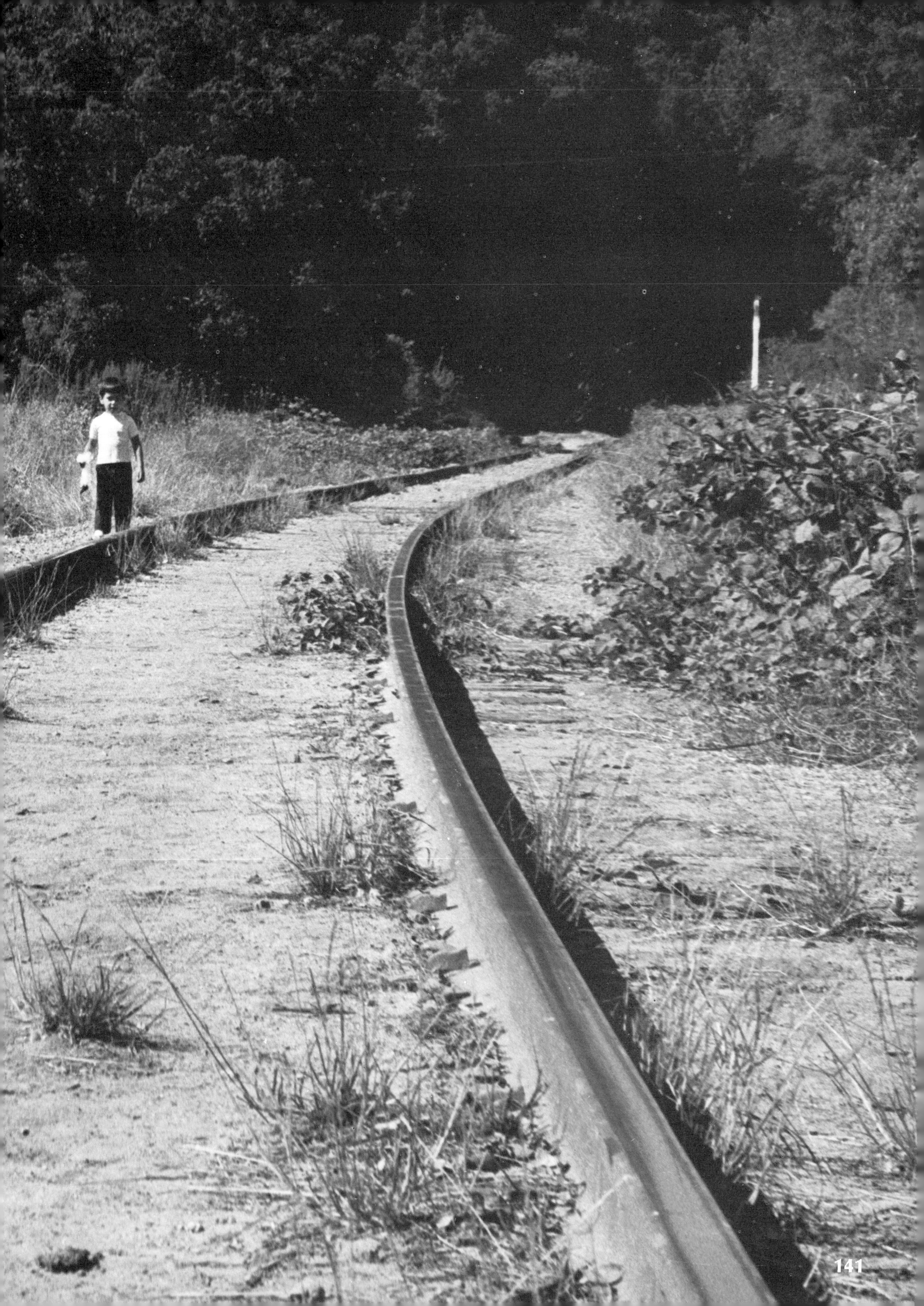

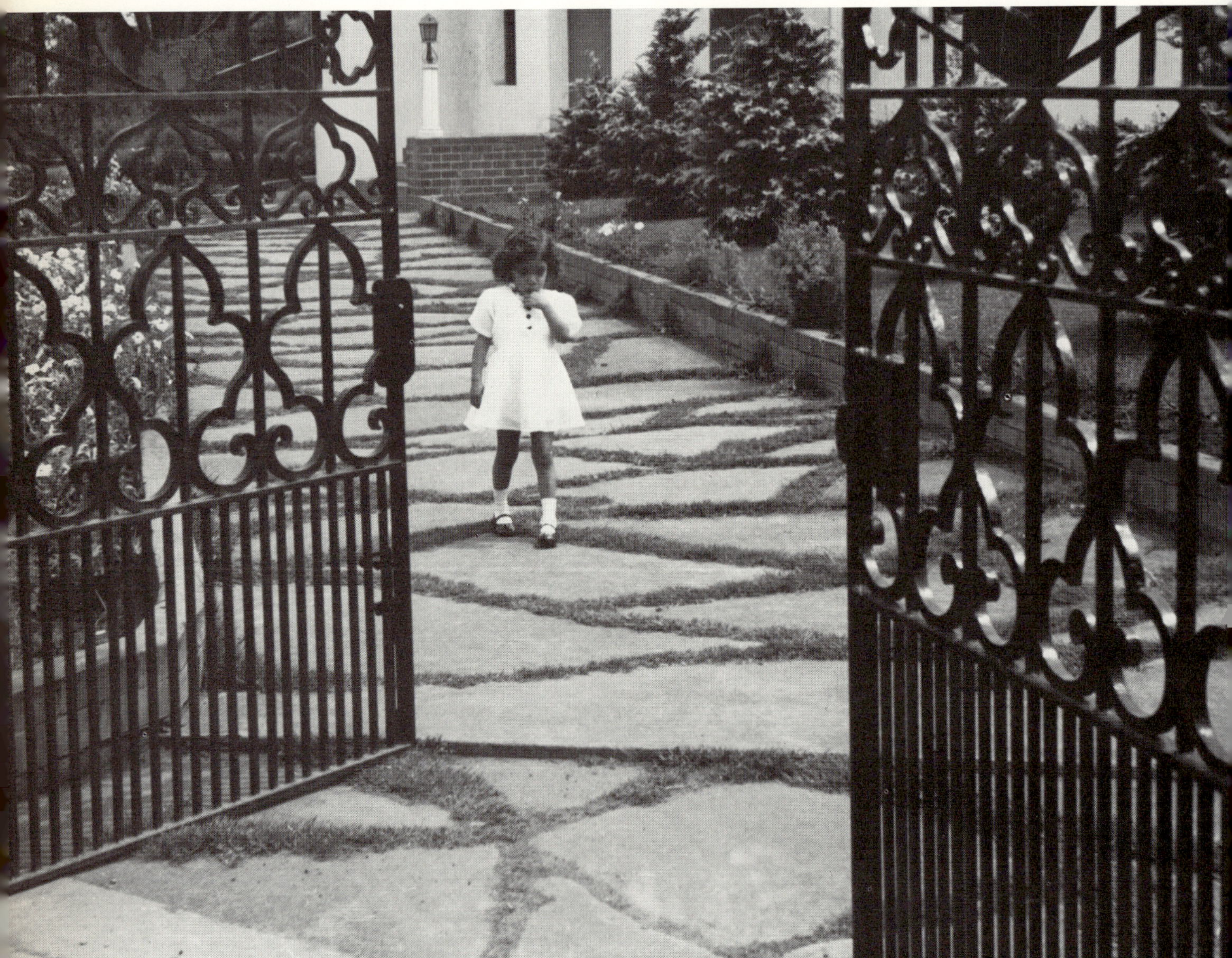

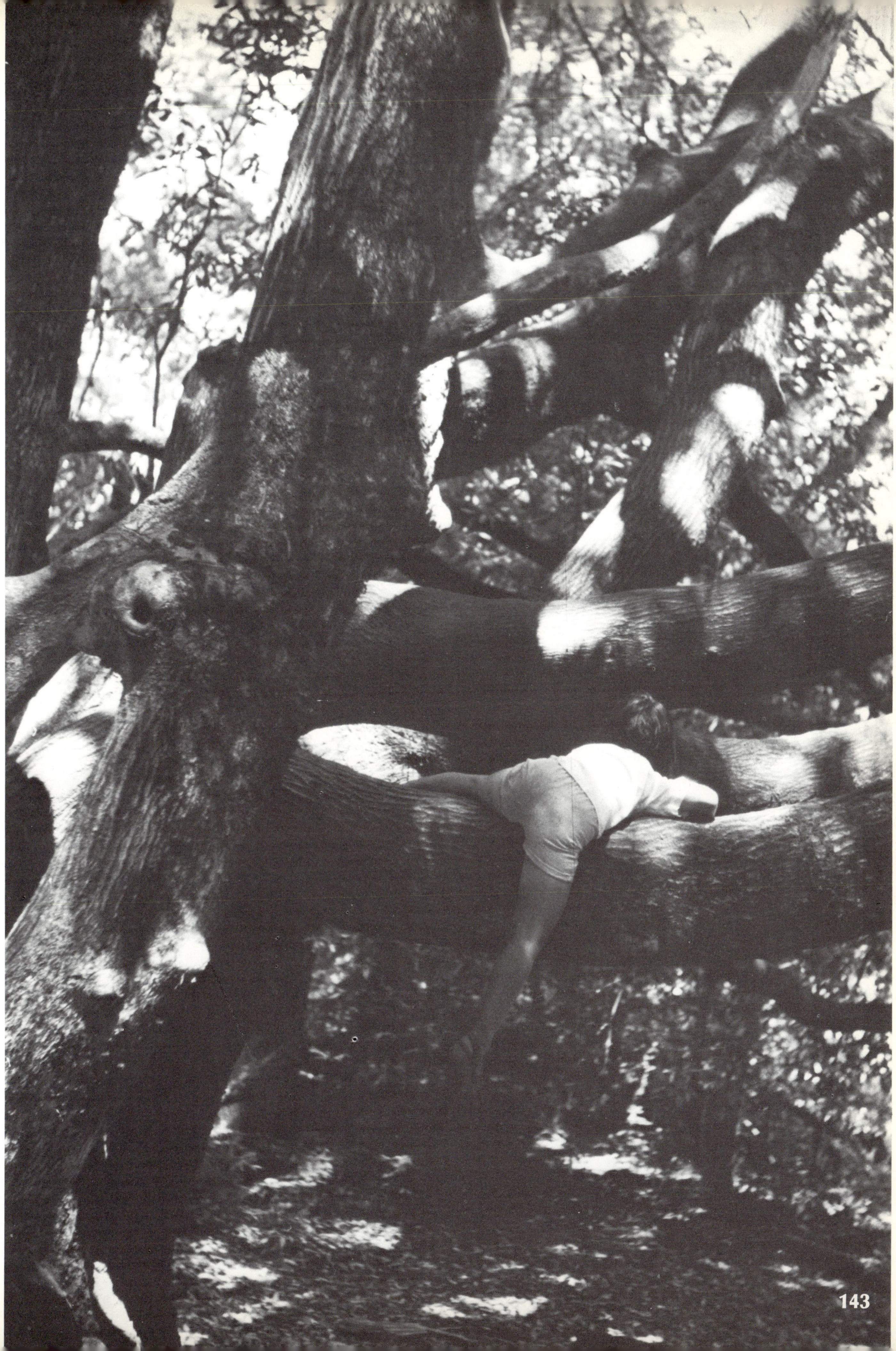

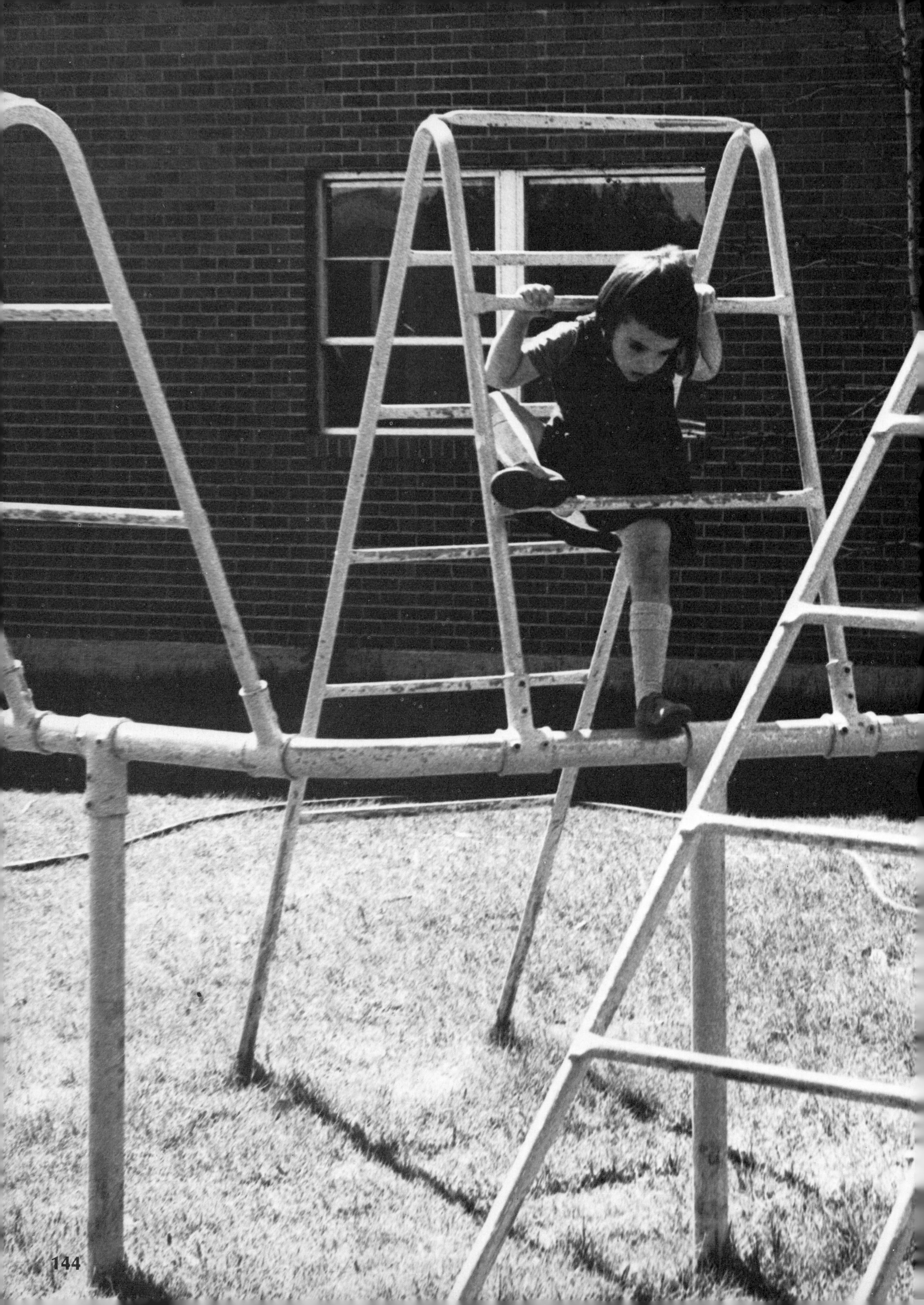

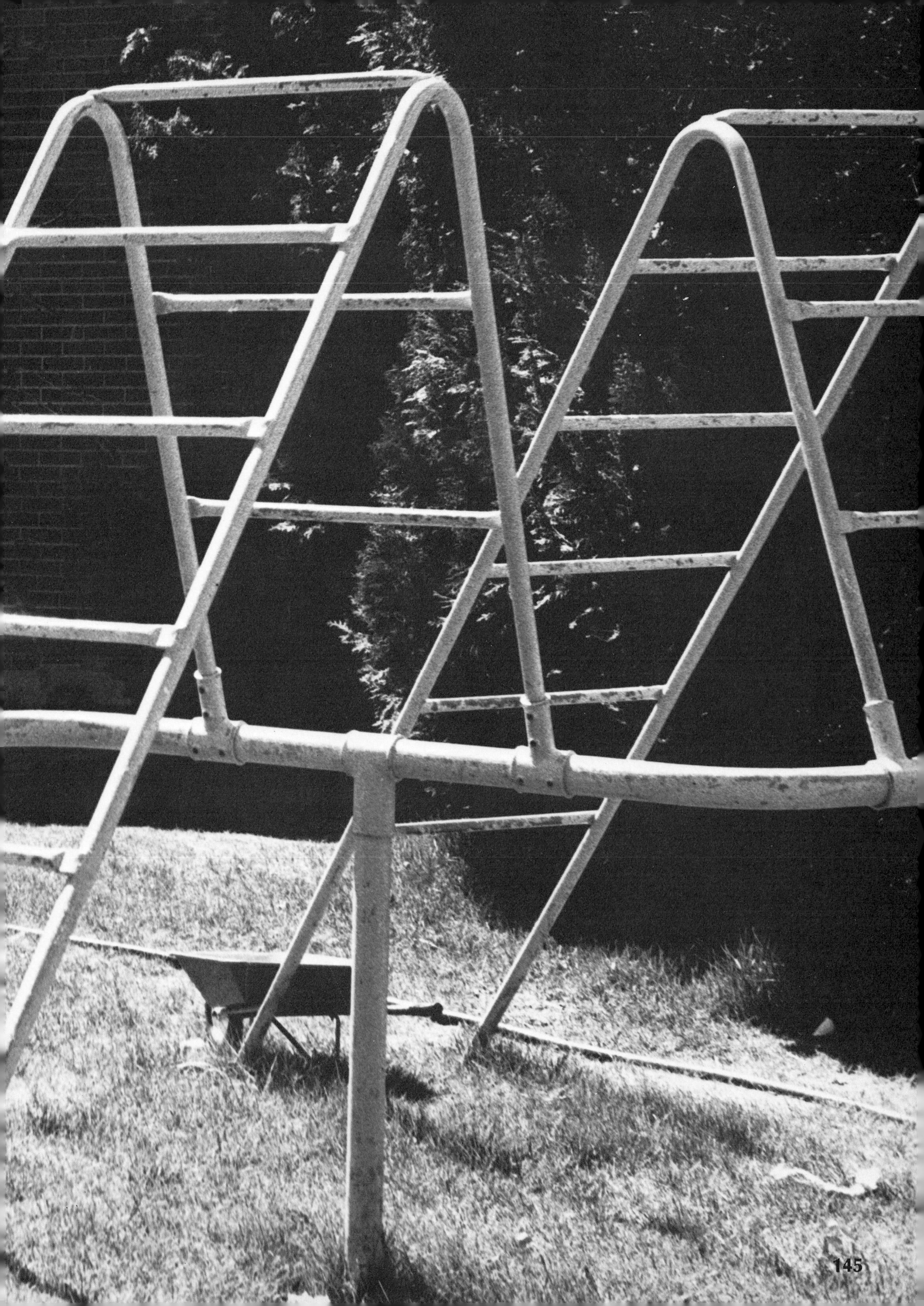

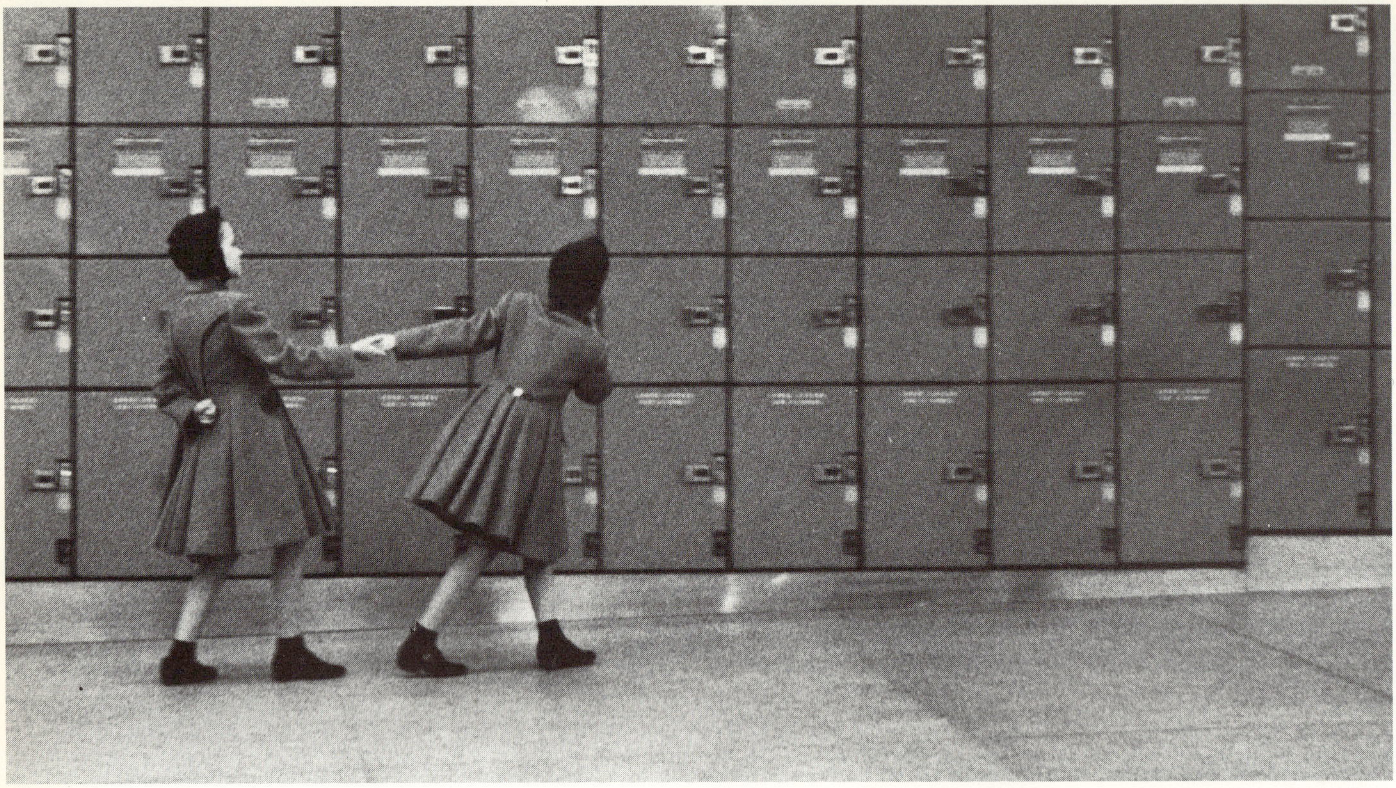

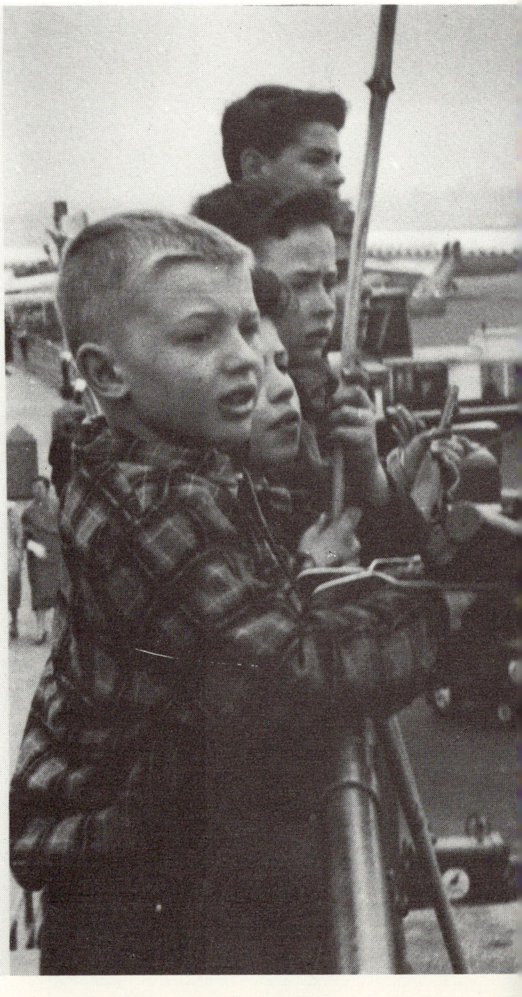

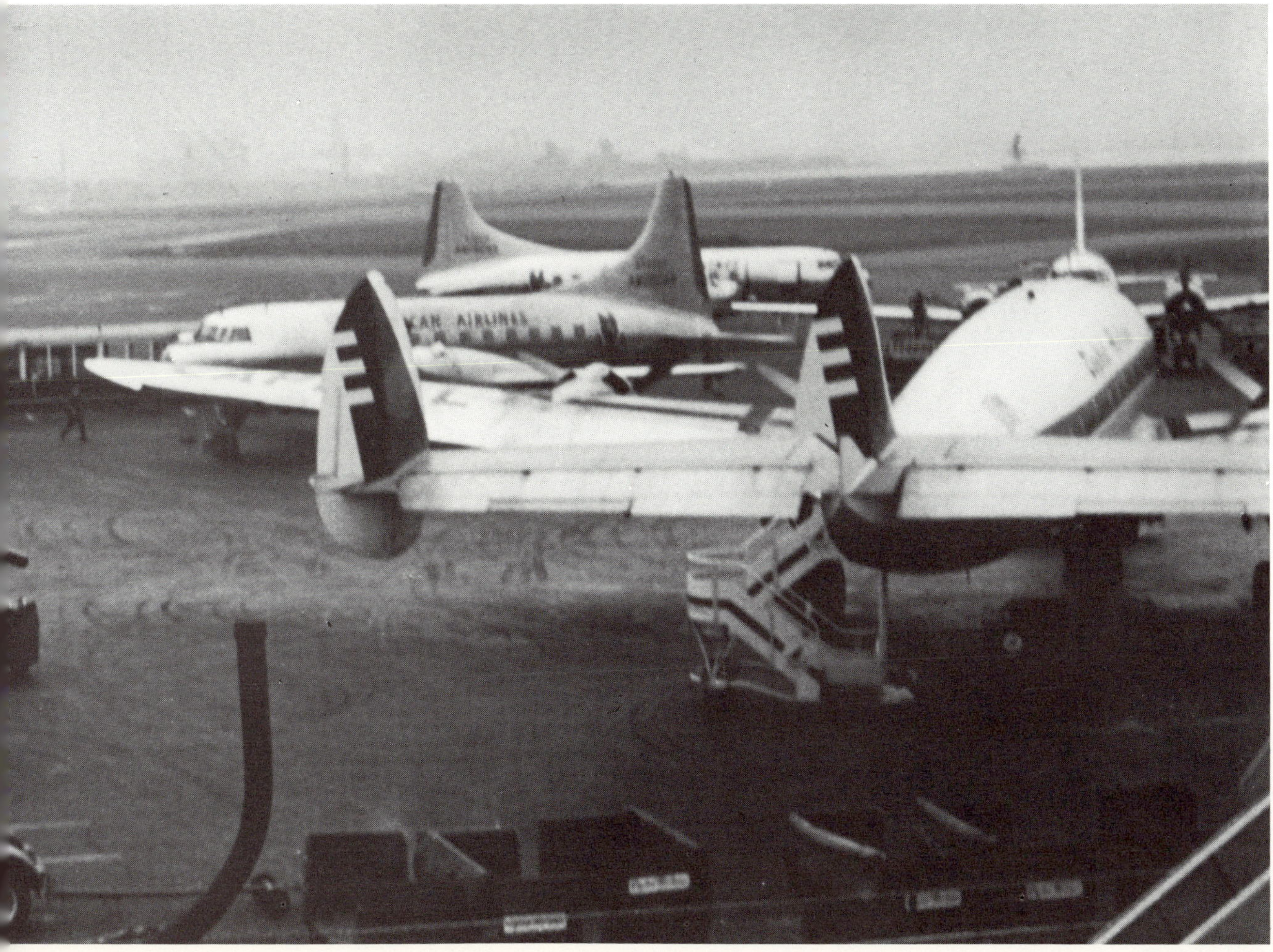
AIRLINES

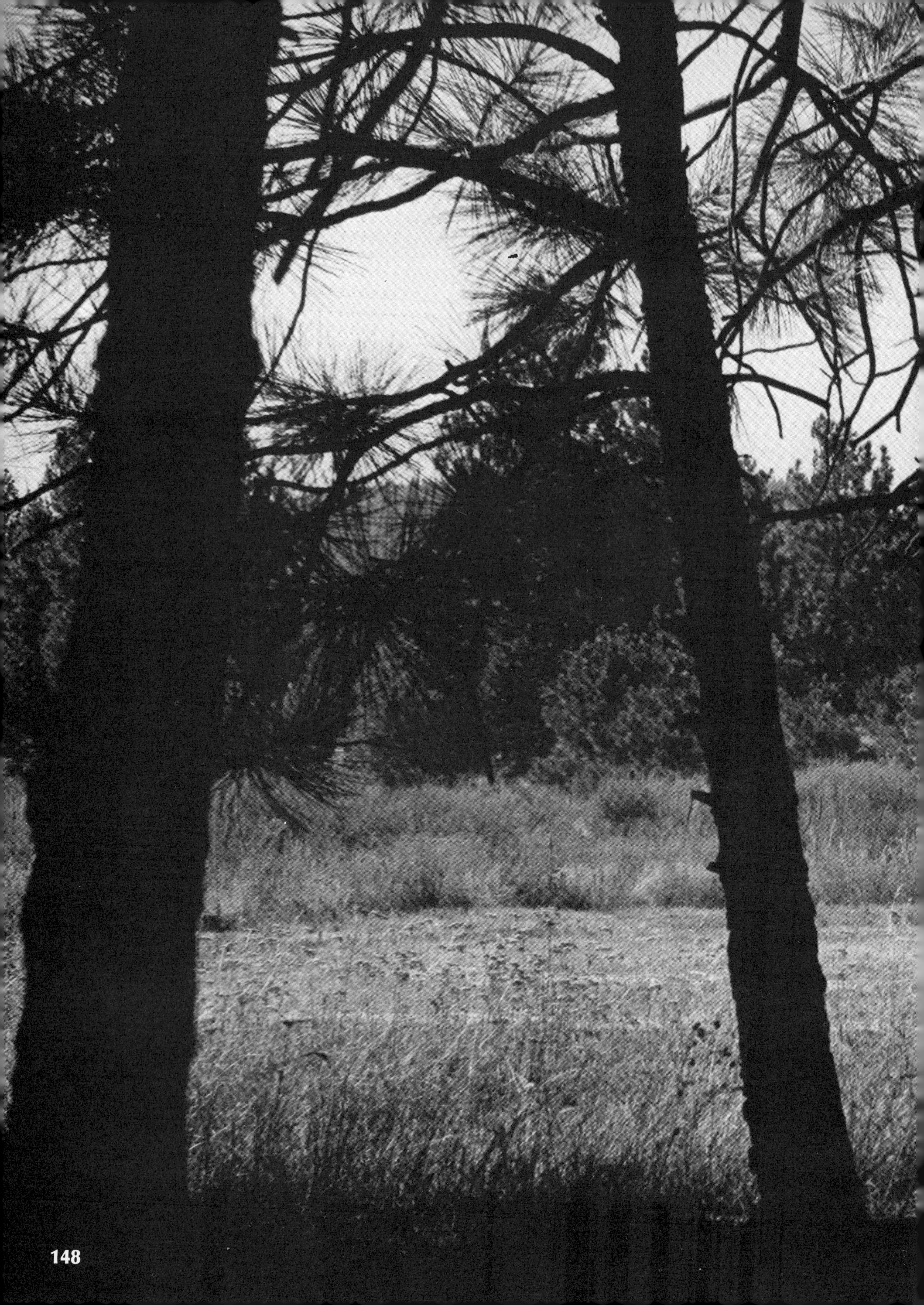

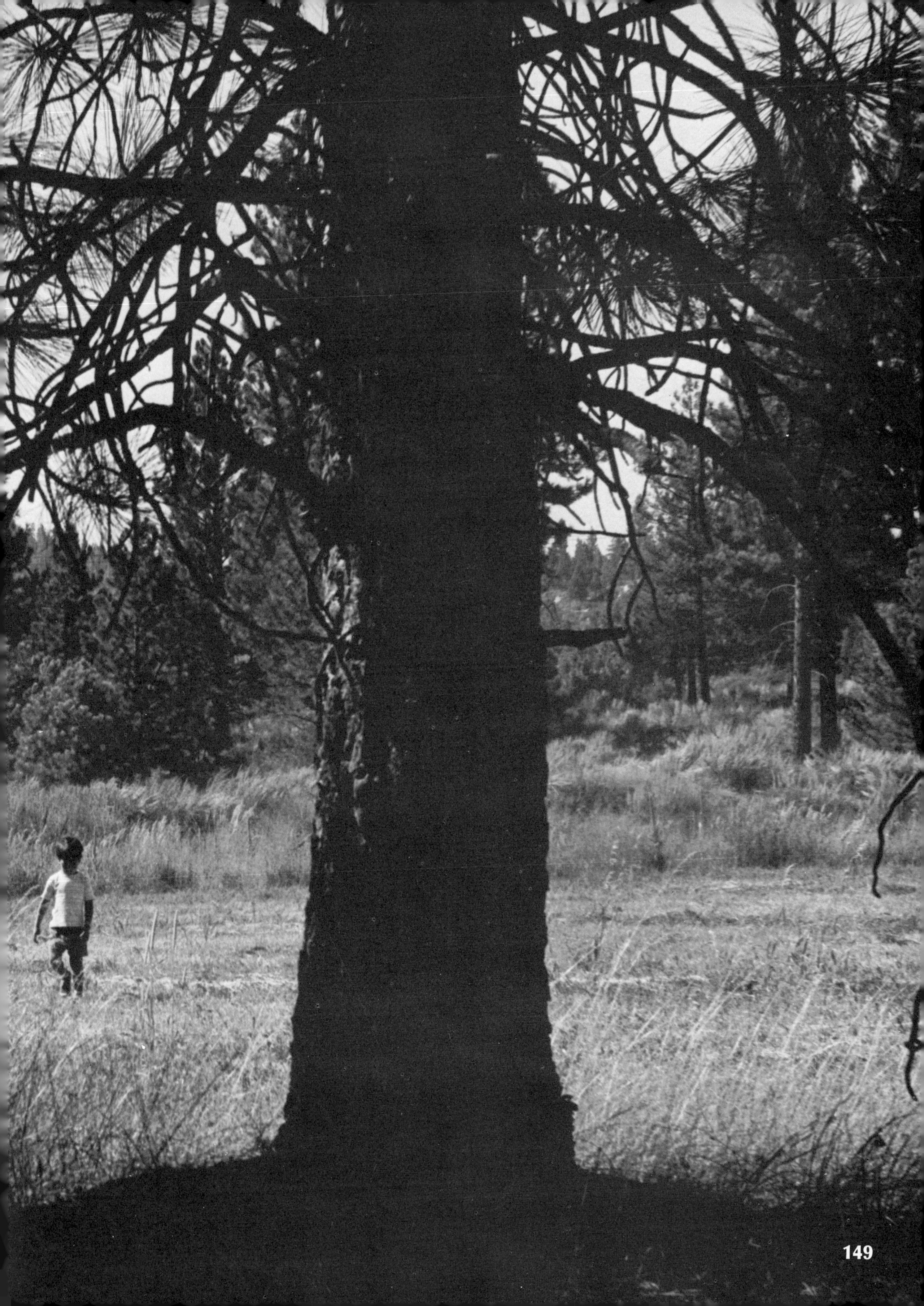

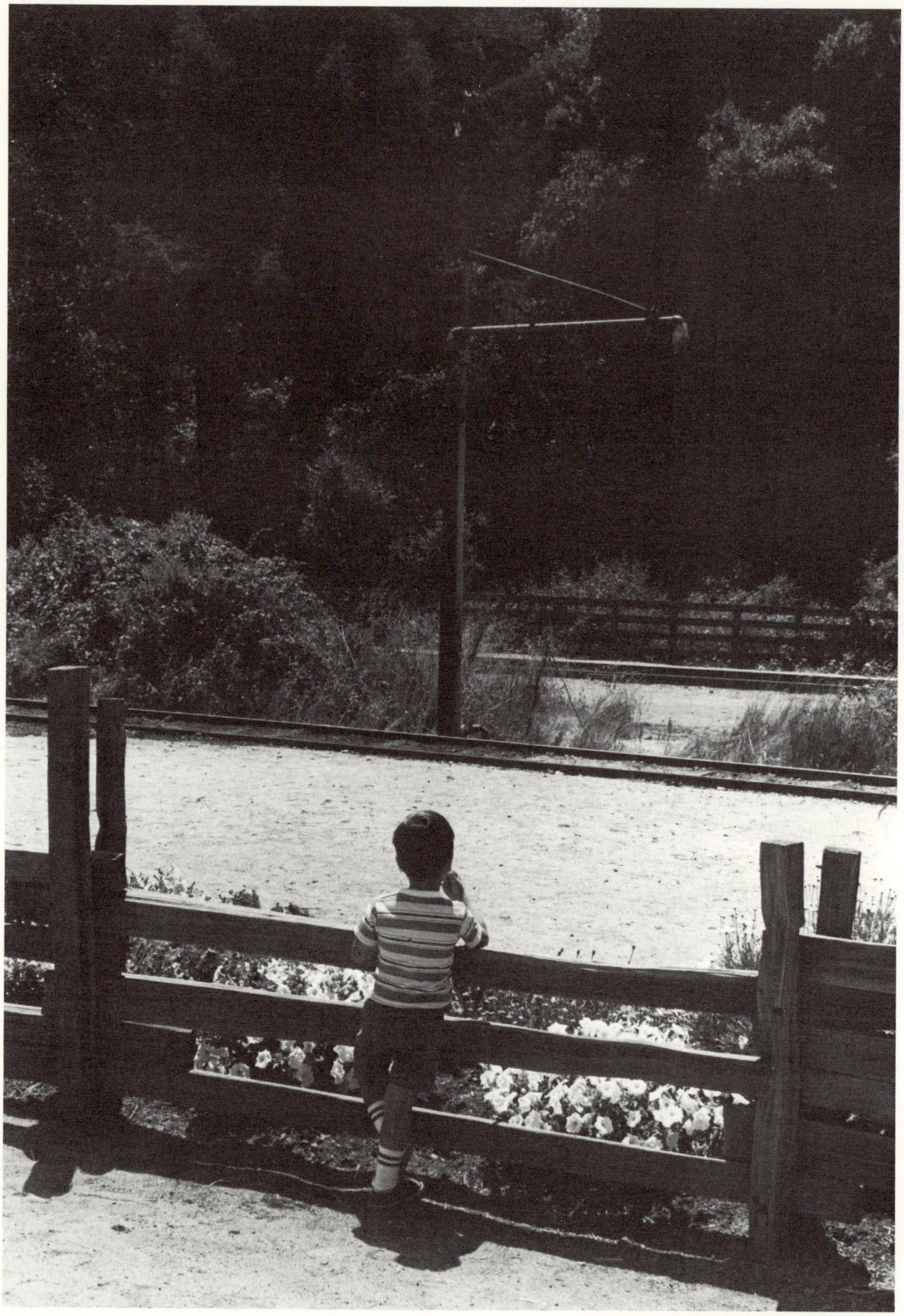

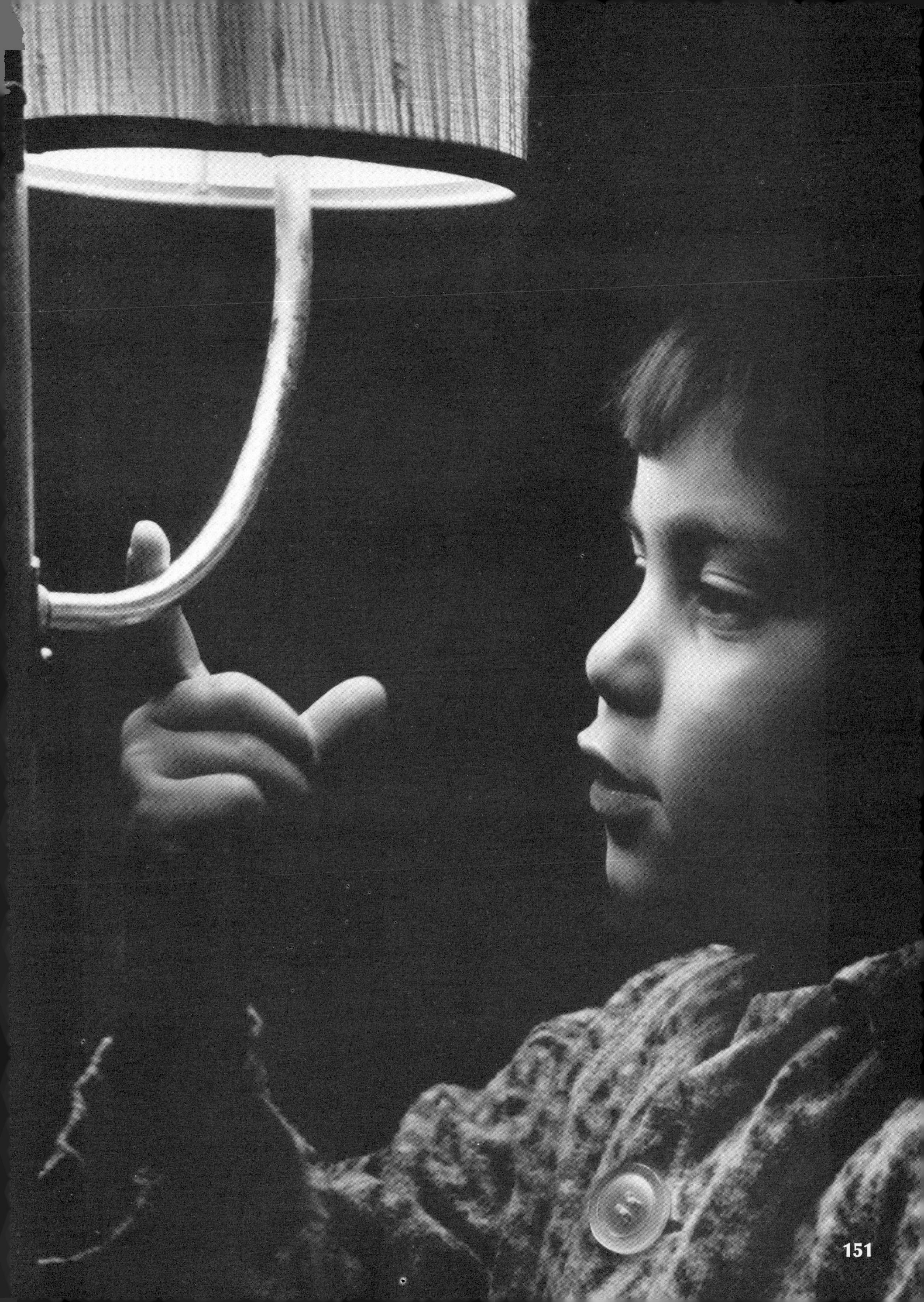

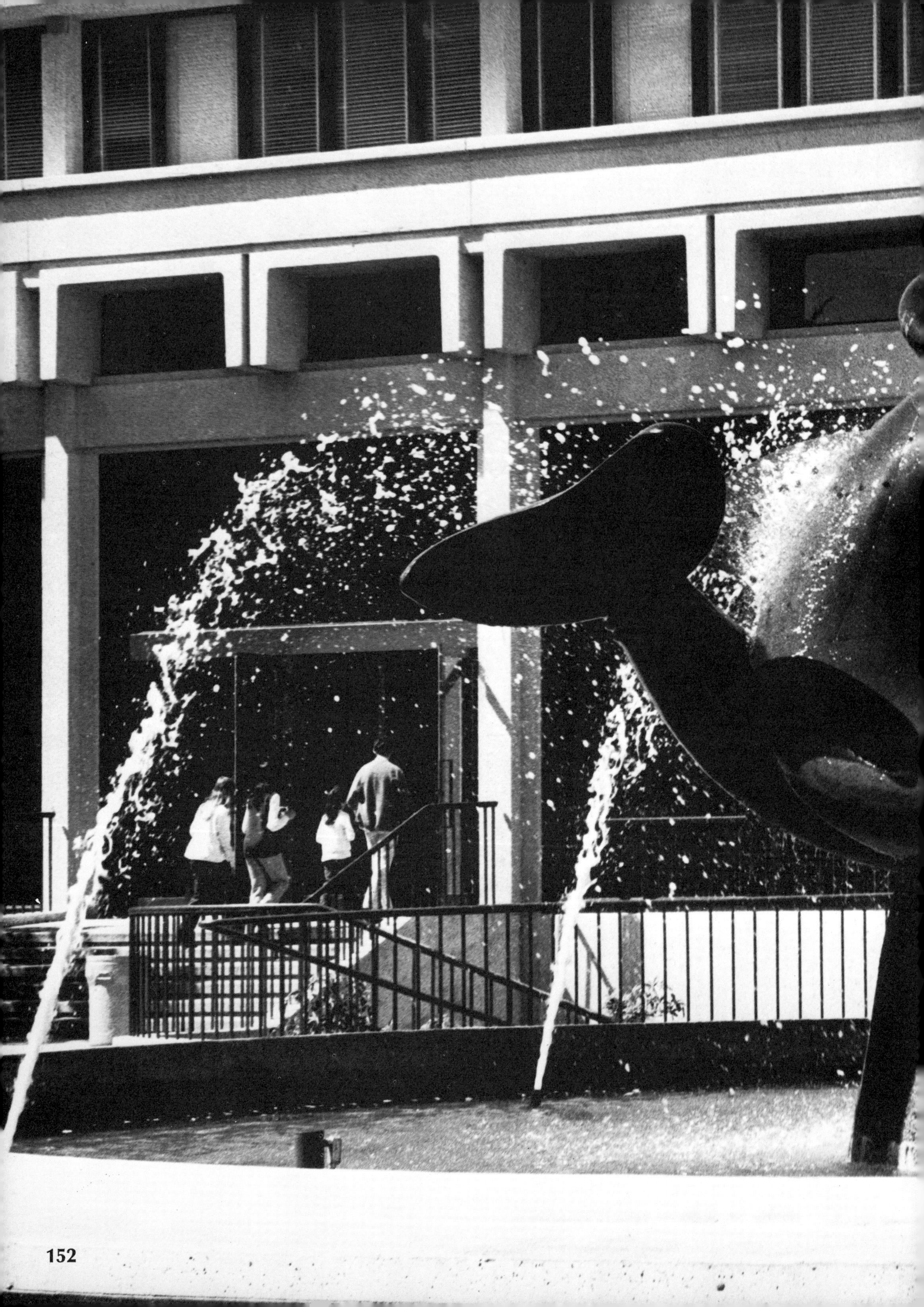

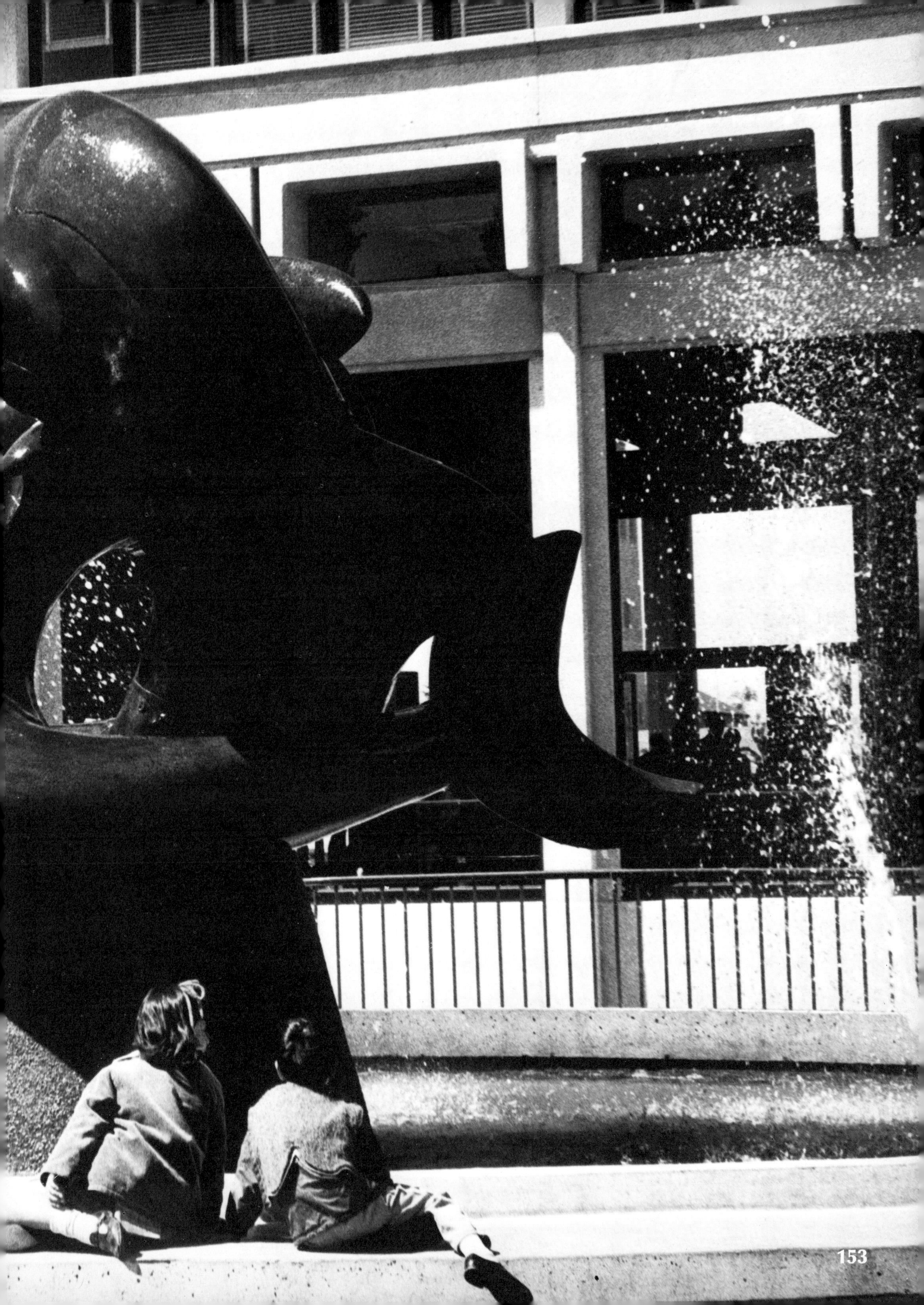

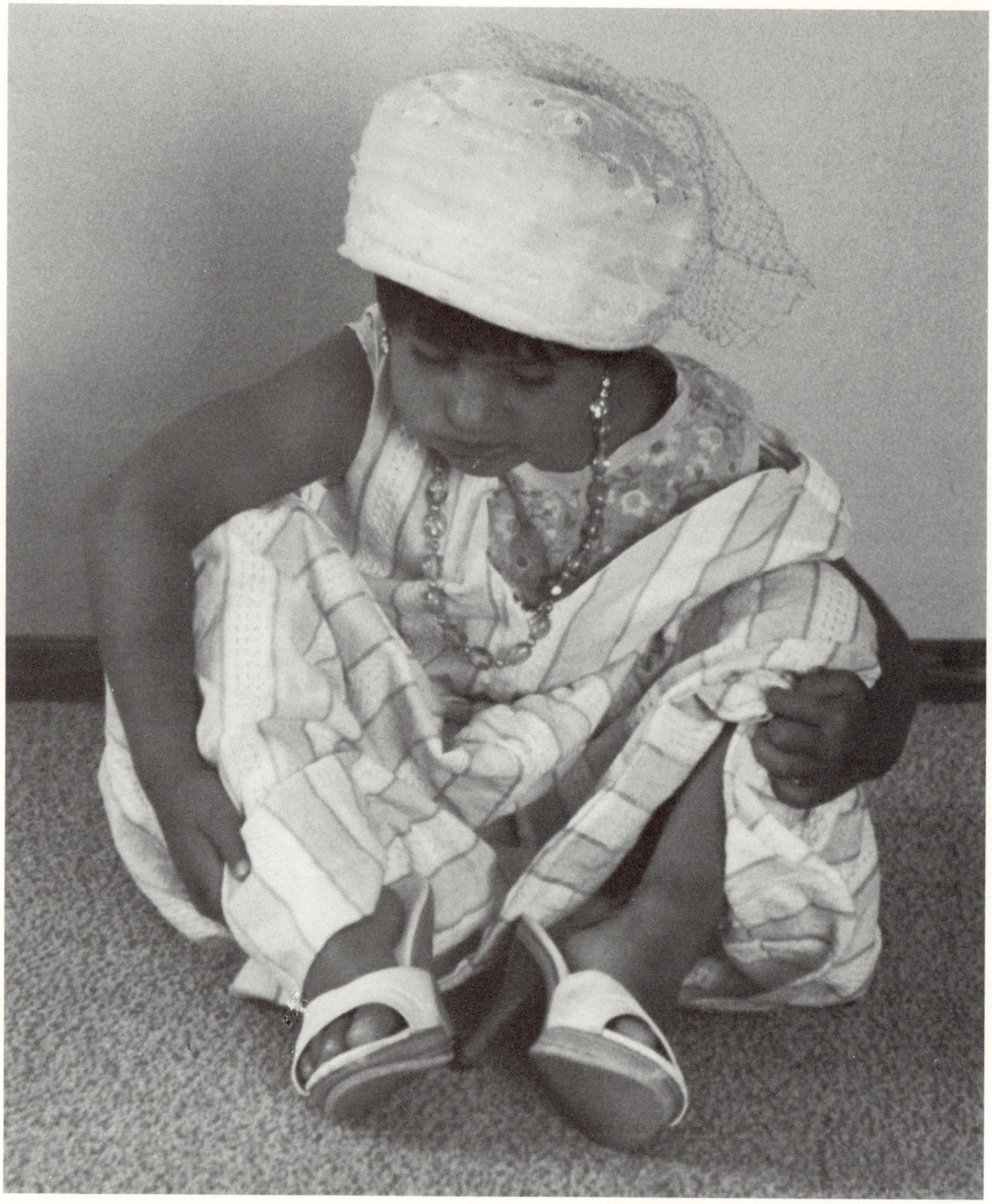

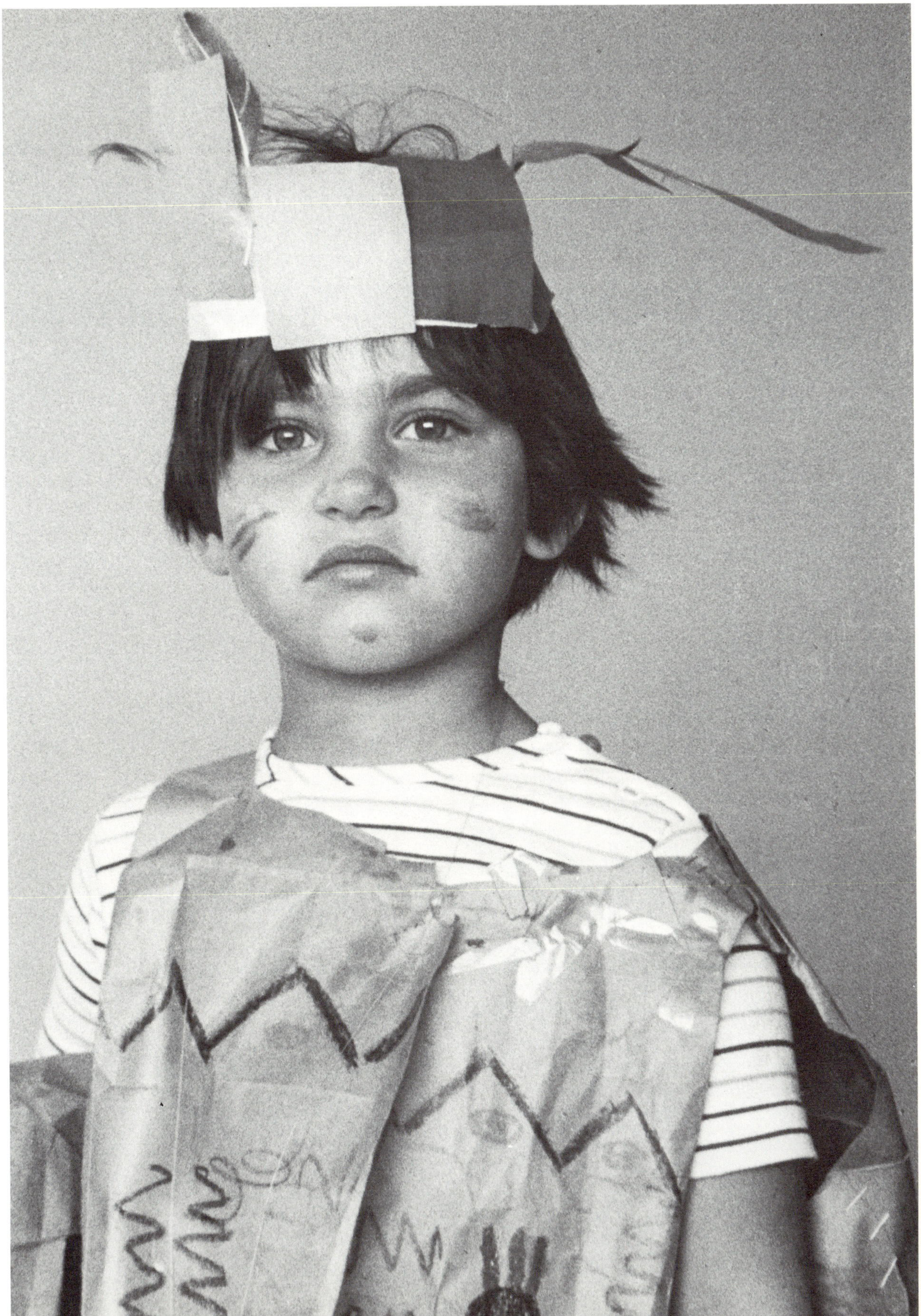

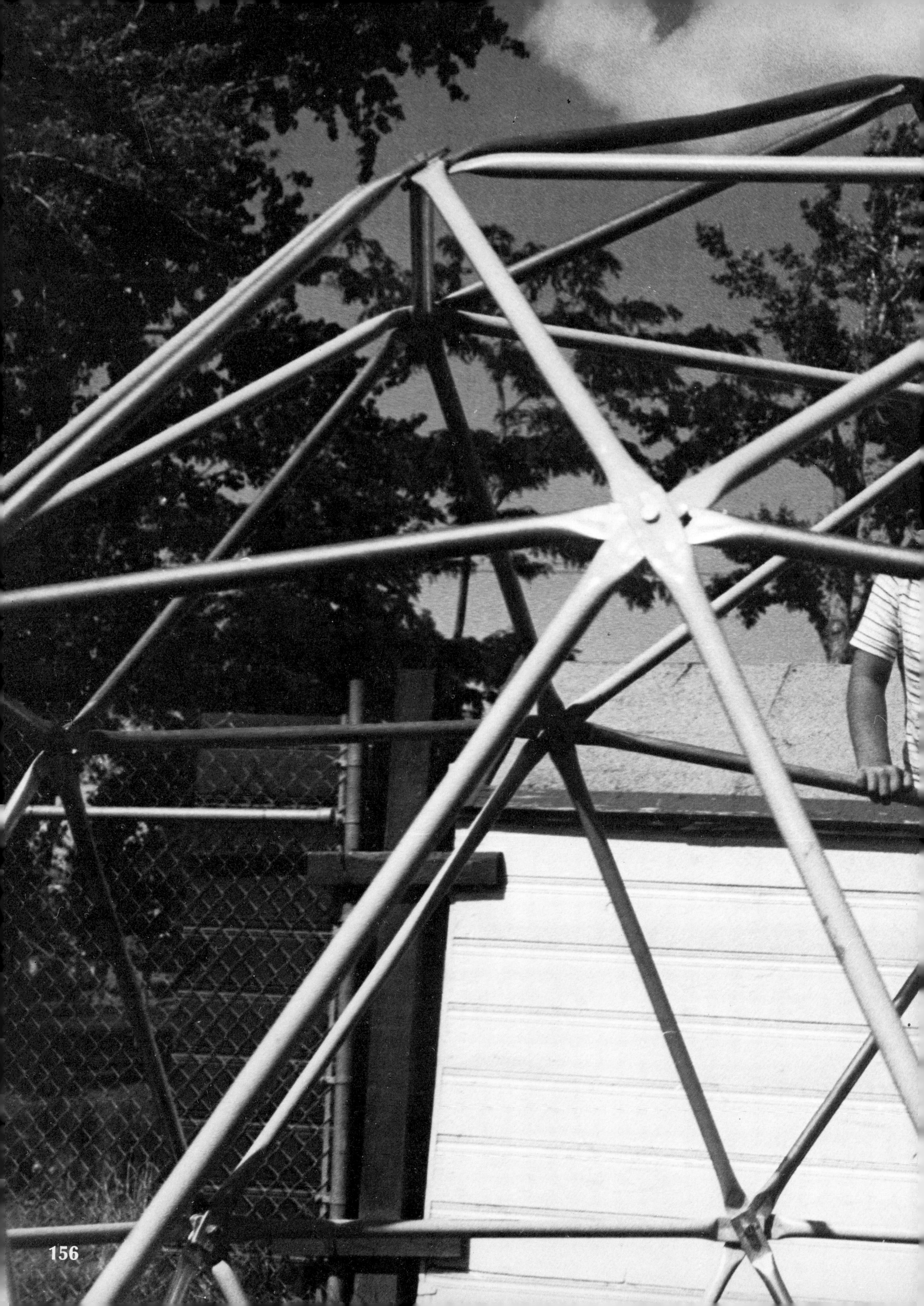

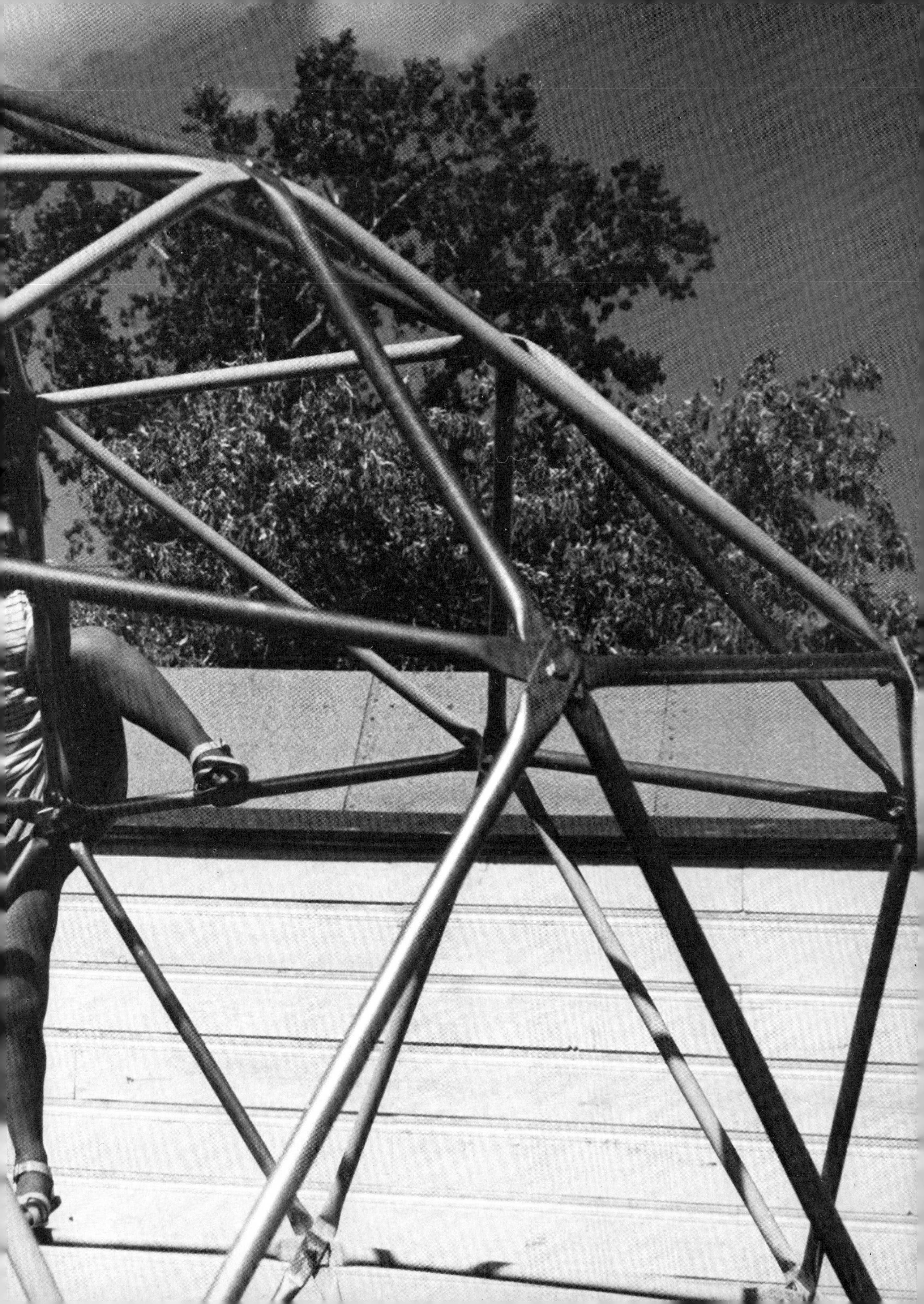

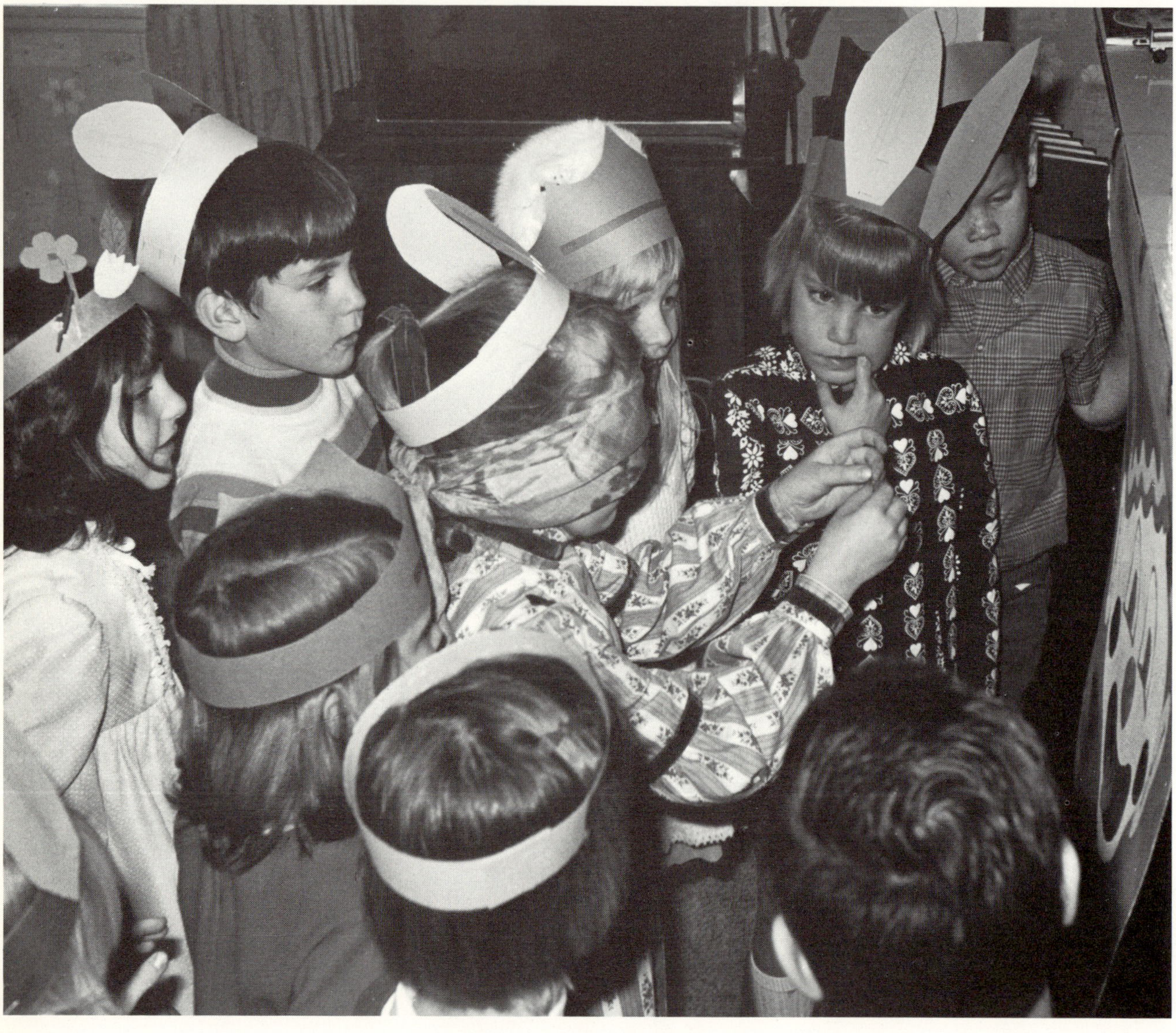

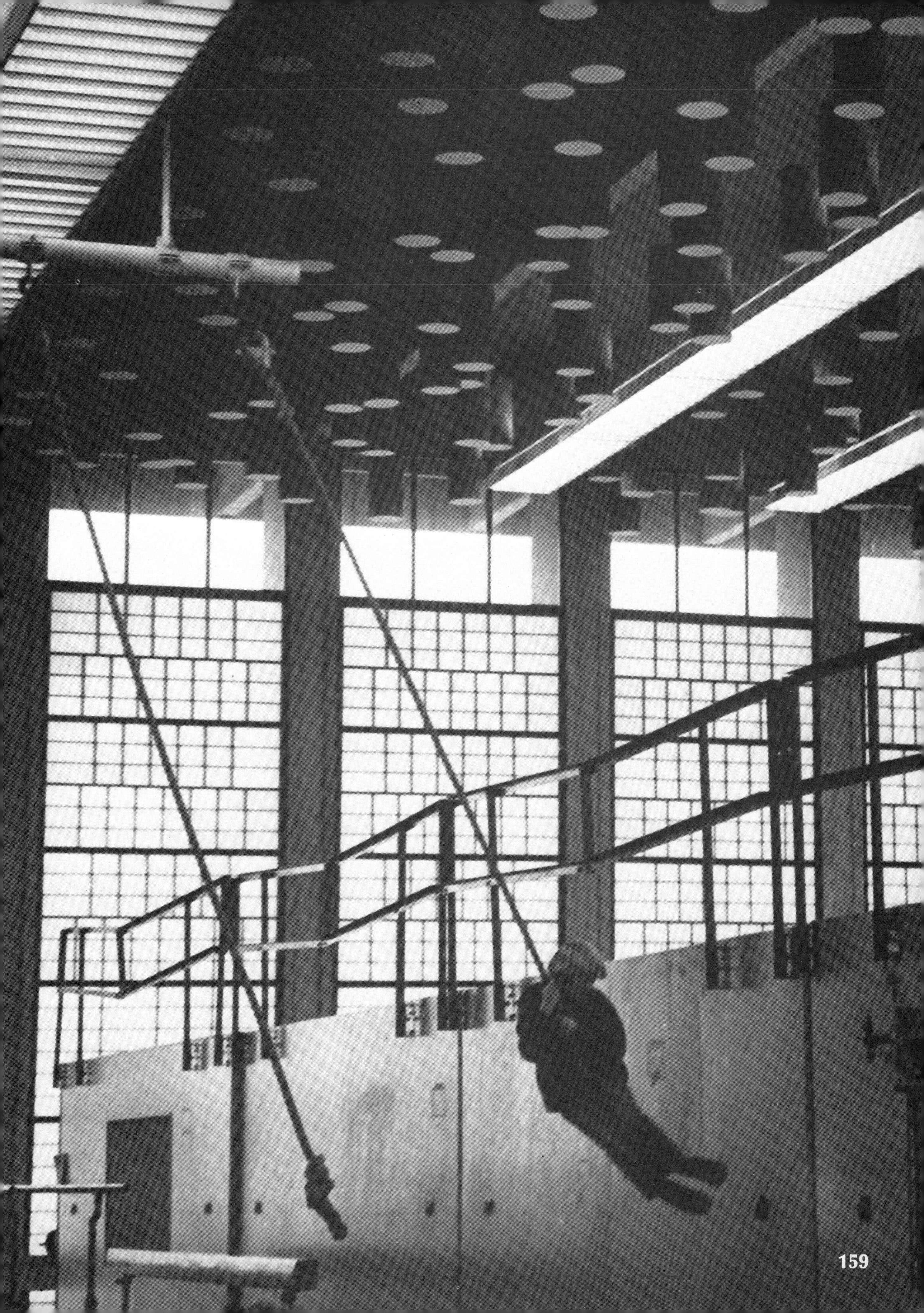

160

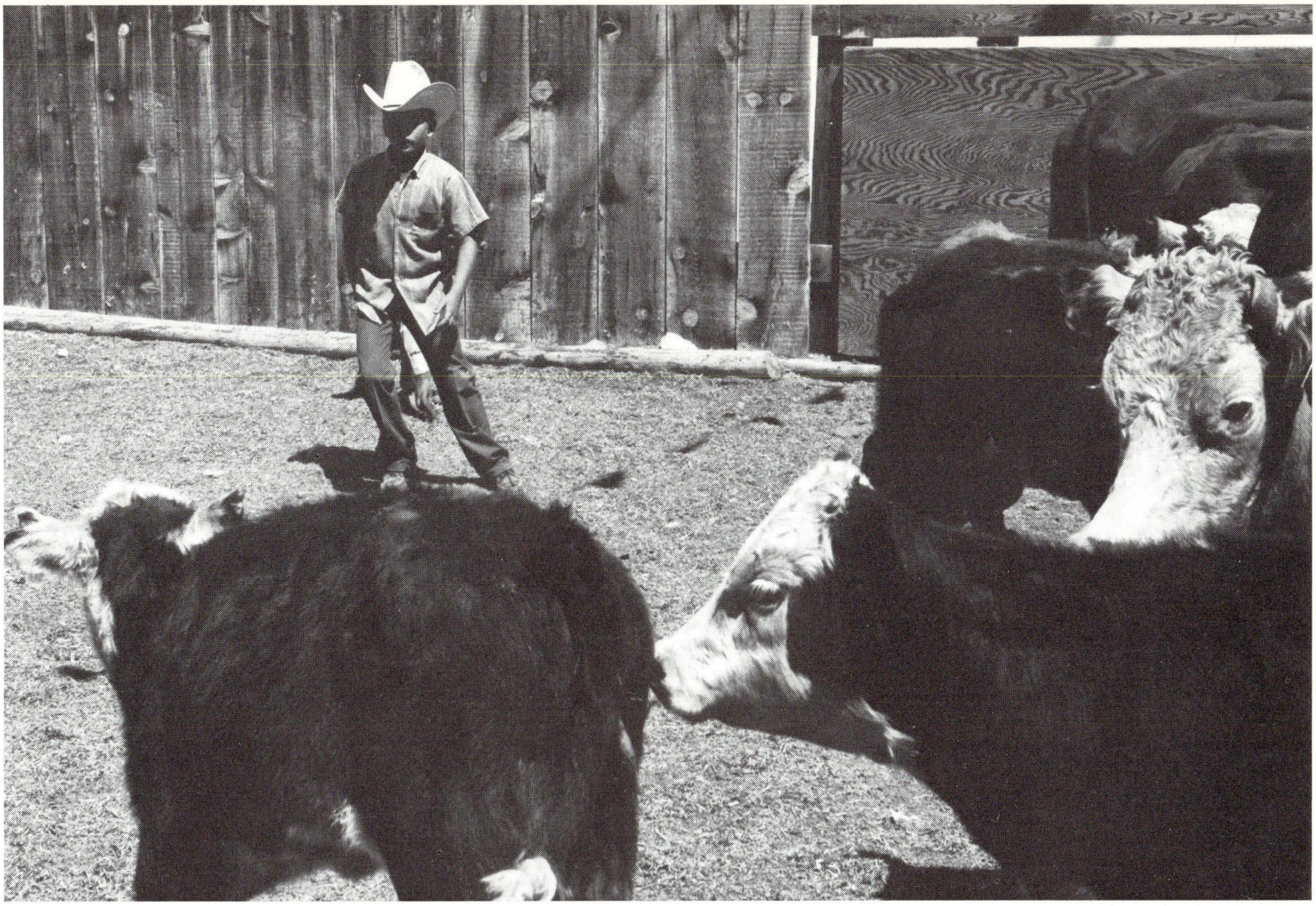

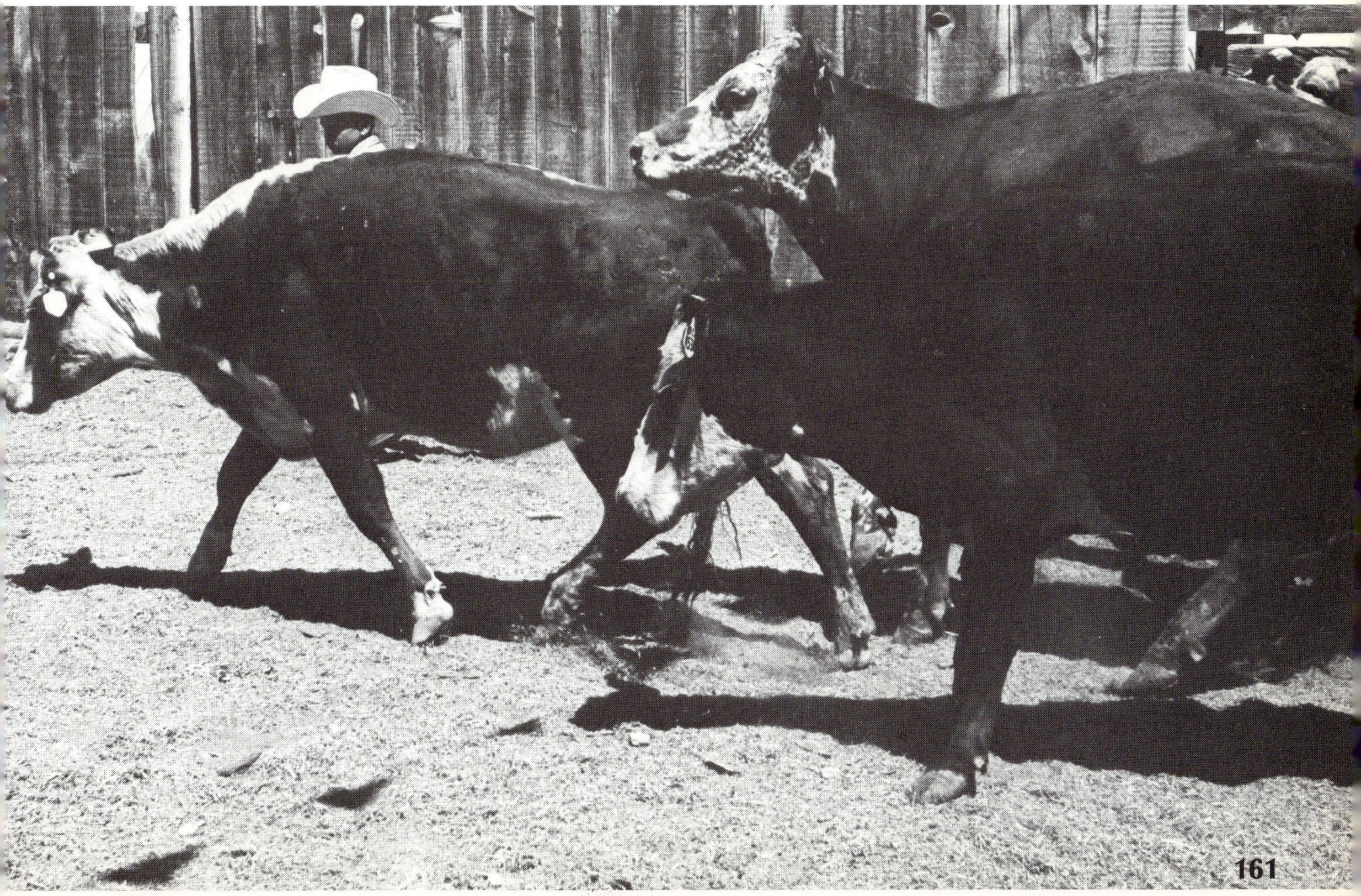

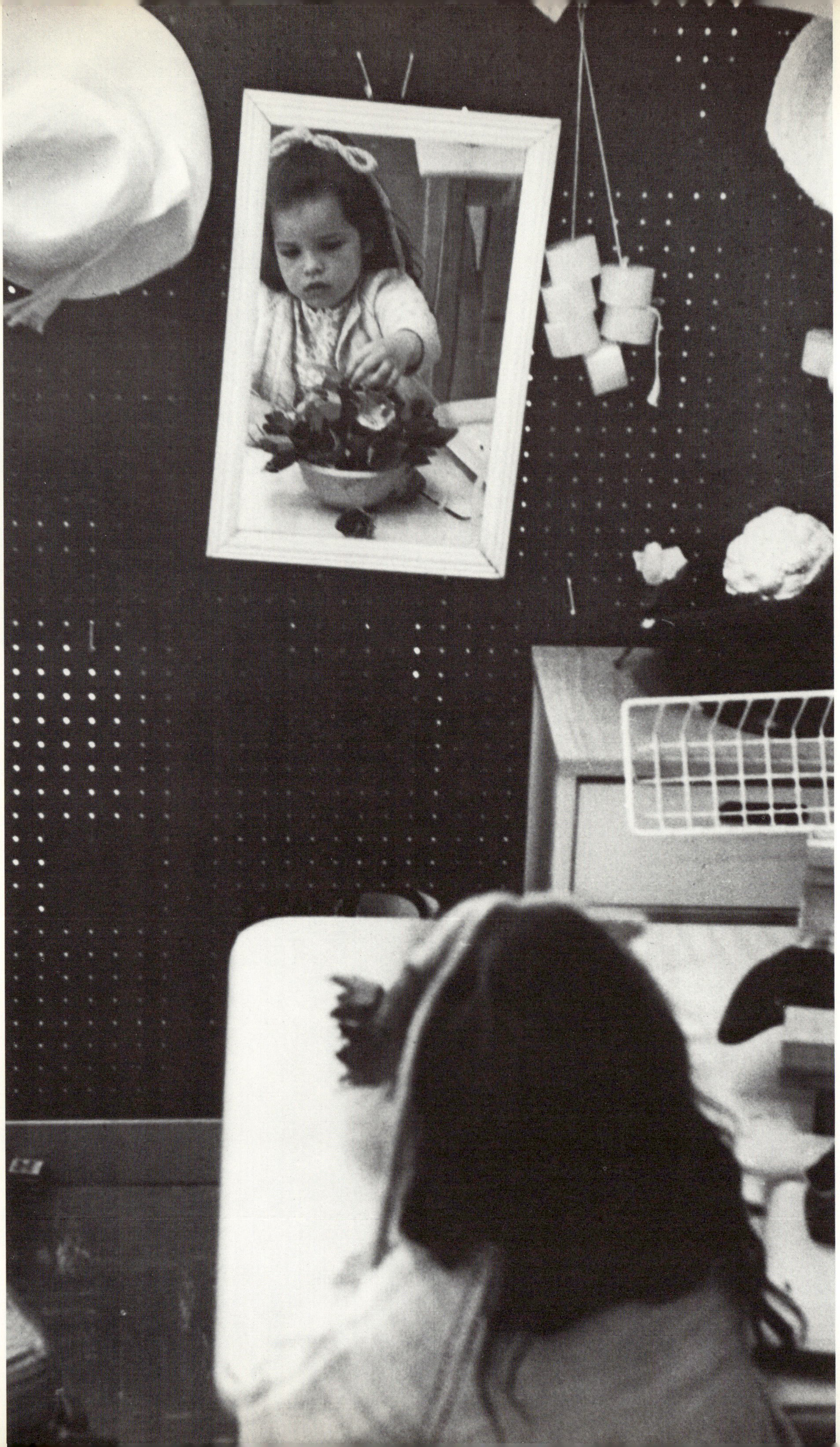

The World of the Child enables the student to confront his surroundings from the viewpoint of the child. It is hoped that the student will be forced to renew his acquaintance with his world and see it from an uninhibited, refreshing viewpoint. The principle underlying the child's way of looking at the world is that the child does not see his surroundings through a veil of abstractions. His experience of the world is immediate, concrete. He is aided by his size, which permits him to get closer to things that are below most people's eye level. He sees details adolescents and adults miss. The child also possesses a sense of wonder that fills him with delight each time he encounters new surroundings. He spends hours fascinated by little things that would bore those older than he, not because such things are insignificant, but because many do not take the time to look.

The photographs in this section can be considered individually or in groups. In groups, they can be used as contrasts, or as contributing different details to support the same viewpoint or theme.

Page 133: This picture can be considered a theme photograph for this chapter and discussed as such. The "girl in the automat" reflects many of the things stated above regarding the world of the child.

Pages 134–135: The child sometimes responds to the world with fear. The picture of the mother and child, together with the contrasting one on the right, is meant to make you wonder why and discuss the reasons.

Pages 136–149: These pictures can be considered individually or together from many viewpoints centering on a dominant theme: the size of the world as it appears to the child. Does size increase the child's sense of wonder and fascination, or does it overwhelm him? Does his nearness to nature awe him, or make him more aware of the significance of nature?

Pages 150–159: These photographs can also be discussed individually or as a group. This time, however, the emphasis is on the child's sense of wonder and on his sense of play. In addition, these pictures portray how the child uses his imagination. In writing about them, the student must use his own imagination in order to see the world the way a child does.

Pages 160–161: This series portrays an adventure that is real as well as imagined. What heightens the adventure is size; look at and examine in detail the adventure from the viewpoint of the size of the boy with the cowboy hat. The role the boy believes he is playing comes from his imagination, which in turn depends on television shows and movies he has seen. In your discussion, take the boy's imagination into account.

Page 162: Do you think a child sees more beauty in a bowl of flowers than an adult? Discuss.

ENVIRONMENT

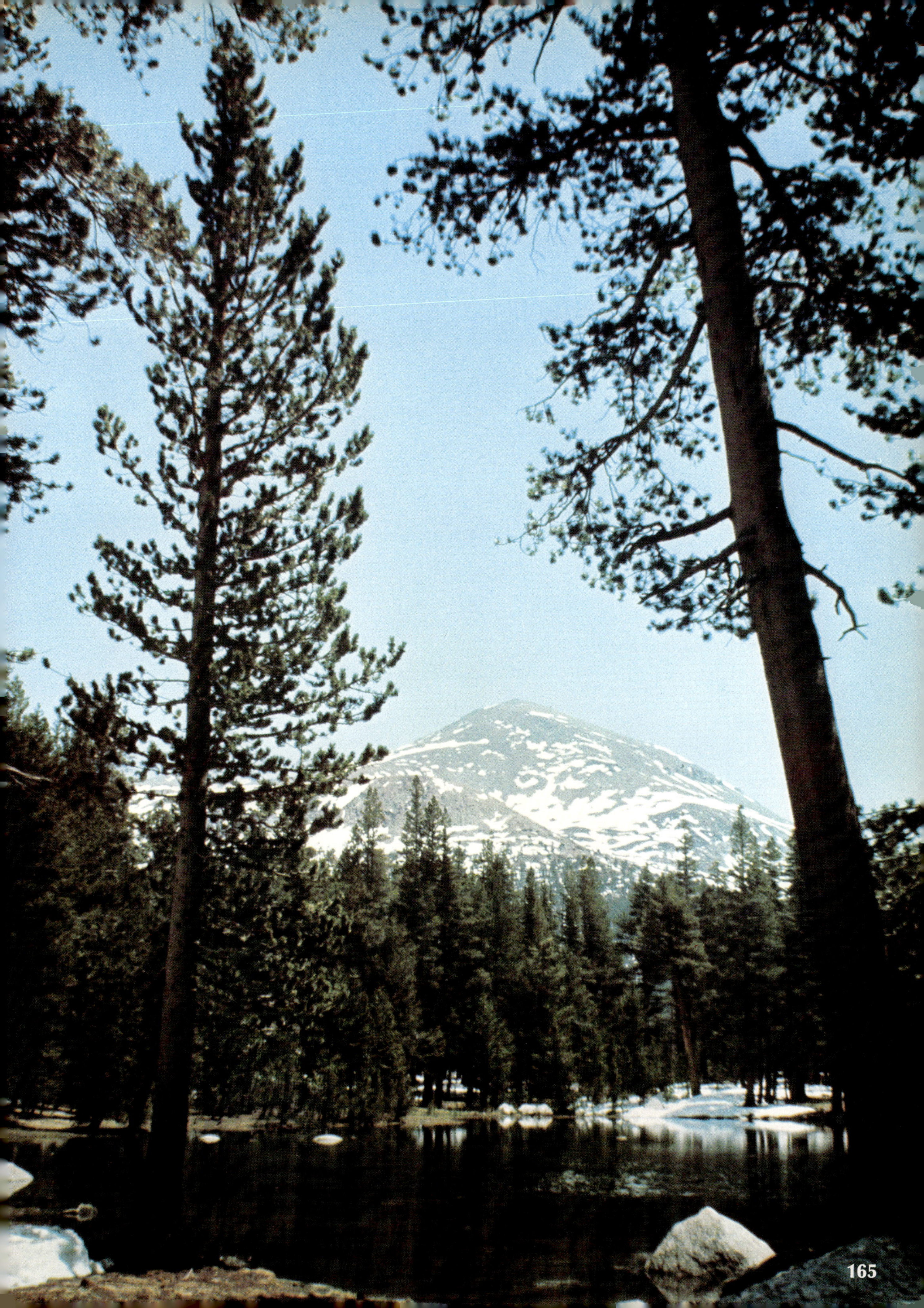

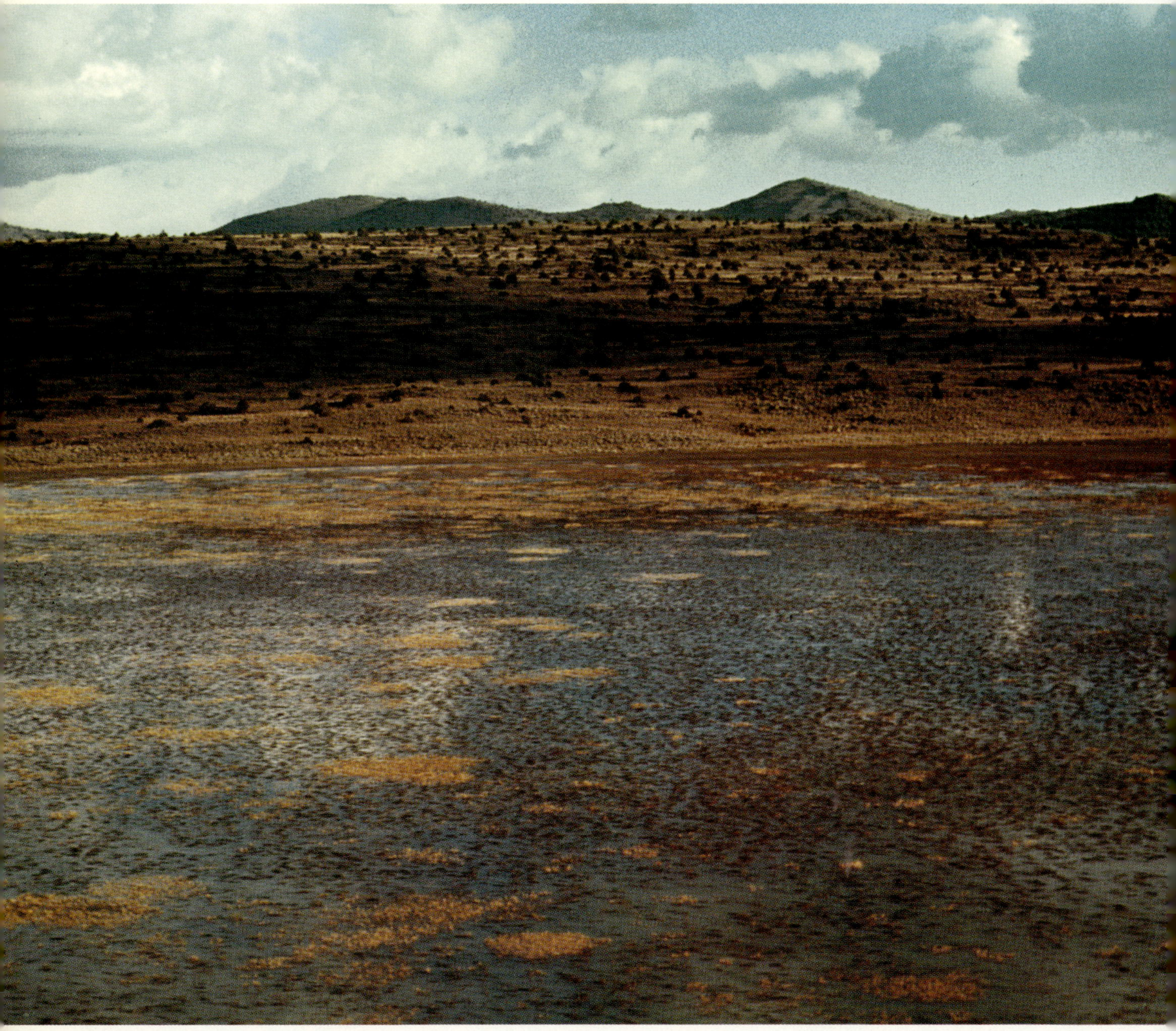

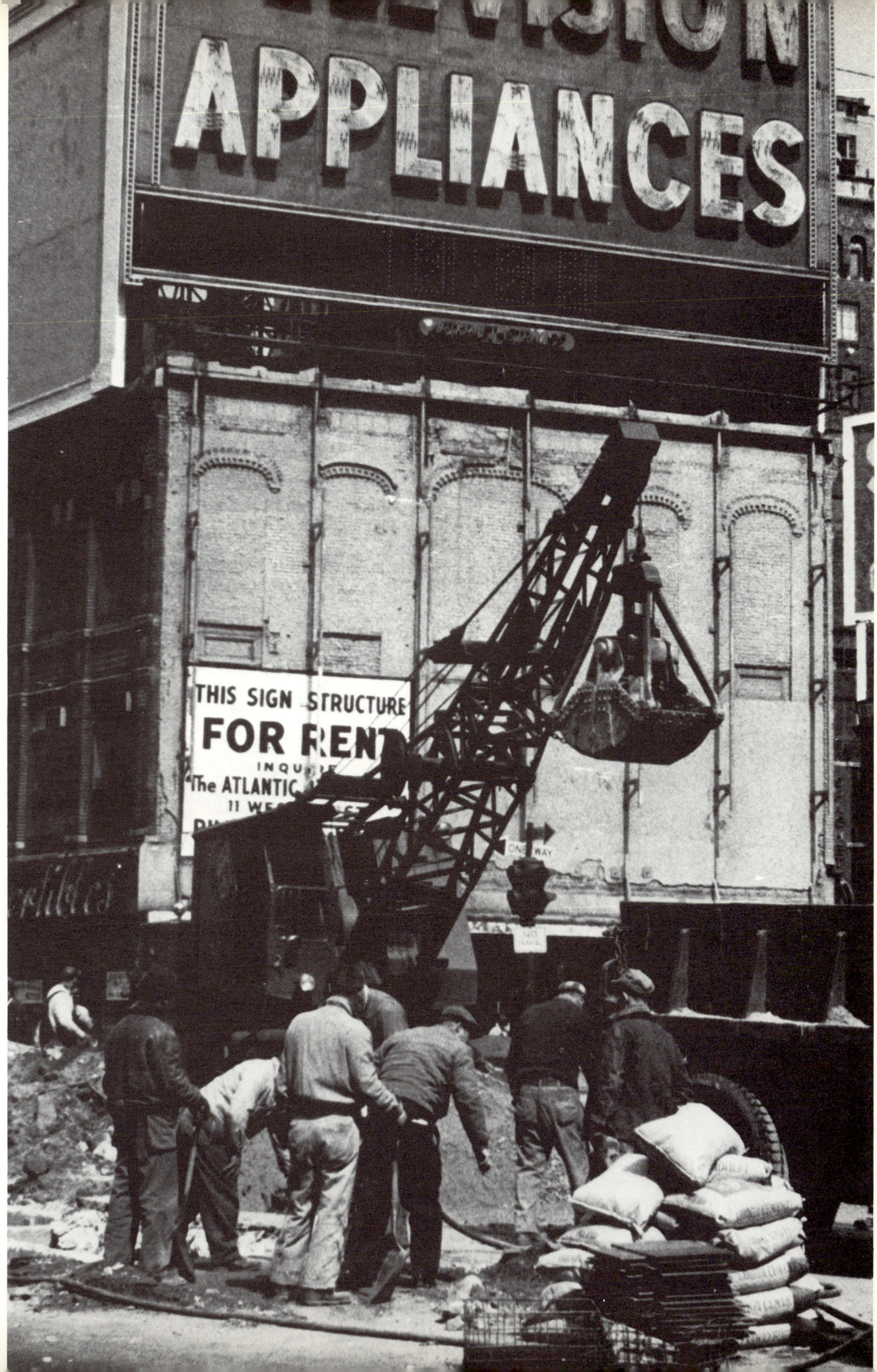
APPLIANCES
THIS SIGN STRUCTURE
ONE WAY

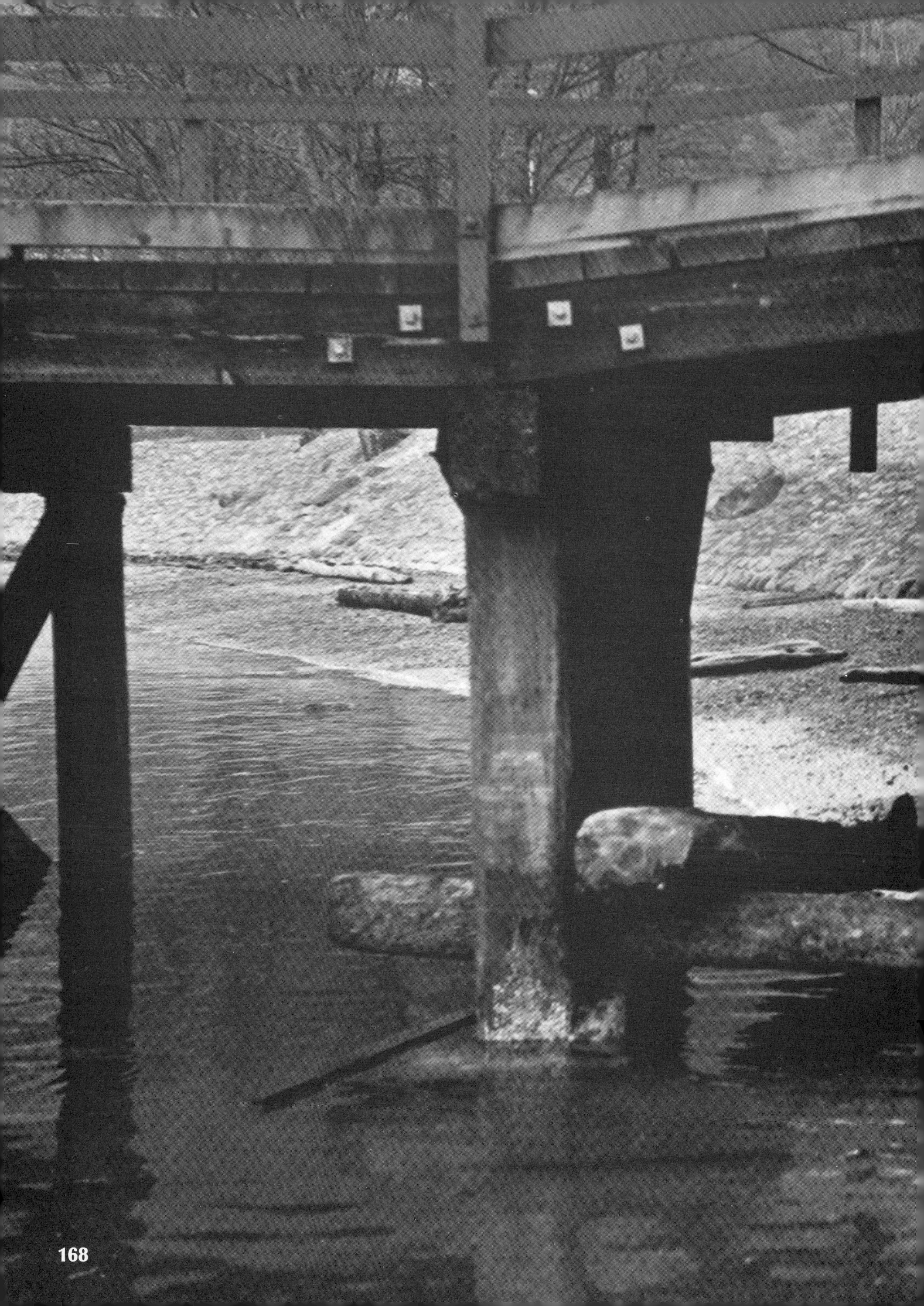

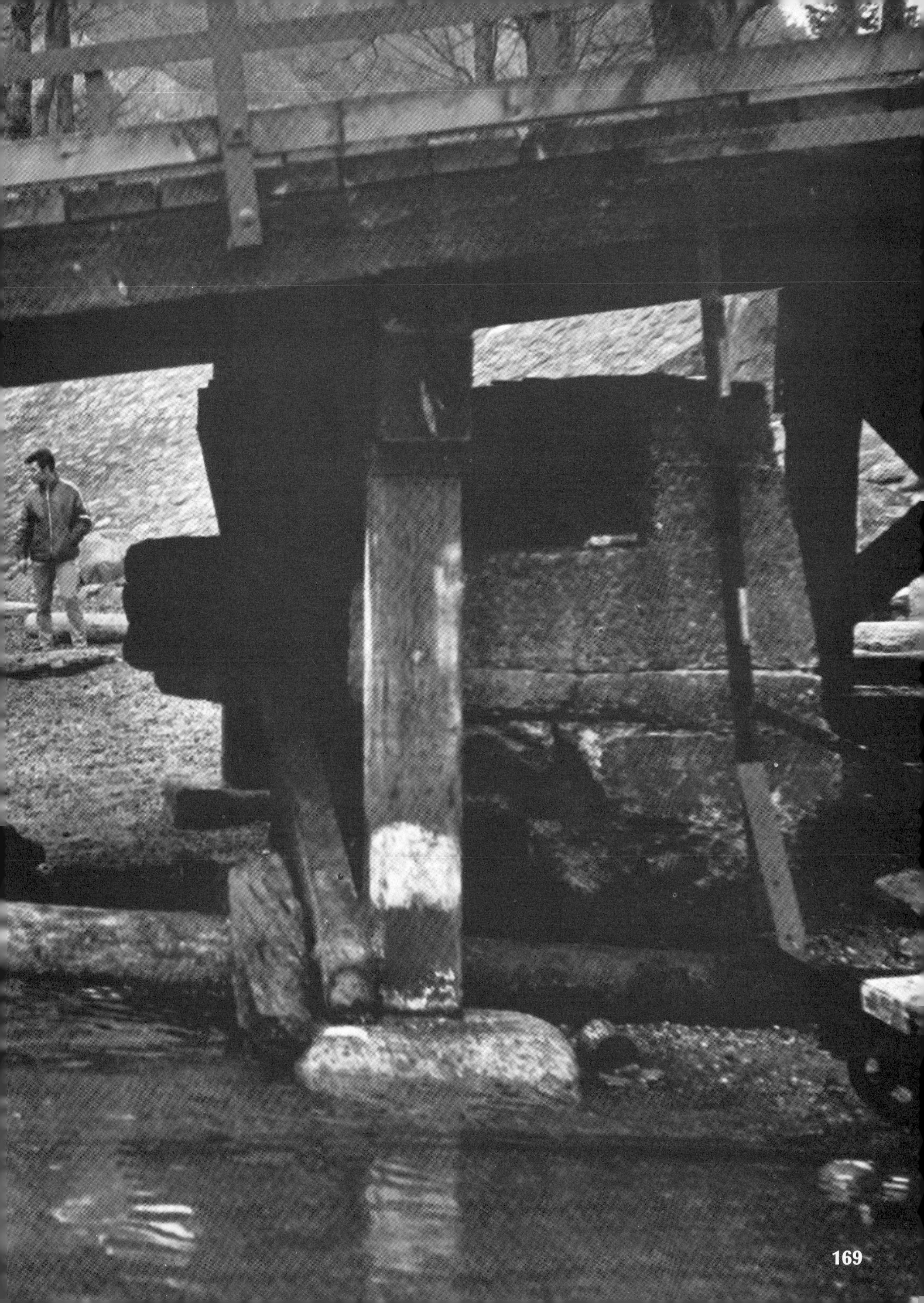

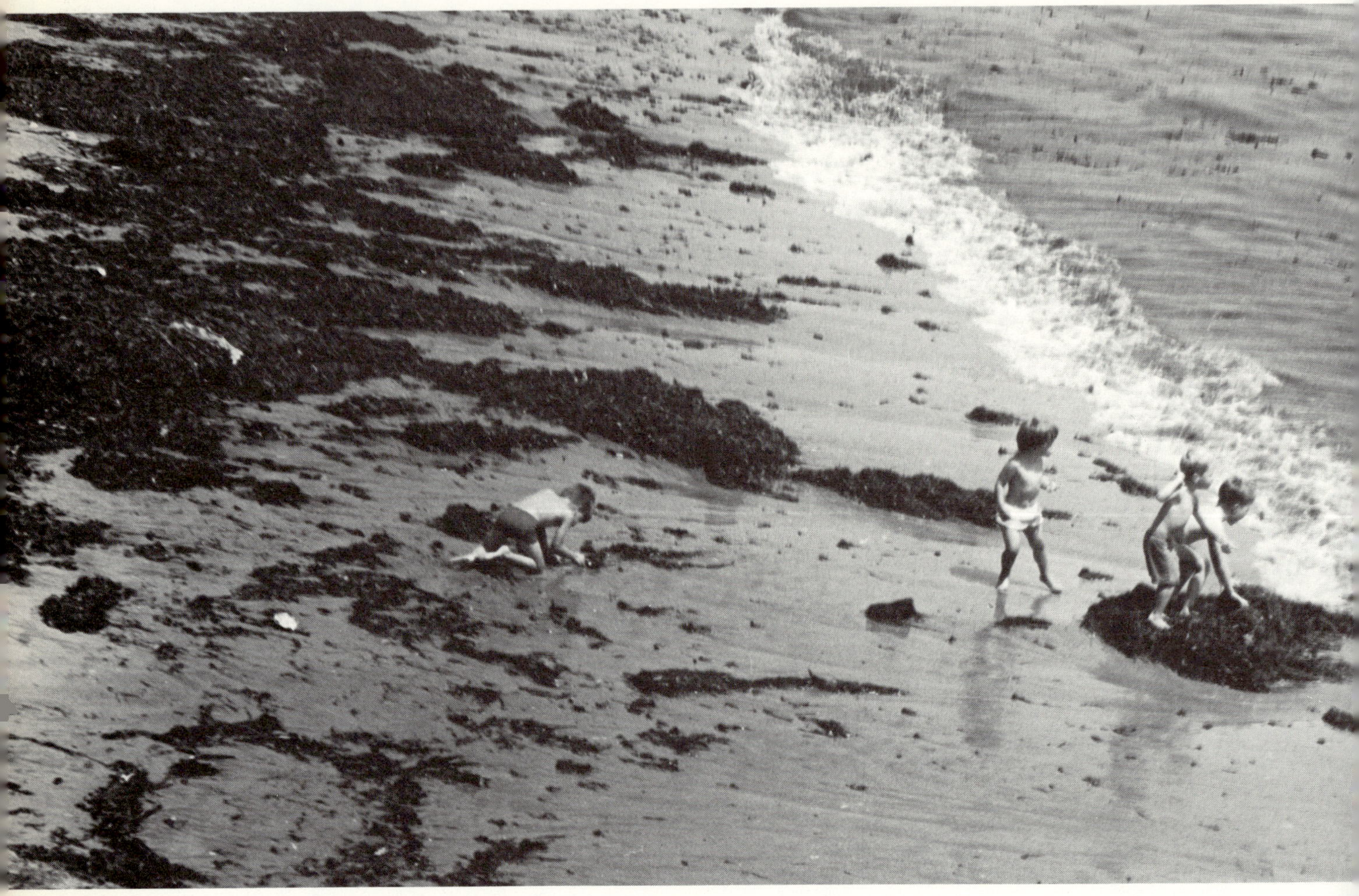

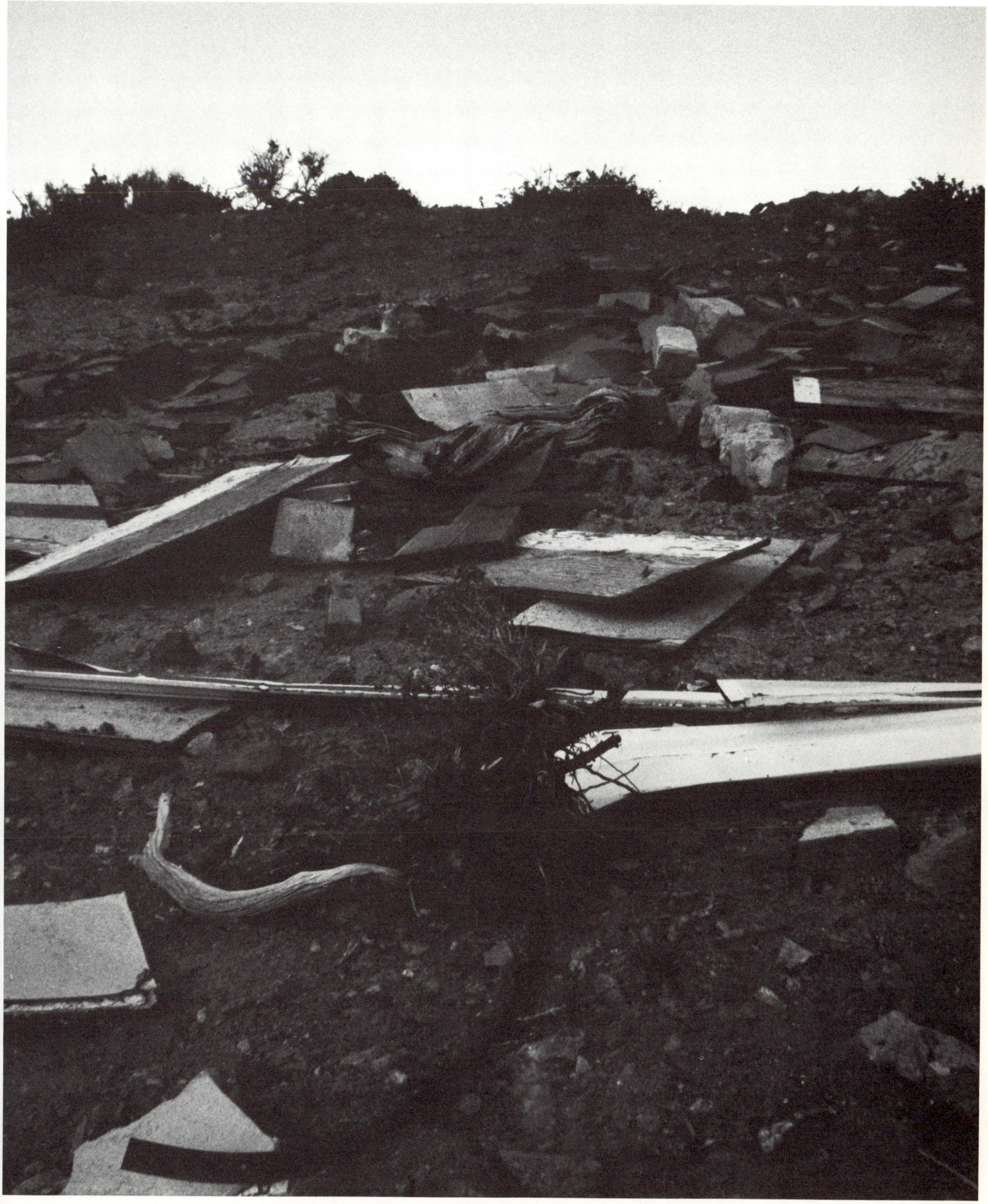

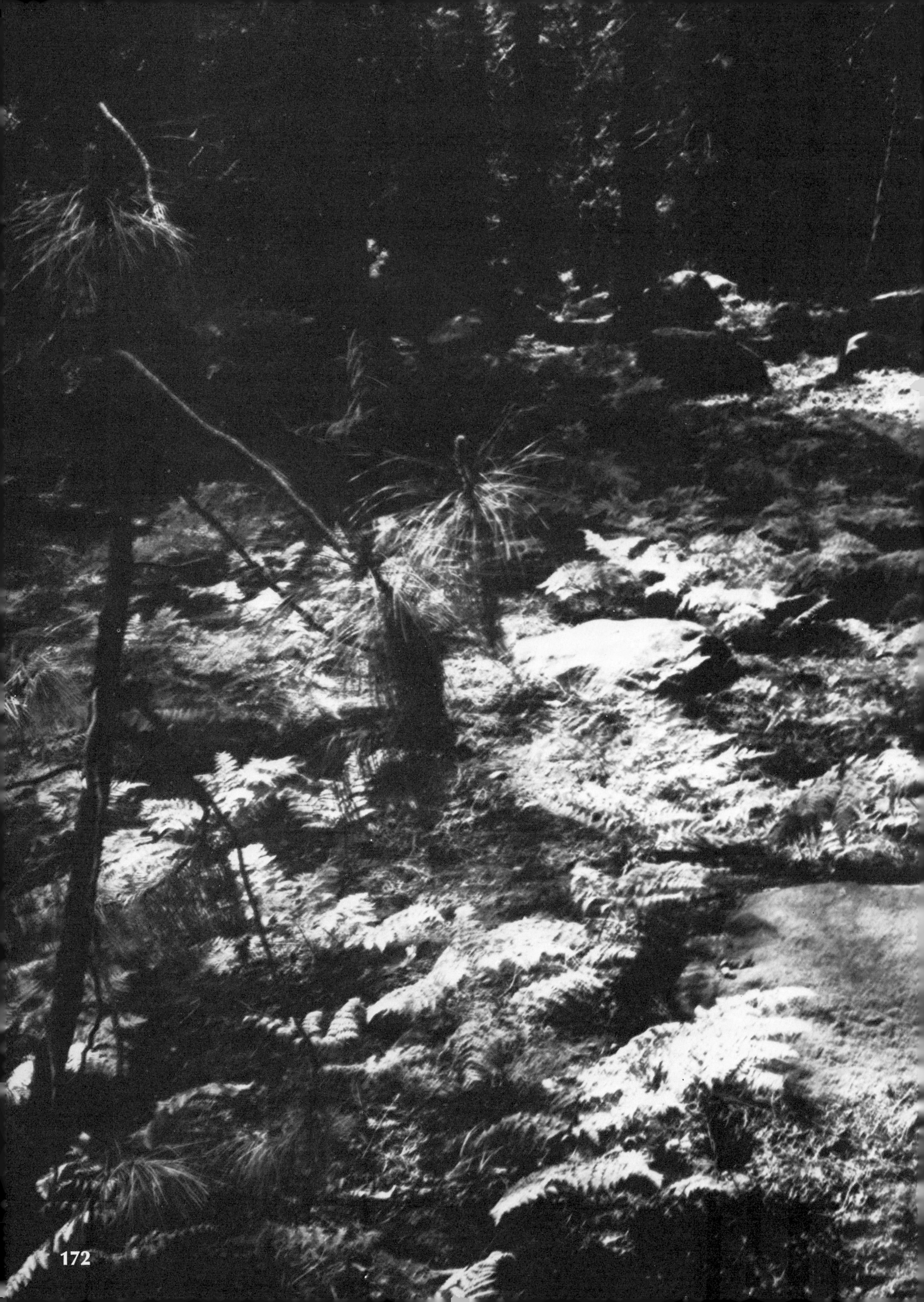

173

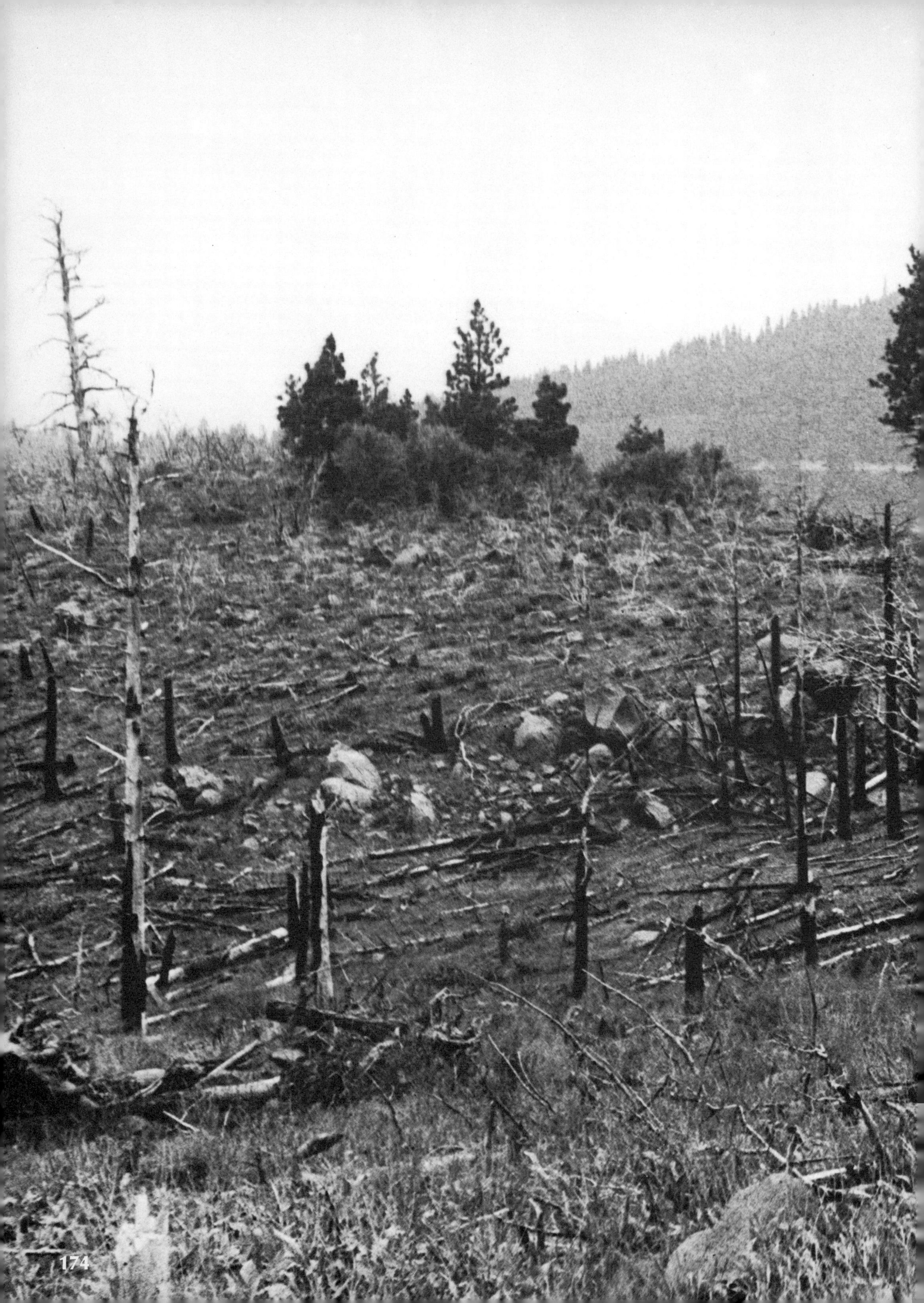

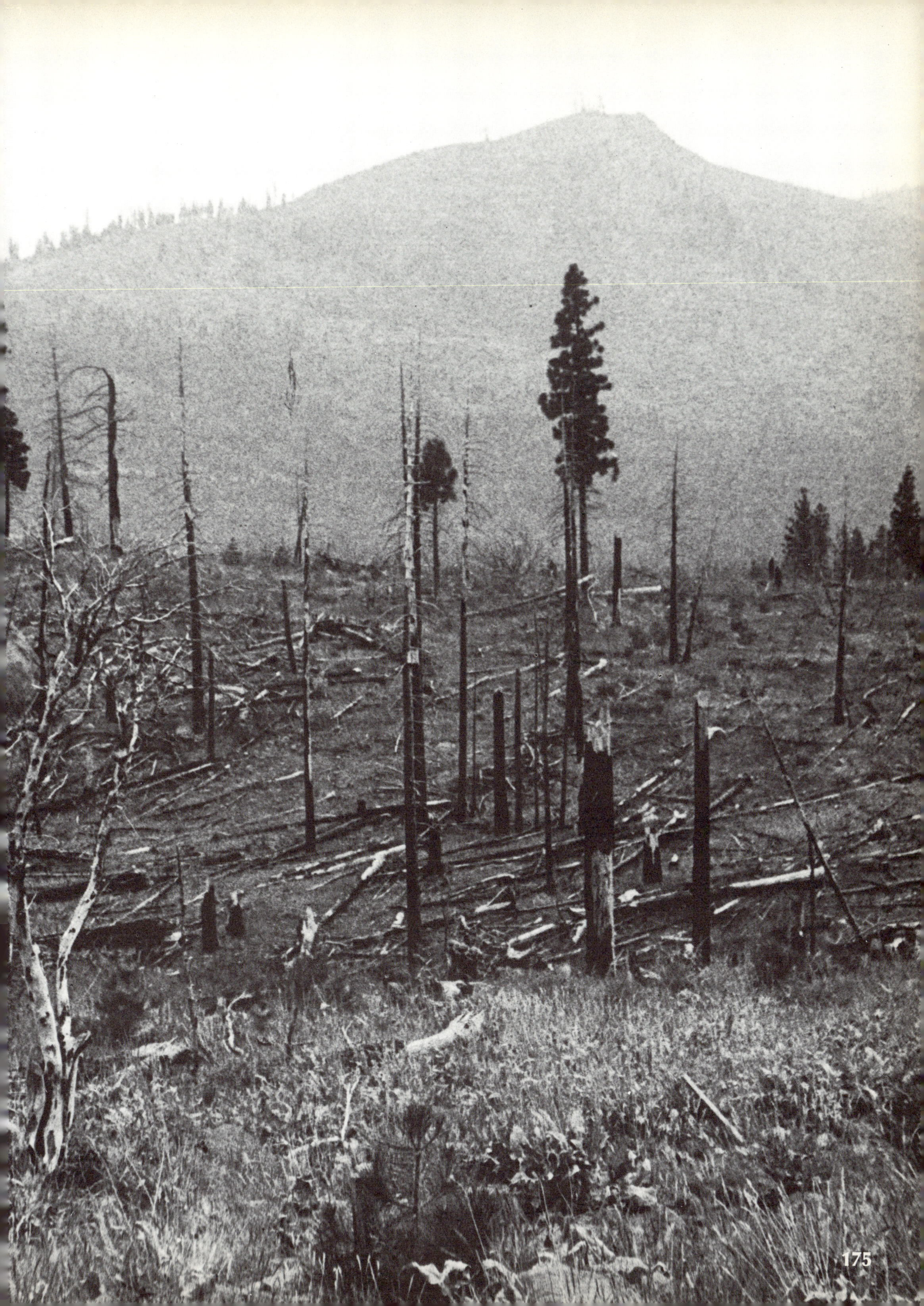

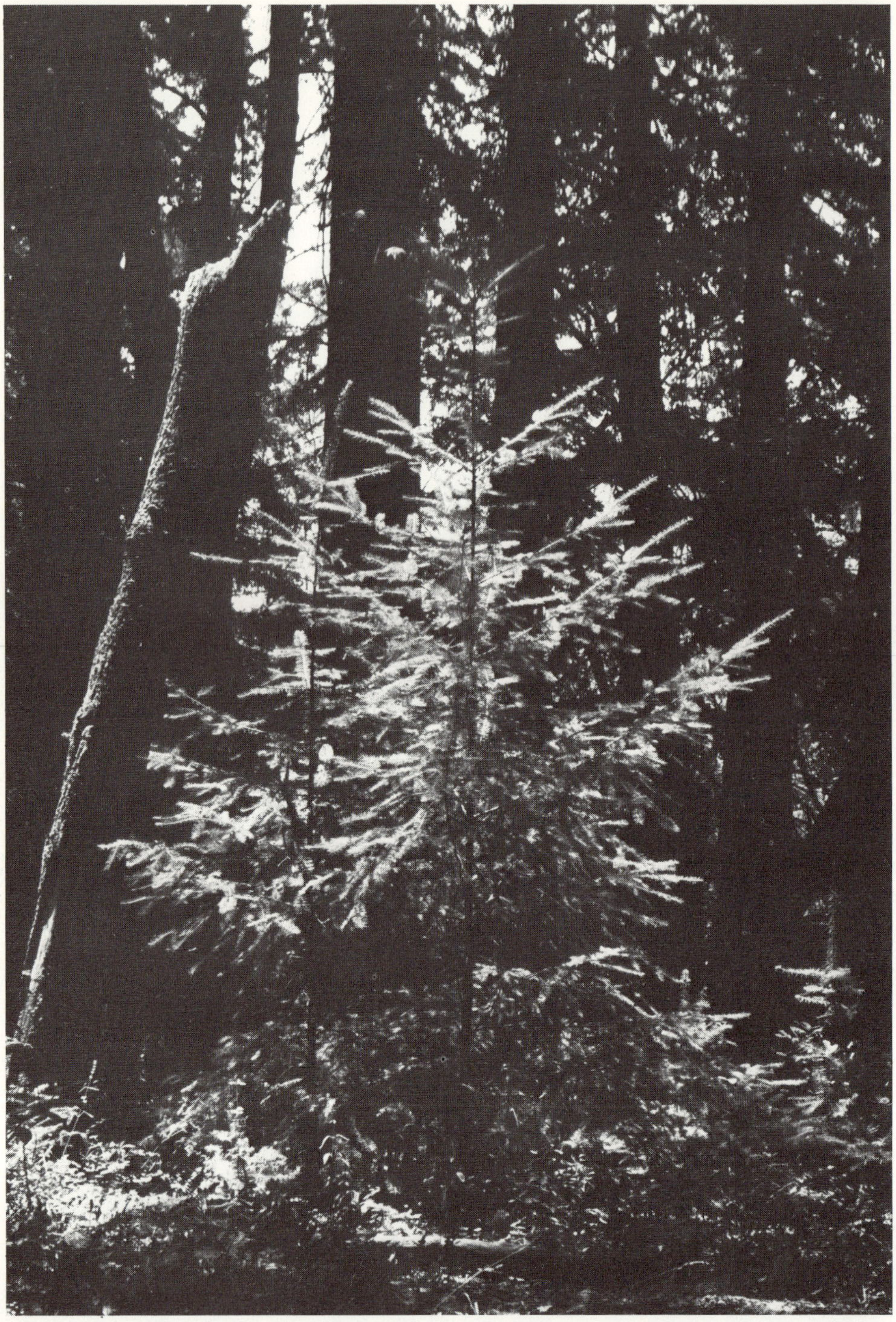

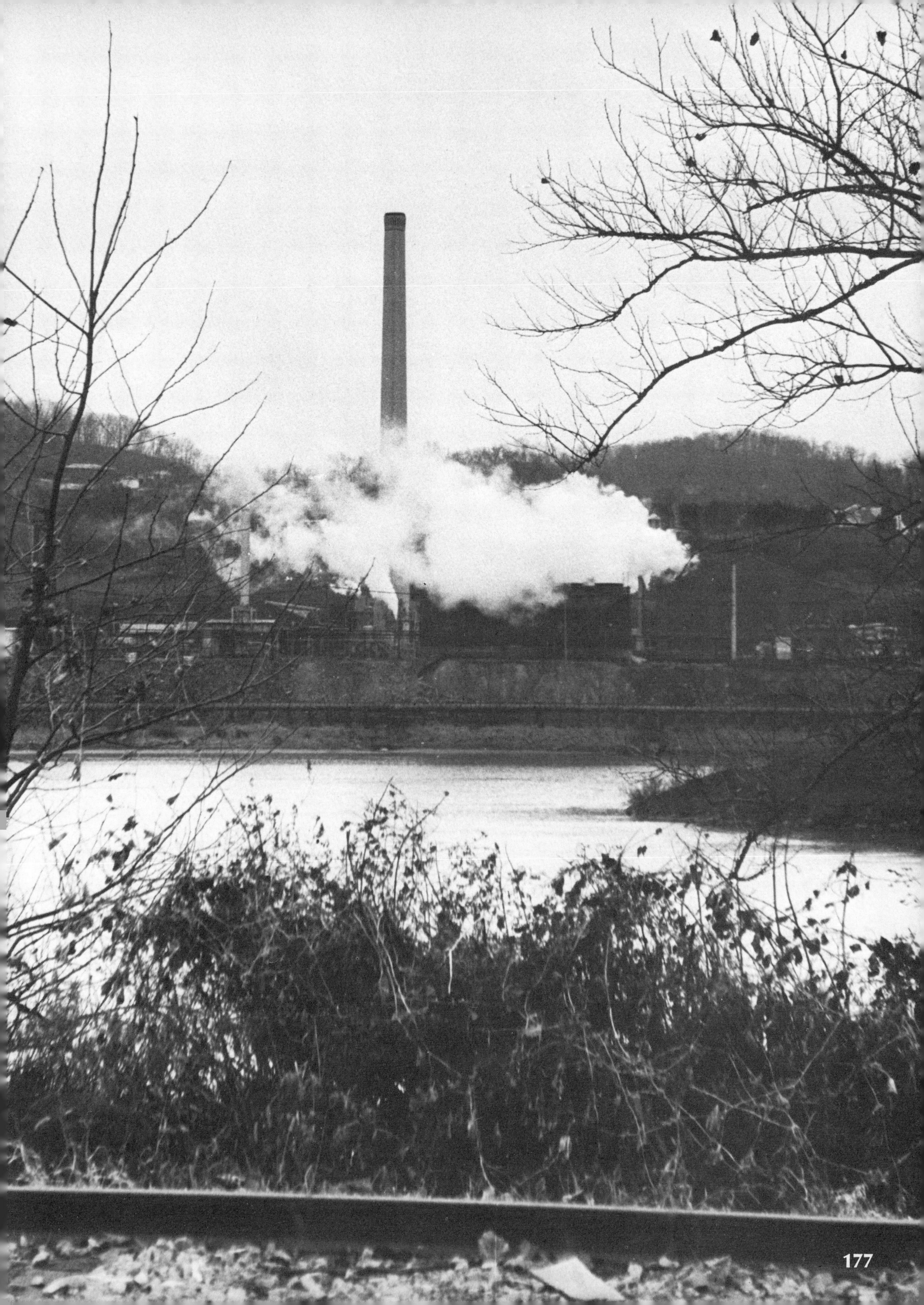

CHEVROLET
GARAGE GARAGE
FOREIGN-AMERICAN
TRIANGLE GARAGE
Mobil

179

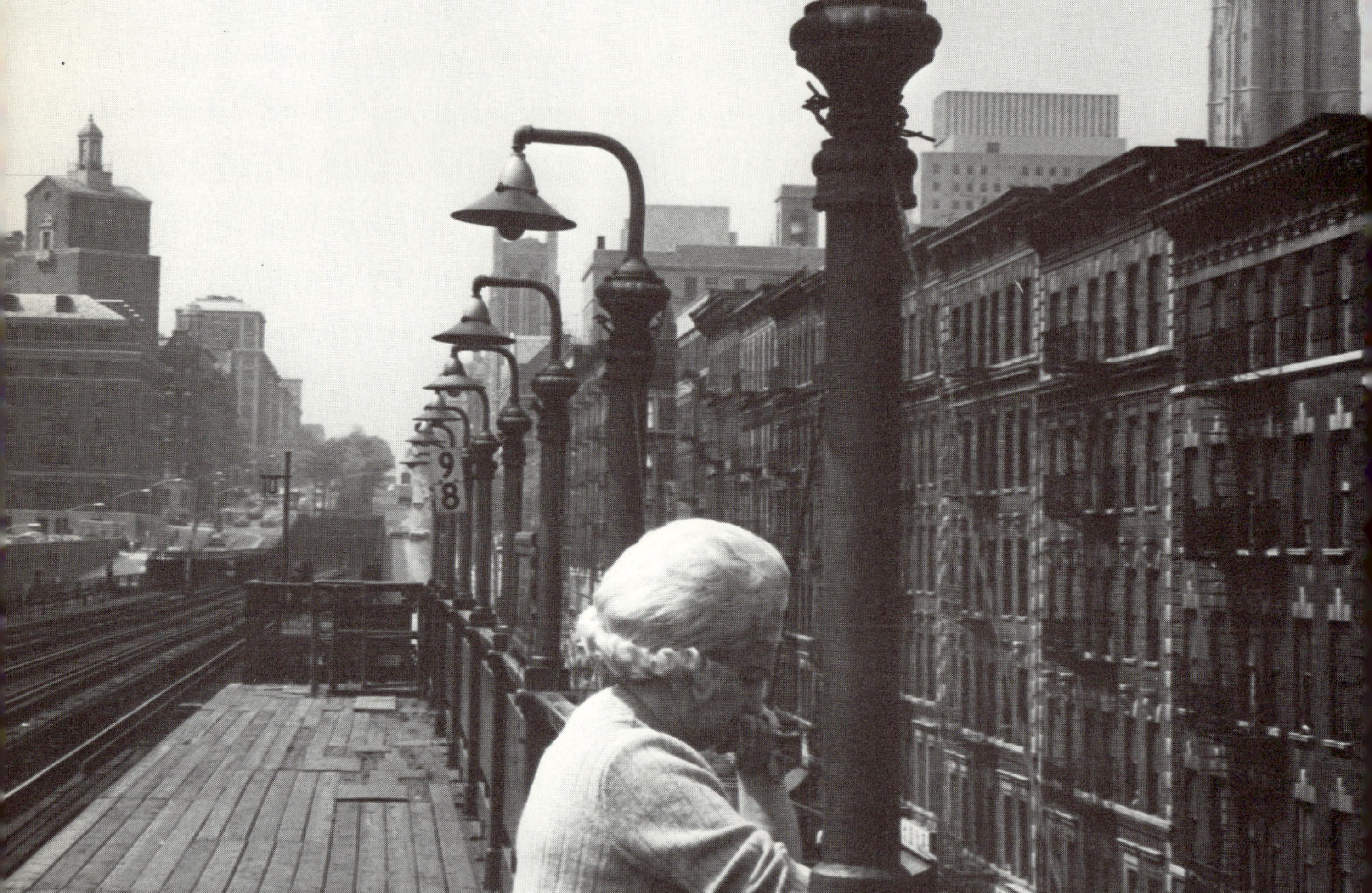
98

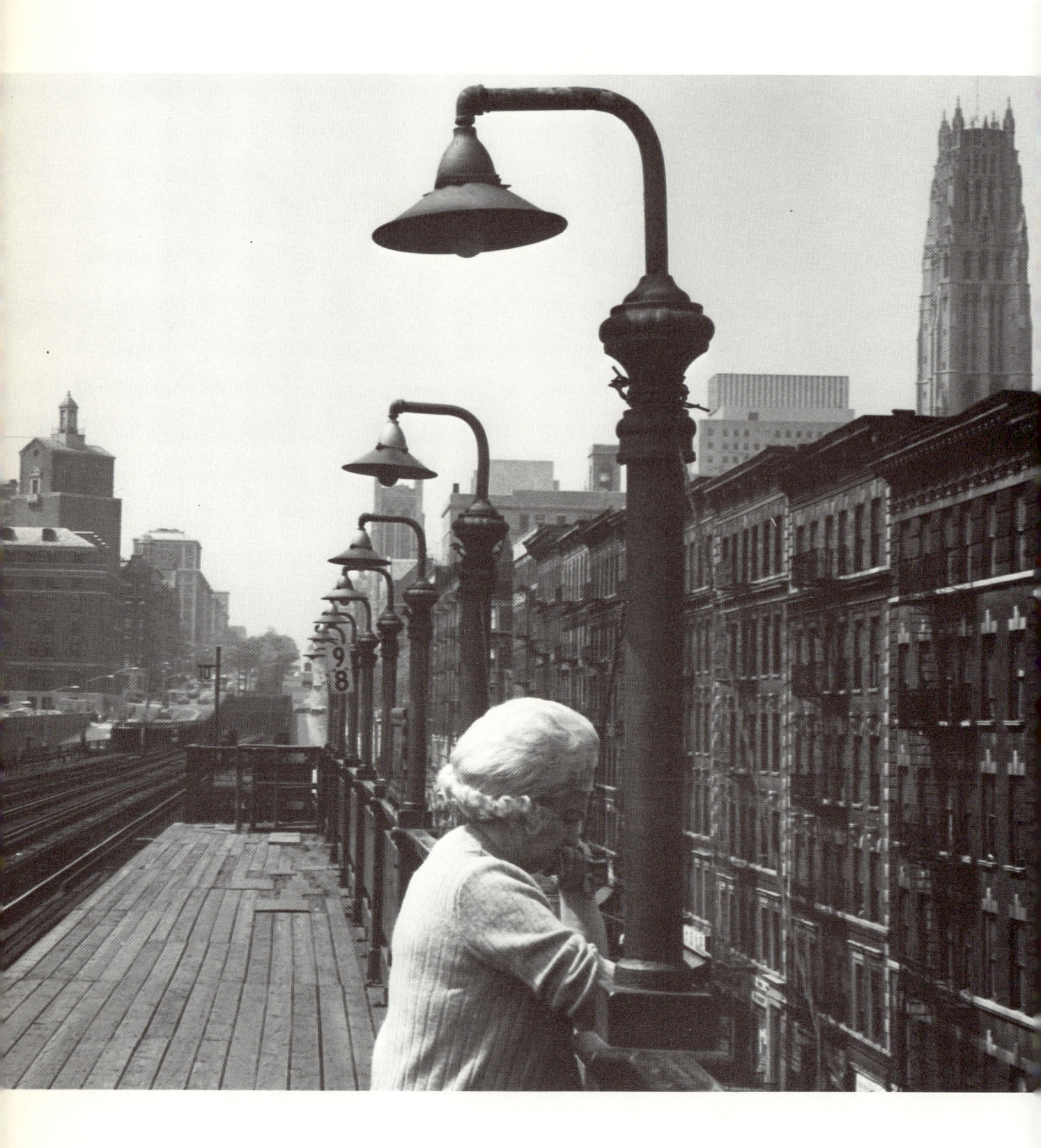

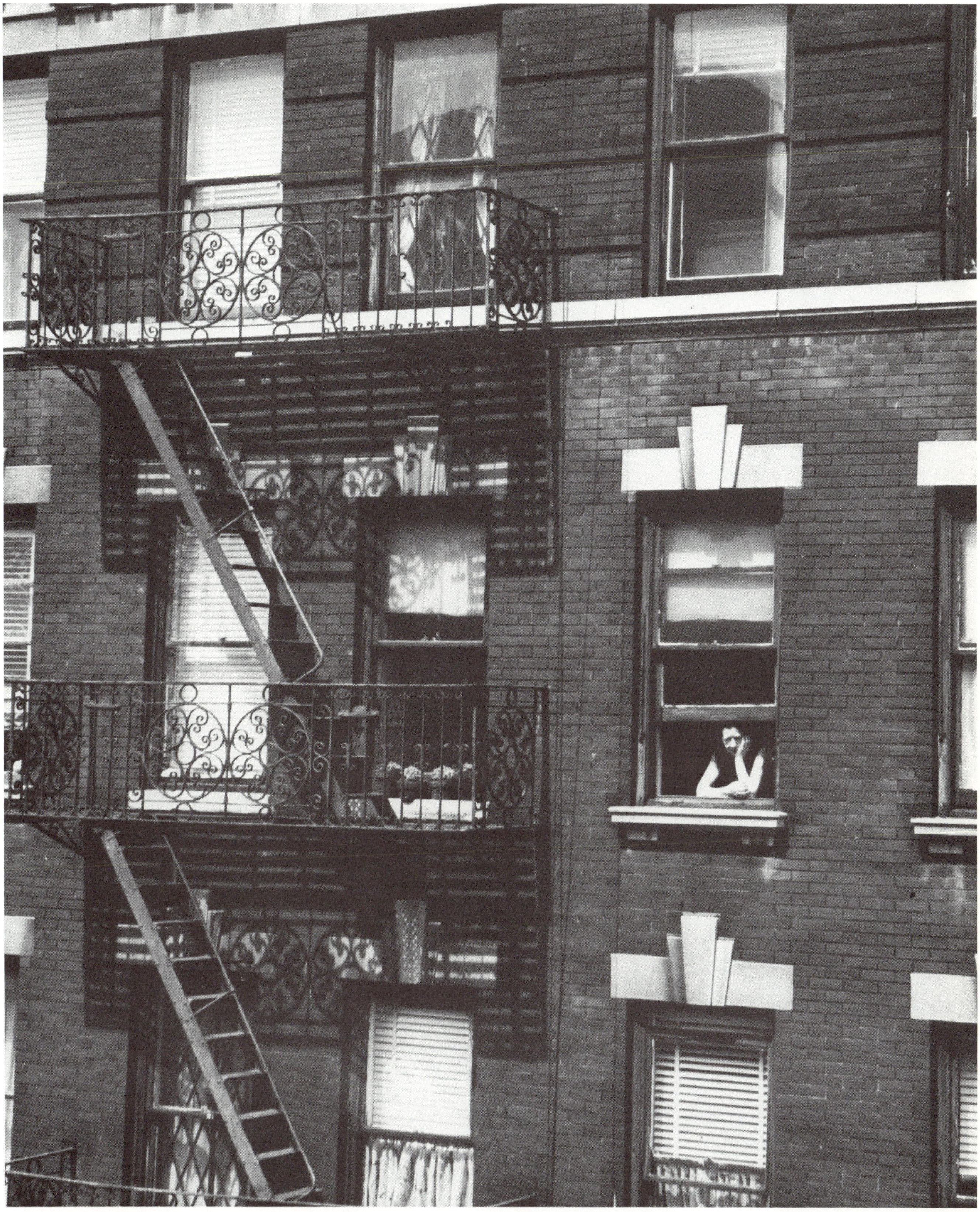

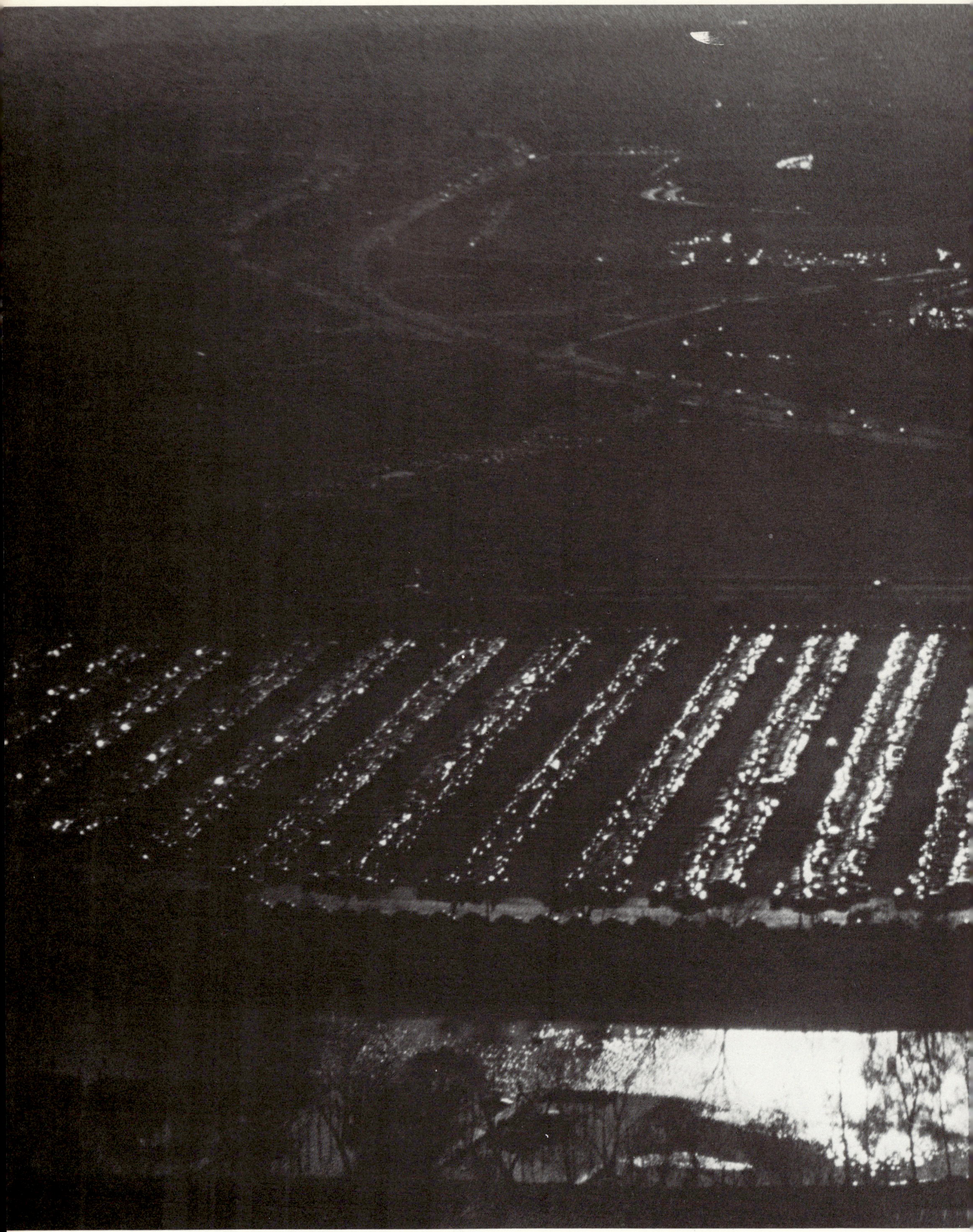

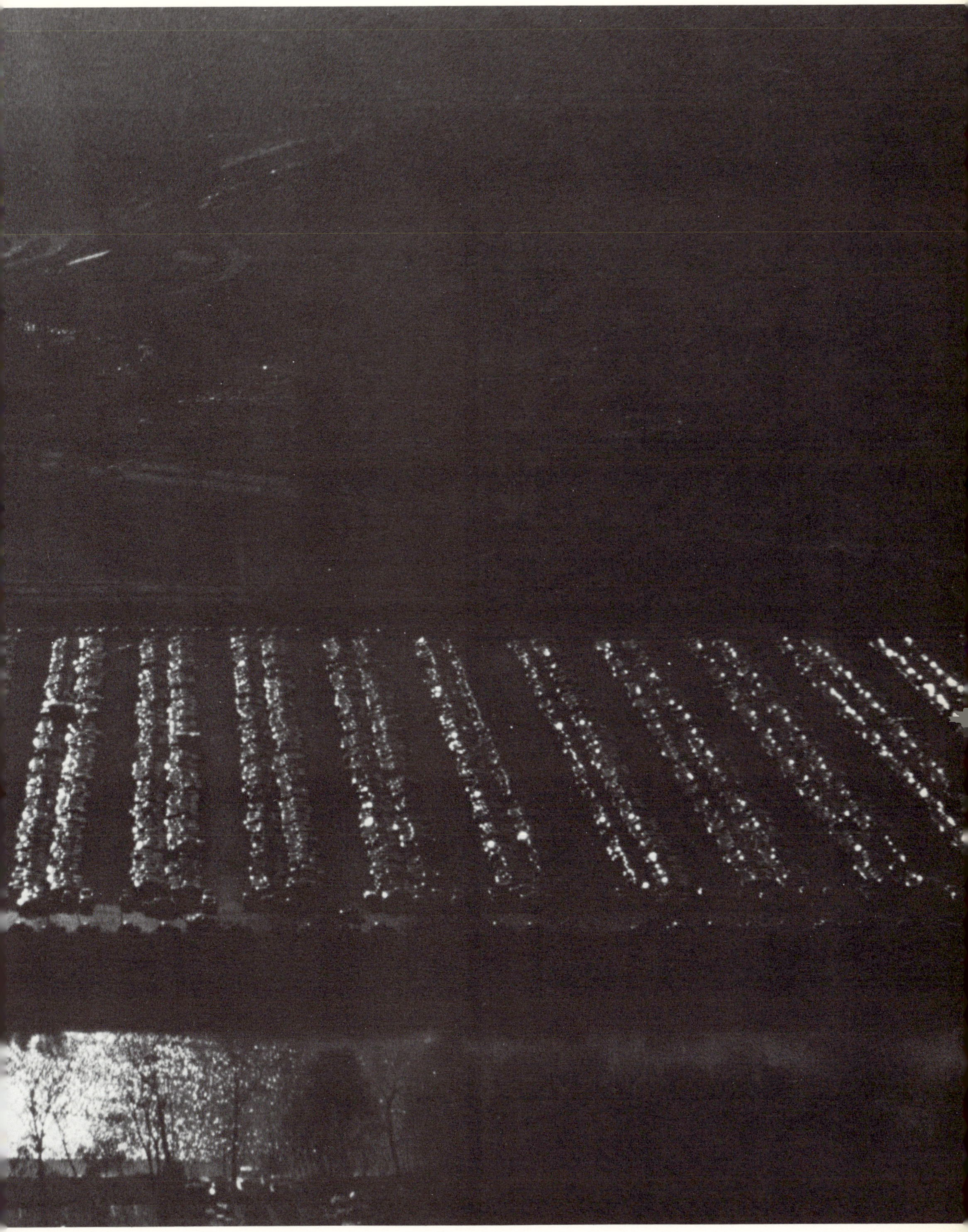

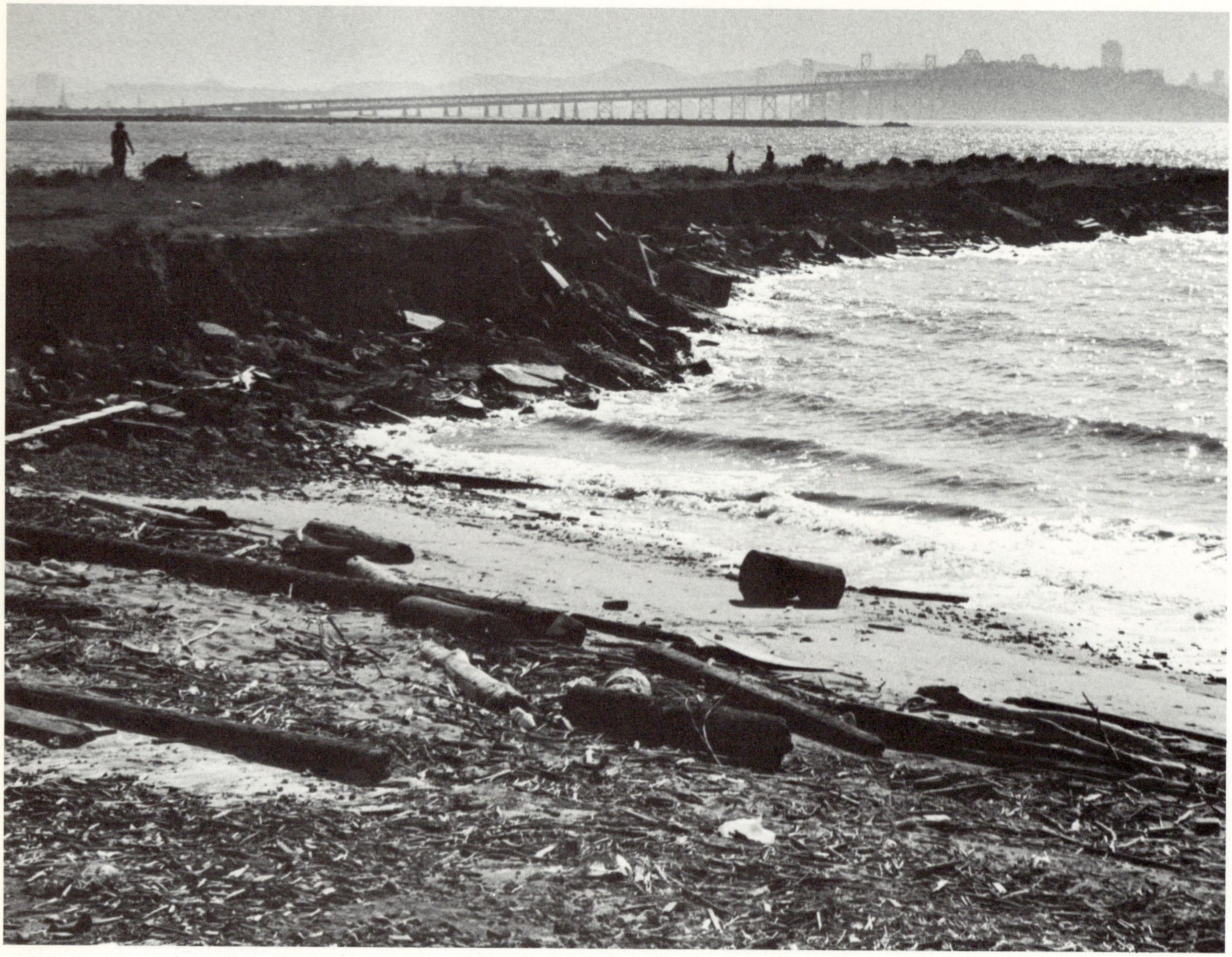

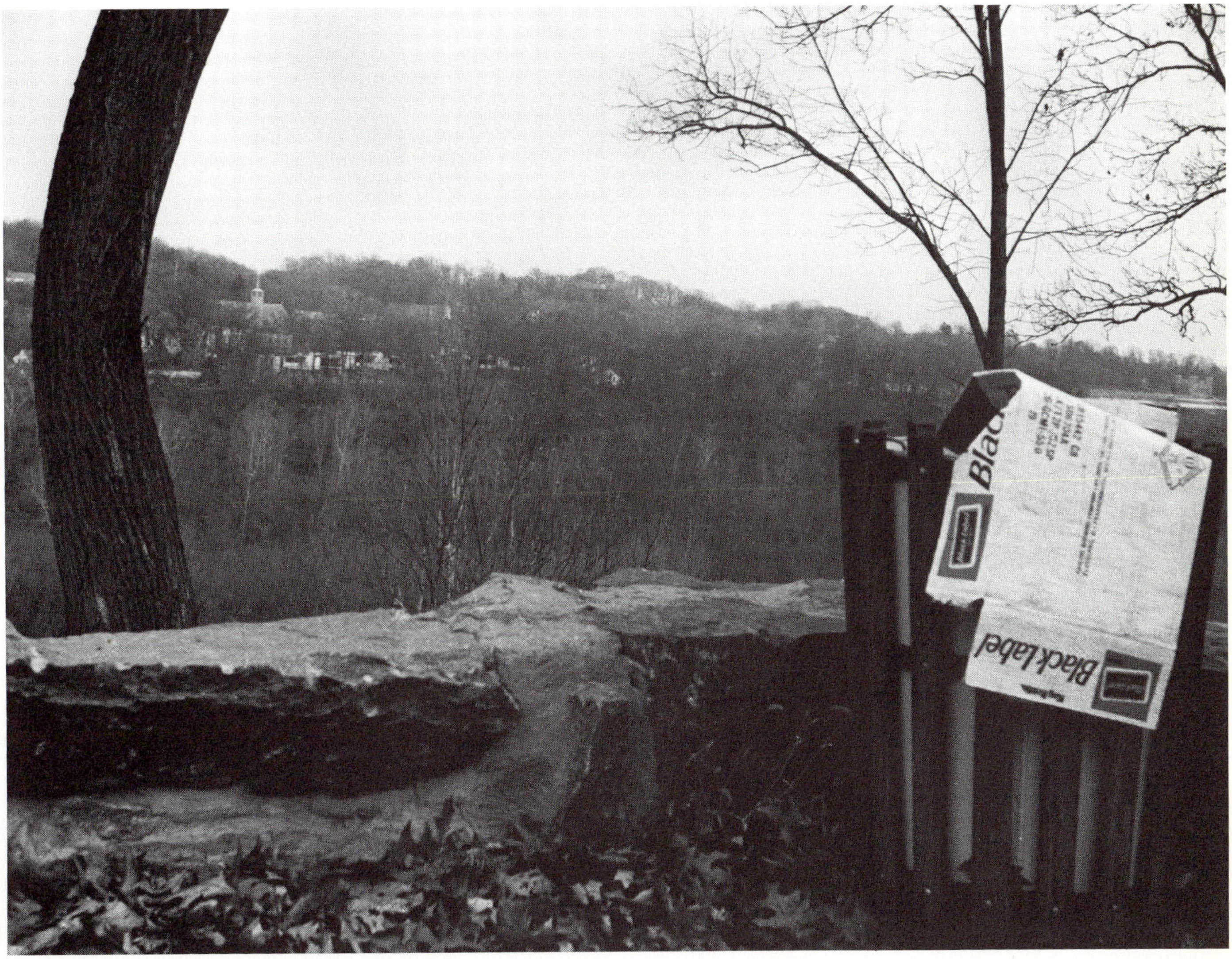
Black-Label
Blac

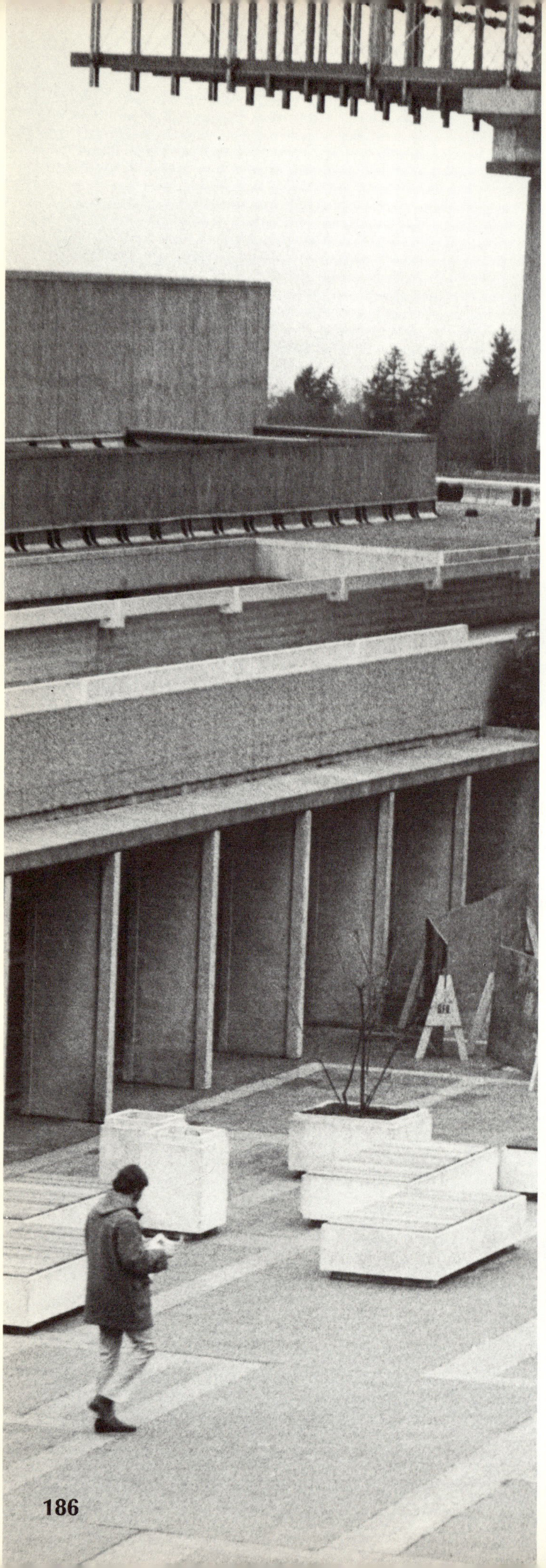

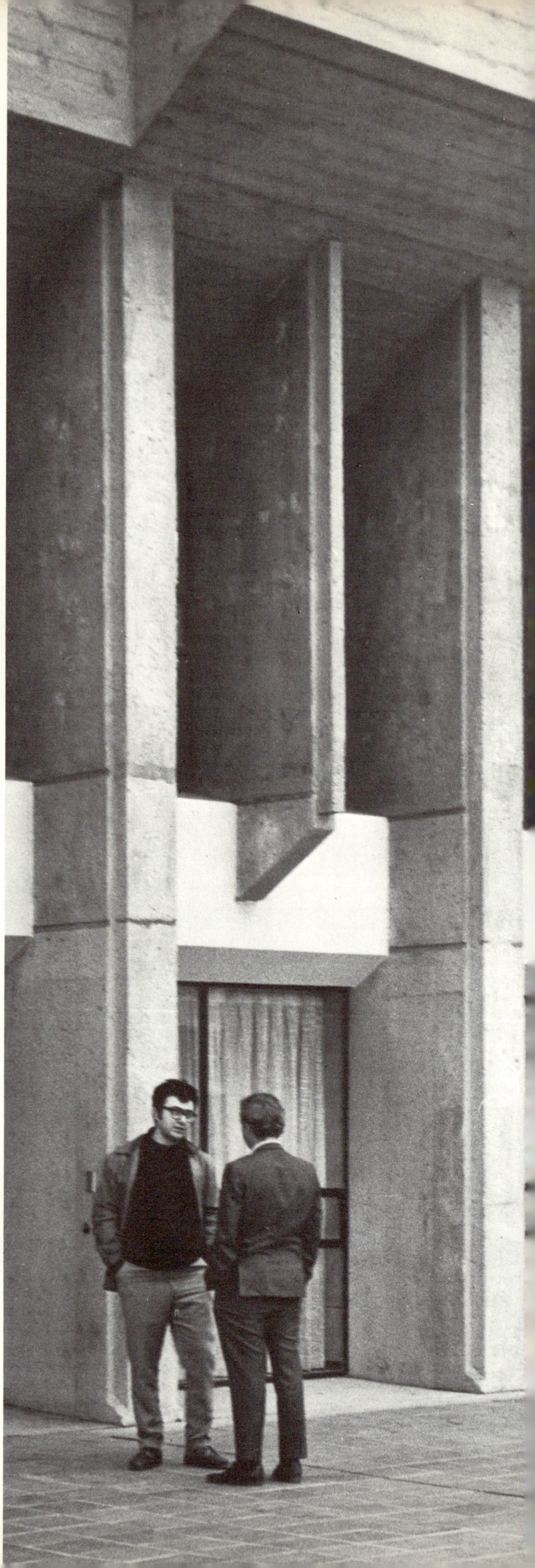

187

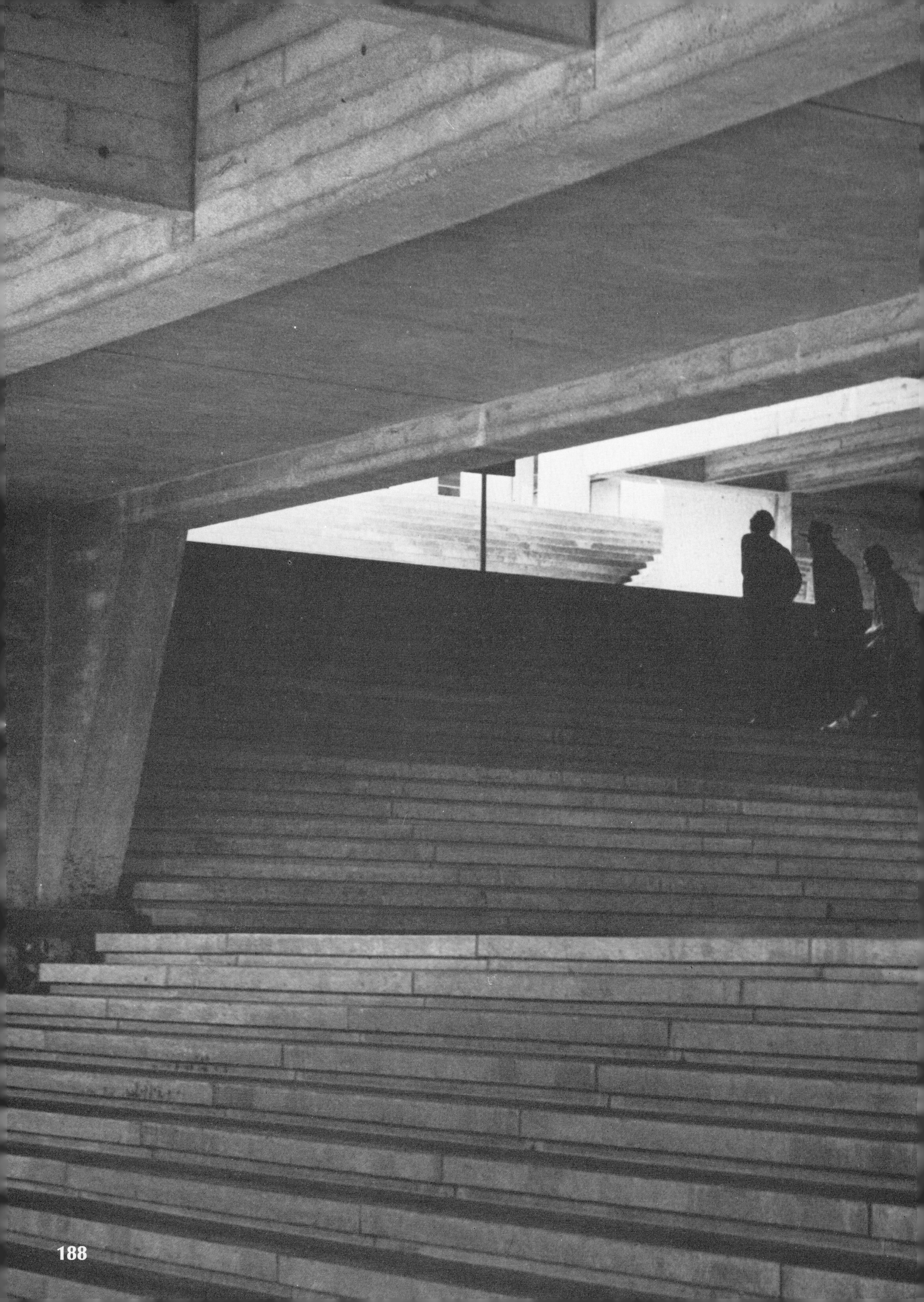

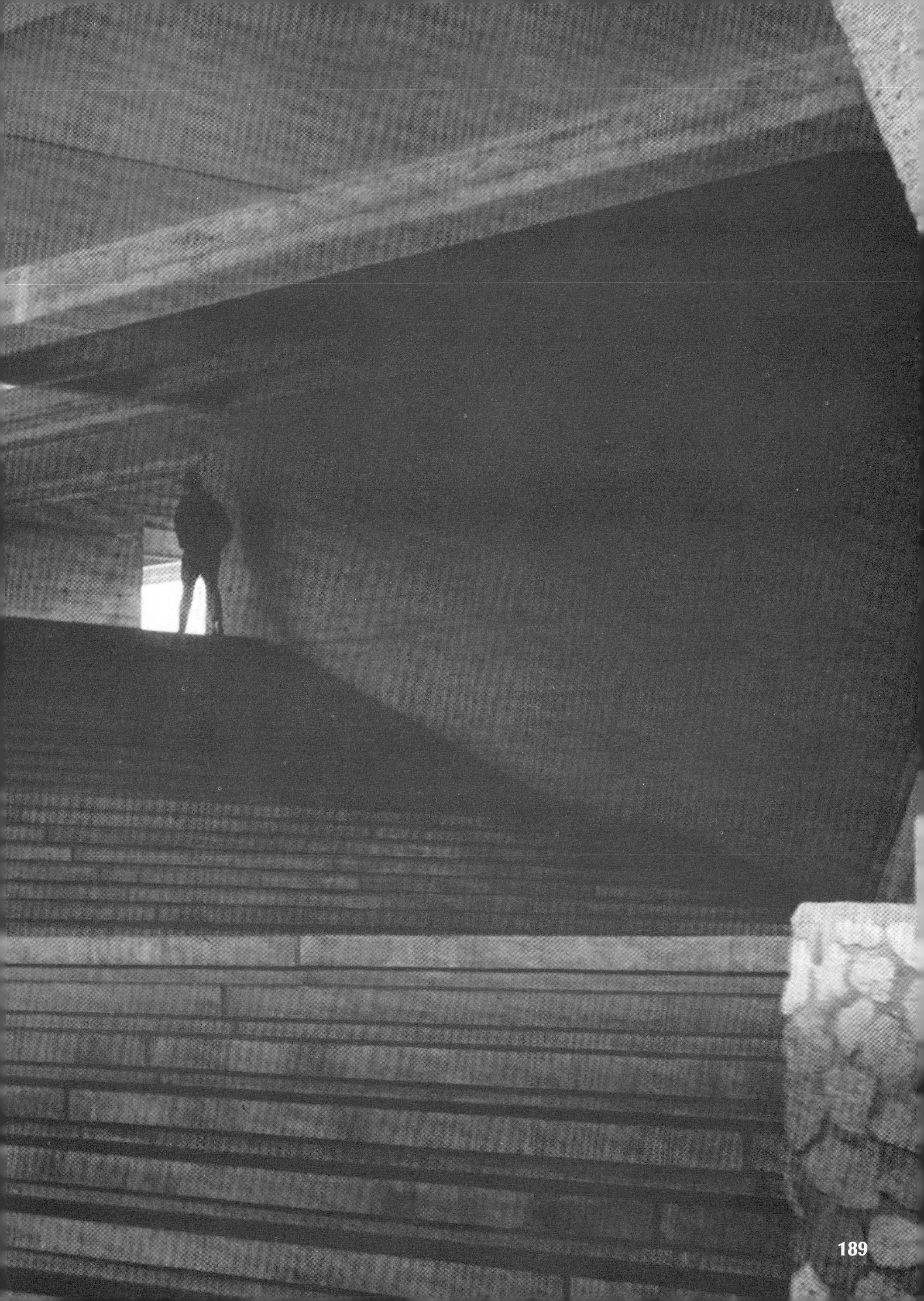

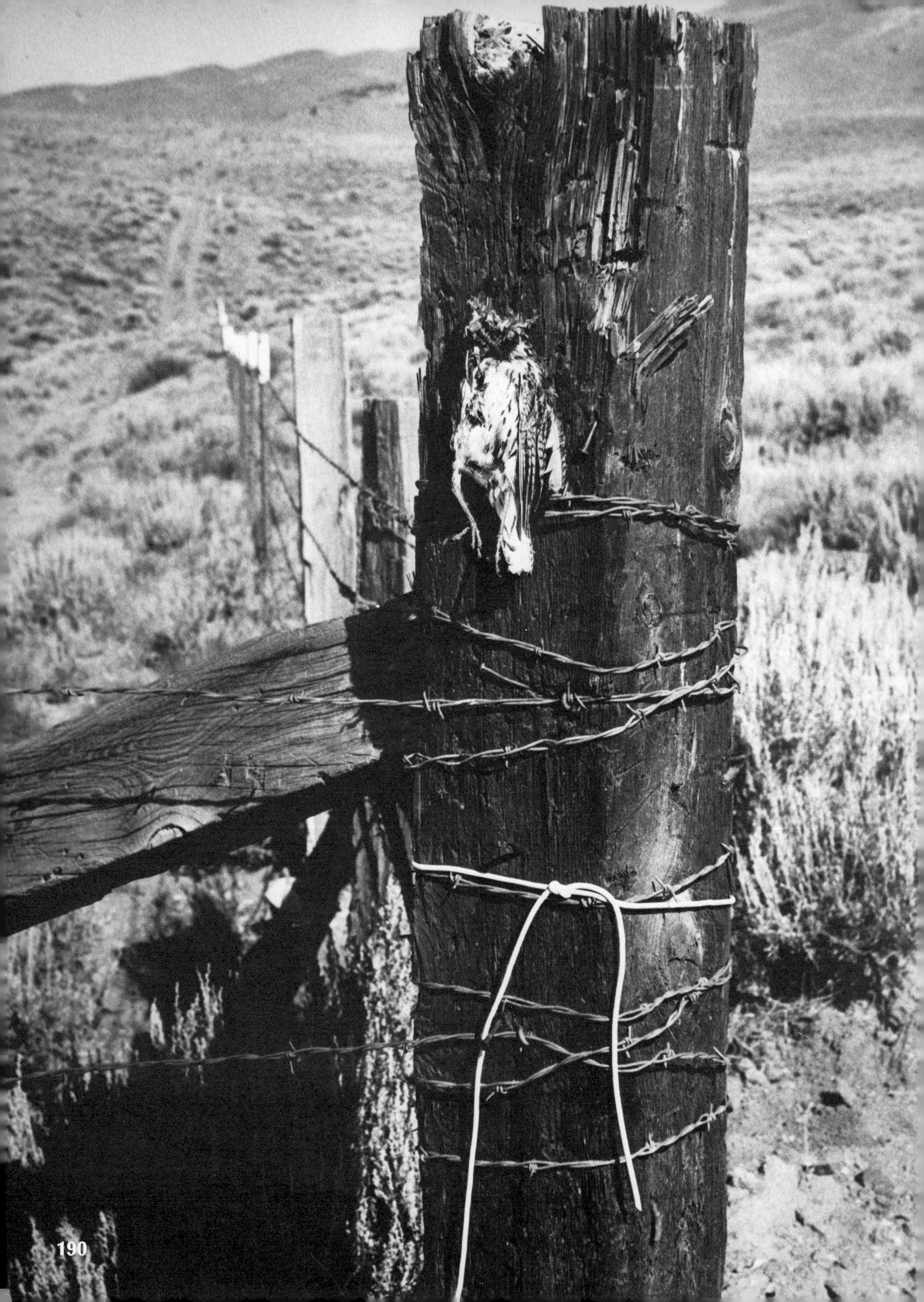

There are so many words about environment and ecology that it is high time for a few images without the words. We pass so many blighted areas without even a glance that it is high time we paused to look. And when we do look, we miss so many details that it is high time we learned to observe, to compare, to use our imaginations. And there are so many times the student is asked to provide answers that it is high time he provided the questions. He can begin with the big question WHY?

The following are brief descriptions of some of the photographs with a very few suggestions on how they are to be utilized for writing assignments. In keeping with the last observation in the above paragraph, there are no questions: the student should begin asking these—especially of himself.

Page 166: Deserts were once forests. Discuss to what extent man is helping to hasten the process.

Page 167: A familiar scene in many towns and cities, this was taken in New York City.

Pages 168–169: A scene on the ocean front in Vancouver, Canada.

Page 170: On the beach in Santa Cruz, California.

Page 171: On the slope of a hill outside a town.

Pages 172–175: The first two pages depict an idyllic forest scene in Yosemite and the next two pages show a forest denuded by fire. Compare the two.

Pages 176–177: Another couple of pictures you can contrast.

Pages 178–179: Discuss this picture from the viewpoint of a person who sees it from his window every morning.

Pages 180–181: Two more photographs you can discuss as if the scenes were part of your neighborhood.

Pages 182–183: A parking lot in Washington, D.C.

Page 184: Part of San Francisco Bay.

Page 185: A turn-off on a Virginia highway, from which one can view a river scene.

Pages 186–189: Five scenes of the "campus" of Simon Fraser University in Vancouver, Canada. Use your imagination to picture the rest of the campus. SFU is being called the university of the future: discuss after doing some research.

Page 190: I came across this bird nailed to a post outside Reno, Nevada. I would rather the student did not write about this photograph: since the picture portrays man's inhumanity to other living creatures, the student ought to ponder over this picture and ask himself endless questions.

PEOPLE

193

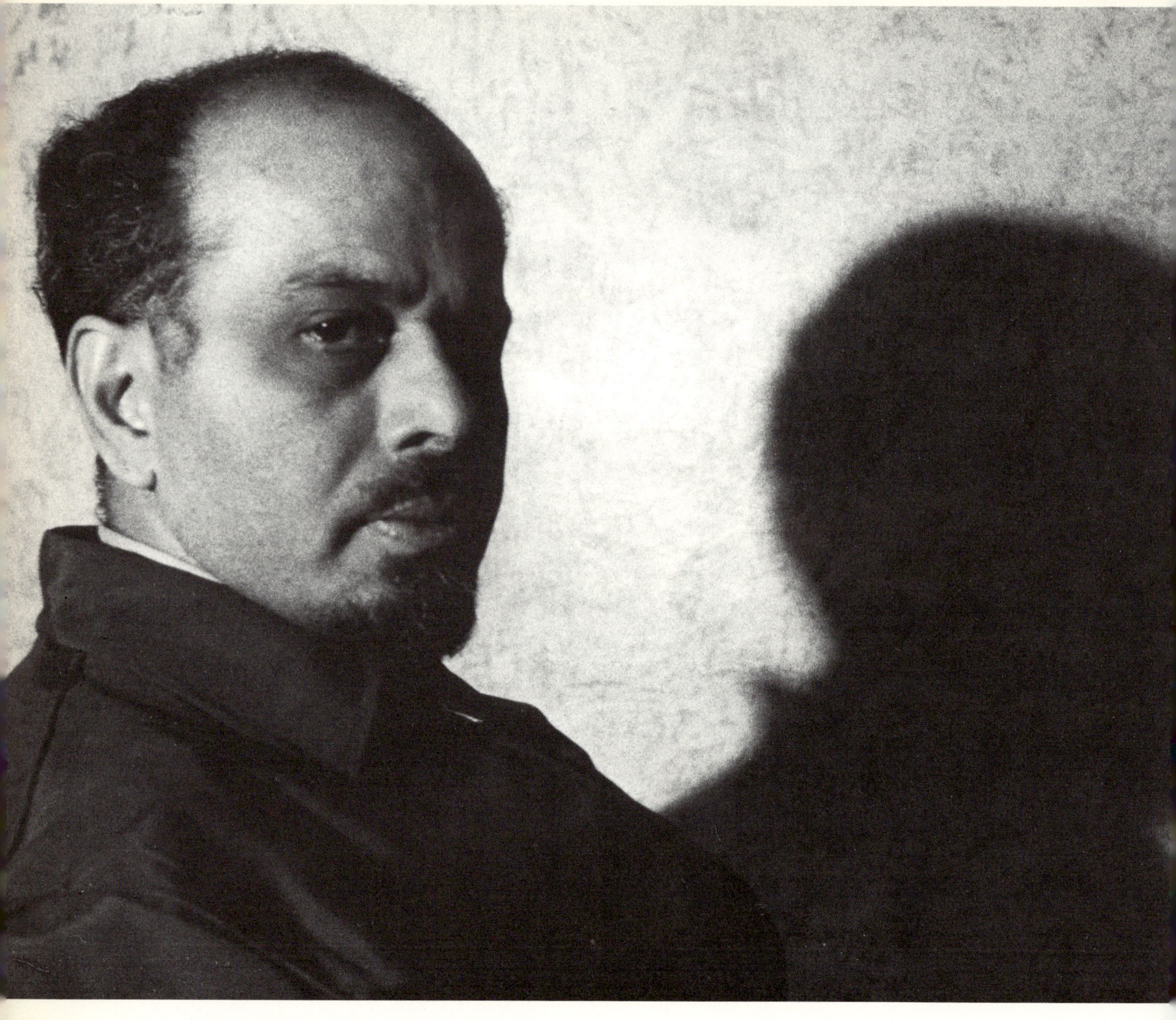

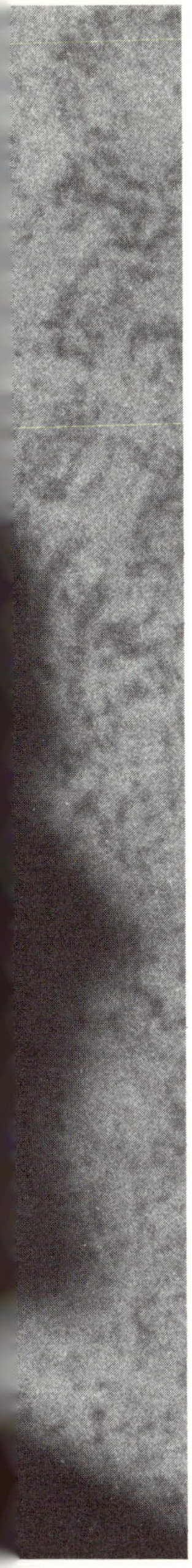

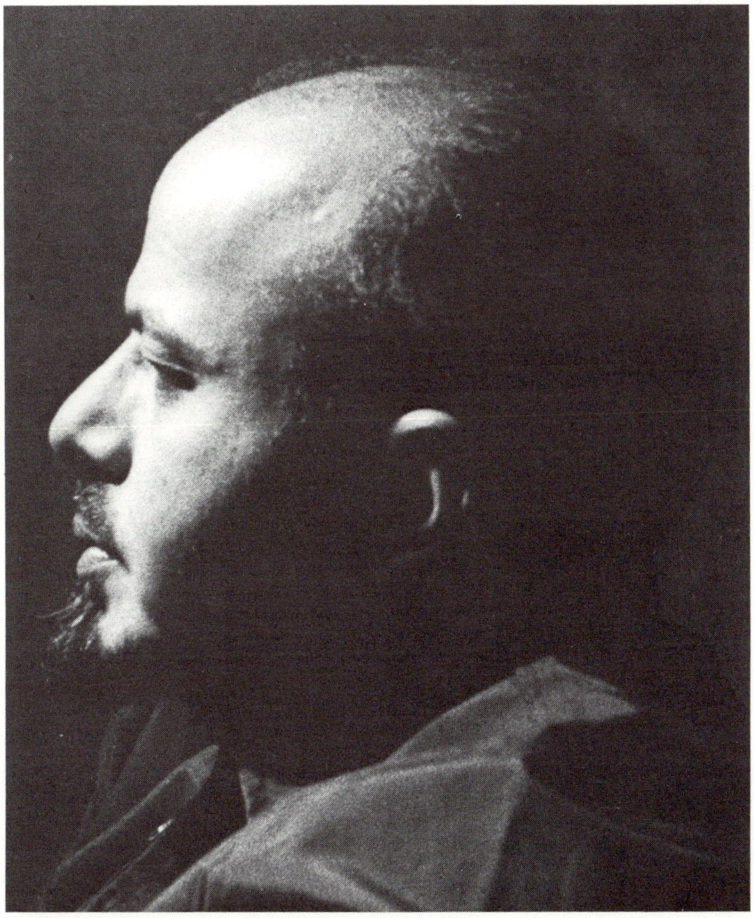

196

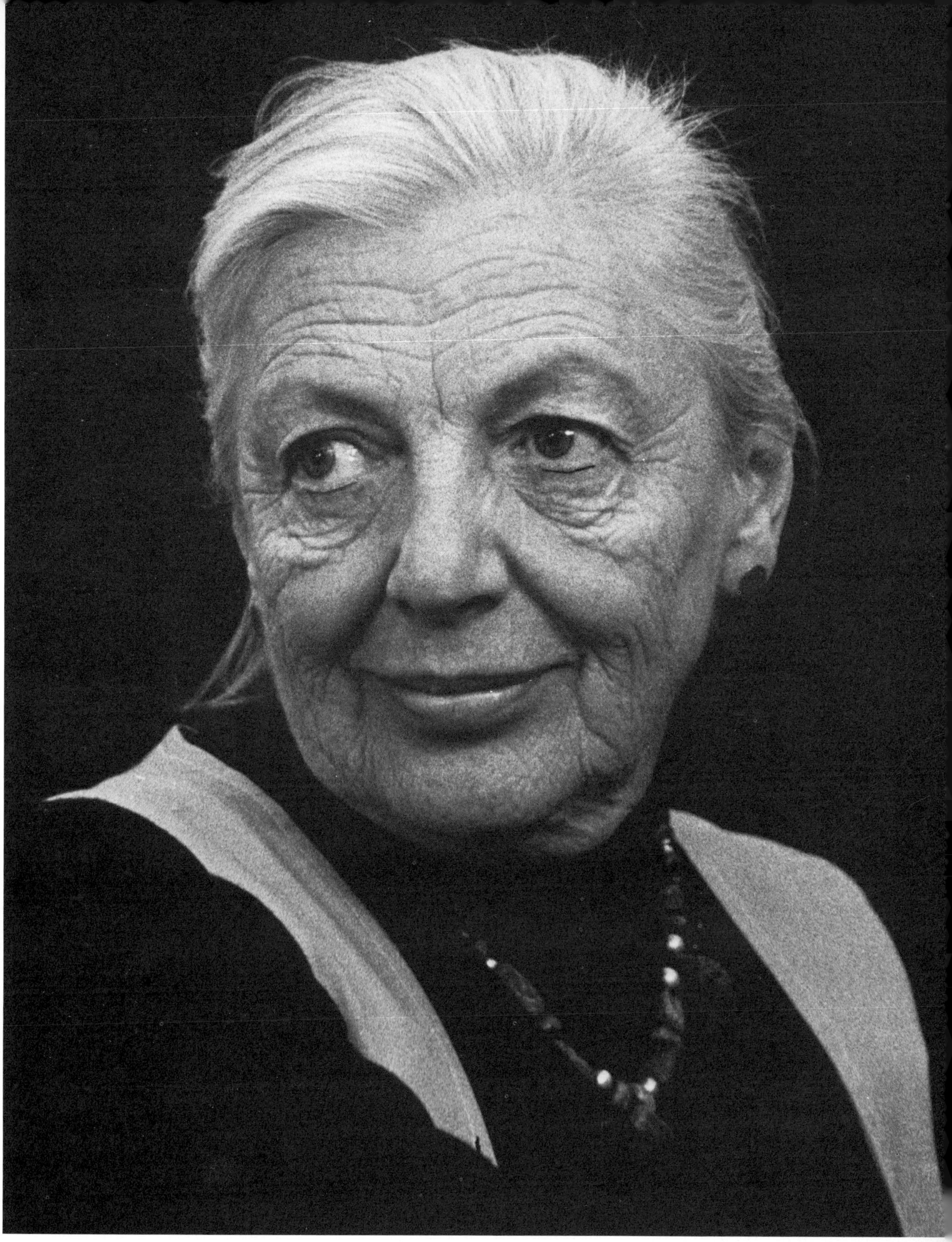

198

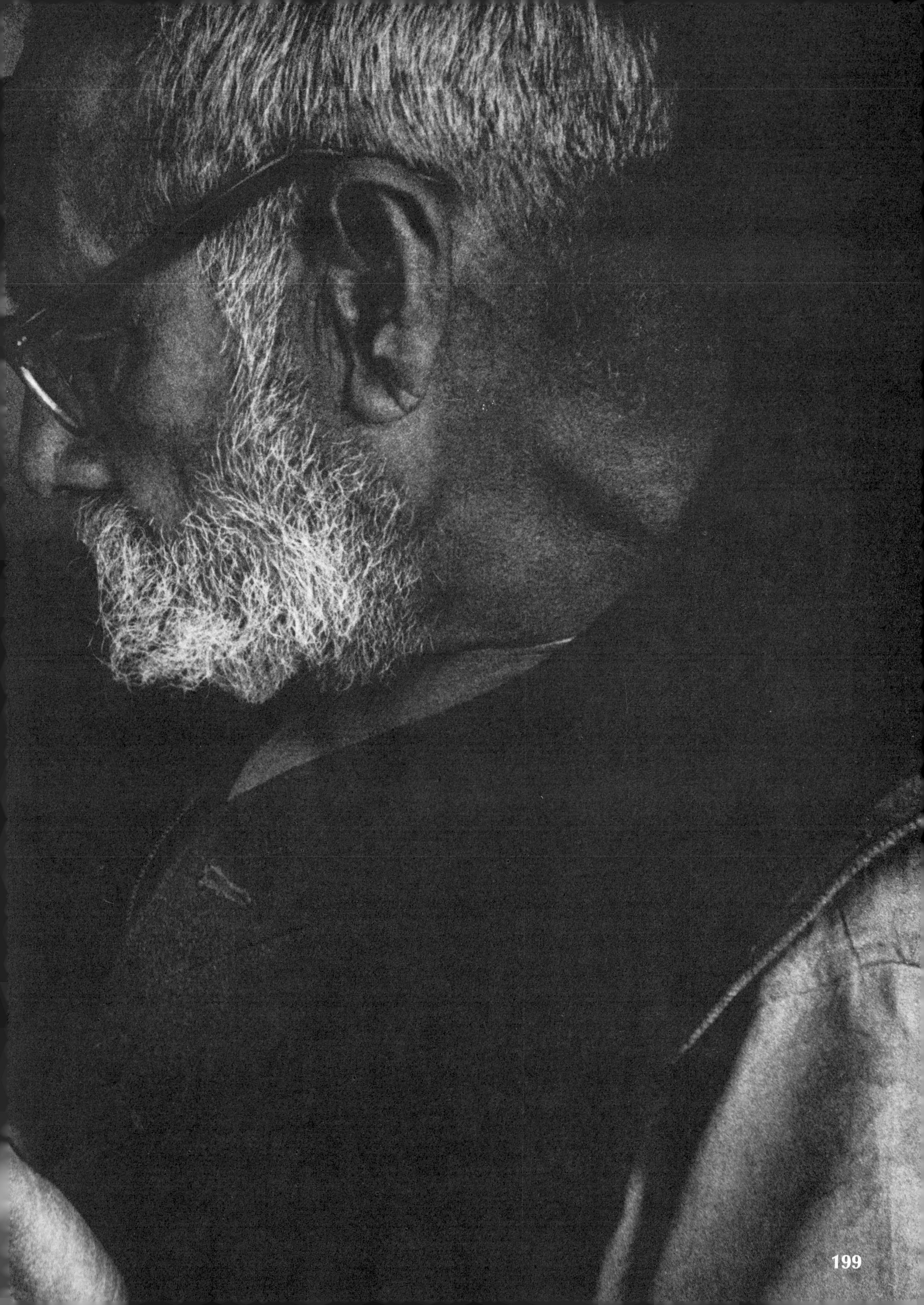

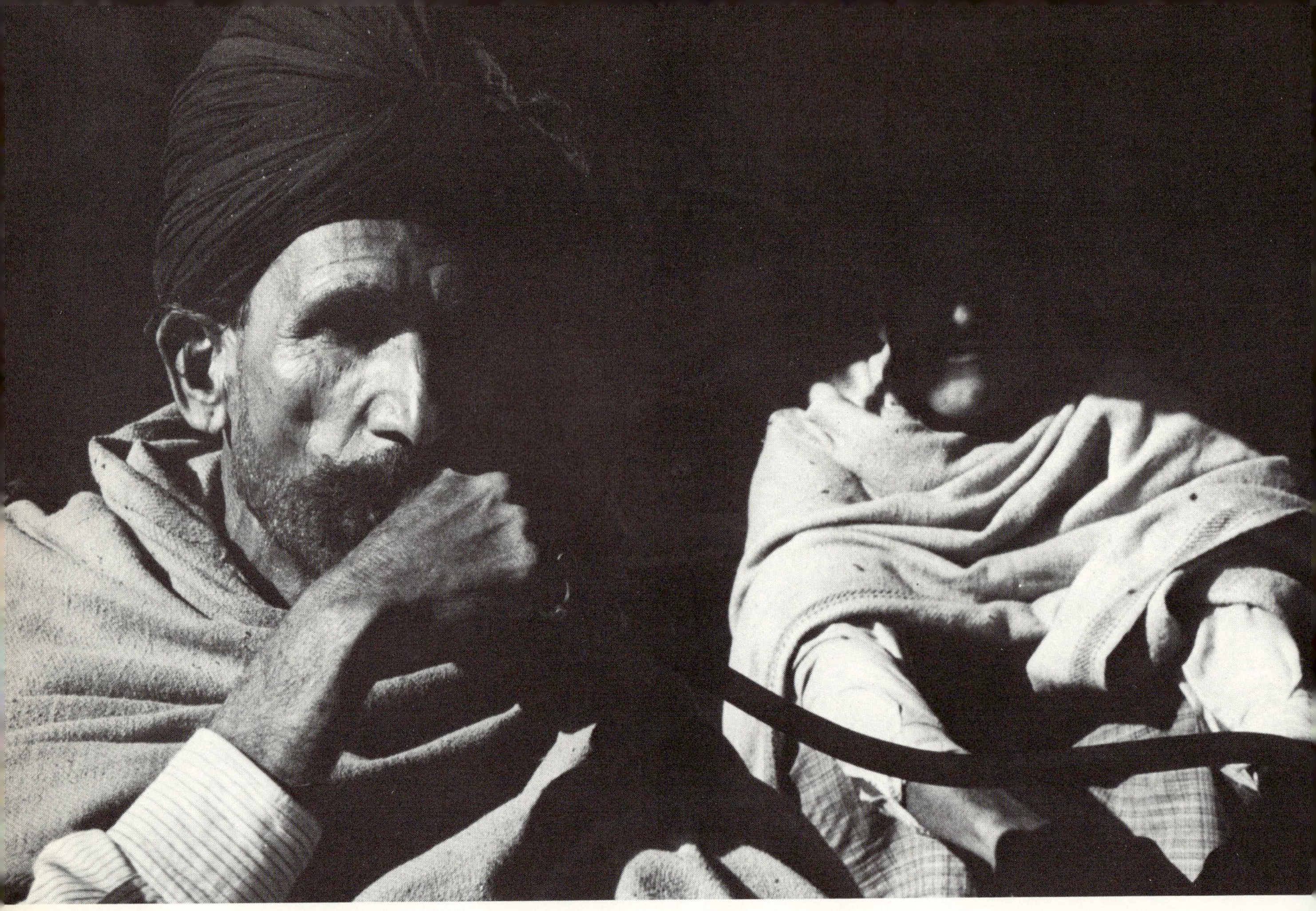

201

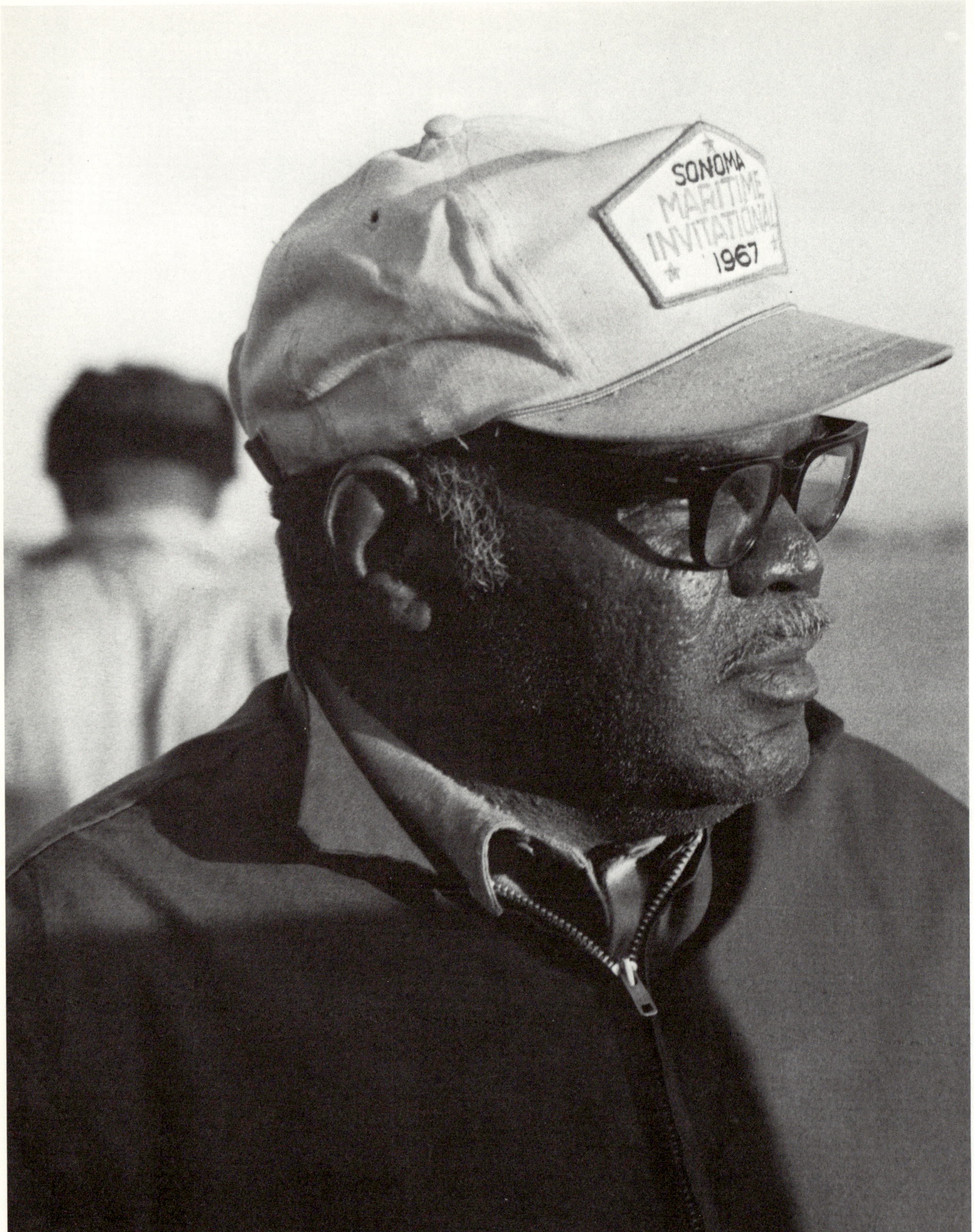
SONOMA
MARITIME
INVITATIONAL
1967

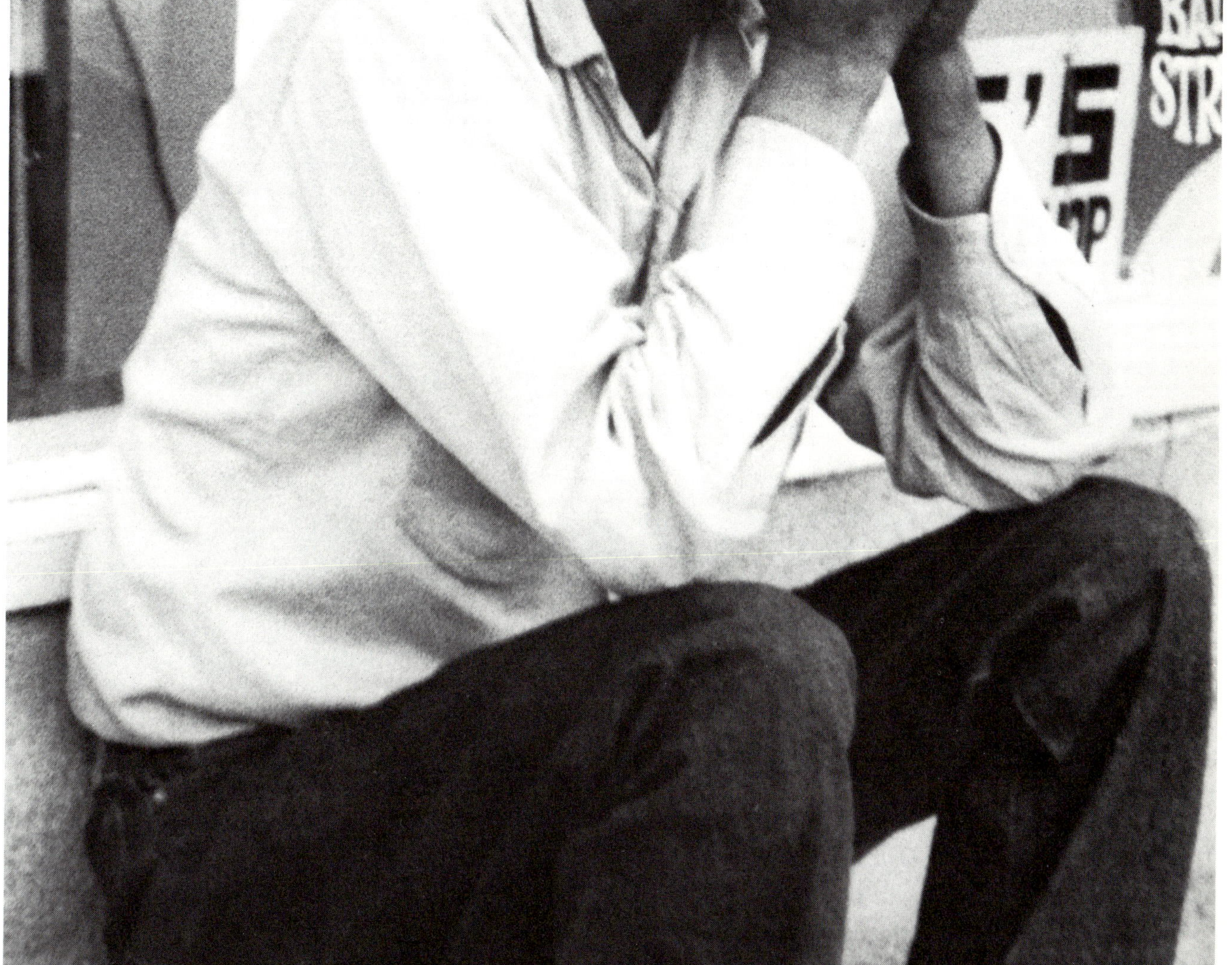

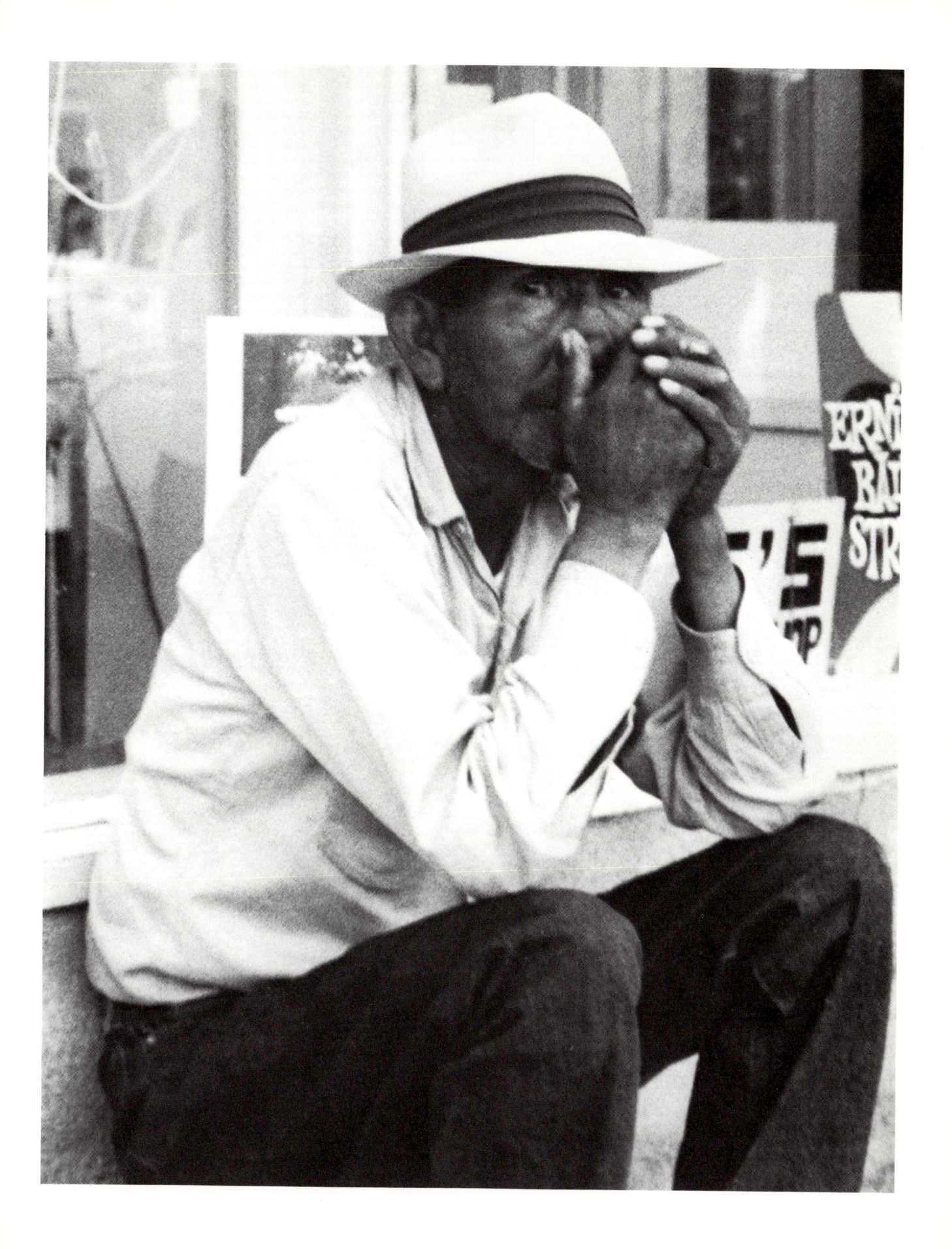

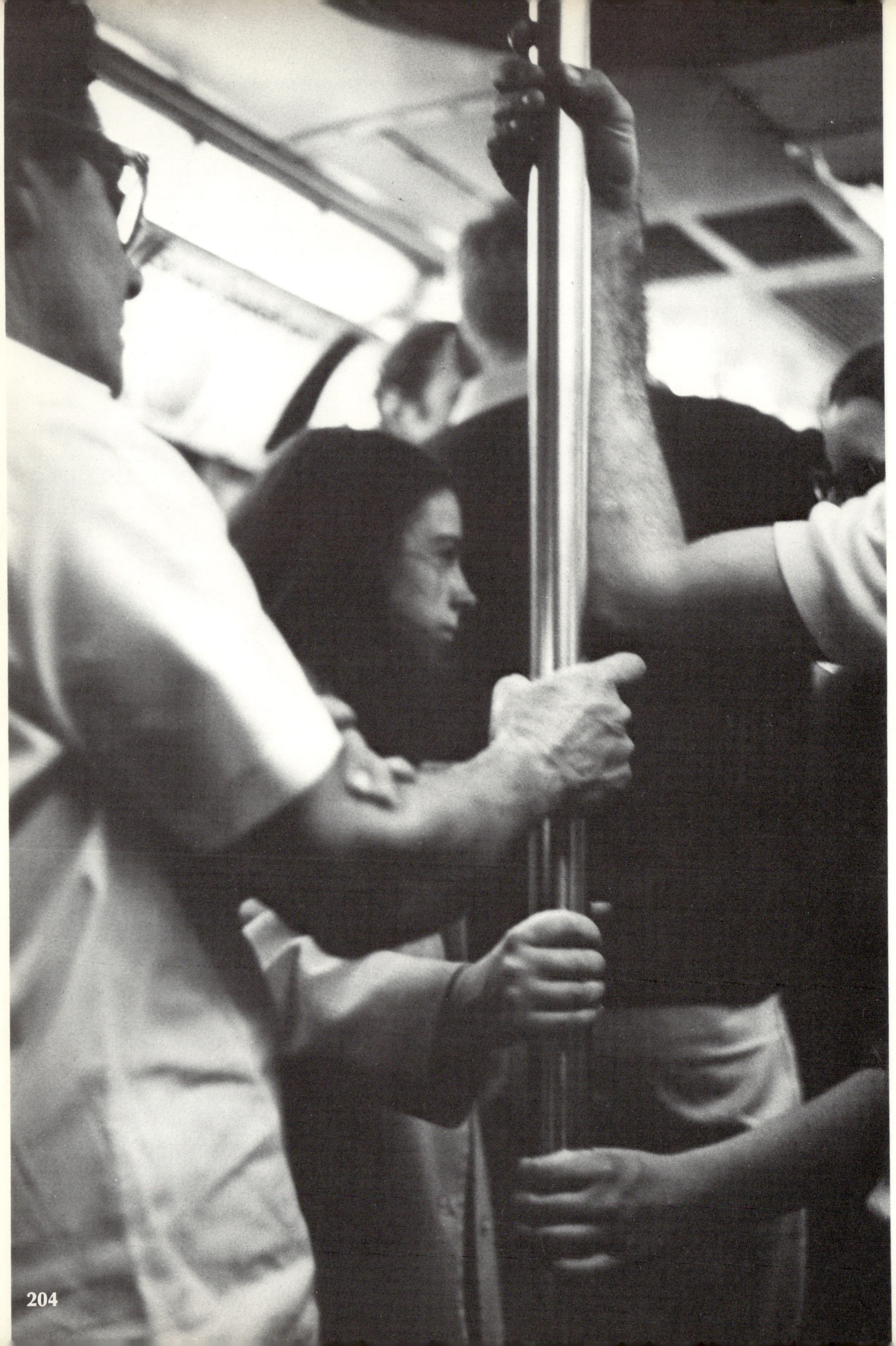

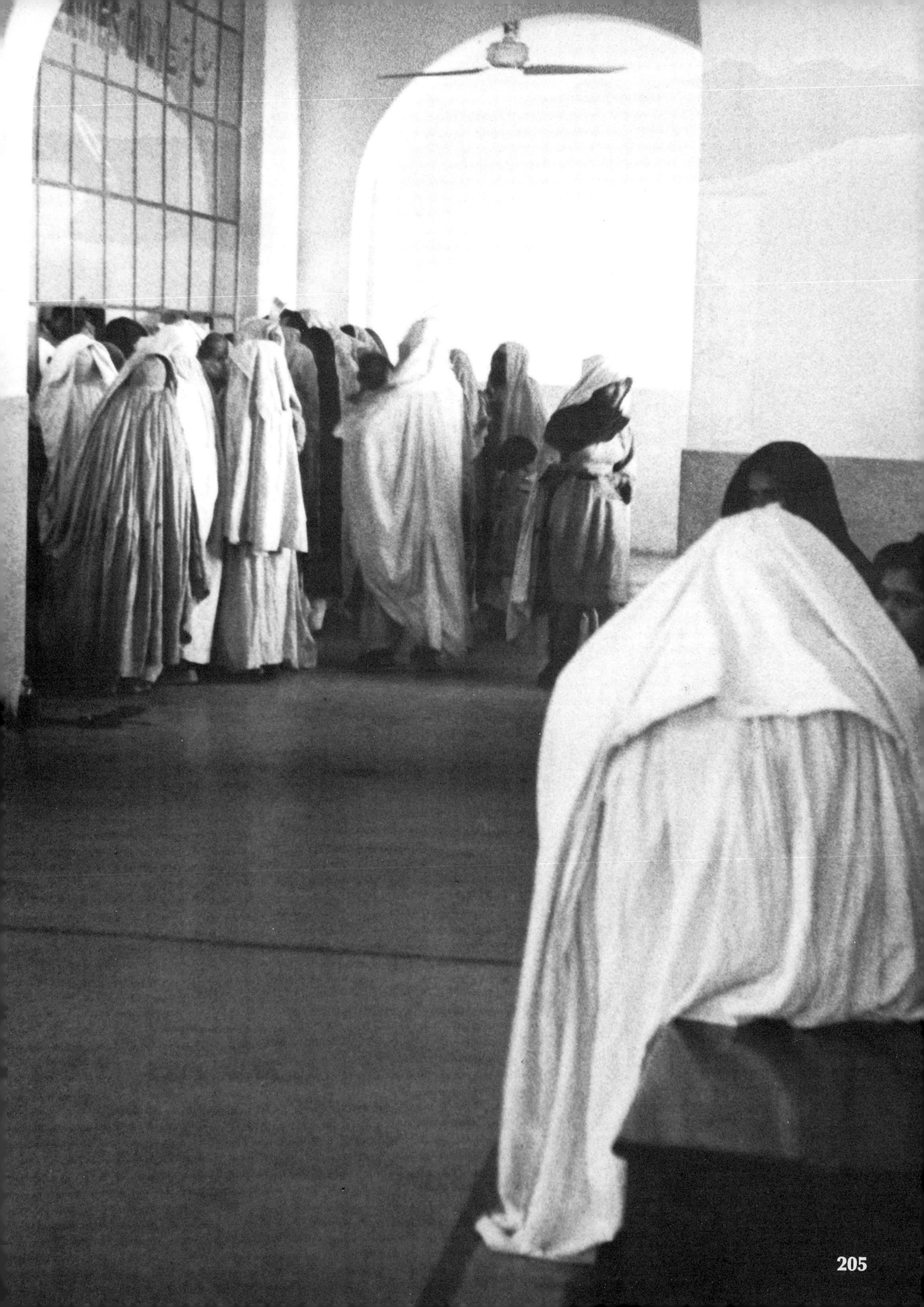

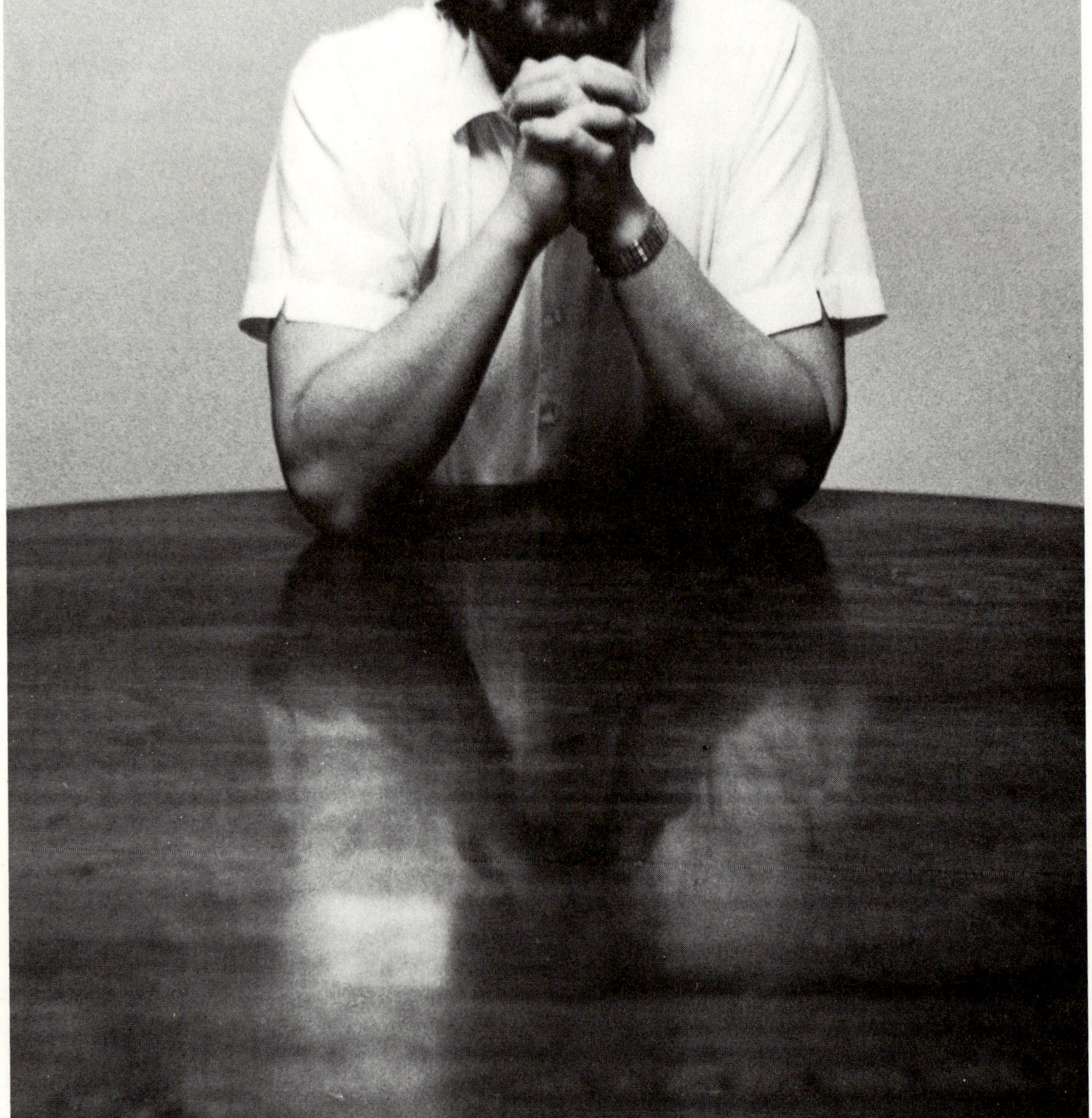

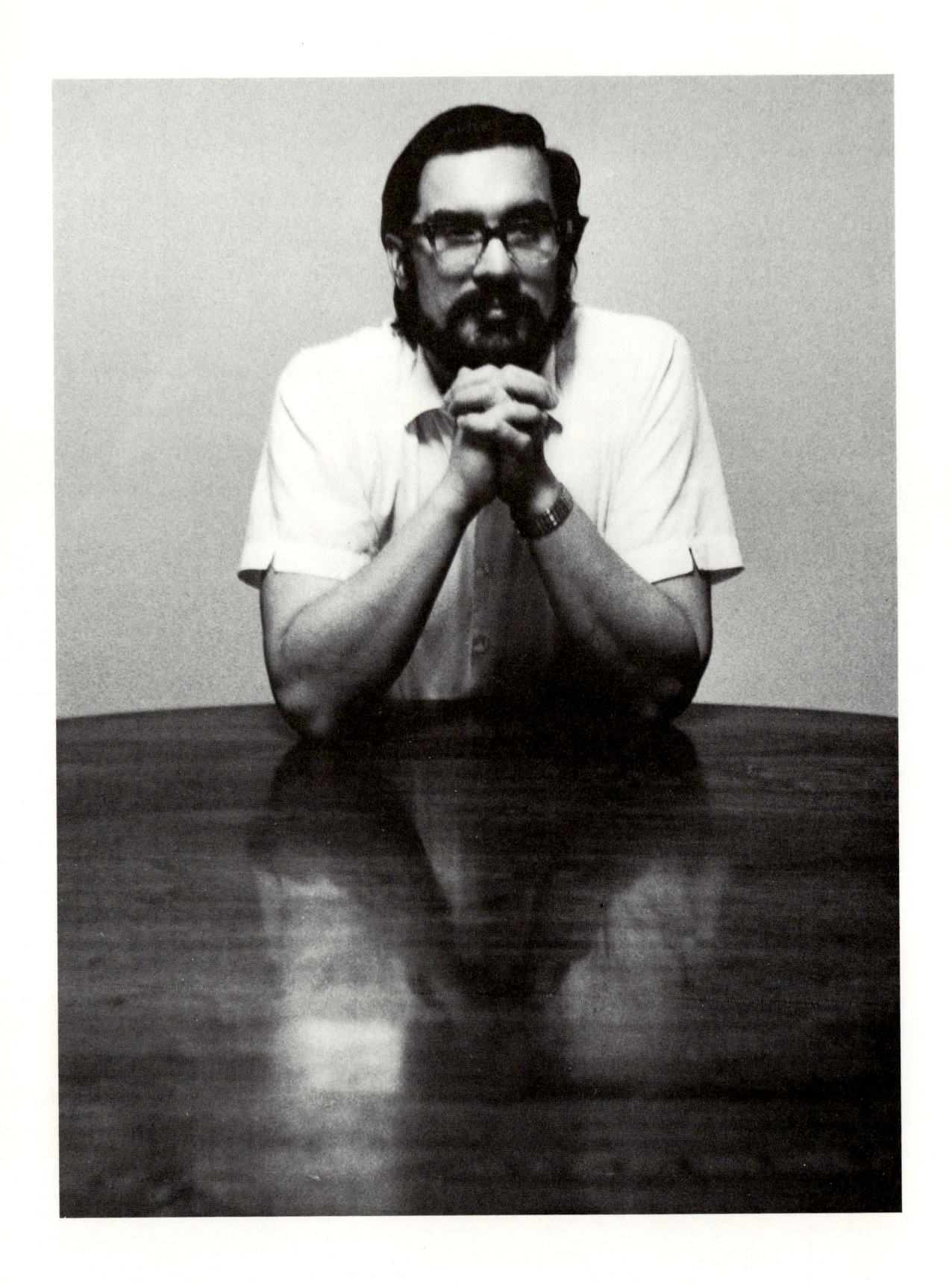

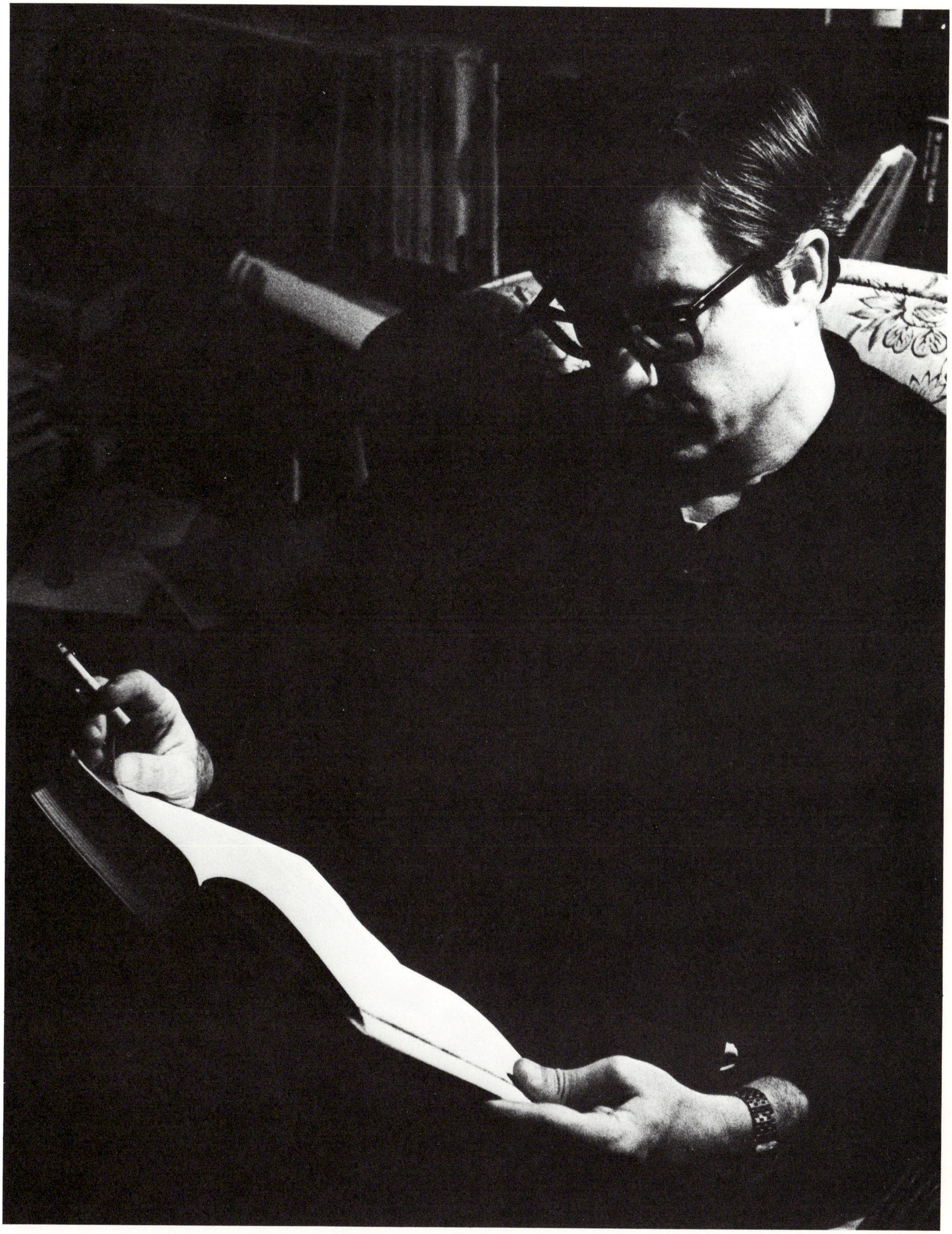

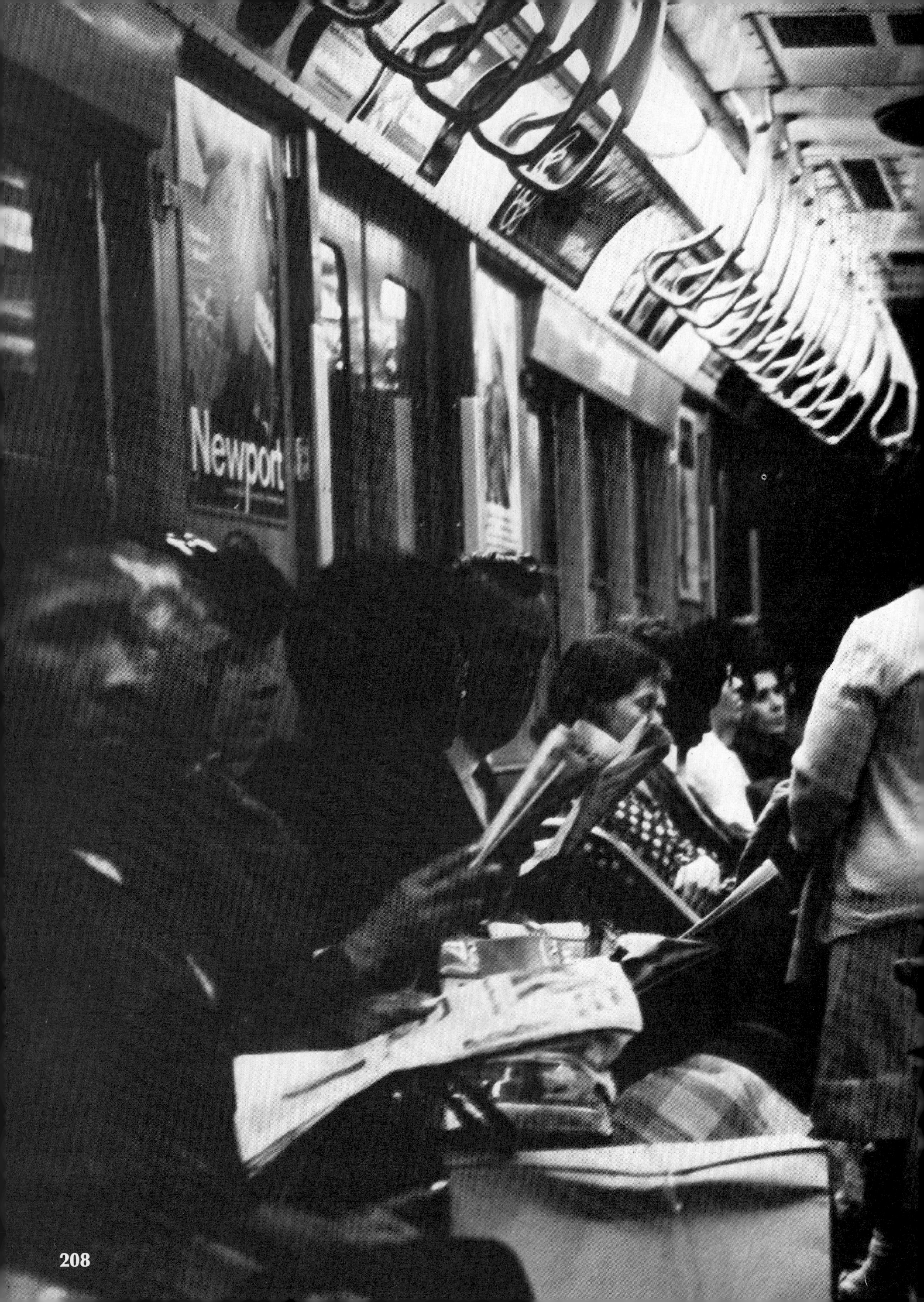
Newport

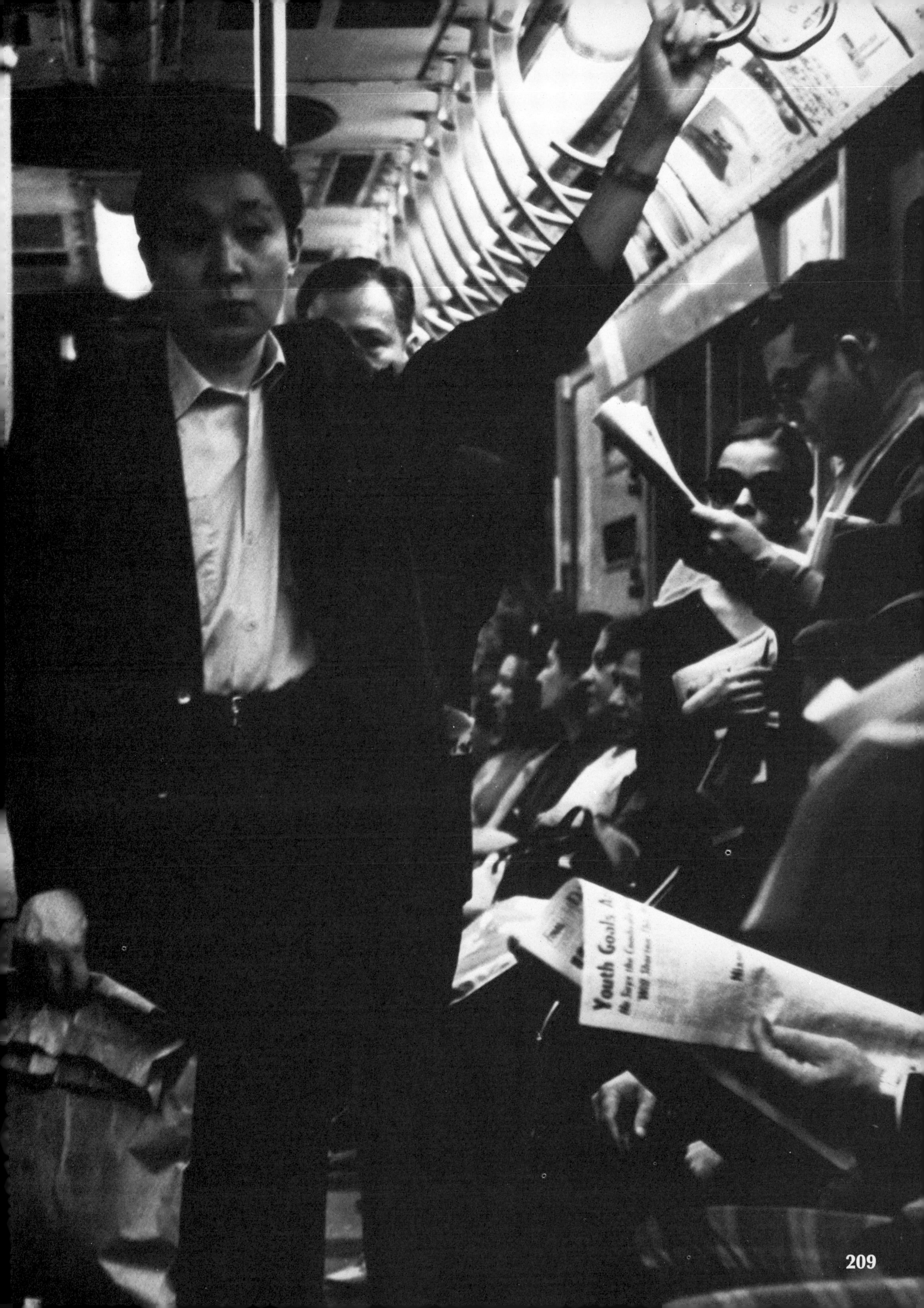
Youth Goals

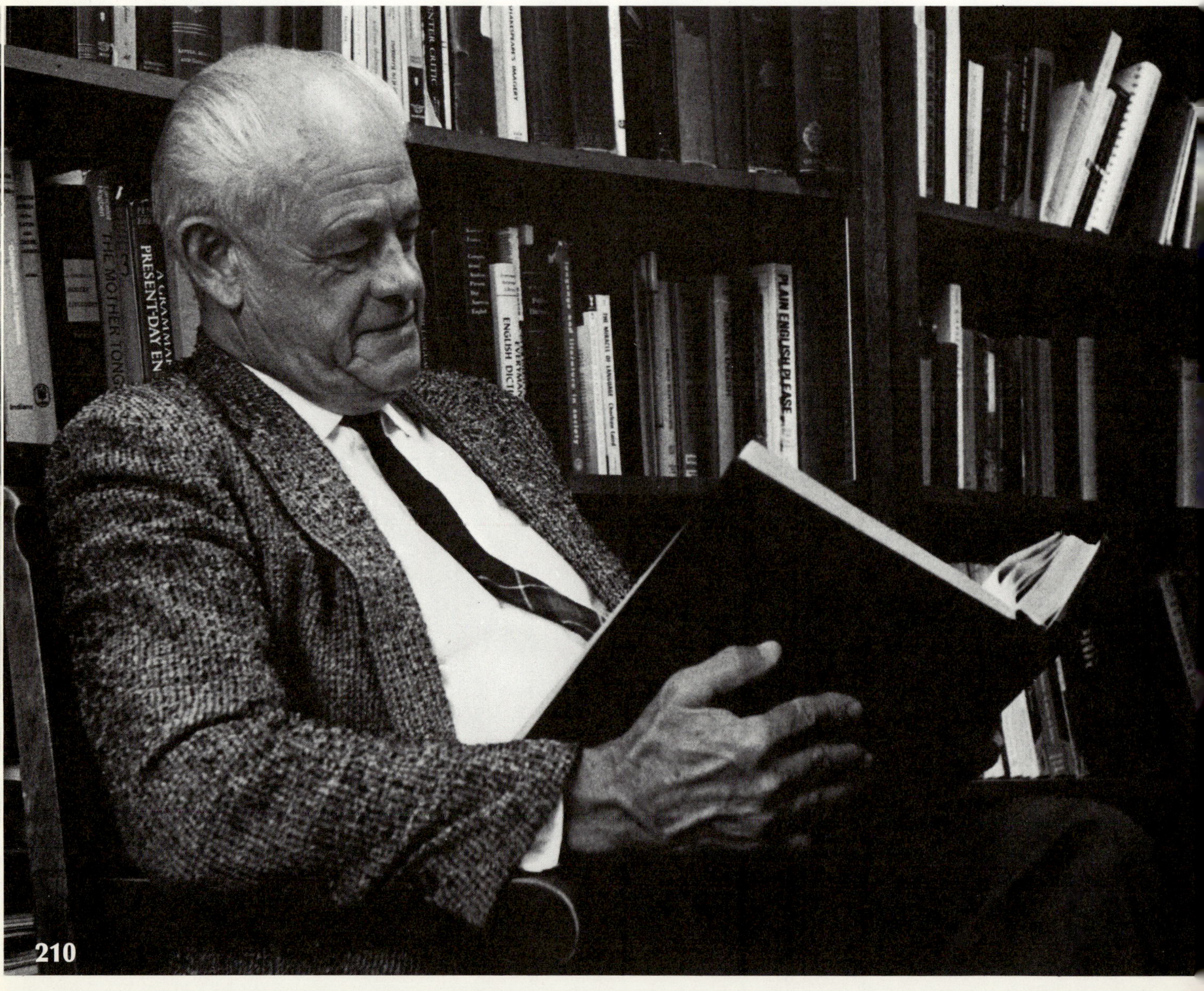
PLAIN ENGLISH PLEASE
SHAKESPEARE'S IMAGERY

211

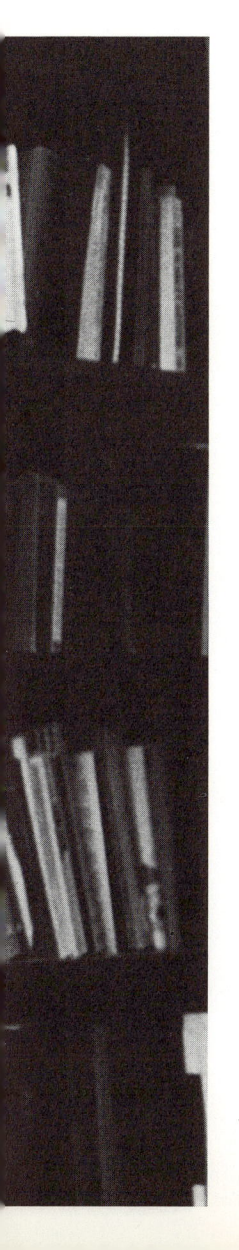

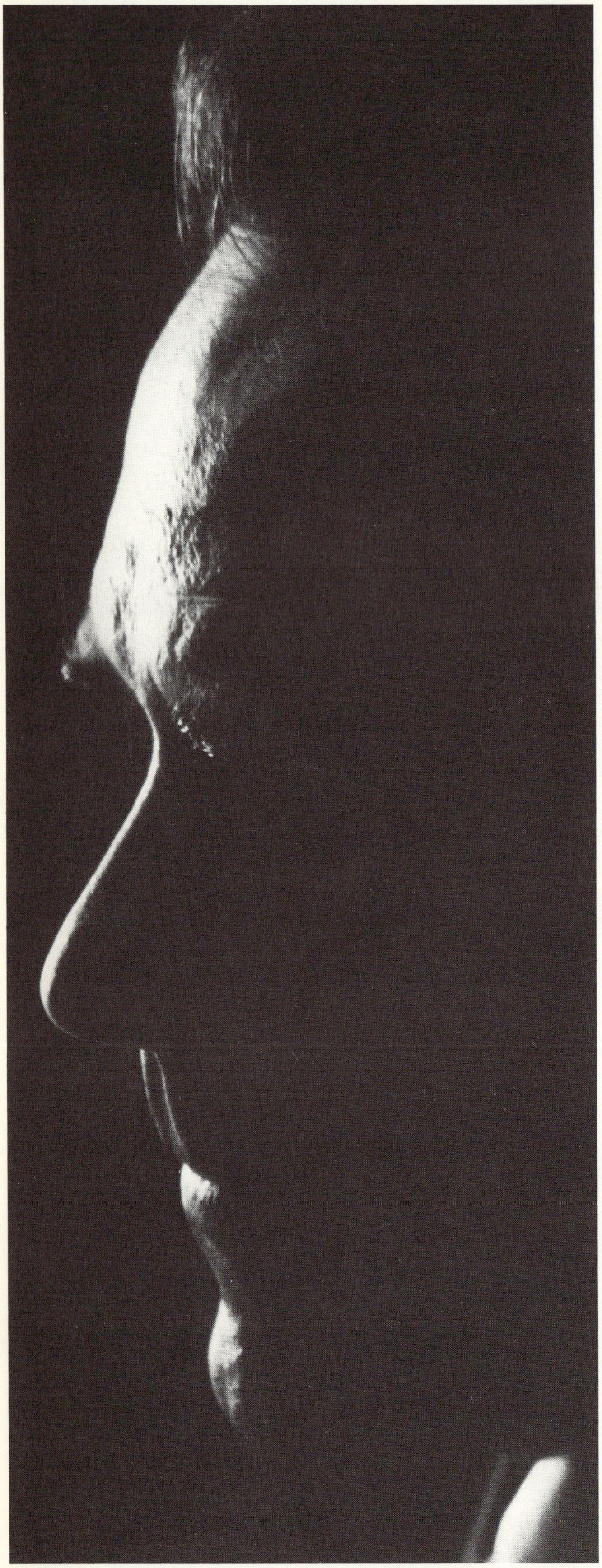

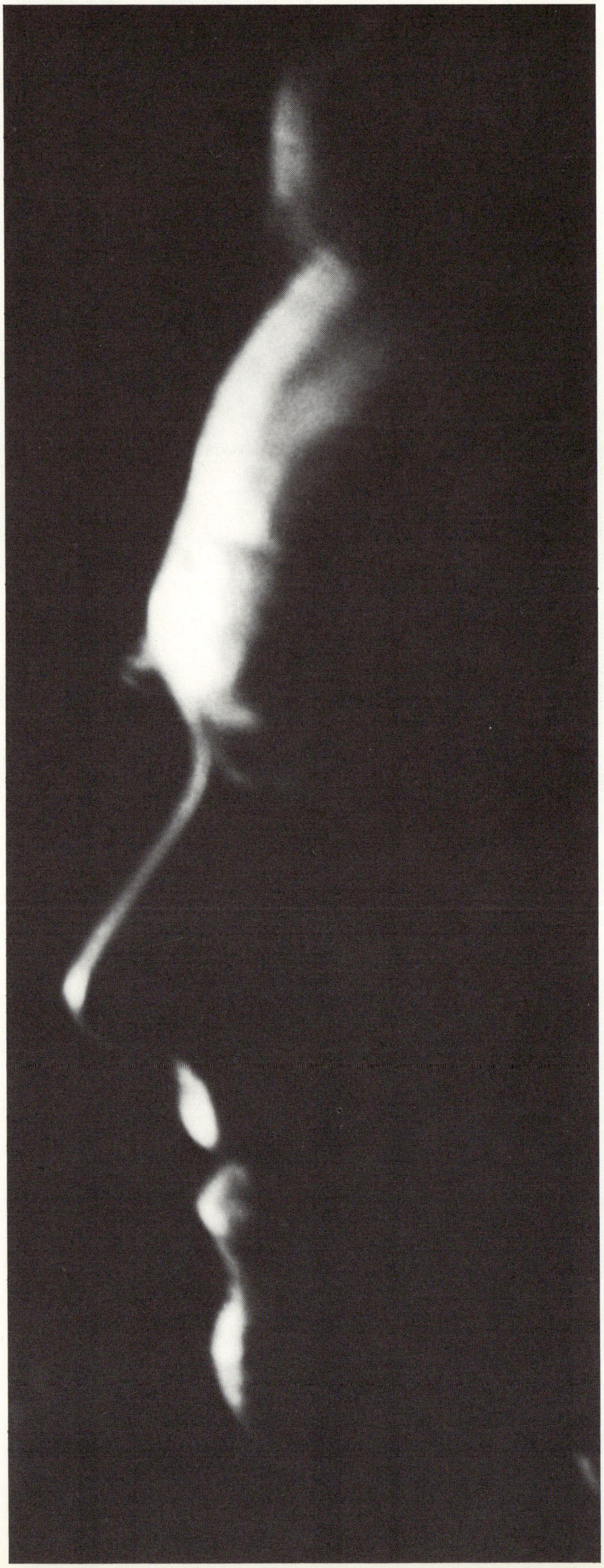

213

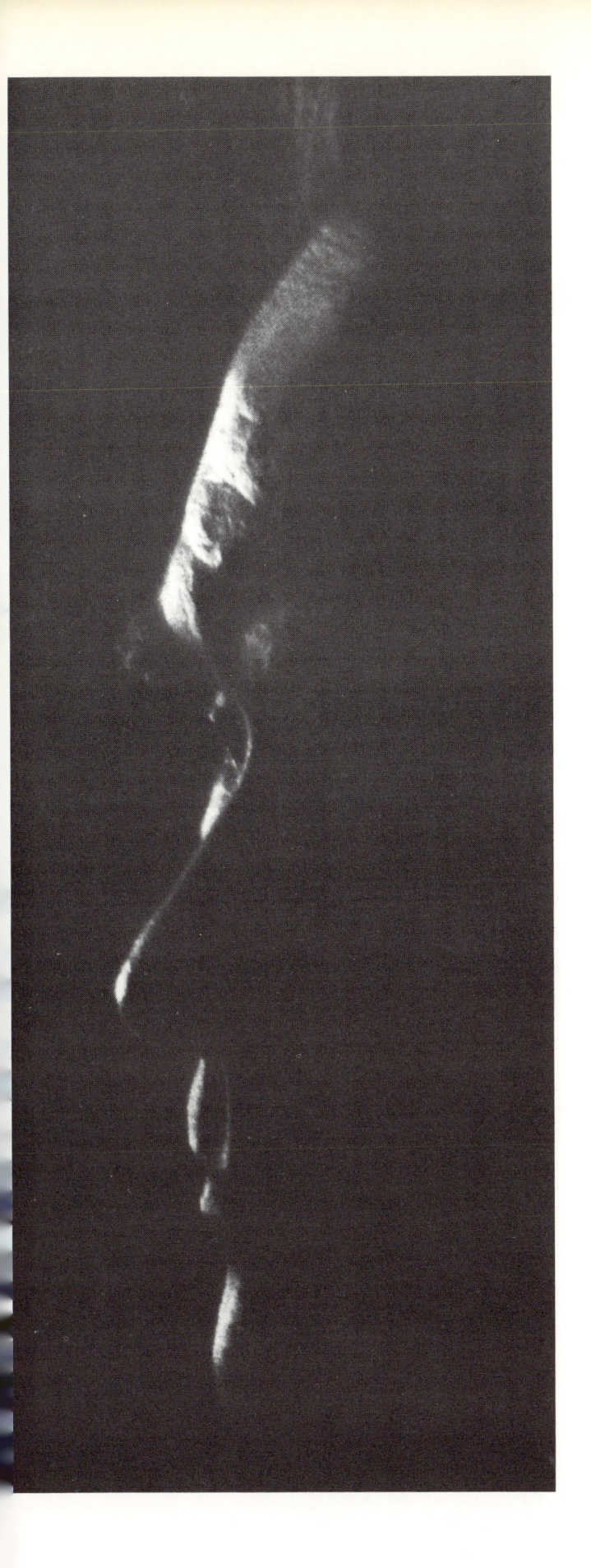

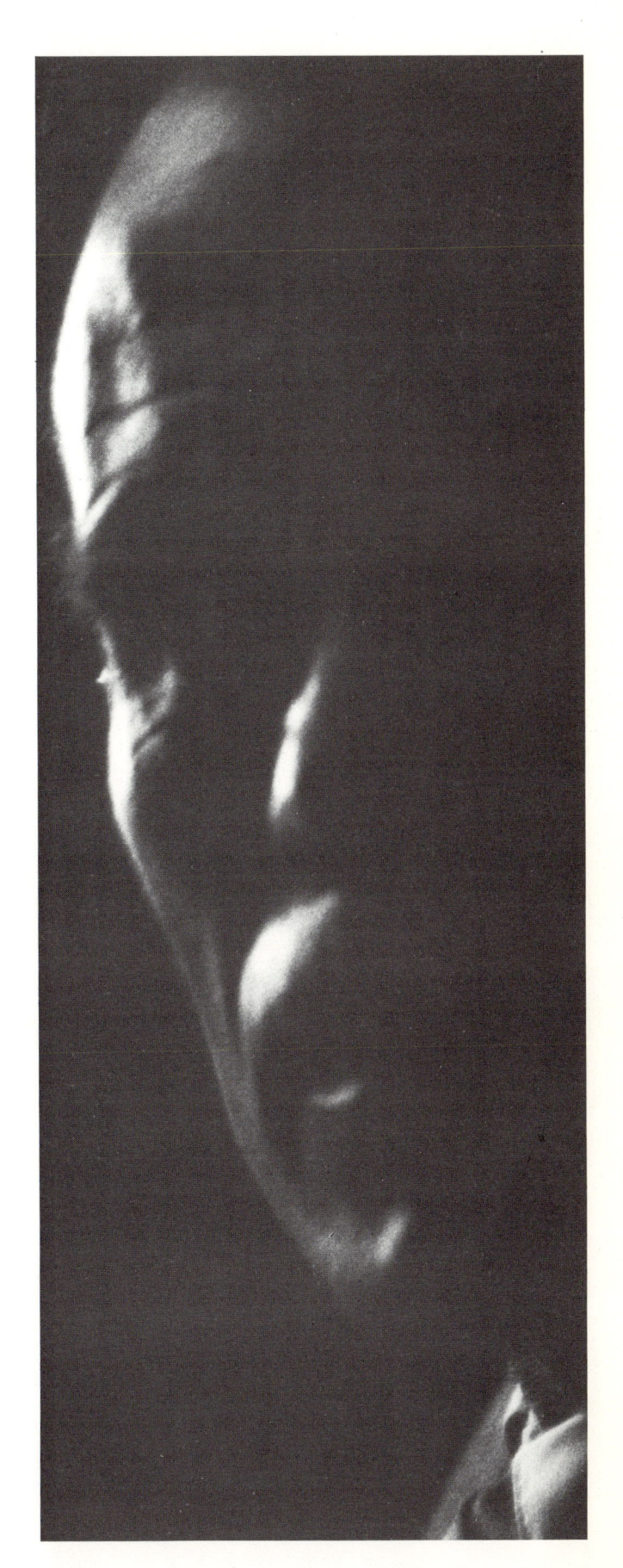

214

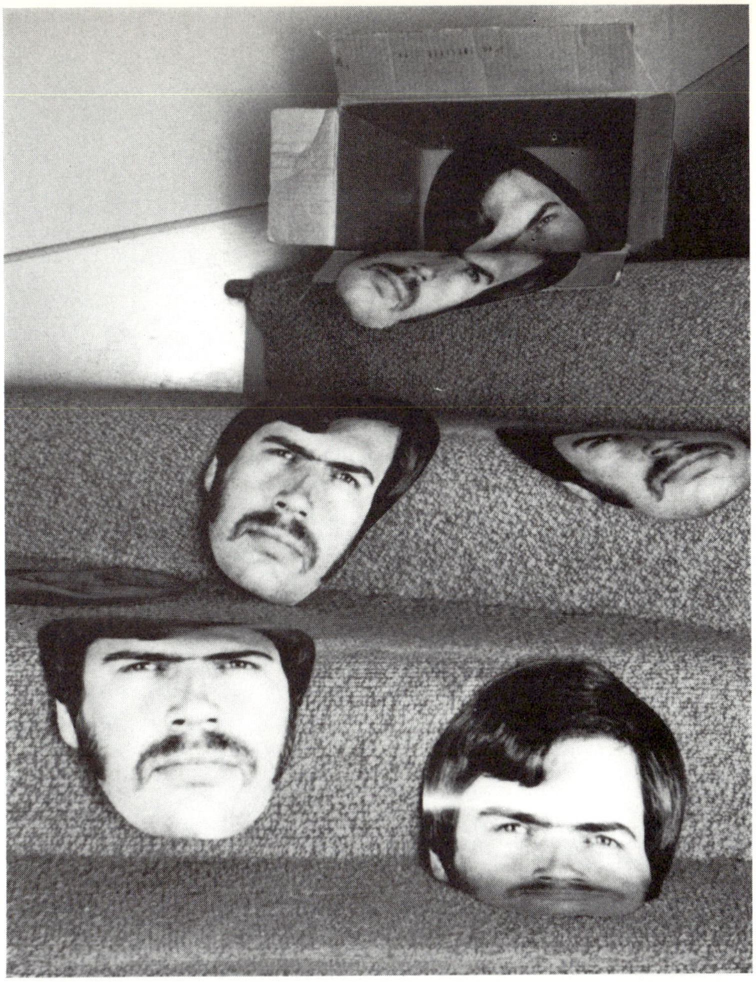

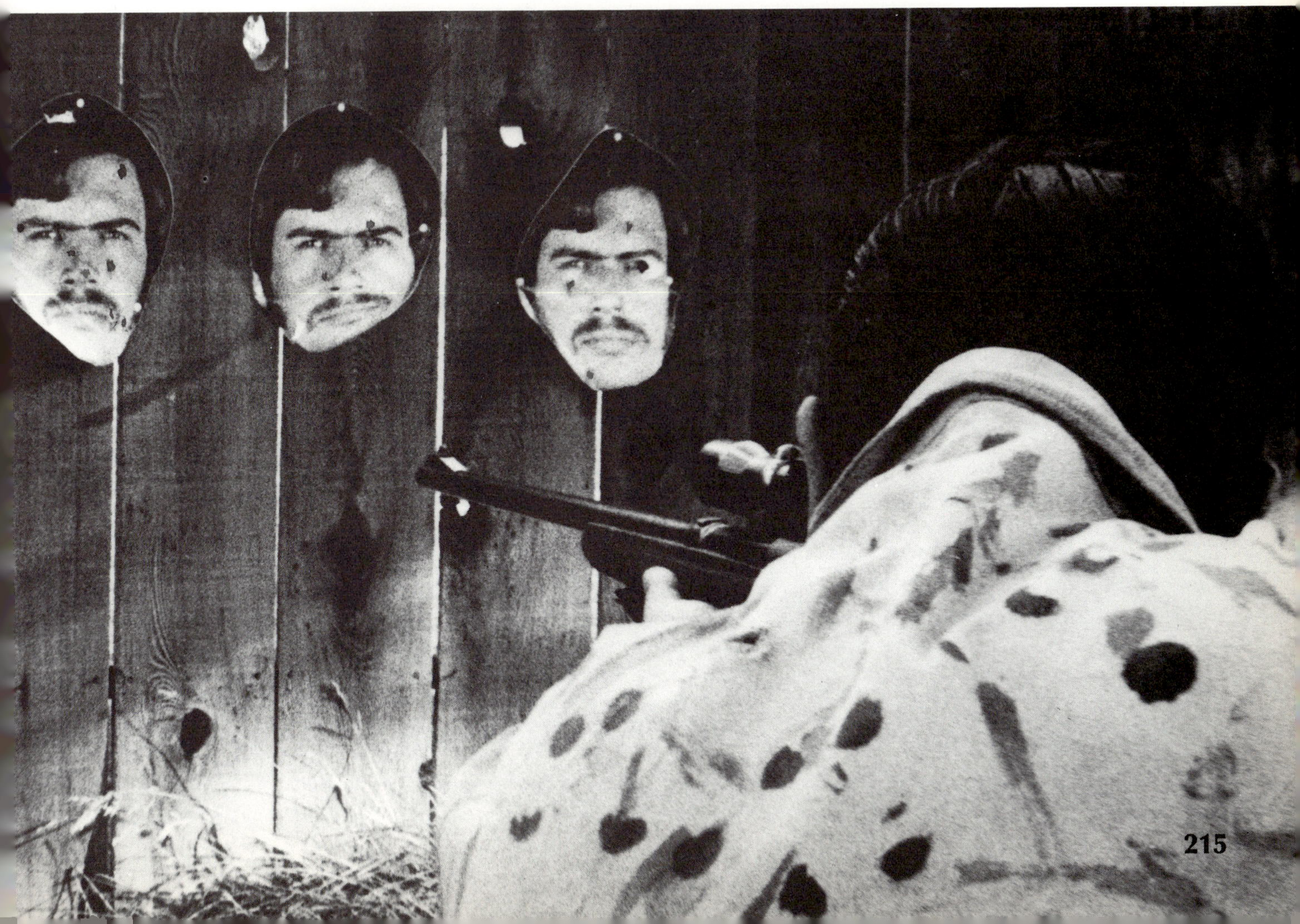

Do you really look at people? The tendency among most of us is to focus on a point a few inches from the face of the person we are talking to. Some look at the person's eyes. In either case, the rest of the features of the person are forgotten, or, worse, ignored. The main reason is that most people do not know how to observe. Also, they make assumptions about others, relying on preconceived notions, and see in the others what they want to see. And there are lots of people who refuse to "face" other people.

It would be nice if the instructor could assign his students to make an effort to observe people and understand them. But can you imagine people putting up with the scrutiny of a whole group of students making notes? Since people do not like to be stared at, the next best thing is this section; you can look at the photographs here all you want. In addition, there is a greater variety of people in these pictures than you would get in most cities.

Some of these photographs should be considered individually. Others lend themselves to being contrasted: these are printed on pages facing each other. Several need to be discussed in relation to their background. The following questions suggest ways the photographs might be considered.

Pages 194–195: Contrast these two photographs of the same person. The different lighting appears to reveal two facets of his character. Does the shadow make a difference?

Pages 196–197: These pictures of a Zulu and an American can also be contrasted—in terms of appearance, clothes, expressions, features, and so on.

Pages 198–199: Discuss this miniaturist in India and the way he maintains the tradition of miniature paintings. Look at similar paintings in art books to help you understand his work.

Pages 200–201: Two families—a father and son in Pakistan and a family riding the subway in New York. Contrast them.

Pages 202–203: Depicted here are two members of minorities in the United States—a black and an Indian. What stereotypes of the two ethnic groups are evident at first glance? Look at these two as people, as individuals, and discuss the difference in your responses.

Pages 204–205: Discuss these two photographs individually or together. The first is a scene in a New York subway and the second is a dental clinic for women in Pakistan.

Pages 206–207: Both these photographs are of scholars and they make different comments about the world of scholarship. What are these comments and in what respect do they differ from each other?

Pages 208–209: Here is a whole subway car full of people to observe, compare, and discuss.

Page 210: There is information in the background of the picture to tell you about the profession of the subject. This is the easy part of the assignment. The difficult part is to take into account the hand. In looking at a person, most people ignore his hands, among other things. What does a hand reveal about a person? In answering this question, begin with this picture.

Page 211: Where would you expect to find a beautiful young lady? Does her being in a tree make a difference in the way you look at her?

Pages 212–213: Four different photographs of the same person, all of them lit with a single light source. Yet each picture appears to reveal a different person. What makes the difference: the lighting, the angle, the expressions, or the way you look at them?

Pages 214–215: These three photographs are an attempt to portray graphically the way people are treated nowadays. Consider each picture individually, or all three together, and discuss the implications of the three portrayals. This assignment can be expanded into a lengthy paper if the student does research on man's treatment of man, either historically or in the contemporary world.

IMAGINATION

IMAGINATION

220

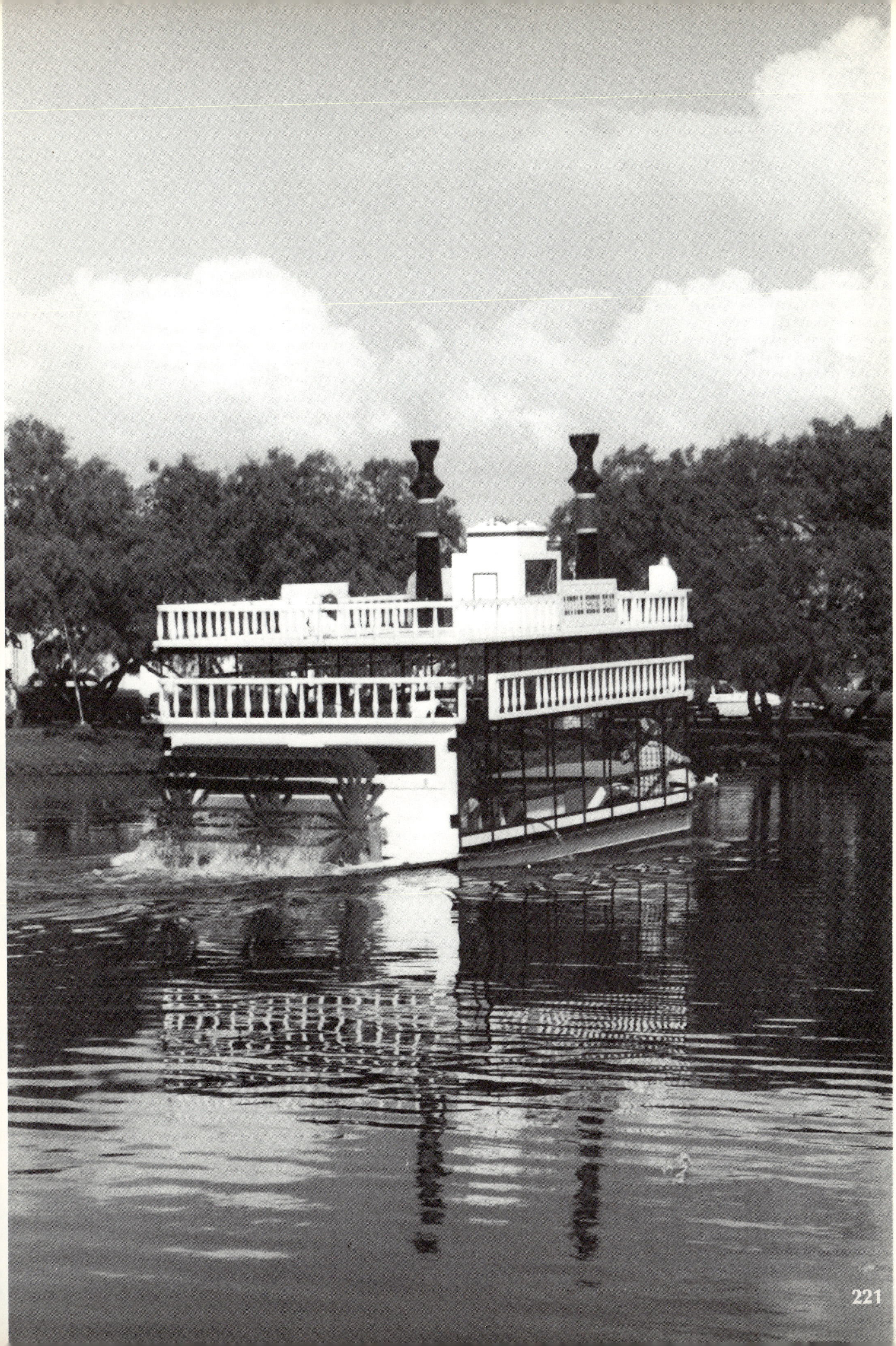

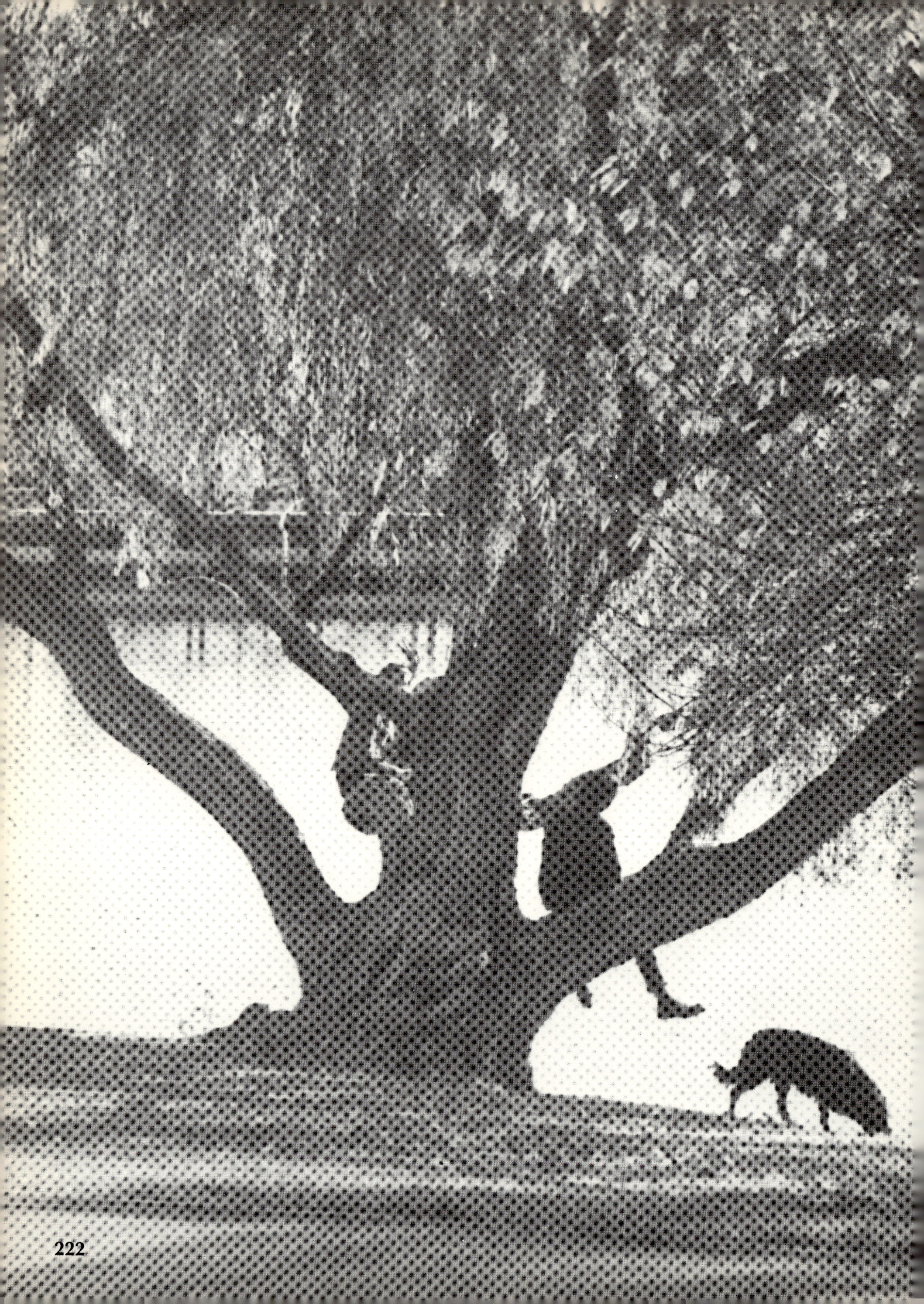

223

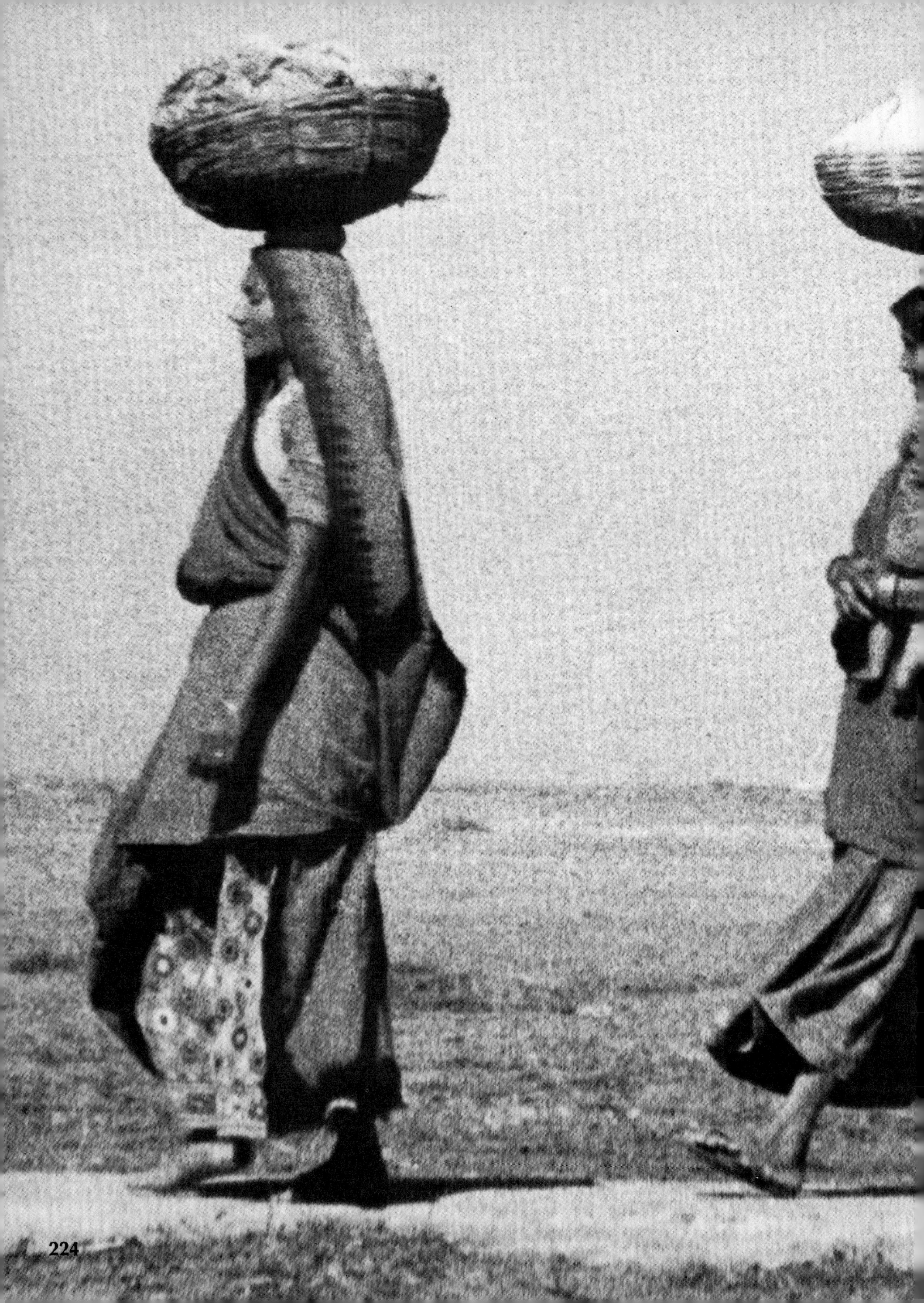

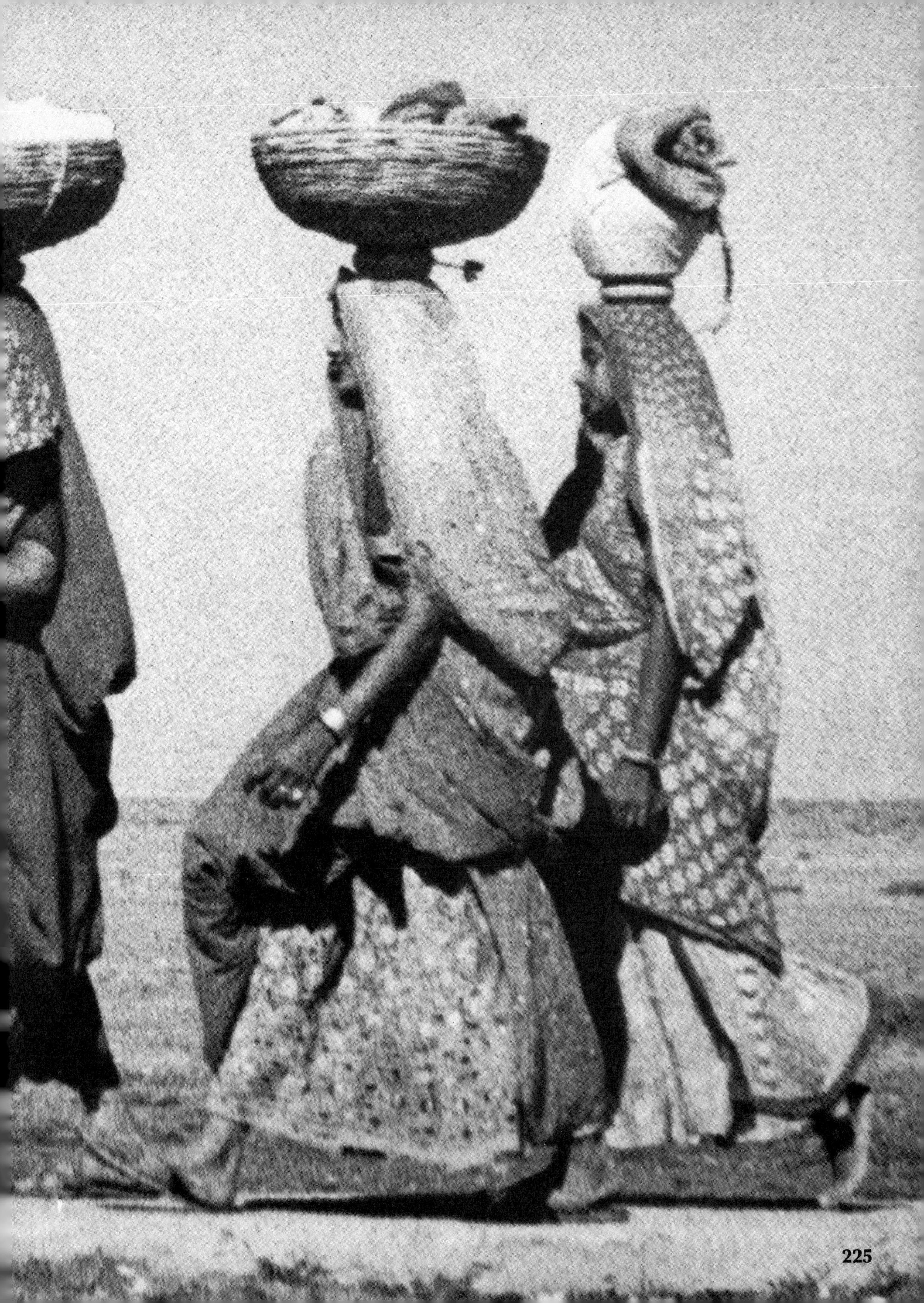

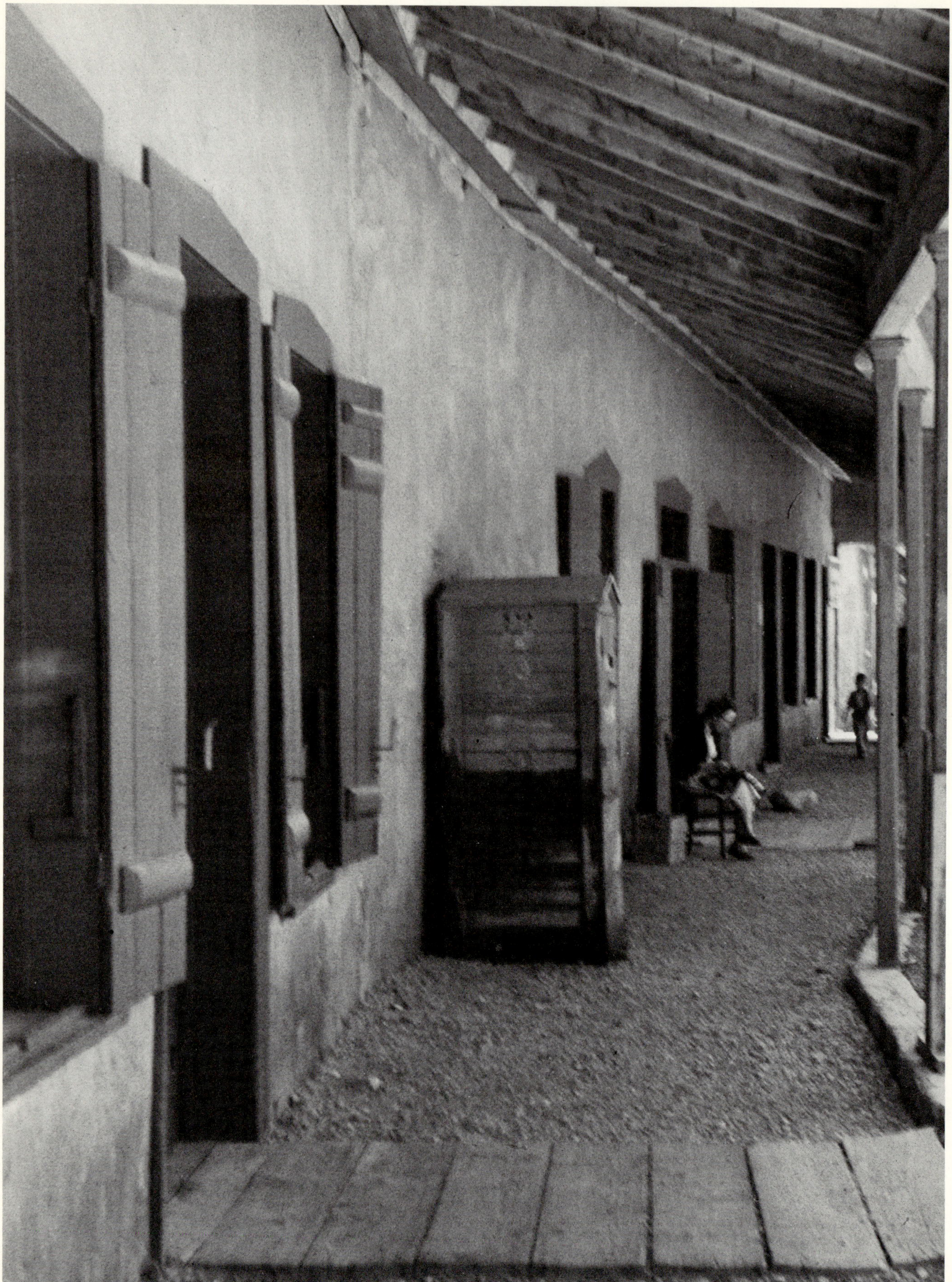

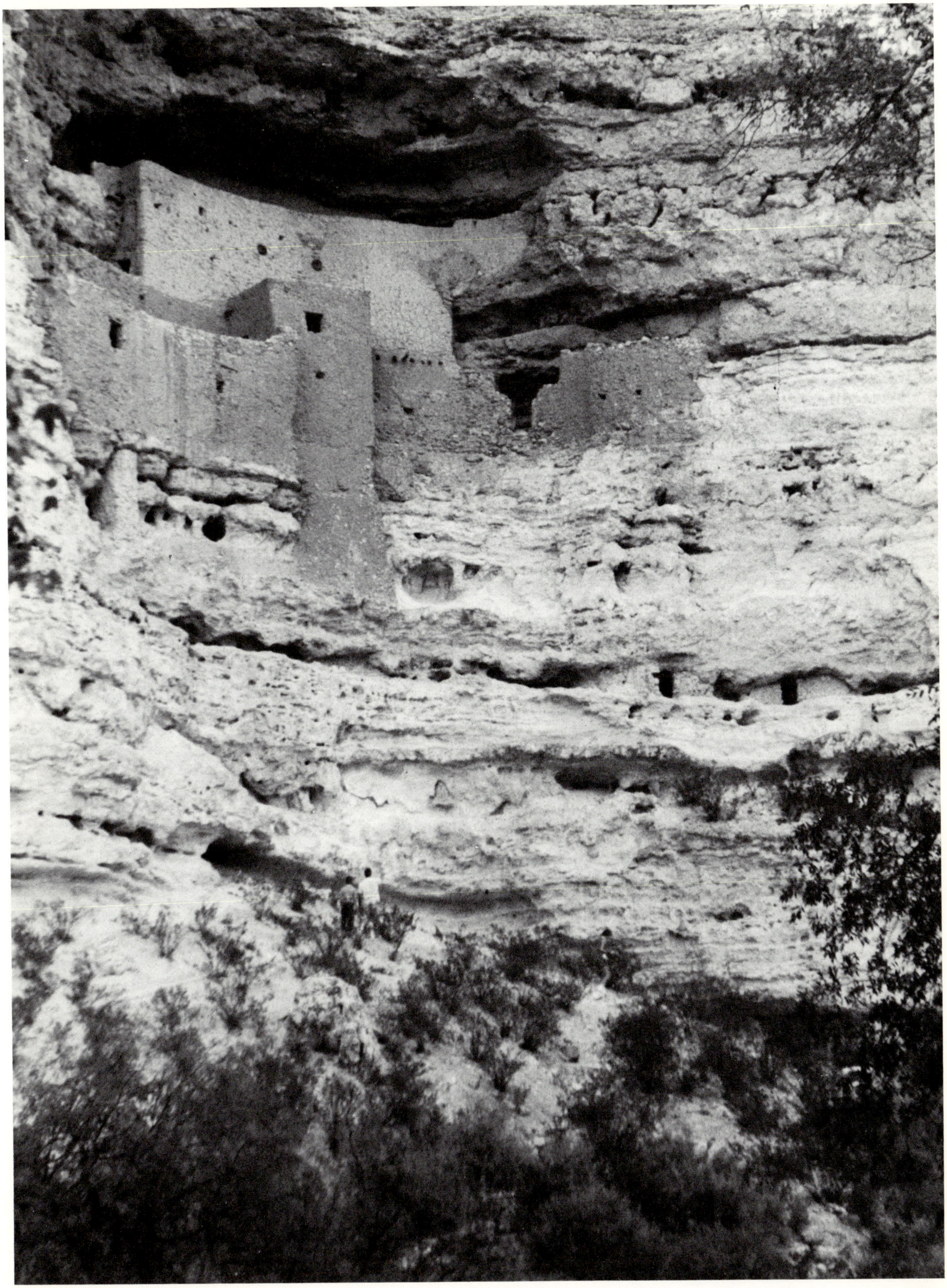

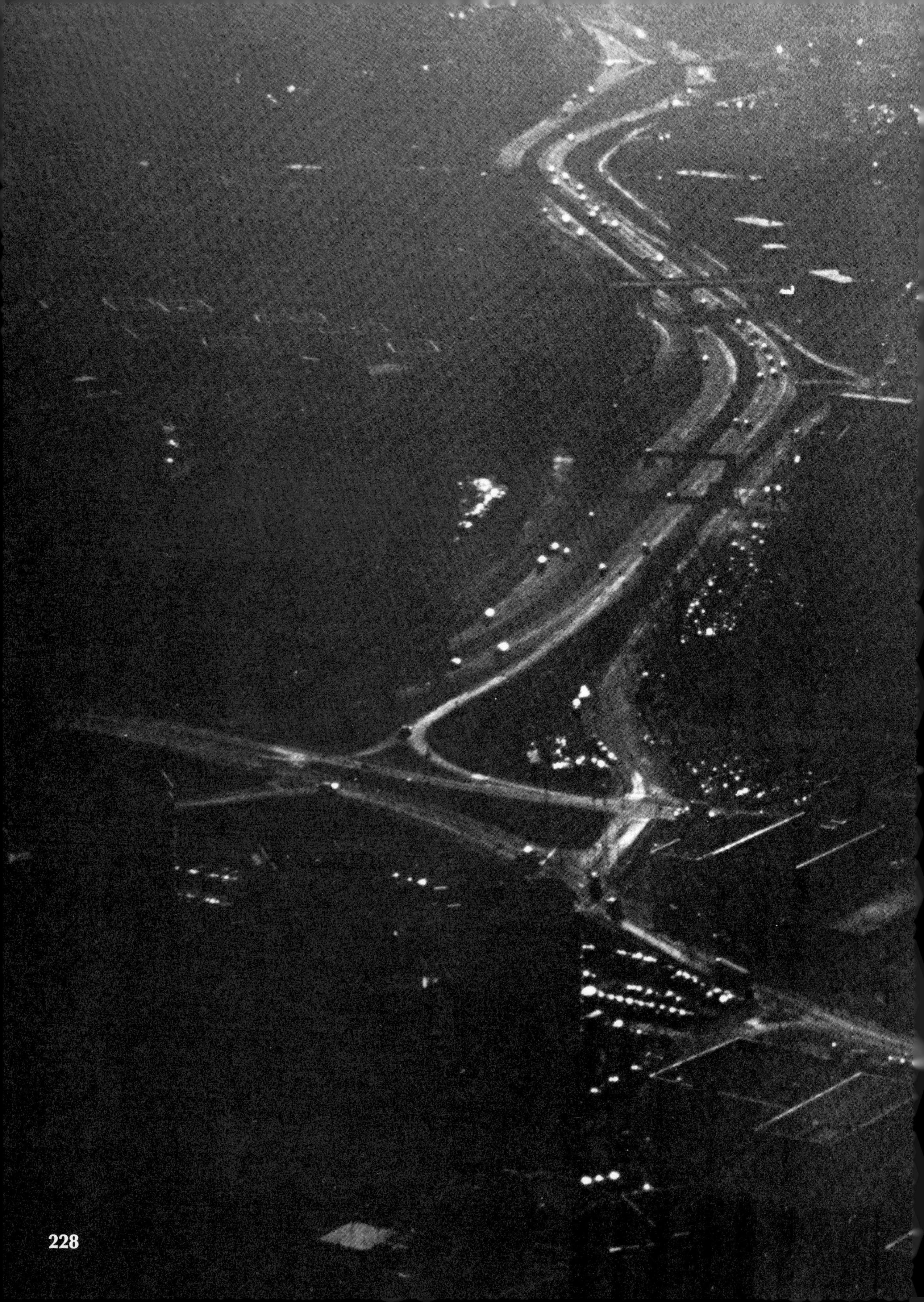

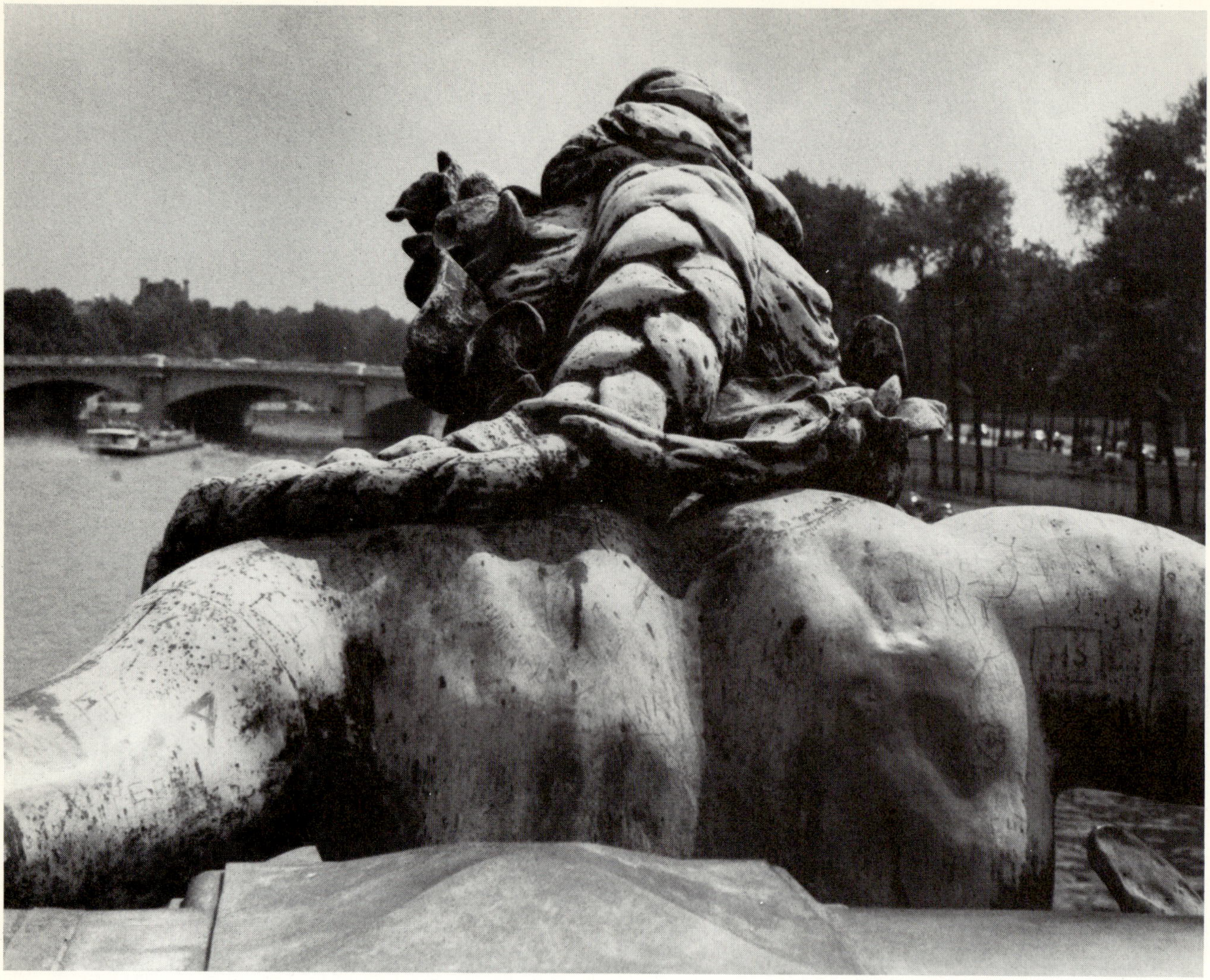

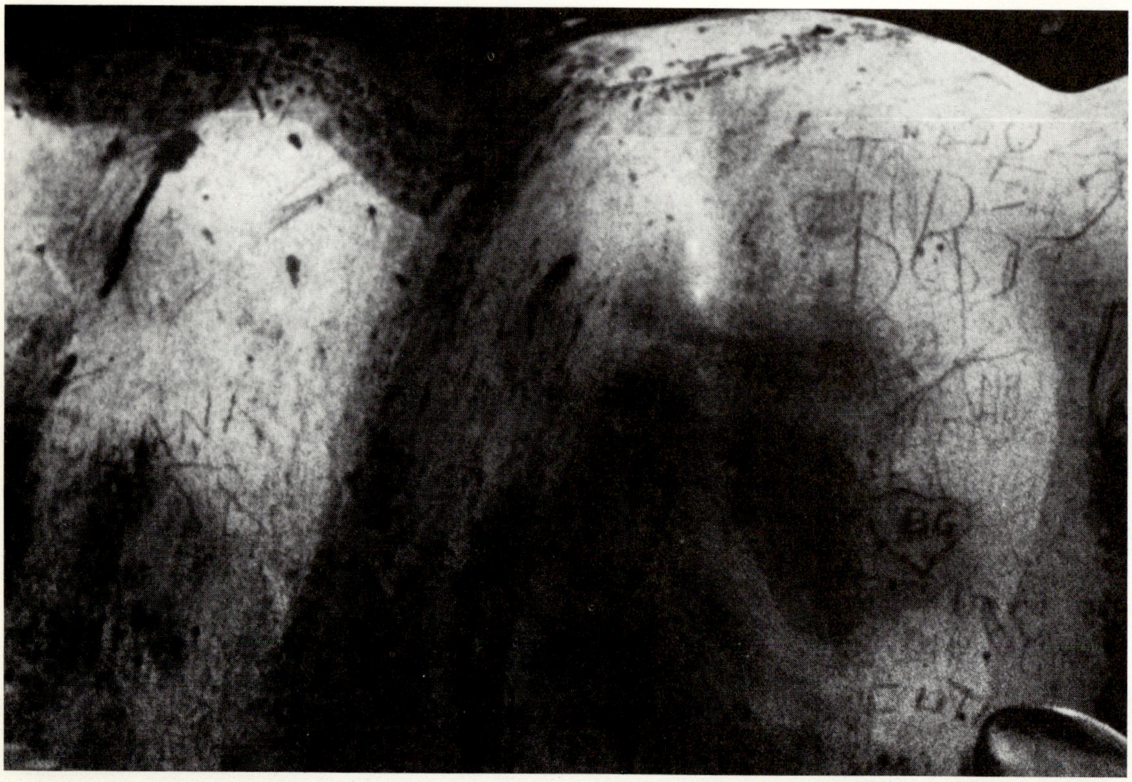

231

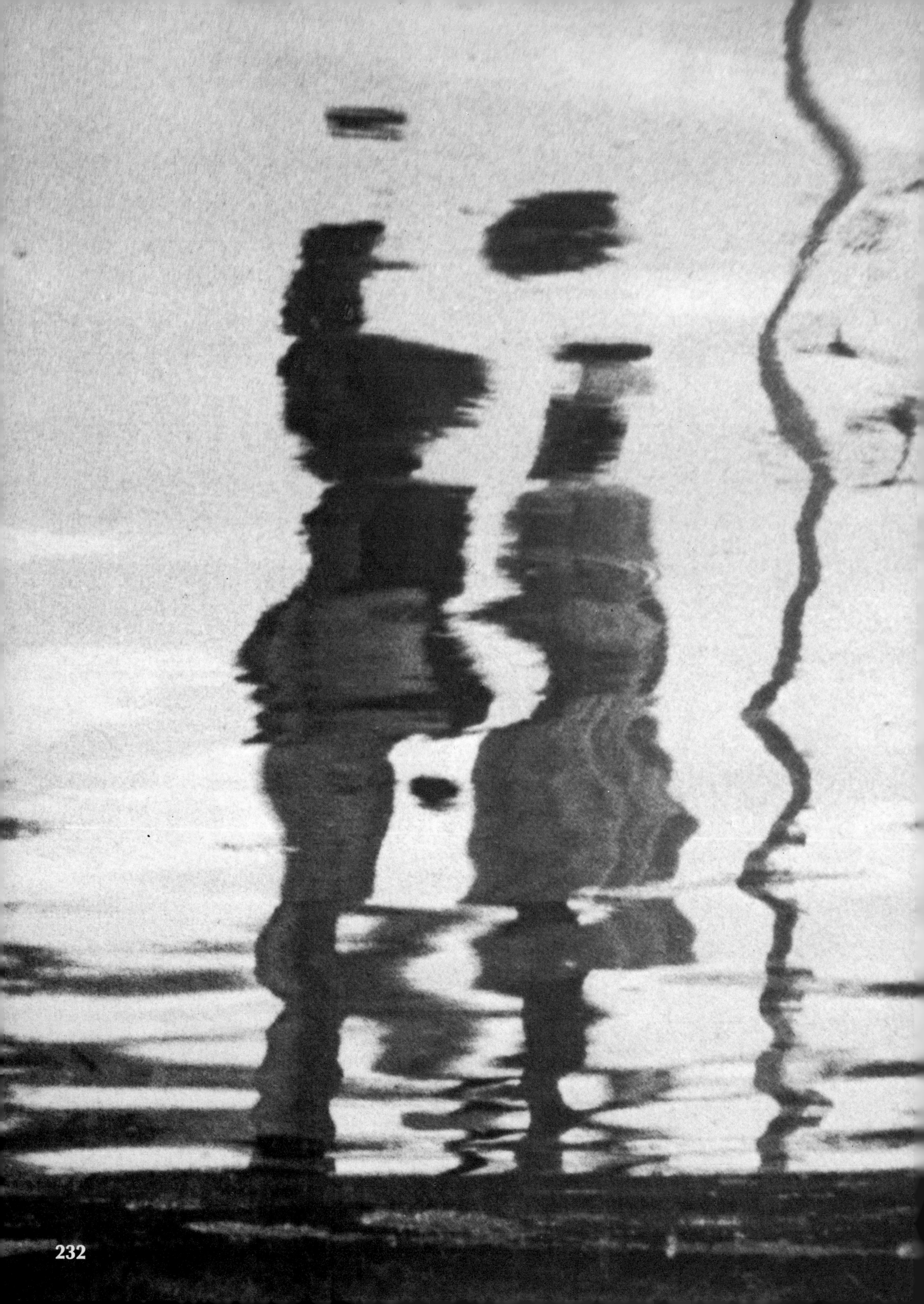

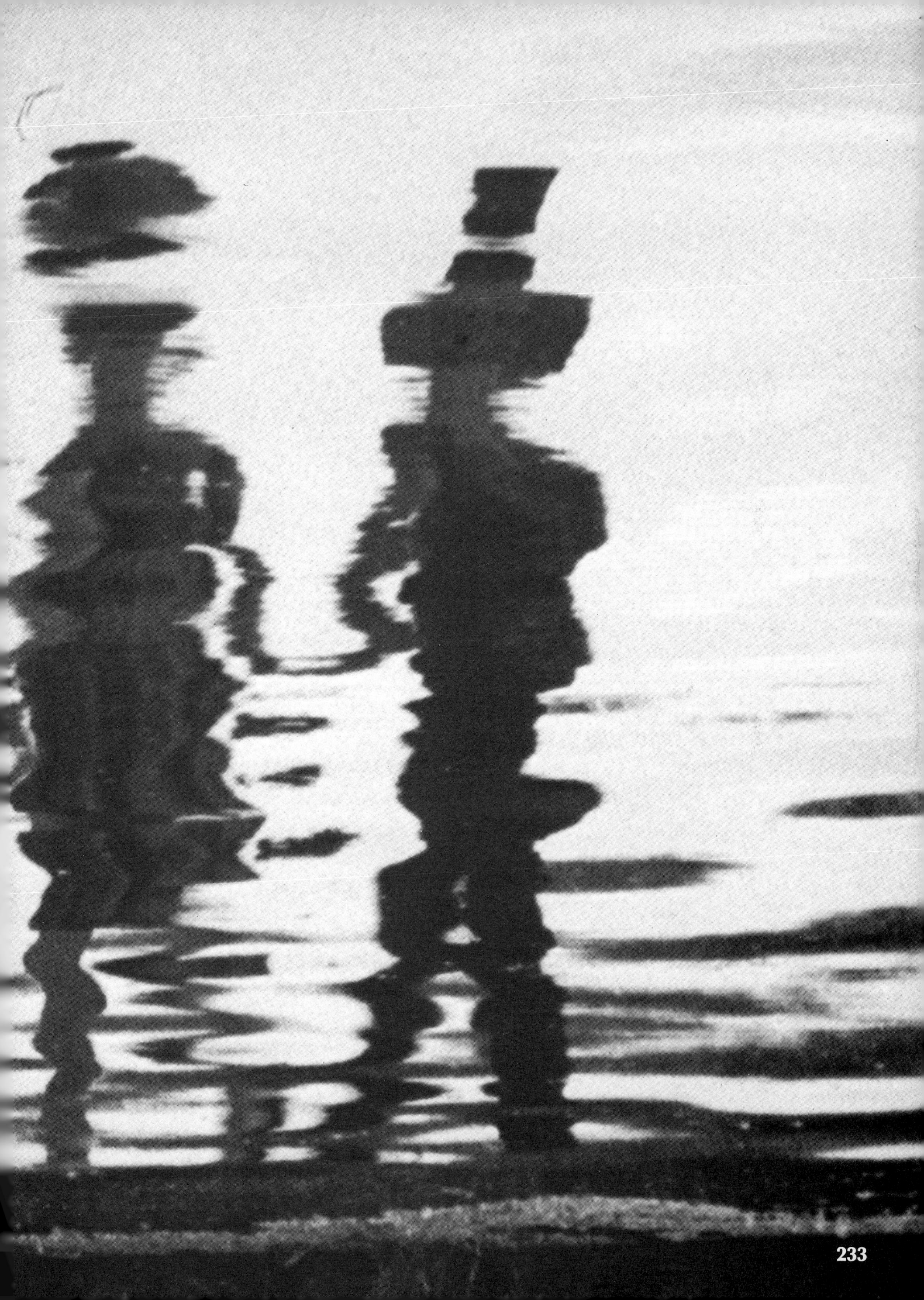

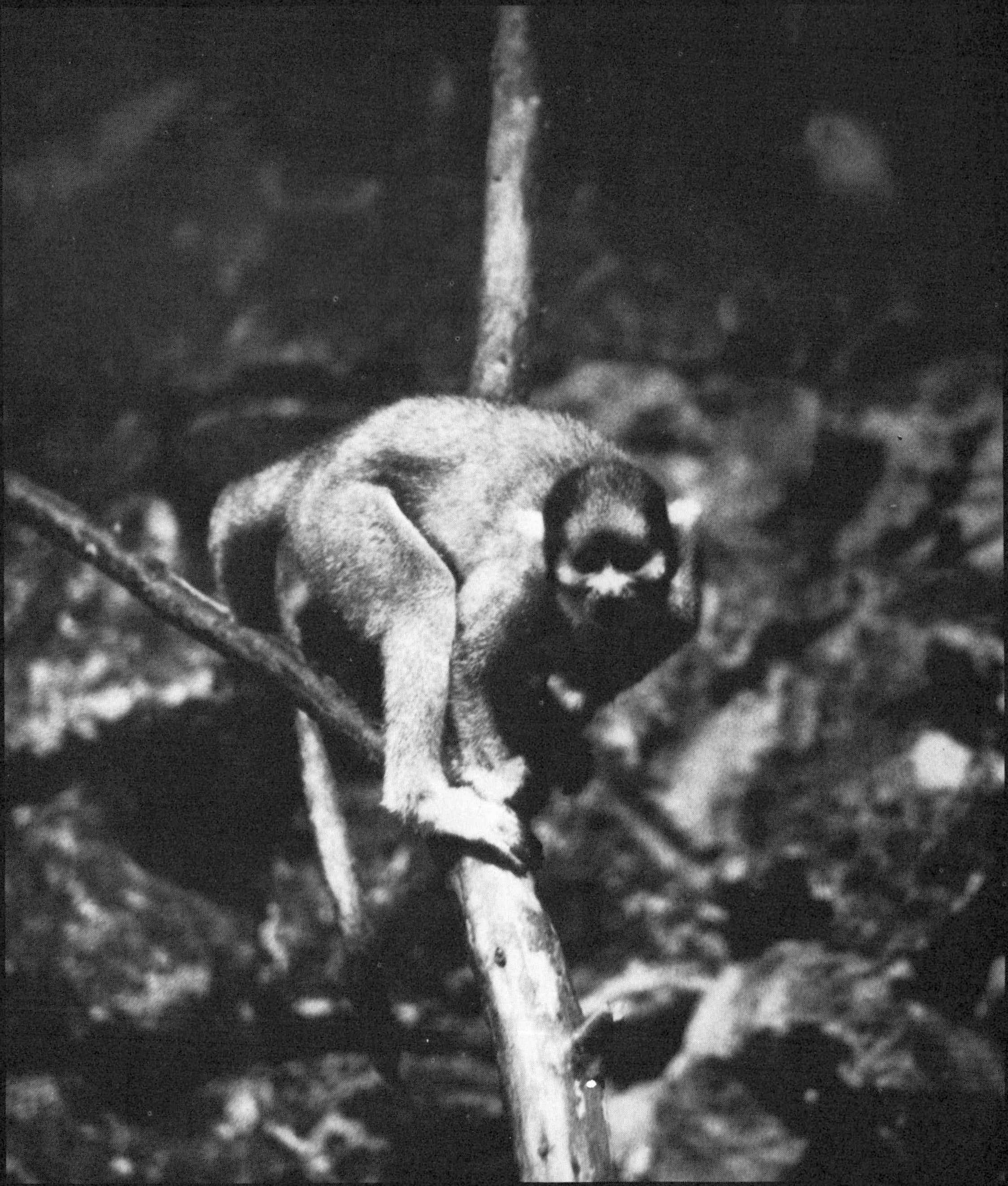

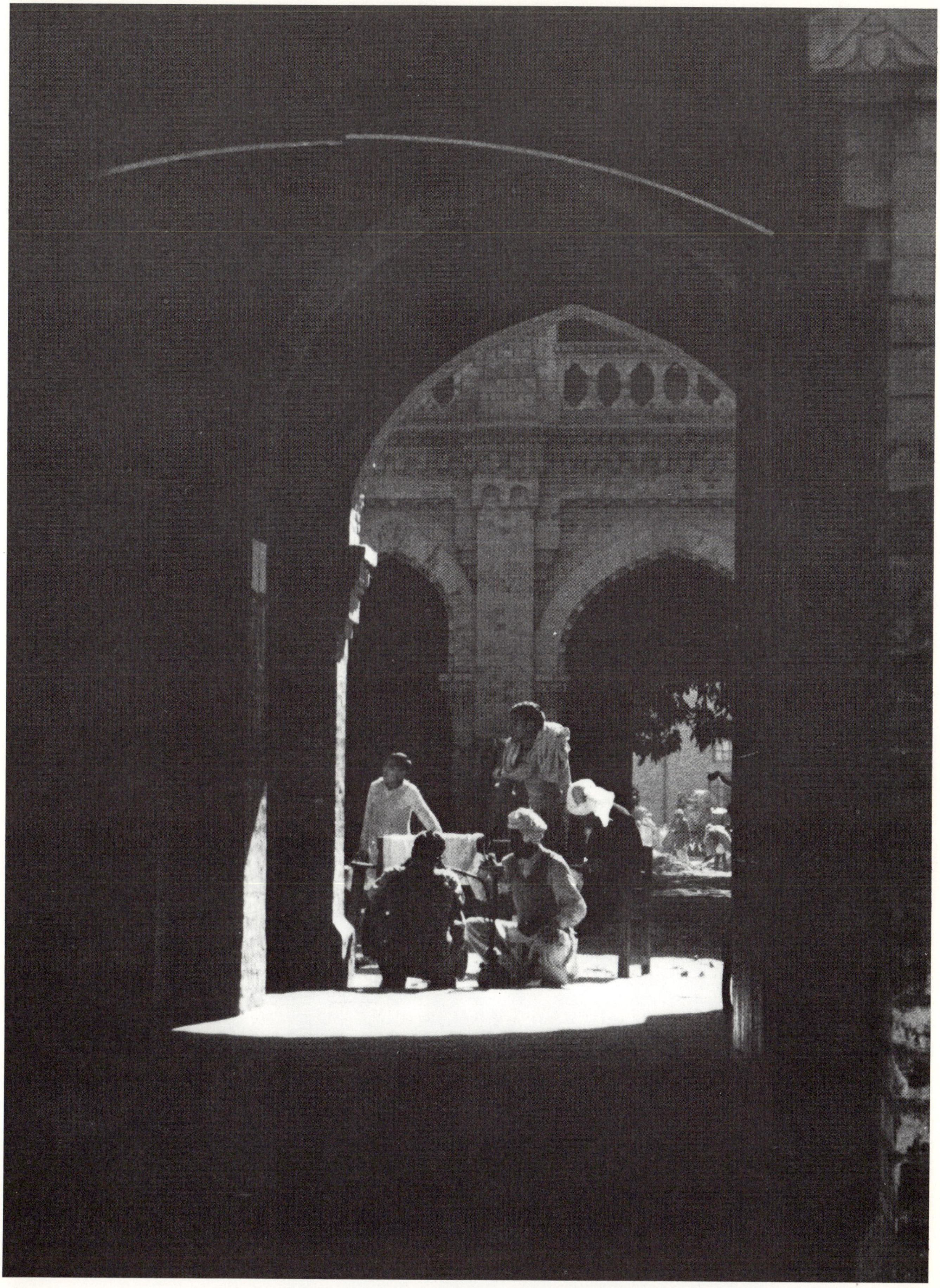

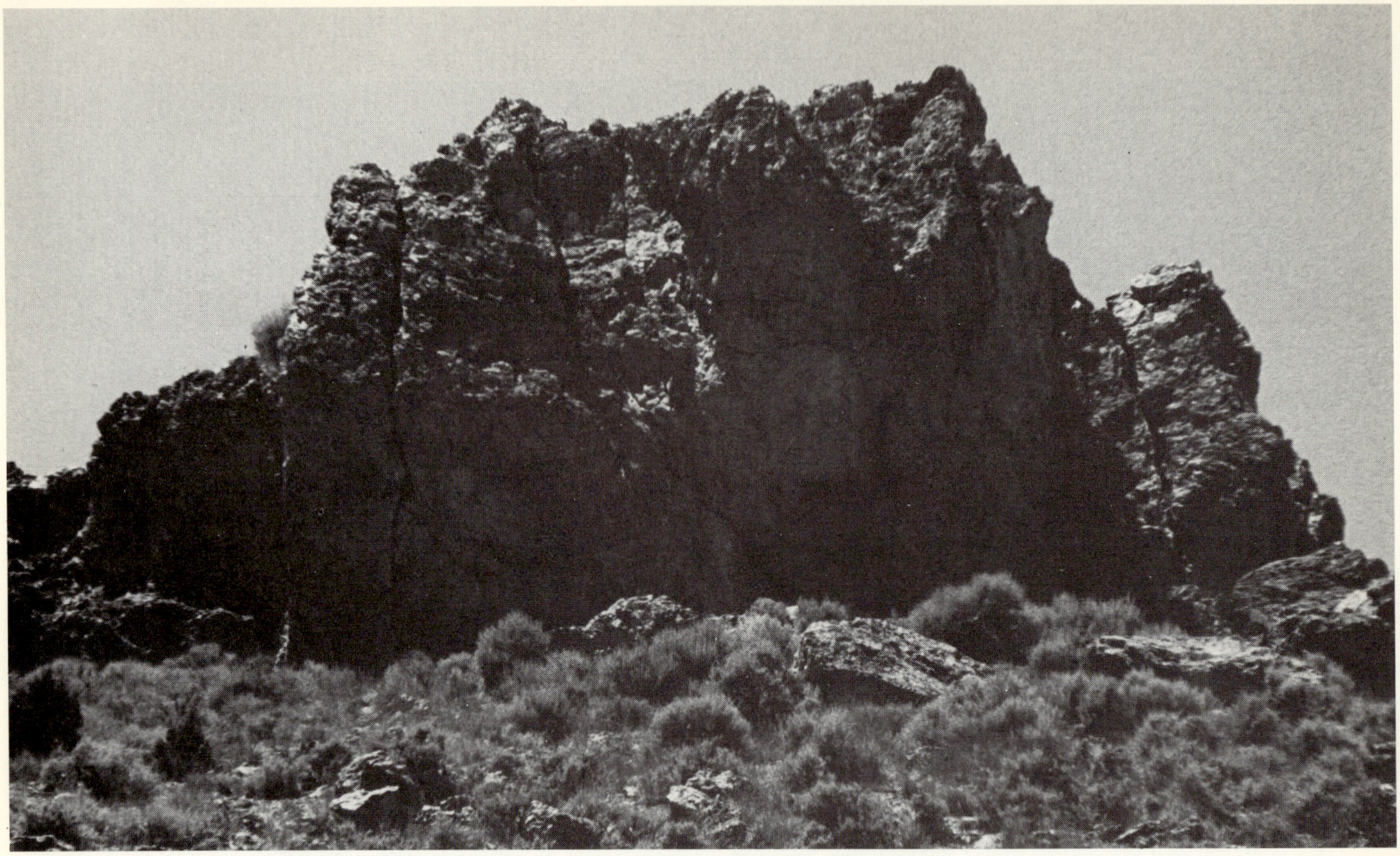

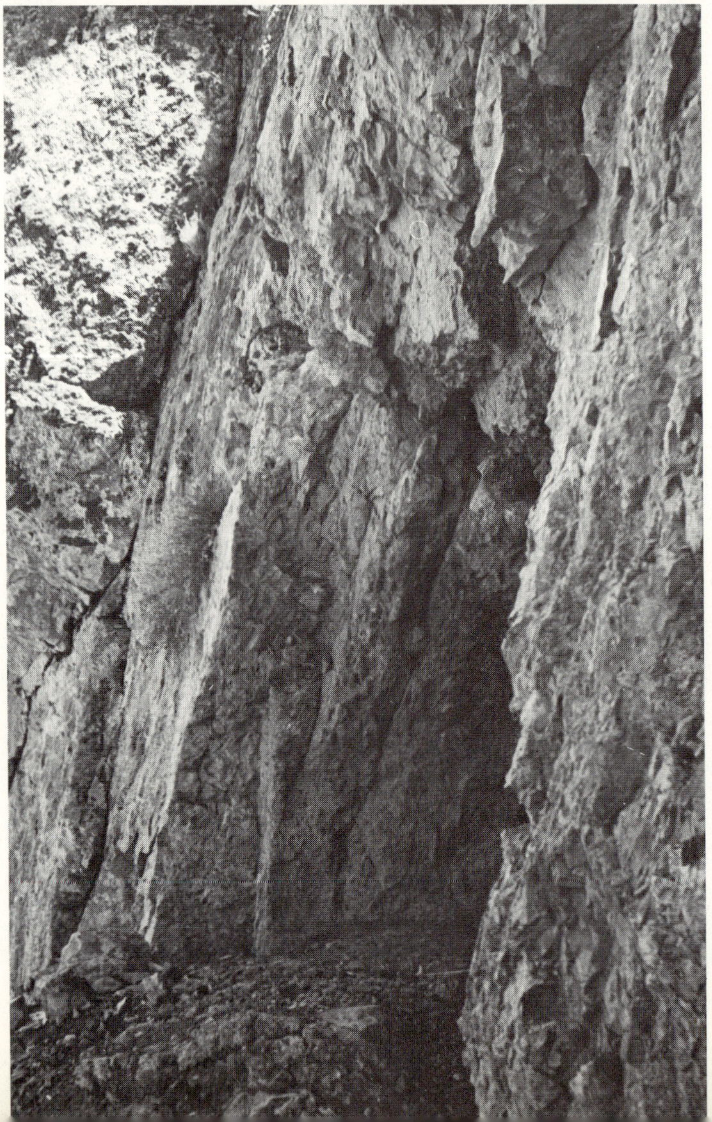

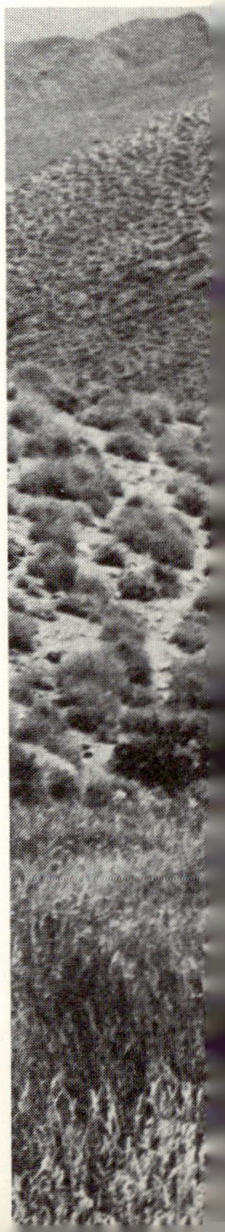

237

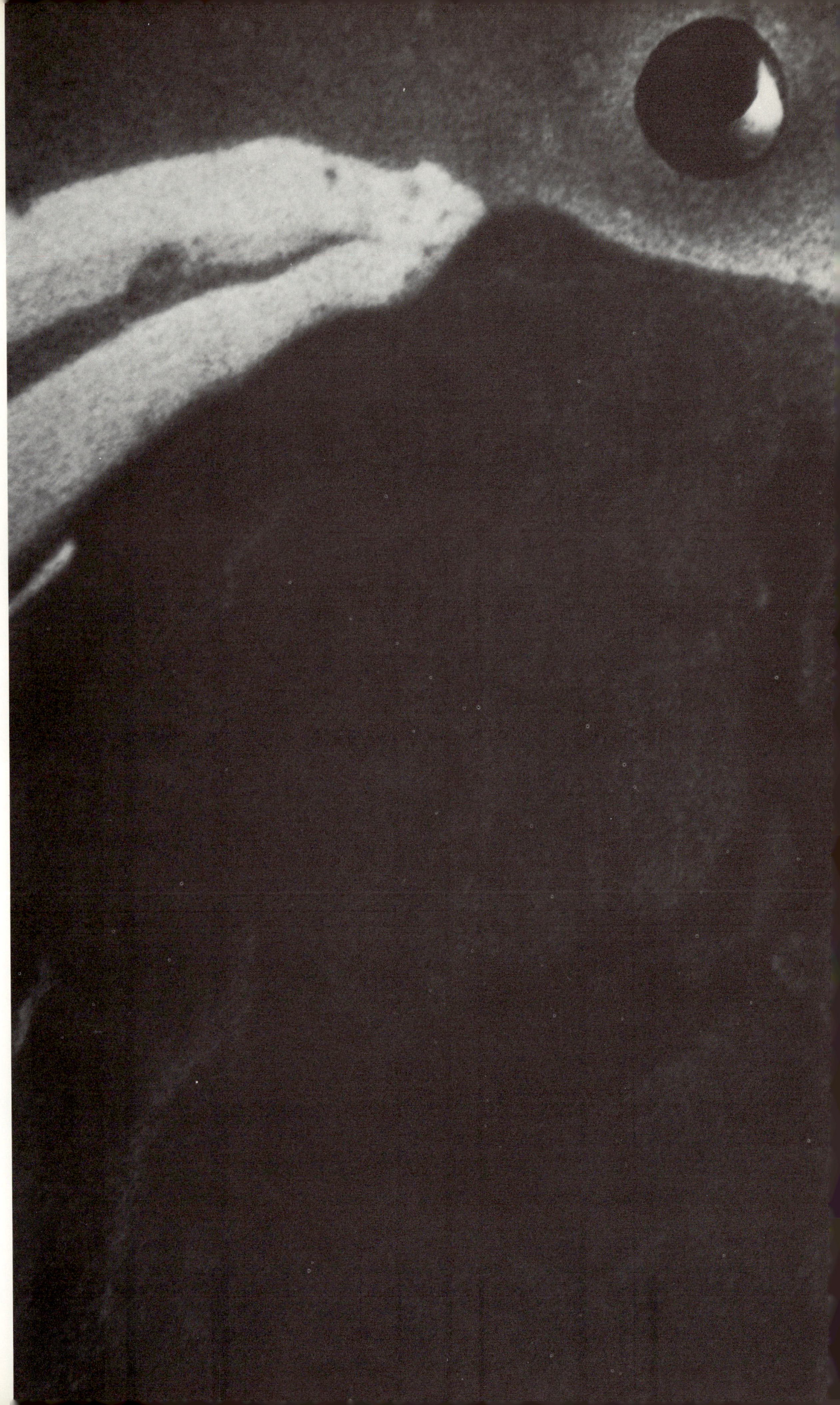

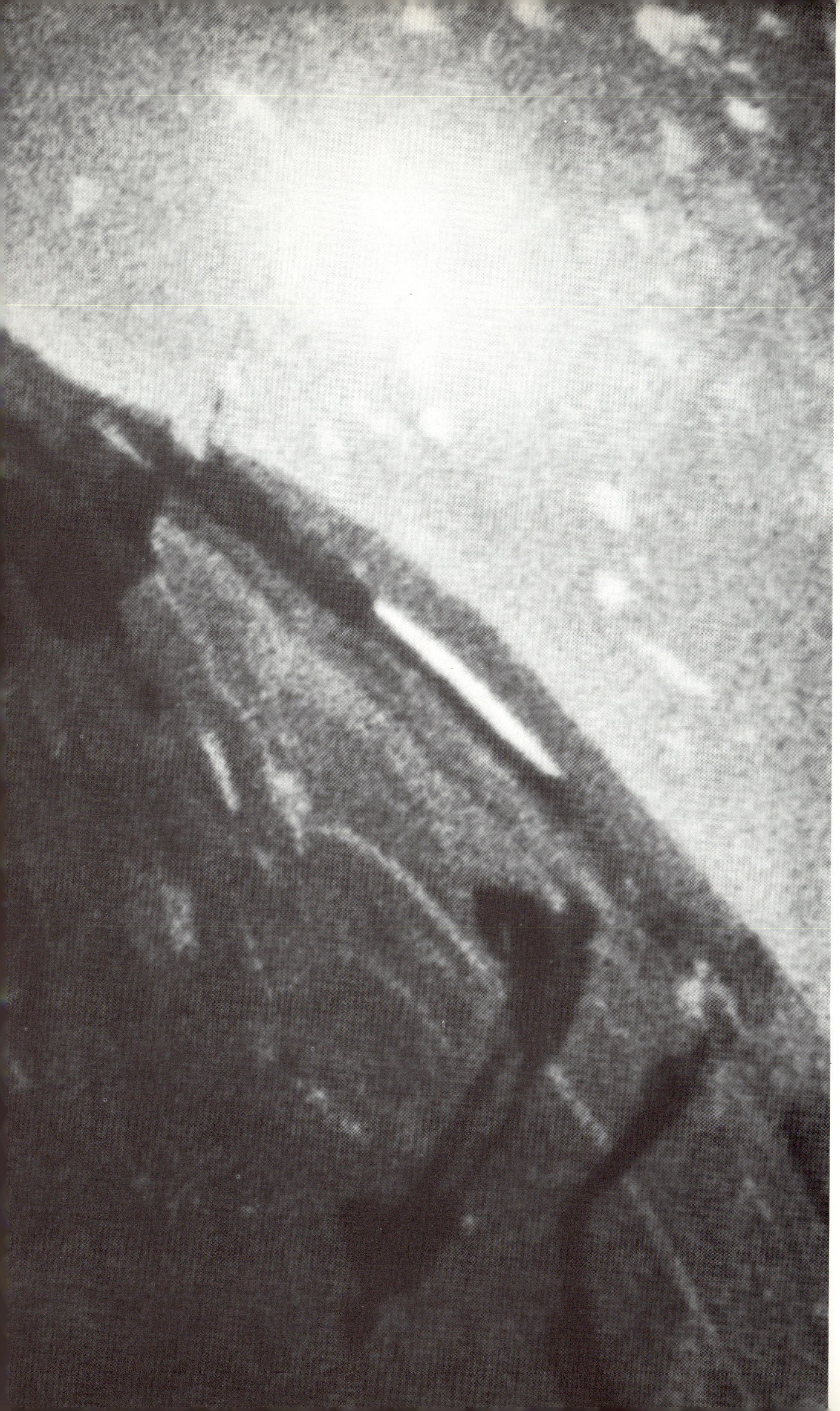

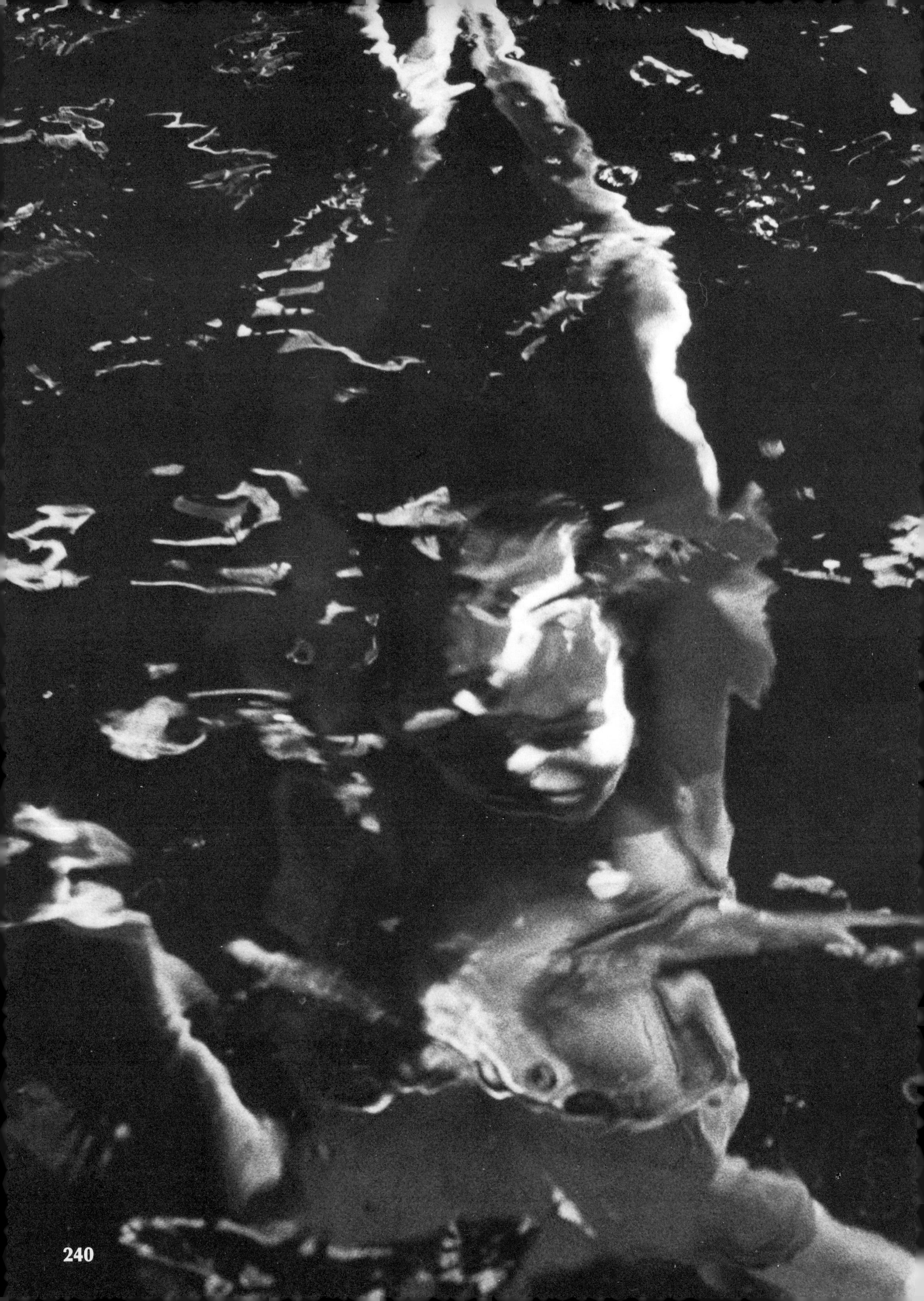

One thing a good photograph always does is stimulate the imagination. One image leads to others and then to more images. Some of the pictures in this section are of this kind. They serve as starting points for voyages of the mind's eye. There are other pictures, however, that rely on a person's imagination for interpretation. Such photographs are rare and the very few I have are included here.

It must be emphasized, though, that this section has been purposely put toward the end of the book; the lessons of the previous sections are necessary if the photographs here are to sufficiently stimulate the imagination. The most important lesson is, of course, observation. In considering these photographs, the student must at first observe closely.

Page 220: The subject of this color photograph always acts as a spark to the imagination. Why?

Page 221: Imagination is the most significant feature of this situation. What does the subject of this picture tell you about the imagination?

Pages 222–225: Examine these photographs closely. We are so used to filling, mentally, the minute blank spaces of a picture that we forget the function of the imagination in helping our eyes perceive. Discuss, after doing the necessary research.

Page 226: This is the hometown of Billy the Kid. How different is this picture from the one perpetuated by Hollywood movies of the Old West? You have to use your imagination in picturing the stereotyped Hollywood picture. Use your imagination further by picturing what life must have really been like in a town like this.

Page 227: Indian cave dwellings in Arizona. Imagine yourself living in one of these dwellings and describe such a life.

Pages 228–229: Have you, on entering a strange town or city, wondered where all the people you see are going? Put yourself into this picture: you are in an airplane, about to land in a big city. Let your imagination wonder about the cars you see here.

Pages 230–231: These pictures appear in the sequence in which I took them in Paris. I asked what the statues would do to the tourists who carved their initials all over the backs of the statues. The last picture was the answer I got. Make wide use of your imagination in writing about the situation in the form of a story.

Pages 232–233: What is this a picture of?

Page 234: What is life like for this creature, caged up day and night?

Page 235: Picture yourself going beyond these gates in a city in India. What would you find?

Pages 236–237: An Indian cave dwelling in Nevada. The first picture is of the cave, the second of the entrance, the third a view from the cave, and the fourth an area below the cave. Imagine what life must have been like in such a dwelling.

Pages 238–239: Outer Space? The End of the World? Fantasy? Let your imagination decide. Describe the picture from the viewpoint of your imagination.

Page 240: What's happening here?

MISCELLA

NEOUS

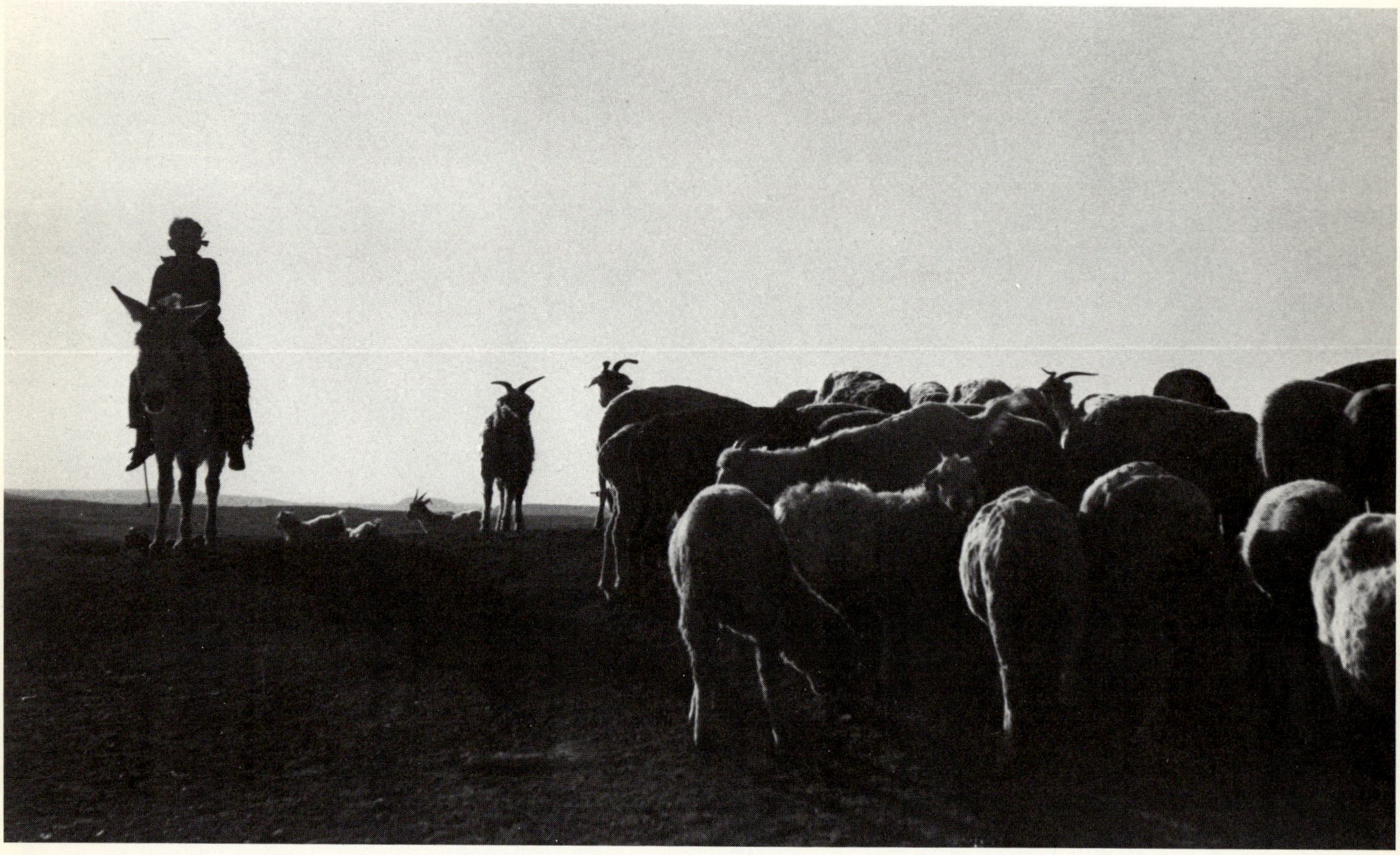

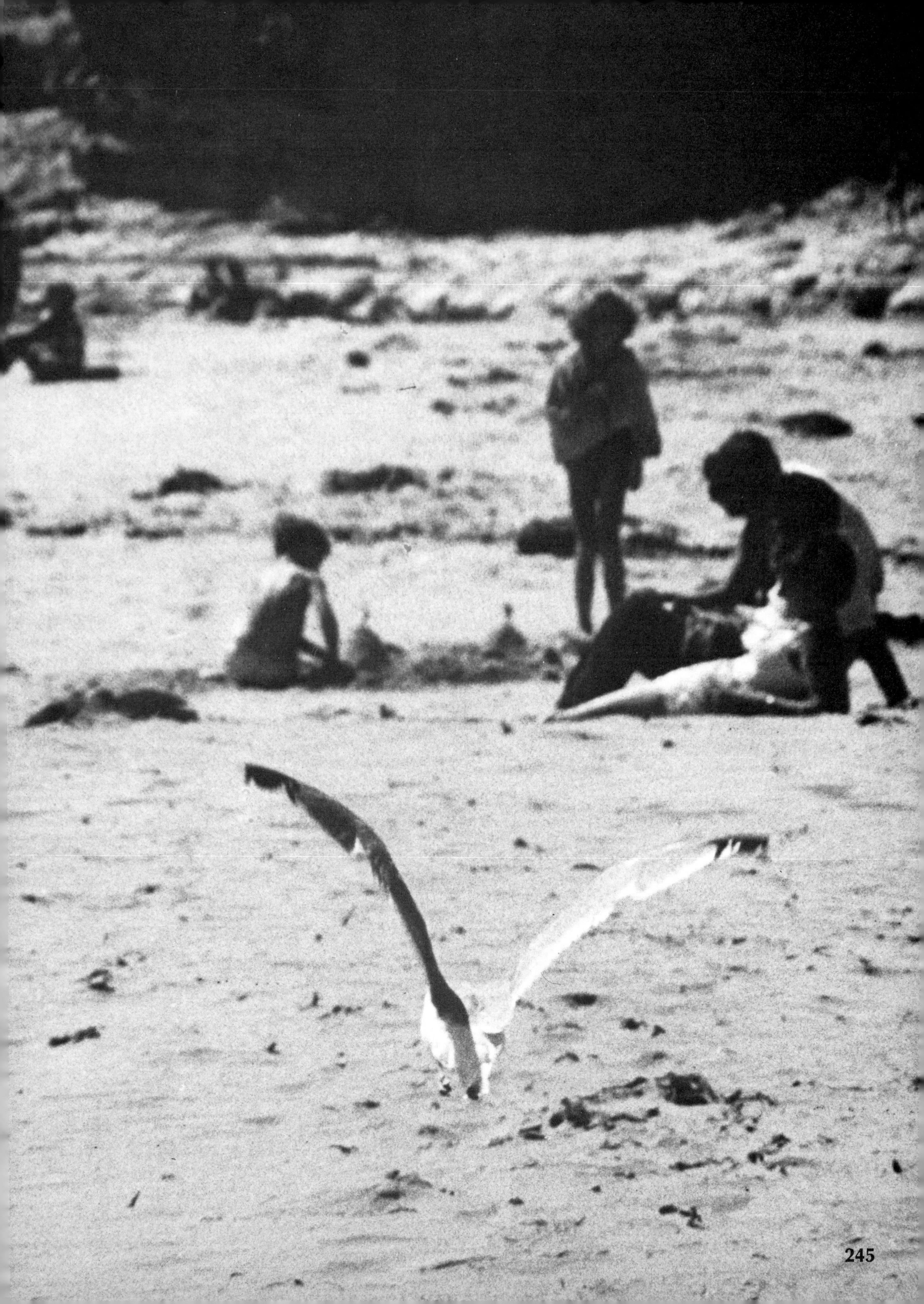

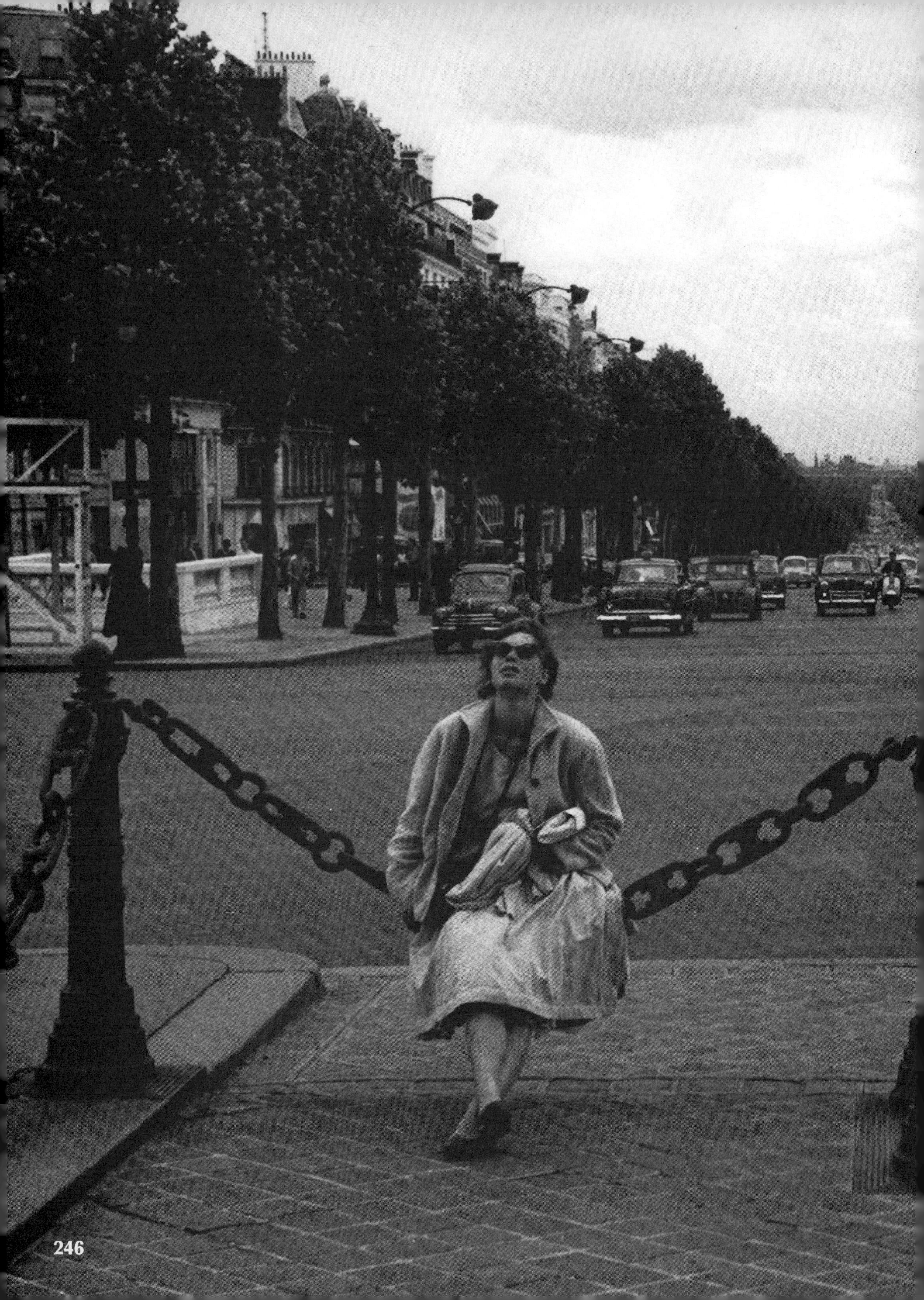

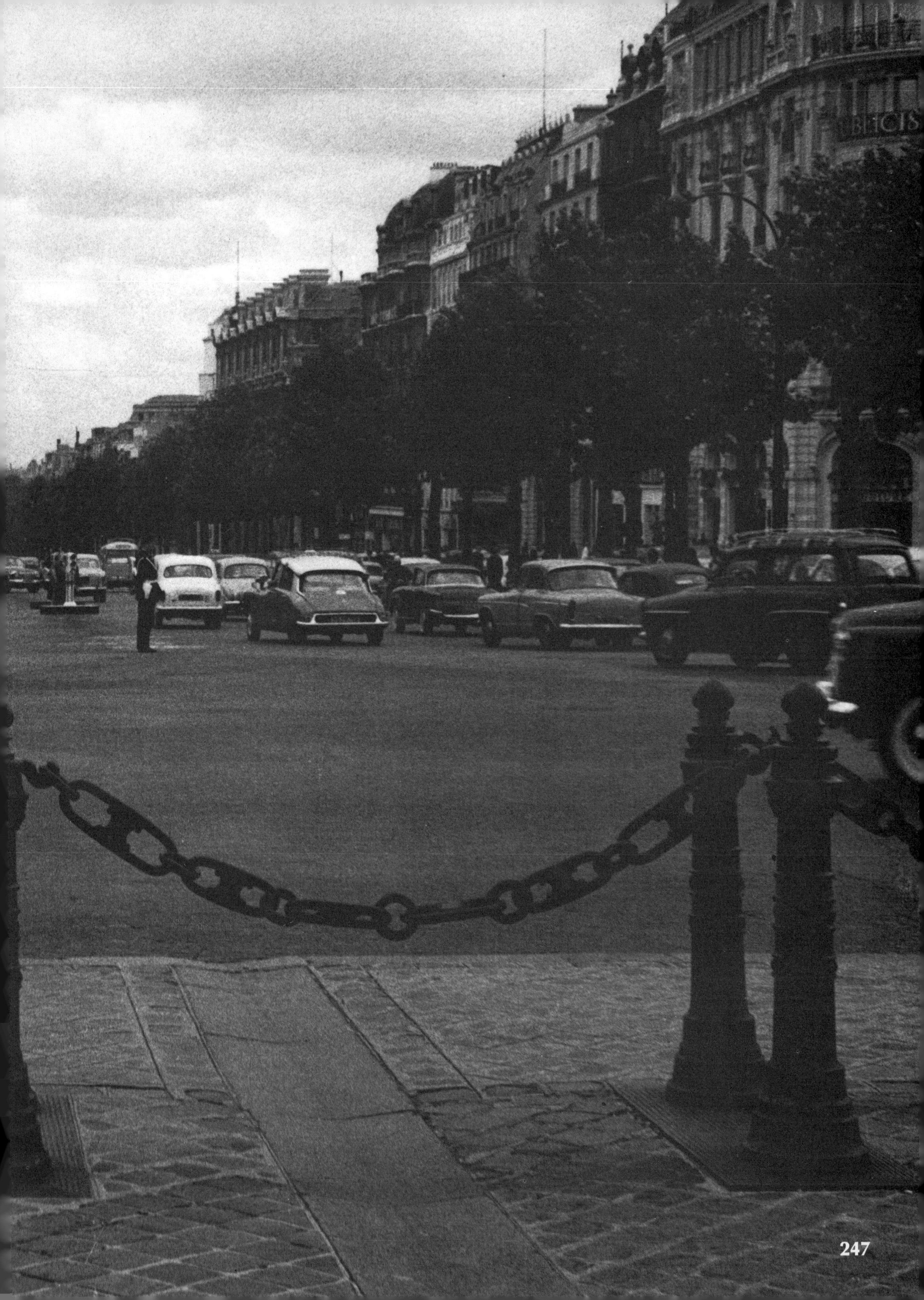

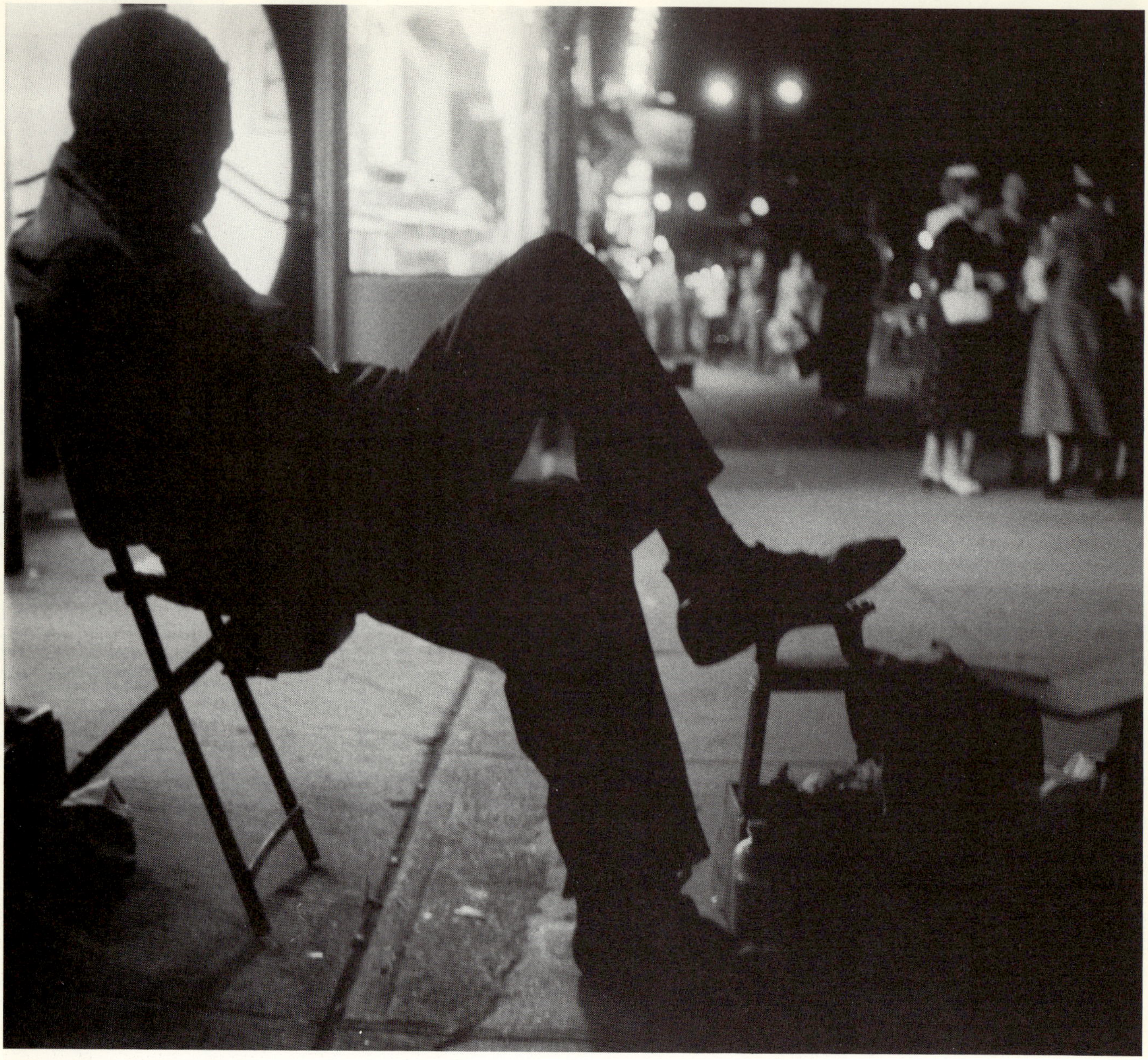

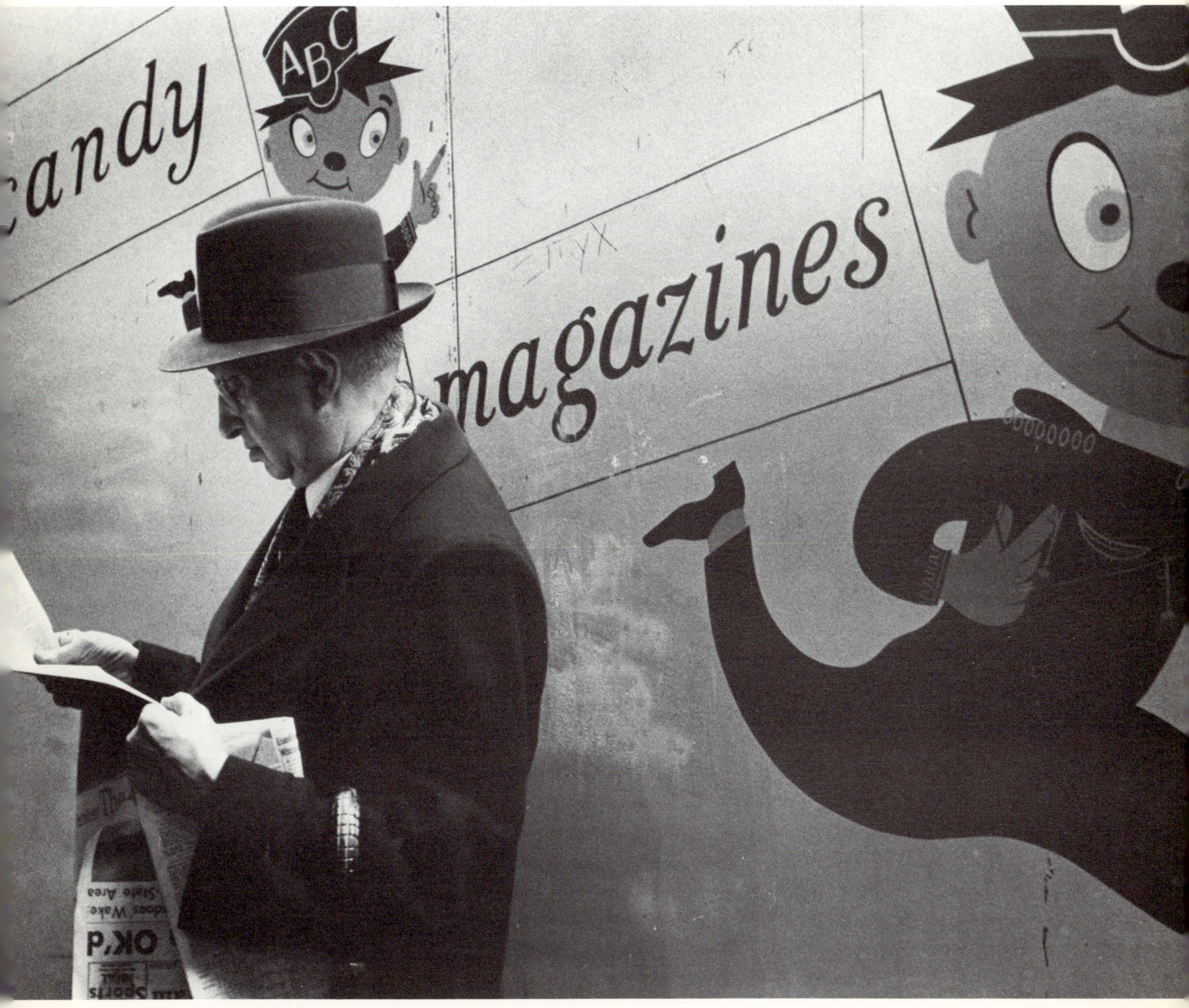
candy
ABC
magazines

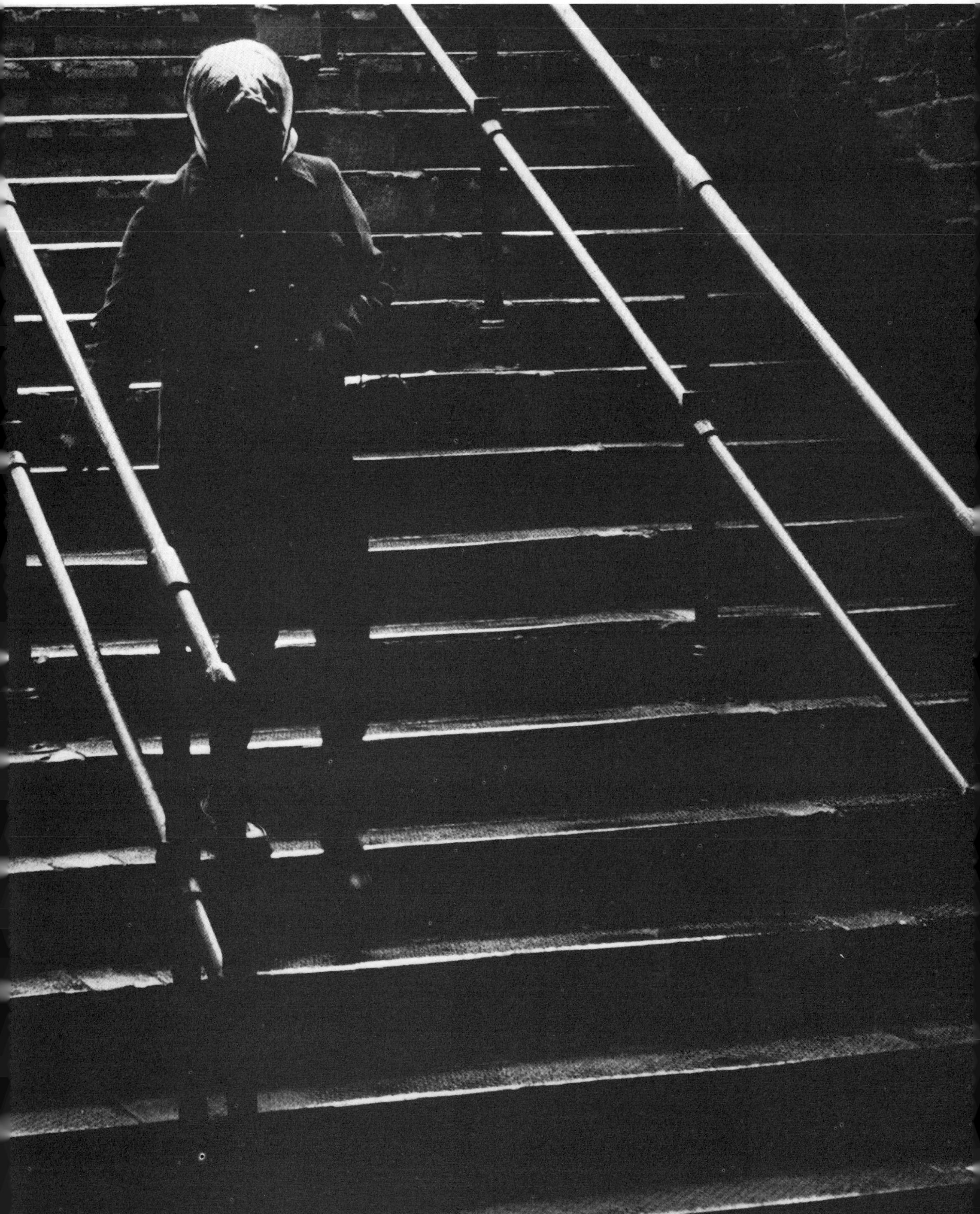

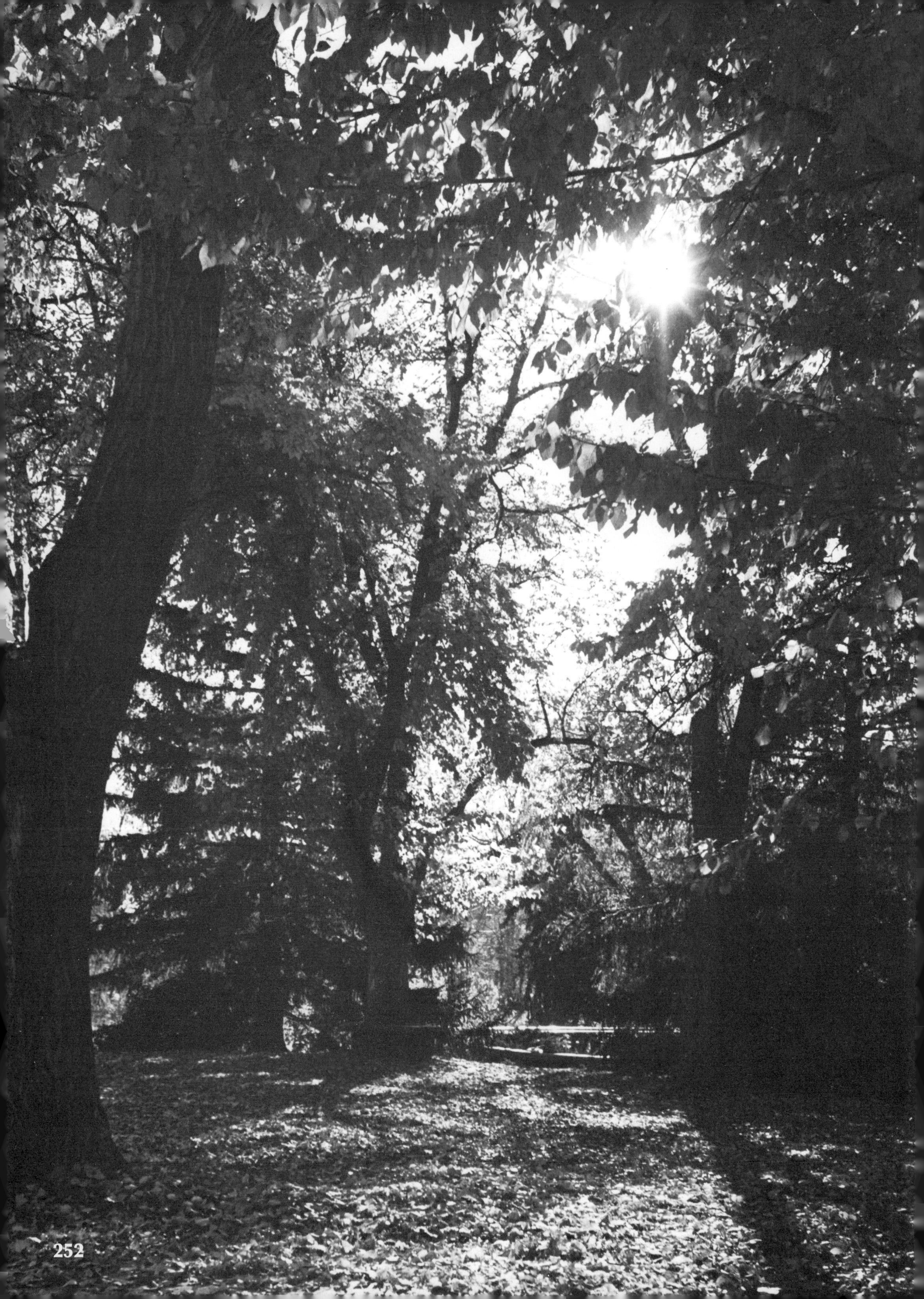

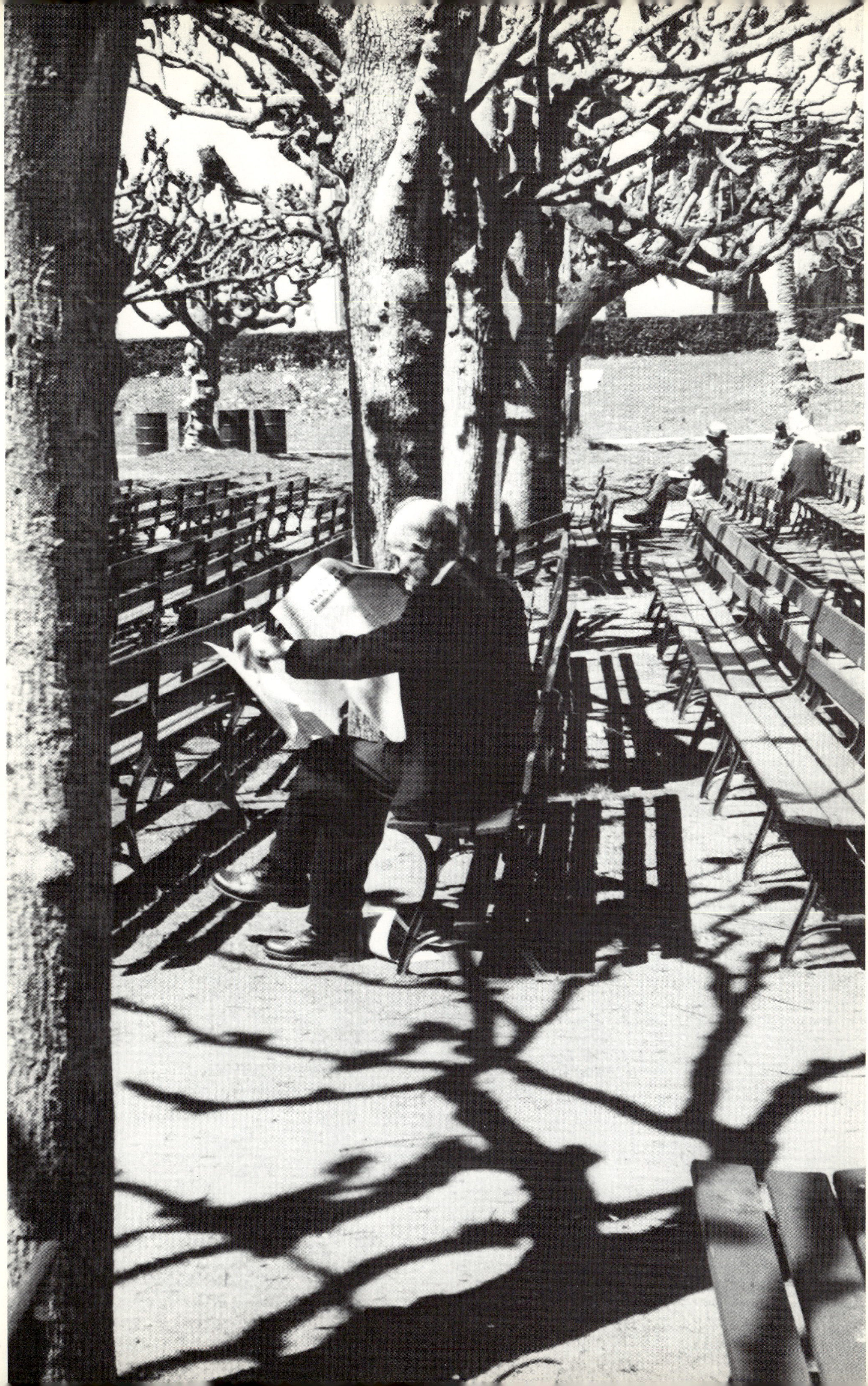

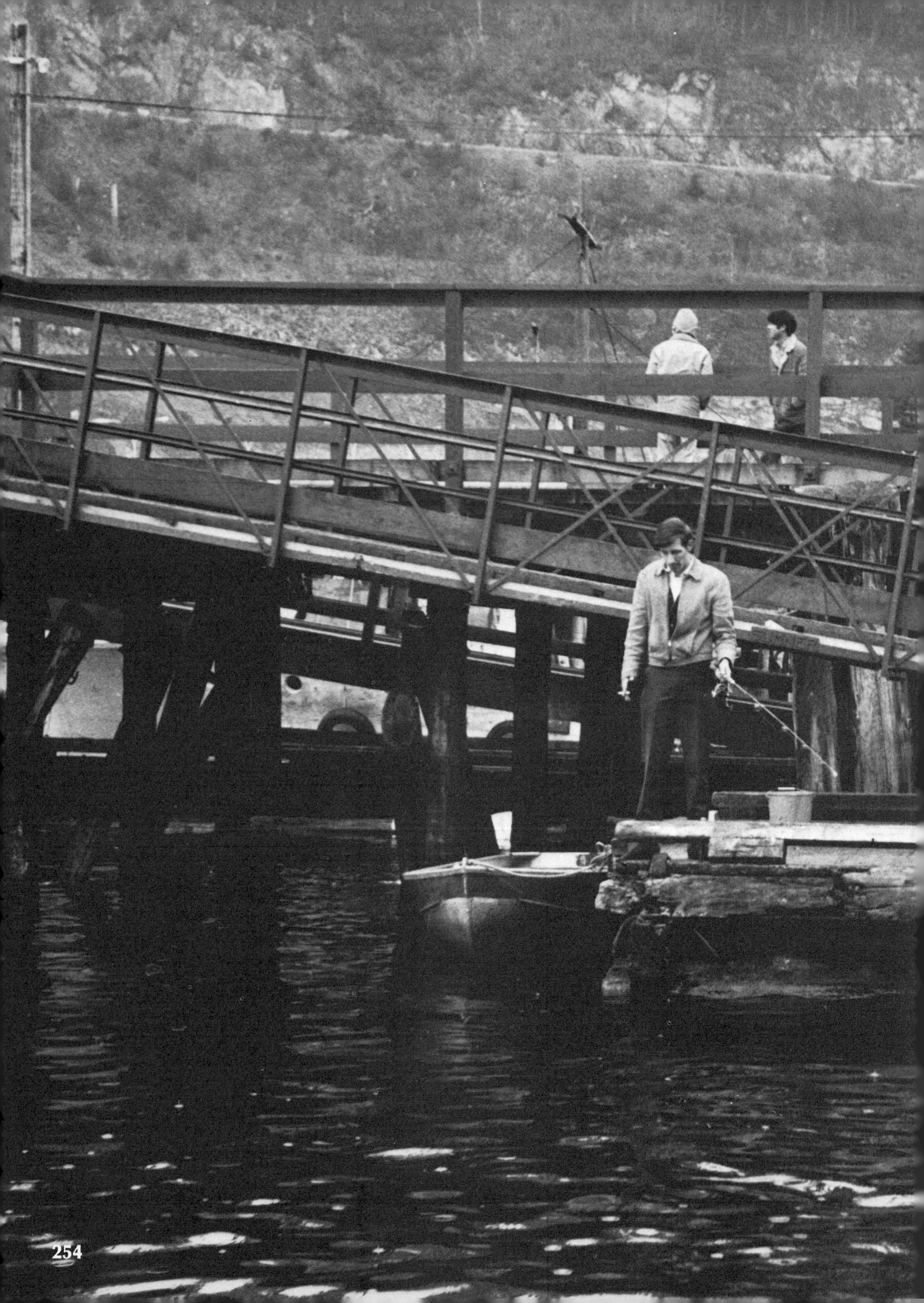

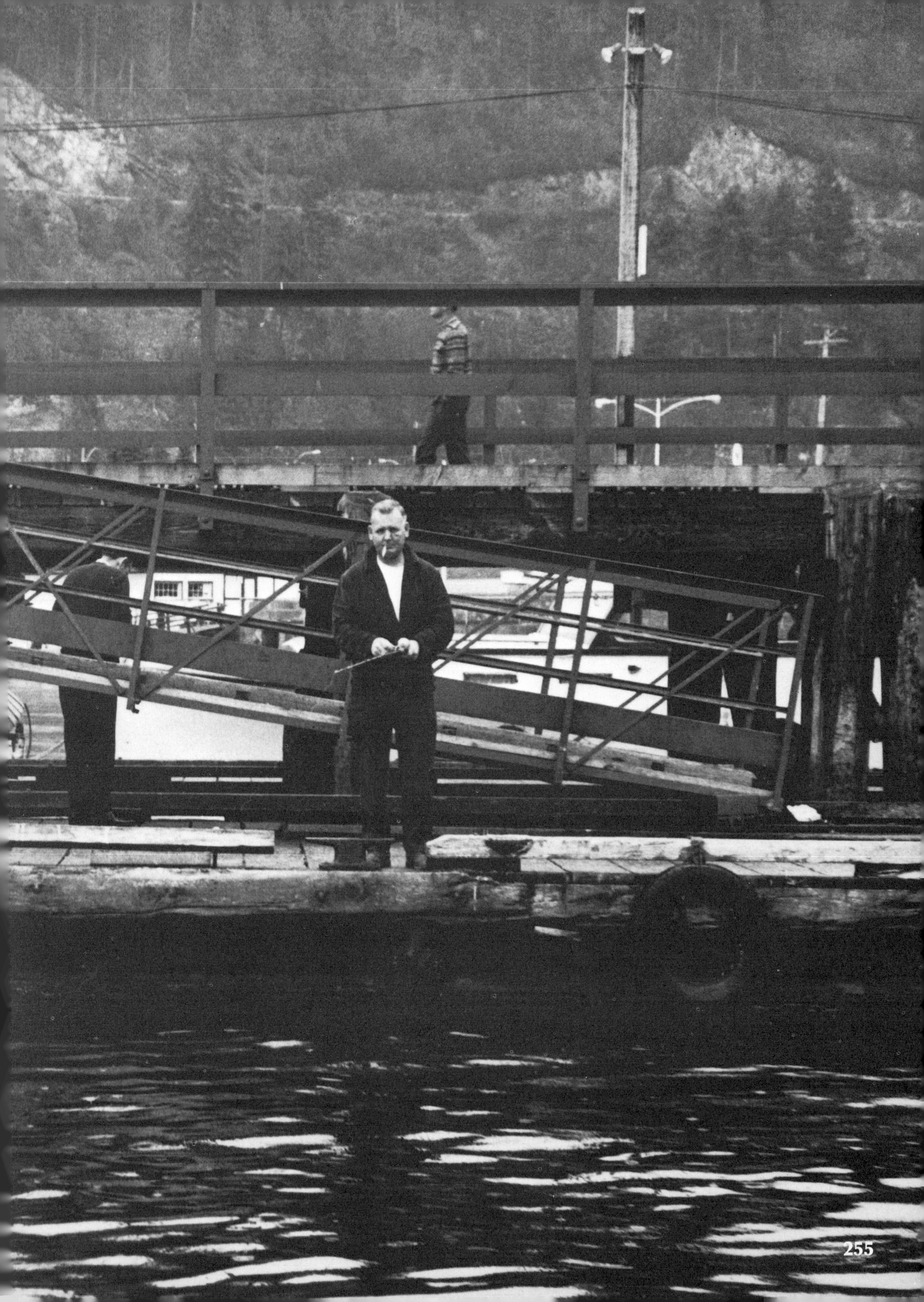

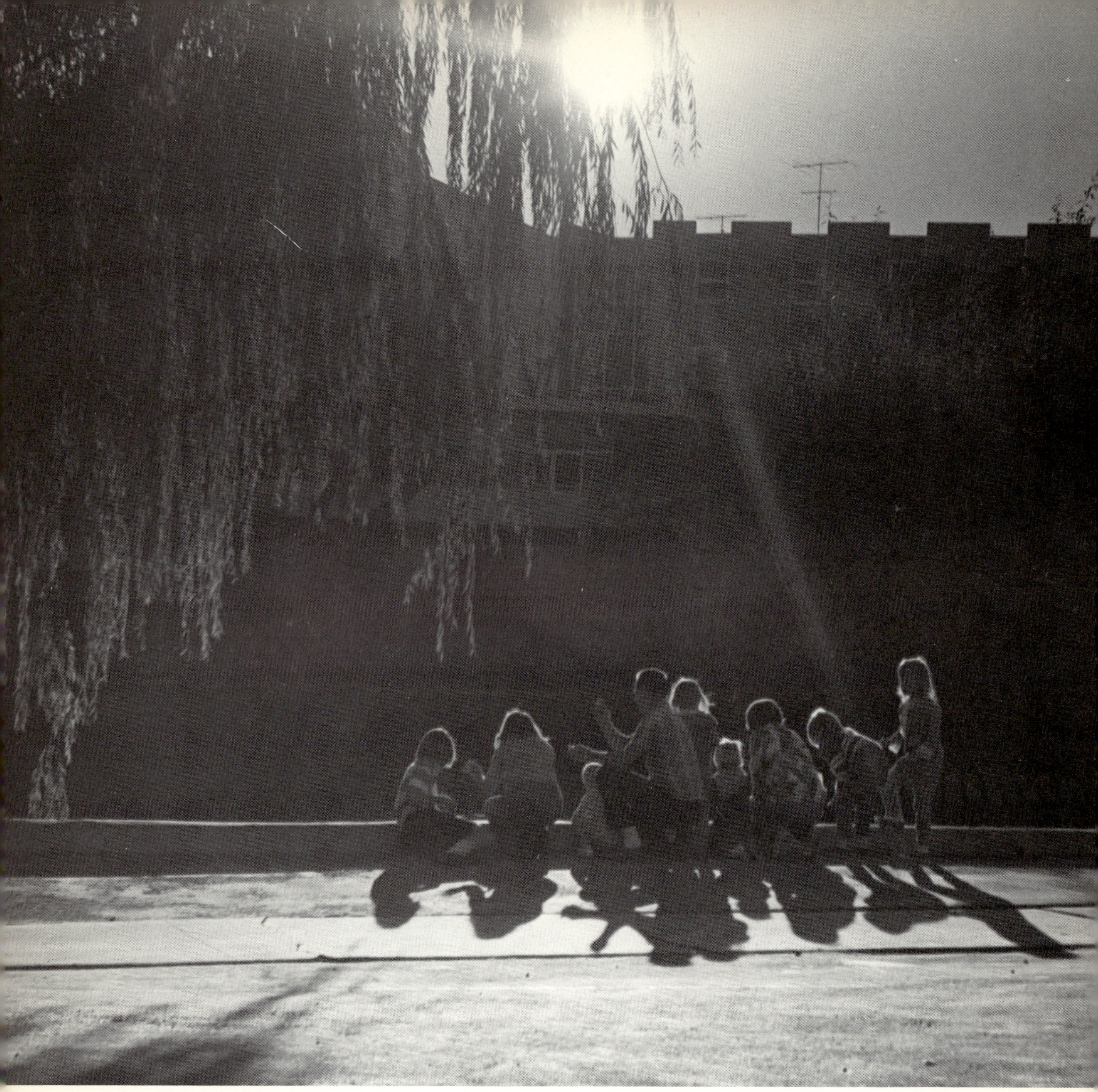

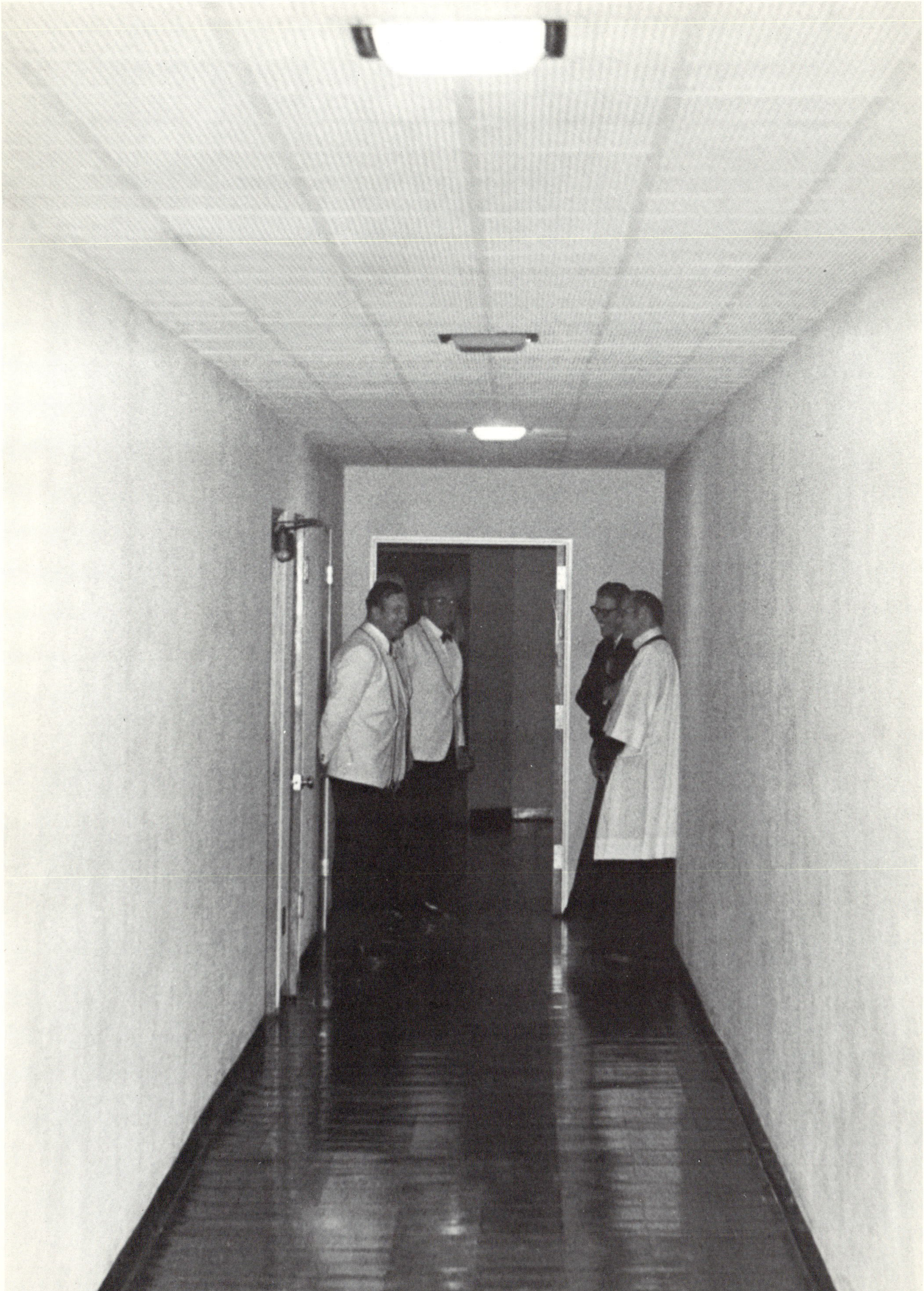

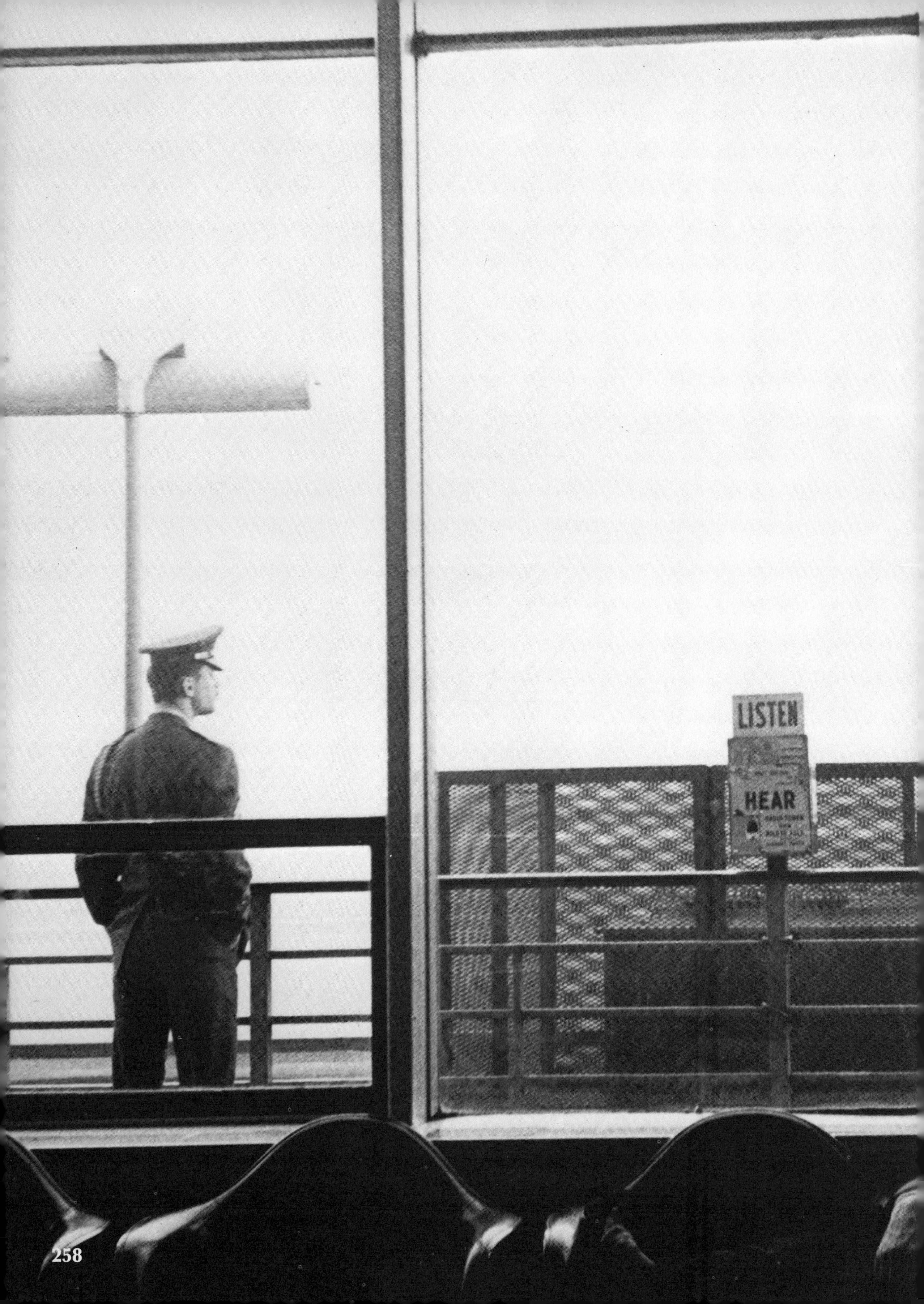
LISTEN
HEAR

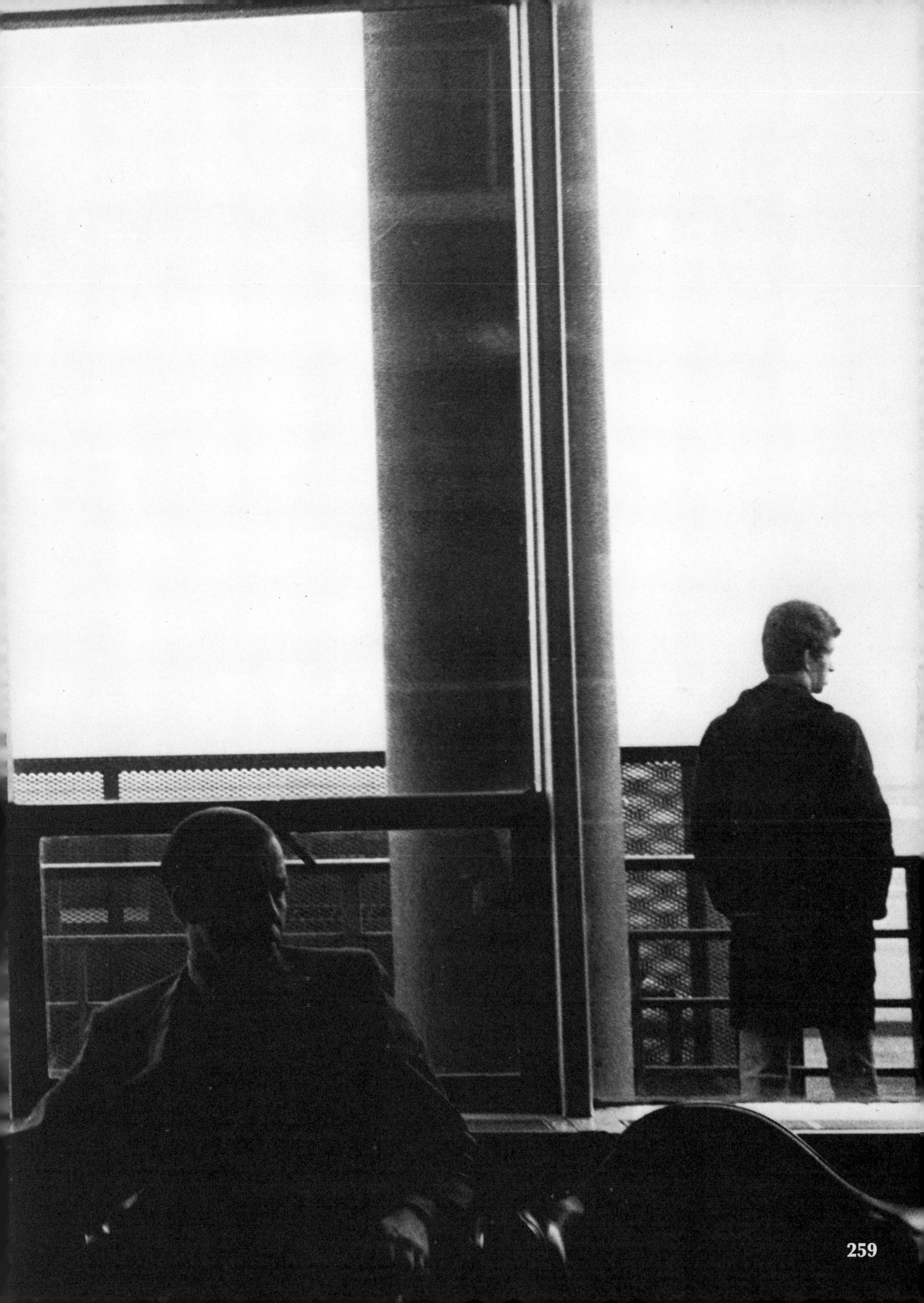

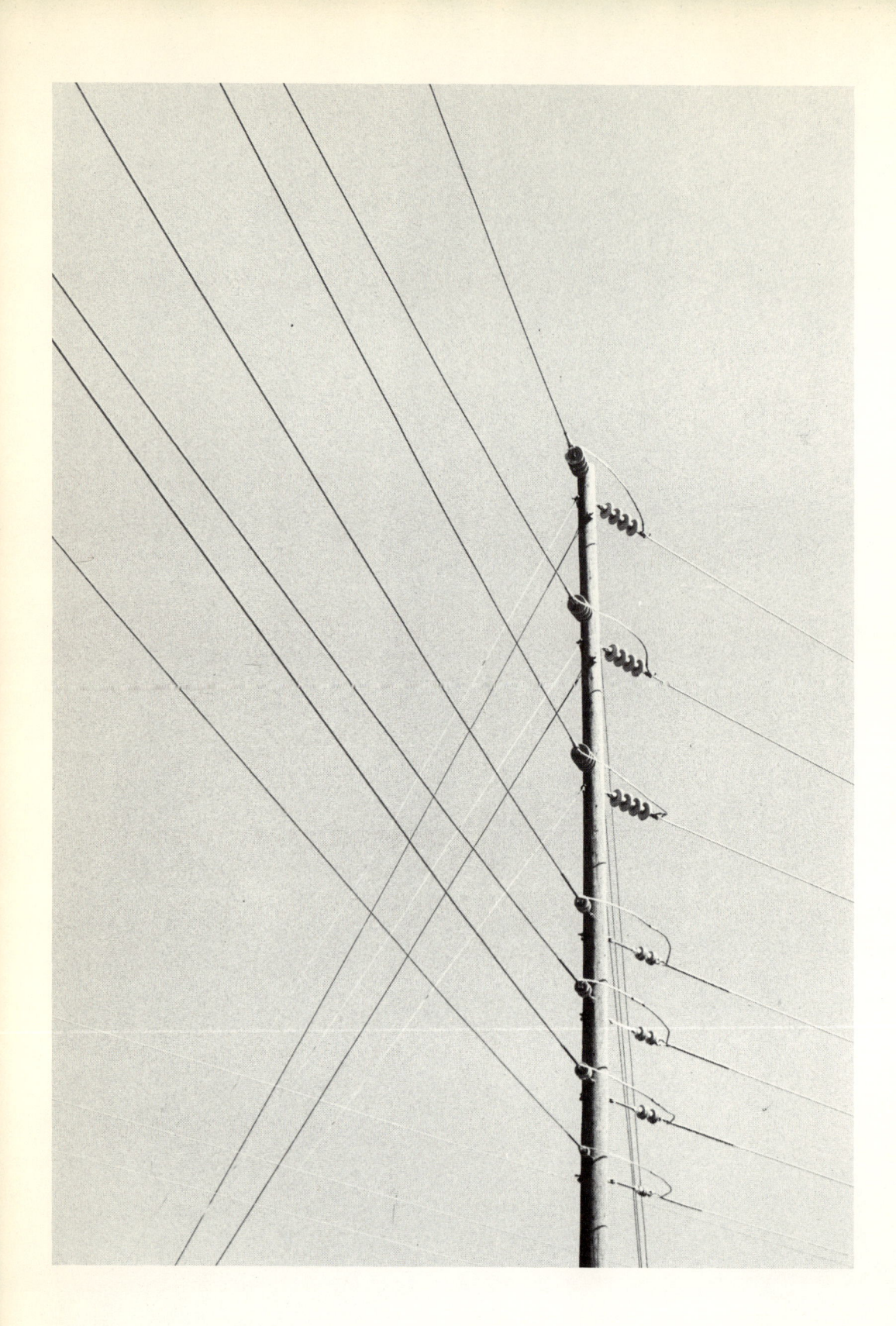

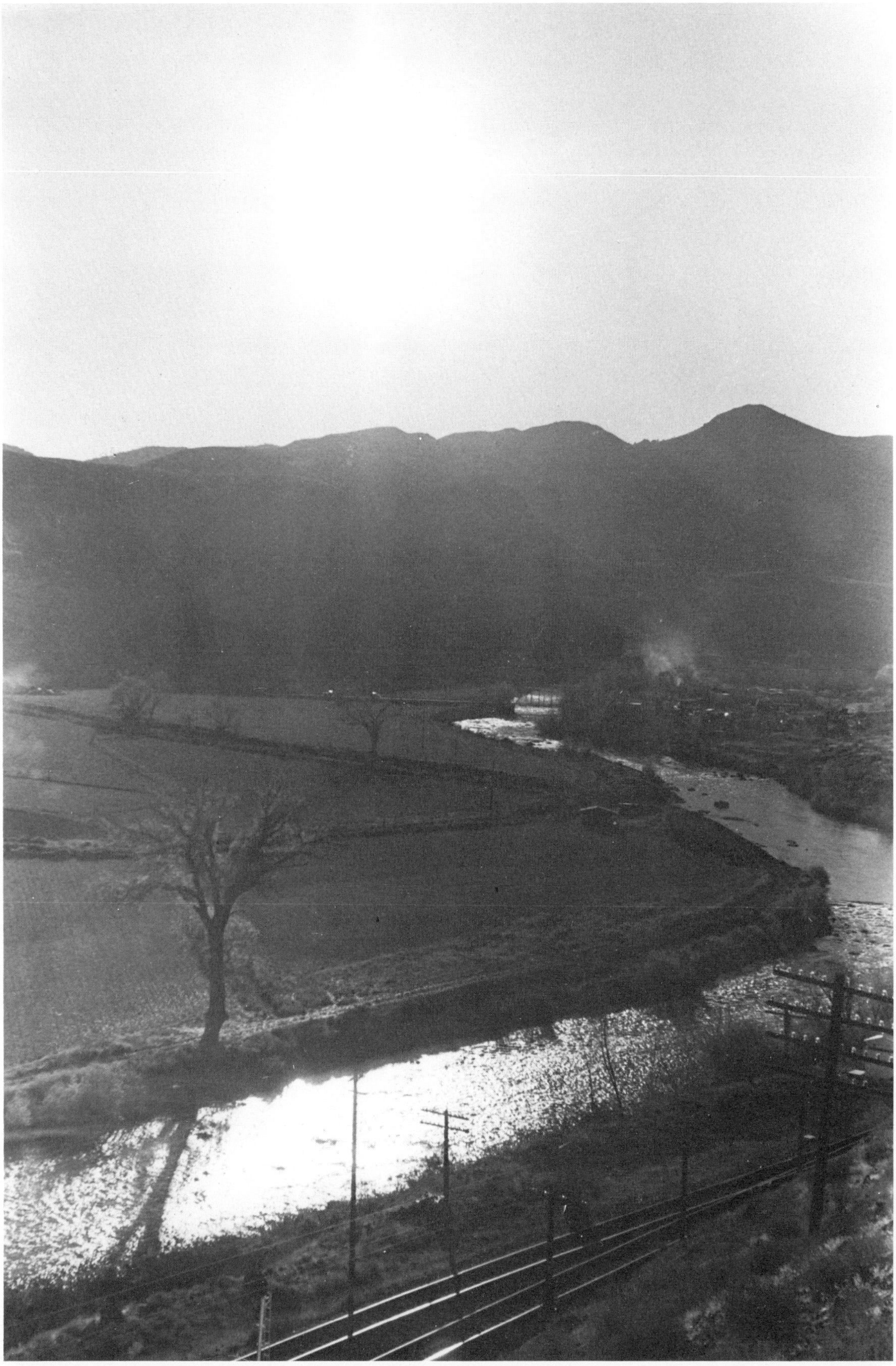

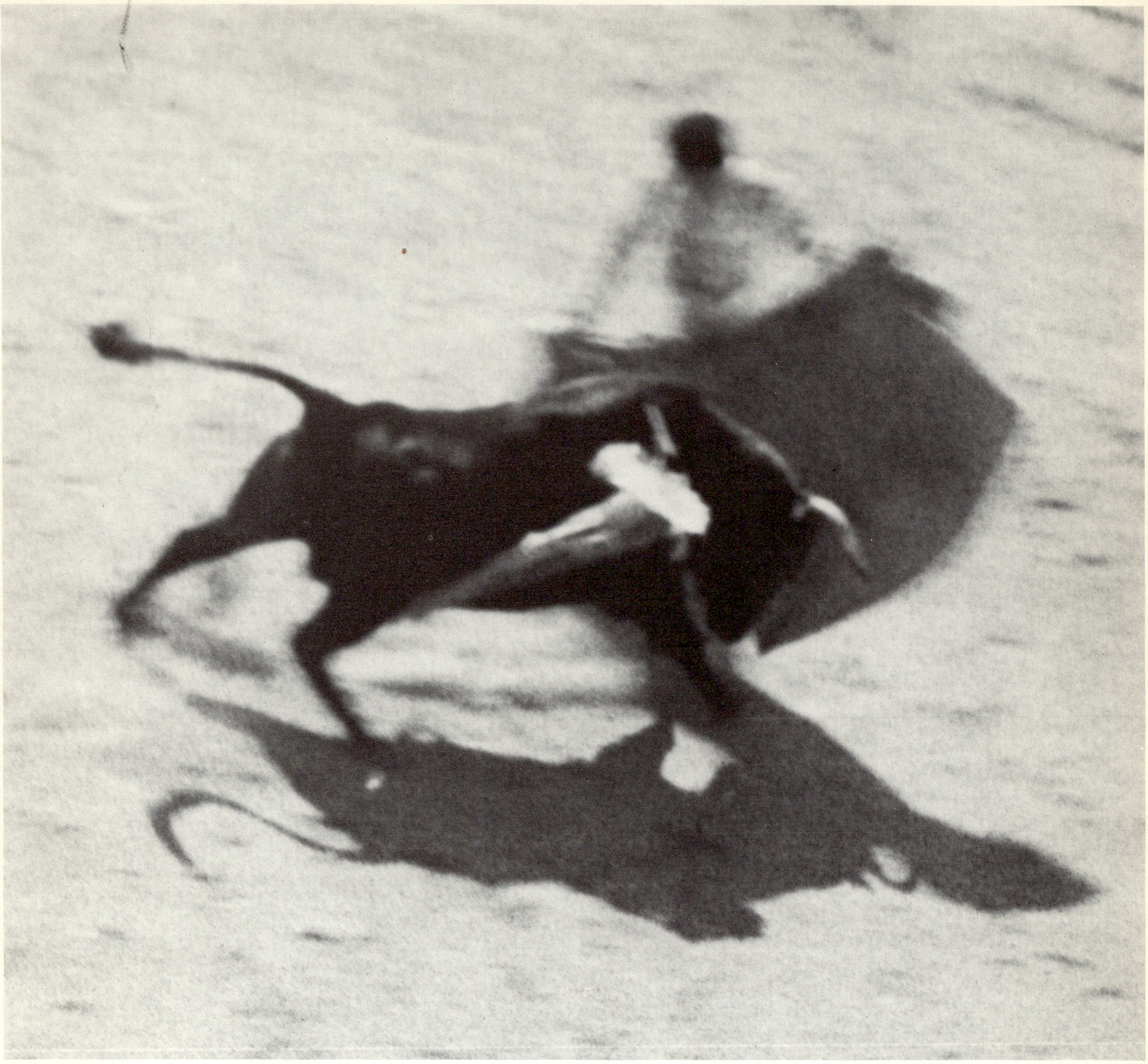